UNIFORMITY OF CUSTOMS ADMINISTRATION IN THE EUROPEAN UNION

Uniform customs administration is of great importance for the EU and the competitiveness of EU businesses in global trade. However, the EU's so-called executive federalism raises the potential for the non-uniform application of EU customs law. This problem has already arisen in the *European Communities—Selected Customs Matters* WTO dispute settlement. Therefore, the central research question of this book concerns the challenge presented to executive federalism in the EU Customs Union by the WTO. It also examines those safeguard measures for uniform customs administration which are in operation. Valuable empirical analysis of the decision-making procedures and practices of the national customs authorities allows for the fullest understanding of the operation of the customs administration. An important feature of the exploration is its analysis of the reform of EU customs law and of the effectiveness of the EU's strategies to enhance uniform customs administration. That analysis helps to identify potential weak points in the decentralised administration of EU customs law and suggests ways in which it might be improved. Scholarly, rigorous and timely, this important study will be required reading for all scholars of EU customs law.

Volume 59 in the Series Modern Studies in European Law

Modern Studies in European Law
Recent titles in this series:

Nationalism and Private Law in Europe
Guido Comparato

EU Asylum Procedures and the Right to an Effective Remedy
Marcelle Reneman

The EU Accession to the ECHR
Edited by Vasiliki Kosta, Nikos Skoutaris and Vassilis P Tzevelekos

The European Court of Justice and External Relations: Constitutional Challenges
Edited by Marise Cremona and Anne Thies

A Critique of Codification
Leone Niglia

Protecting Vulnerable Groups: The European Human Rights Framework
Edited by Francesca Ippolito and Sara Iglesias Sanchez

EU International Relations Law Second Edition
Panos Koutrakos

Fundamental Rights in the EU: A Matter for Two Courts
Edited by Sonia Morano-Foadi and Lucy Vickers

What Form of Government for the European Union and the Eurozone?
Federico Fabbrini, Ernst Hirsch Ballin and Han Somsen

The UK and European Human Rights: A Strained Relationship?
Edited by Katja S Ziegler, Elizabeth Wicks and Loveday Hodson

The European Union in International Organisations and Global Governance: Recent Developments
Edited by Christine Kaddous

Nudge and the Law: What Can EU Law Learn From Behavioural Sciences?
Edited by Alberto Alemanno and Anne-Lise Sibony

Fundamental Rights in EU Internal Market Legislation
Vasiliki Kosta

For the complete list of titles in this series, see 'Modern Studies in European Law' link at www.hartpub.co.uk/books/series.asp

Uniformity of Customs Administration in the European Union

Kathrin Limbach

·HART·
PUBLISHING
OXFORD AND PORTLAND, OREGON
2018

Hart Publishing
An imprint of Bloomsbury Publishing Plc

Hart Publishing Ltd
Kemp House
Chawley Park
Cumnor Hill
Oxford OX2 9PH
UK

Bloomsbury Publishing Plc
50 Bedford Square
London
WC1B 3DP
UK

www.hartpub.co.uk
www.bloomsbury.com

Published in North America (US and Canada) by
Hart Publishing
c/o International Specialized Book Services
920 NE 58th Avenue, Suite 300
Portland, OR 97213-3786
USA

www.isbs.com

First published in hardback, 2015
Paperback edition, 2018

British Library Cataloguing-in-Publication Data
A catalogue record for this book is available from the British Library.

ISBN: PB: 978-1-50992-002-0
HB: 978-1-78225-672-4

Typeset by Compuscript Ltd, Shannon
Printed and bound in Great Britain by
Lightning Source UK Ltd

Acknowledgements

This book adapts the doctoral research that I conducted on uniformity of customs administration in the European Union at the German Research Institute for Public Administration Speyer (FÖV), and which I defended at the German University of Administrative Sciences Speyer (DHV) in July 2014.

In being able to perform this research, I am greatly indebted to many people. First and foremost, I wish to thank Professor Dr Wolfgang Weiß, for his excellent supervision and continuous encouragement. Without him, I would never have ventured upon this challenging project. I am also very grateful to Professor Dr Ulrich Stelkens and Professor Dr Hermann Hill for serving as members of my thesis examination committee and for all their comments and suggestions. I would also like to express my gratitude in particular to Professor Dr Jan Ziekow from the FÖV for supporting the project.

I also owe much gratitude to former research assistant Dr Markus Haberkamm of the DHV Department of Public Law with focus on International and European Law, who over the past years has been of great assistance to me at highly critical moments and has become more than a colleague but also a friend. I have been very fortunate to find myself among colleagues who have been incredibly supportive and helpful during the whole research process and completion of this book. I wish to thank in particular Dr Jesse Lehrke from the FÖV, whose ceaseless efforts to correct my English and improve the manuscript I appreciate highly.

Beyond the FÖV and the DHV, I am very grateful to Jörg Schöneck from the German Federal Ministry of Finance for supporting the interviews with the German customs administration and making introductions for me with the British customs administration, HMRC. I want to acknowledge, in particular, the many German customs officials who have taken part in the German customs administration interviews, and the many British customs officials who have taken part in the interviews with the British customs administration.

I am very grateful for the work done by Julia Ebert, who had the job of being the first person to correct my English. I also wish to thank Natalie Agostinis for her swift French translation during a difficult situation. I thank my family and friends for their supportive and understanding companionship and wish to mention especially my best friend Jenny.

I wish to dedicate this book to my parents, Andrea and Peter, for their constant and generous support in all ways; to my husband Dominik, without whose support and patience it would not have been possible for me to complete this book; and to my sister Elena for being such a wonderful person and for putting everything in its right perspective.

Kathrin Limbach
Speyer, July 2014

Acknowledgements

Contents

Table of Cases

Decisions of the Court of Justice of the European Union (ECJ):

ECJ, Case C-375/07, *Staatssecretaris van Financiën v Heuschen & Schrouff Oriëntal Foods Trading BV*, [2008] European Court Reports I-8691, 20th of November 2008
Citation: ECJ of 20 November 2008, Case C-375/07, *Heuschen & Schrouff Oriëntal Foods Trading BV II*, [2008] ECR I-8691, para (…) 258
ECJ, Case C-403/07, *Metherma GmbH & Co KG v Hauptzollamt Düsseldorf*, [2008] European Court Reports I-8921, 27th of November 2008
Citation: ECJ of 27 November 2008, Case C-403/07, *Metherma GmbH & Co KG*, [2008] ECR I-8921, para (…) 264
ECJ, Case C-510/06 P, *Archer Daniels Midland Co v Commission of the European Communities*, [2009] European Court Reports I-1843, 19th of March 2009
Citation: ECJ of 19 March 2009, Case C-510/06 P, *ADM II*, [2009] ECR I-1843, para (…) 236
ECJ, Case C-150/08, *Siebrand BV v Staatssecretaris van Financiën*, [2009] European Court Reports I-3941, 7th of May 2009
Citation: ECJ of 7 May 2009, Case C-150/08, *Siebrand BV*, [2009] ECR I-3941, para (…) 265
ECJ, Case C-428/07, *The Queen, on the application of Mark Horvath v Secretary of State for Environment, Food and Rural Affairs*, [2009] European Court Reports I-6355, 16th of July 2009
Citation: ECJ of 16 July 2009, Case C-428/07, *Horvath*, [2009] ECR I-6355, para (…) 141
ECJ, Joined Cases C-125/07 P, C-133/07 P, C-135/07 P and C-137/07 P, *Erste Group Bank AG (C-125/07 P), Raiffeisen Zentralbank Österreich AG (C-133/07 P), Bank Austria Creditanstalt AG (C-135/07 P) and Österreichische Volksbanken AG (C-137/07 P) v Commission of the European Communities*, [2009] European Court Reports I-8681, 24th of September 2009
Citation: ECJ of 24 September 2009, Joined Cases C-125/07 P, C-133/07 P, C-135/07 P and C-137/07 P, *Erste Group Bank AG*, [2009] ECR I-8681, para (…) 236
ECJ, Case C-260/08, *Bundesfinanzdirektion West v HEKO Industrieerzeugnisse GmbH*, [2009] European Court Reports I-11571, 10th of December 2009
Citation: ECJ of 10 December 2009, Case C-260/08, *HEKO Industrieerzeugnisse*, [2009] ECR I-11571, para (…) 232, 241–42
ECJ, Case C-456/08, *European Commission v Ireland*, [2010] European Court Reports I-859, 28th of January 2010
Citation: ECJ of 28 January 2010, Case C-456/08, *Commission v Ireland*, [2010] ECR I-859, para (…) 31
ECJ, Case C-373/08, *Hoesch Metals and Alloys GmbH v Hauptzollamt Aachen*, [2010] European Court Reports I-951, 11th of February 2010
Citation: ECJ of 11 February 2010, Case C-373/08, *Hoesch Metals and Alloys GmbH*, [2010] ECR I-951, para (…) 231
ECJ, Case C-75/09, *Agra Srl v Agenzia Dogane—Ufficio delle Dogane di Alessandria*, [2010] European Court Reports I-5595, 17th of June 2010
Citation: ECJ of 17 June 2010, Case C-75/09, *Agra Srl*, [2010] ECR I-5595, para (…) 149

Decisions of the General Court:

Dispute Settlement Body (DSB):

Part I

Introduction

1

Uniform Customs Administration in the European Union

IN THE CURRENT era of increasing globalisation, the European administrative area cannot be understood in isolation from worldwide harmonisation processes. The scope for European and Europeanised administration is determined in part by external forces. Of especial importance in this context is the World Trade Organization (WTO), an international organisation of which the European Union (EU)[1] is a member, as are the individual EU Member States, and which has developed an extensive legal order of its own. The WTO even has at its disposal a Dispute Settlement Body and a Panel and Appellate Body that have their own dynamics. In the area of EU customs administration that is the focus of this book, the WTO has specific requirements binding on its members and, therefore, has an impact that cannot be ignored. To some extent, it can even challenge the decentralised concept of the administration of customs law in the EU, the so-called 'Executive Federalism'.

In the area of EU customs administration, several levels interact with each other. On the one hand, the EU is a customs union[2] and its customs law is extremely harmonised because it is enacted centrally on the EU level. There exist several EU regulations that determine the European customs tariff rate and deal with other questions of substantive customs law, including even customs procedures. Therefore, the EU Customs Union is based on common legislation and policy.[3] On the other hand, EU customs law is applied and implemented by the national customs authorities of the EU Member States. Therefore, customs administration in the EU is decentralised, which makes the operational functioning of the EU Customs Union rather complex.[4]

[1] After the Treaty of Lisbon came into force on 1 December 2009, the European Union (EU) is now legal successor to the European Communities (EC), pursuant to Art 1 para 3 Treaty on European Union (hereinafter TEU), and has its own legal personality, pursuant to Art 47 TEU, and can sign international agreements, pursuant to Art 216 para 1 Treaty on the Functioning of the European Union (hereinafter TFEU). Therefore, in this document the term 'European Union'/'EU' is used instead of 'European Communities'/'EC', even when describing a time of the past where actually the European Communities had been acting. Only in literal citations or in case there is the potential risk of confusion single exceptions will be made.

[2] By 'Customs Union', this document refers exclusively to the EU Customs Union and territory as defined in Chapter 1 TFEU, excluding customs unions with Turkey, Andorra and San Marino.

[3] COM (2012) 791 final, p 9.

[4] ibid, p 9.

This decentralised approach to EU customs administration raises the potential for the non-uniform application of EU customs law, since the national customs administrations in the different EU Member States are organised autonomously, and to some extent can act independently from each other. The European Commission is not a supervisory authority for the national customs administrations and thus cannot give instructions. EU customs law is open to interpretation, because many provisions contain undefined legal terms, while other provisions provide for a margin of discretion when making certain customs decisions. Therefore, customs procedures can differ significantly in different EU Member States. Especially in a paper-based environment, without common criteria and standards, the conditions for uniform customs administration are not ideal.

Nonetheless, uniform administration of EU customs is of great importance for the EU and the competitiveness of EU businesses in global trade. Non-uniform customs administration limits effectiveness and efficiency, giving rise to duplication, inconsistency and mismatches of resources.[5] Moreover, non-uniform customs administration has the potential to weaken the strong economic position of the EU by producing legal uncertainty, expensive and drawn out judicial proceedings, and loss of revenue (customs duties are part of the EU's own resources). It can even have negative economic/political or security/political consequences, by leading to trade diversion and security vulnerabilities. Uniform administration of EU customs is a legal obligation and a necessity for the proper functioning and security of the EU Customs Union.

In this context, the national customs authorities not only have to administer EU regulations, but simultaneously have to respect the requirements of the WTO. In Article X of the General Agreement on Tariffs and Trade of 1994 (GATT 1994), the WTO established certain standards regarding the uniform administration of customs law. The requirement for uniformity in the administration of EU customs law is defined not only by the interest of the EU in the coherent administration of EU law, but also by the demands of the WTO, which have considerably different consequences. It is this very request for uniformity in customs administration that can challenge the Executive Federalism of the EU as a decentralised approach to the administration of EU customs law.

This problem has already arisen in the WTO dispute settlement *EC—Selected Customs Matters*,[6] which took place from 2004 until 2006. In this WTO dispute, the United States claimed that EU customs law was administered non-uniformly, in the sense of Article X:3(a) GATT 1994, by the national customs authorities of the EU Member States, and that, therefore, the EU was violating its obligations as a member of the WTO. However, the main question was left open, as the Panel in the WTO dispute settlement did not analyse whether the EU was indeed

[5] ibid, p 15.
[6] WT/DS315.

administering EU customs law in a non-uniform manner in the sense of Article X:3(a) GATT 1994—it only discussed single cases of allegedly non-uniform administration, not the EU customs administration system as a whole.

Therefore, a central research question of this book is the challenge presented to Executive Federalism in the EU by the WTO with regard to the administration of EU customs law. Is Executive Federalism in the administration of EU customs law compatible with the obligations of WTO membership? What safeguard measures exist to provide for uniformity in EU customs administration even given decentralised implementation through national customs authorities?

To answer these questions this book will analyse to what extent Article X:3(a) GATT 1994 promotes processes in the decentralised EU customs administration through its binding requirements for a uniform customs administration, especially in the interpretations of the WTO Dispute Settlement Body. Furthermore, an analysis will also be made of the safeguard measures for the uniform administration of EU customs law that are in operation, that can meet the standards of both EU law and WTO law, and in how far the EU succeeds in doing so. This requires identification of the potential deficits in the EU legal framework regarding uniform customs administration.

Apart from the legal analysis, it is also of some interest to look at whether and how the European instruments for securing uniform administration actually work. Therefore, a short empirical analysis of the decision-making procedures and practices of the national customs authorities is included herein. This short analysis supplements the legal findings with impressions based on empirical conclusions, regarding to what extent the European mechanisms for securing the uniform application of EU customs law work in actual administrative practice, and how aware the customs administrations of the EU Member States are of WTO law when making decisions. For this analysis, 20 customs officials of the customs administrations in Germany and in the United Kingdom were interviewed, using the same interview guide for both groups. Those two national customs administrations were chosen because of certain differences between them, one of which played a role in the *EC—Selected Customs Matters* WTO dispute settlement, already mentioned.

Part II of the book takes a look at the legal system of the EU Customs Union and its potential shortcomings with regard to uniform customs administration, as well as the role of the WTO in this matter. Chapter 2 will discuss the EU Customs Union and outline its legal framework, including its structure, functions and potential deficits with regard to uniform implementation. The focus will be on the Common Customs Tariff (CCT) and the Customs Code with its implementing provisions, as these legal texts constitute the main parts of EU customs law.

In Chapter 3, the role of WTO law in EU customs administration and the degree of uniformity in customs law implementation that is required by Article X:3(a) GATT 1994 will be discussed. This will include a detailed analysis of the relevance of the obligation of uniform customs administration with regard to the EU system of customs administration.

Part III of the book analyses the efforts to reform the current legal system of the EU Customs Union. Chapter 4 covers the 'great reform' of EU customs law that began at the time of the WTO dispute settlement *EC—Selected Customs Matters*. It also discusses the EU's strategies to enhance uniform customs administration. The main strategies are the simplification of EU customs law with regard to its structure and legal terminology and, simultaneously, the adoption of detailed provisions, supported by administrative guidance, that restrict the margins of discretion in EU customs law held by EU Member States in implementing EU customs law. Another important strategy is the establishment of an electronic customs environment with central databases and interoperable IT systems capable of standardising working processes as well as criteria and standards. A further strategy is the promotion and coordination of cooperation in order to promote best practices and common understandings among the national customs authorities of the EU Member States. Thus, this extensive reform agenda includes legal aspects, IT aspects and operational aspects, all intended to prepare EU customs for current and future challenges in a globalised world with severe security issues. In fact, the whole Customs Code has been rewritten, and EU customs is to be a paperless environment based on electronic customs systems.

However, this reform of the EU customs system is still ongoing, as it has turned out to be even more difficult than was first expected. In fact, a recasting of the reform has already been started and the final outcome of this long-term process, now to be concluded presumably in the year 2020,[7] cannot be forecast with certainty. This recasting of these reforms and its potential to improve uniform customs administration will be the object of analysis in Chapter 5. This study covers the period until 31 December 2013.

The largest part of the book (Part IV) analyses the implementation of EU customs law and the effectiveness of the EU's strategies, including a discussion of its possible features as a customs procedure union as well as a customs administration union (Chapter 6). Administrative cooperation (Chapter 7) and the role and competences of the European Commission (Chapter 8) in the implementation of EU customs law will be analysed in order to outline the possible features of an integrated administration in the EU Customs Union. A brief summary will close this part (Chapter 9).

Part V takes a closer look at customs areas of special interest for this study. Herein, Chapter 10 does not focus on the overall uniform functioning of the EU Customs Union, but instead concentrates on special tools and mechanisms for 'uniformisation' of EU customs law implementation in three specific areas of EU customs administration: classification, valuation and rules of origin. These fields of EU customs constitute the main parts of EU customs law and are of special importance in day-to-day customs work. Furthermore, they were areas criticised in the *EC—Selected Customs Matters* WTO dispute settlement.

[7] COM (2012) 791 final, p 13; Zeilinger, in: Koszinowski (ed), 2013, pp 103–07 (105); Witte, 2012 AW-Prax 4, p 119 (119); Boysen, in: von Arnauld (ed), 2014, § 9 pp 447–514, para 75.

The analysis of the challenge presented to Executive Federalism by Article X:3(a) GATT 1994 regarding the uniform administration of EU customs law allows for a more thorough understanding of the relevance that WTO law has for administrative practice. It can contribute to the identification of potential weak points in the decentralised administration of EU customs law, and provide information for the improvement of the uniform customs administration. The results and recommendation of this study are presented in the Final Conclusion (Part VI, Chapter 11).

Part II

The EU Customs Union and the WTO

2

The EU Customs Union in the European Union's Legal System

ACCORDING TO ARTICLE 28 TFEU, the EU comprises a customs union for which the Union itself has exclusive and all-encompassing competence, determining its legal organisation in the form of a common tariff customs law as well as a common customs procedural law pursuant to Articles 31, 207 TFEU. The EU's exclusive competence is laid down in Article 3 paragraph 1 section (a) TFEU. The harmonisation of customs law in the EU was basically completed on 1 January 1993 with the realisation of the European Single Market, through the abolition of goods control at the borders between the EU Member States.[1] Since this point, no physical customs controls at the internal frontiers of the EU have been carried out, as all the goods within the customs area of the EU count as Union goods.[2]

I. EU CUSTOMS LAW AS A PIONEER FOR THE EUROPEANISATION OF ADMINISTRATIVE LAW

When it comes to the 'Europeanisation' of national administrative law, it is EU customs law that has had the pioneering role.[3] When the Community Customs Code (CCC) came into force in 1994, it replaced more than 100 single regulations and directives which themselves had already displaced the national administrative laws in the field of customs.[4] The Community Customs Code and its implementing provisions are the first comprehensive and the most extensive harmonised codification of law on the EU level[5] and also codify for the first time principles of common administrative law.[6] For example, Article 5 CCC regulates the right of representation—for customs-related legal matters—and establishes indirect representation as well as direct representation, which was new for some EU Member

[1] Wolffgang, in: Witte/Wolffgang (eds), 2012, p 5, para 6; similar: Gormley, 2009, p 1, para 1.01.

[2] Wolffgang, in: Witte/Wolffgang (eds), 2012, p 11, para 15.

[3] Rogmann, in: Kluth/Müller/Peilert (eds), 2008, pp 797–819 (798); similar: Lyons, 2008, pp 23, 24.

[4] Rogmann, in: Kluth/Müller/Peilert (eds), 2008, pp 797–819 (798).

[5] Witte, in: Witte (ed), 2013, Introduction CCC, para 3; Hohrmann, in: Hübschmann/Hepp/Spitaler (eds), 2013, Vol XIV, Introduction CCC, para 19.

[6] Rogmann, in: Kluth/Müller/Peilert (eds), 2008, pp 797–819 (798).

States.[7] Articles 8 and 9 CCC contain rules concerning the annulment of decisions, which also differ from the terminology for withdrawal and revocation of administrative acts used in some EU Member States, for example in Germany.[8] Consequently, the Community Customs Code has been called an 'agleam example for successful harmonisation of a part of European administrative law',[9] and 'a milestone in the development of Union law.'[10] Thus, inter alia, EU customs law, with its established principles, could pave the way for the subsequent Europeanisation of administrative law.[11] It also includes some procedural regulations that could be considered as the basis of common administrative law,[12] for example the immediate enforcement of decisions (Article 7 CCC), information (Article 11 CCC) and binding information (Article 12 CCC), and extension of a period and deferment of time limits (Article 17 CCC). Therefore, it is possible that EU customs law could serve as a model of how to meet the challenges of enforcing European administrative law in the EU Member States.[13]

Furthermore, EU customs law is also partly economic law. Beyond customs duties, prohibitions and restrictions also have to be considered, in the cross-border movement of goods.[14] Economic losses incurred as a result of brand piracy and plagiarism are enormous, and still increasing. The number of shipments suspected of violating intellectual property rights (IPR) is consistently high, as shown by recent statistics published by the European Commission.[15] In 2012, customs registered almost 91,000 such cases, and nearly 40 million products were held at the external border of the EU.[16] This level of activity by customs administrations in the EU to protect consumers and ensure fair competition highlights the economic importance of EU customs law beyond the collection of duties.[17] It is because of this service function[18] that EU customs law must also consider the interests of economic operators.[19] However, to play a role in paving the way for the Europeanisation of this function, EU customs law must ensure that its enforcement in the EU Member States is both effective and uniform.[20] The uniform administration of customs law is also a requirement of the WTO, pursuant to Article X:3(a) GATT 1994. Thus, the uniform implementation of EU customs law constitutes a genuine obligation of the EU.

[7] Witte, in: Witte (ed), 2013, Art 5 CCC, para 2.
[8] Alexander, in: Witte (ed), 2013, Art 9 CCC, para 2.
[9] Stober, 2003 NJW 8, p 572 (572).
[10] Terra, in: Terra/Wattel (eds), 2012, p 162.
[11] Rogmann, in: Kluth/Müller/Peilert (eds), 2008, pp 797–819 (798).
[12] Wolffgang, in: Witte/Wolffgang (eds), 2012, p 13, para 17 and p 26, para 32.
[13] Rogmann, in: Kluth/Müller/Peilert (eds), 2008, pp 797–819 (799).
[14] Möller/Schumann/Sibum, 2010, p 15.
[15] European Commission, 2012 Report on Intellectual Property Rights Enforcement.
[16] European Commission, 2012 Report on Intellectual Property Rights Enforcement, pp 7, 8.
[17] Möller/Schumann/Sibum, 2010, p 15.
[18] Stober, 2001, p 9.
[19] See para 2 of the preamble of the Community Customs Code.
[20] Rogmann, in: Kluth/Müller/Peilert (eds), 2008, pp 797–819 (799).

II. HISTORY OF THE EU CUSTOMS UNION

According to Article 28 TFEU (ex Article 23 TEC), the EU comprises a customs union which covers all trade in goods and which prohibits customs duties on imports and exports between EU Member States, as well as all charges having equivalent effect, and which entails the adoption of a common customs tariff in their relations with third countries. Today's Single European Market would be unimaginable without the EU Customs Union as a foundation, as such, market integration needs the instruments of the EU Customs Union to harmonise the intra-community trade of the EU Member States.[21]

When the Treaty establishing the European Economic Community (TEEC) was concluded in 1957, the main objectives were to create a customs union (Article 9 TEEC) and Common Market (Article 2 TEEC). Therefore, all customs duties and import quotas on trade between the Member States were to be discontinued after a transitional period of 12 years (Part 1 Title I TEEC) and a common customs tariff vis-á-vis third countries was to be created by 1 January 1970 (Part 1 Title II TEEC). The EU Customs Union was also accompanied with a common commercial policy (Part 3 Title II Chapter 3 TEEC); this fact makes clear its basic difference from a simple free trade area.

The term 'customs union' has two official definitions: that of the World Customs Organization (WCO), and that of the World Trade Organization (WTO). In the view of the WCO, a customs union is an:

> entity forming a Customs territory replacing two or more territories and having in its ultimate state the following characteristics: A common Customs tariff and a common or harmonized Customs legislation for the application of that tariff; the absence of any Customs duties and charges having equivalent effect in trade between the countries forming the Customs Union in products originating entirely in those countries or in products of other countries in respect of which import formalities have been complied with and Customs duties and charges having equivalent effect have been levied or guaranteed and if they have not benefited from a total or partial drawback of such duties and charges; the elimination of restrictive regulations of commerce within the Customs Union.[22]

The WTO, in Article XXIV:8(a) GATT 1994, states that:

> a customs union shall be understood to mean the substitution of a single customs territory for two or more customs territories, so that (i) duties and other restrictive regulations of commerce … are eliminated with respect to substantially all the trade between the constituent territories of the union or at least with respect to substantially all the trade in products originating in such territories, and, (ii) …, substantially the same duties and other regulations of commerce are applied by each of the members of the union to the trade of territories not included in the union.

[21] Rogmann, in: Kluth/Müller/Peilert (eds), 2008, pp 797–819 (799).

[22] WCO, 'Glossary of International Customs Terms', 2013, D/2013/0448/20, p 13.

The main features of a customs union are therefore free trade, in principle, between its members, and a common external trade policy, which means the administration of common rules and a common customs tariff in external trade. One can say that the crux of a customs union is for the member states to waive sovereignty and autonomy in the field of customs.[23]

Even before the target date of 1 January 1970, the European Customs Union had been realised by the six original Member States of the European Economic Community (EEC6). On 1 July 1968, the Common Customs Tariff came into force—at least in the commercial sector—as Regulation (EC) 950/68 of 28 June 1968,[24] as did regulations regarding the customs area,[25] customs valuation[26] and the concept of origin of goods.[27] Furthermore, customs duties and import quotas for trade were no longer imposed between the Member States and, on 1 January 1970, the Common Customs Tariff was extended to the agricultural sector.[28]

Next to the abolition of customs duties on imports and exports between the Member States, as well as all charges having equivalent effect, the adoption of a common customs tariff in their relations to third countries was of decisive importance for the establishment of the EU Customs Union pursuant to (now) Article 28 TFEU.[29] With the creation of the Common Customs Tariff as a solely external tariff, the internal tariffs between the EU Member States were completely abolished and tariff sovereignty passed to the EU. Furthermore, with the enactment of the Common Customs Tariff not only was the customs tariff union realised—long before the Single European Market was established in 1993—but also the entry of the EU (at this time, the EEC6) into the obligations under the General Agreement on Tariffs and Trade (GATT).[30] Nevertheless, until the creation of the Single European Market in 1993, customs controls were still carried out at the internal borders of the EU Member States, especially because of different customs formalities, but also for tax collection or consumer protection and economic protection.[31] In the absence of a further harmonisation of customs law, which stagnated for a

[23] Rüsken, in: Rüsken (ed), 2013, Vol I, Introduction CCC, para 41.

[24] [1968] OJ L172/1–402, repealed by Council Regulation (EEC) 2658/87 of 23 July 1987 on the tariff and statistical nomenclature and on the Common Customs Tariff, [1987] OJ L256/1–675, last amended by Council Regulation (EC) 254/2000 of 31 January 2000, [2000] OJ L28/16–18.

[25] Council Regulation (EEC) 1496/68 of 27 September 1968 on the definition of the customs territory of the community, [1968] OJ L238/1–2.

[26] Council Regulation (EEC) 803/68 of 27 June 1968 on the valuation of goods for customs purposes, [1968] OJ L148/6–12.

[27] Council Regulation (EEC) 802/68 of 27 June 1968 on the common definition of the concept of the origin of goods, [1968] OJ L148/1–5.

[28] Council Regulation (EEC) 2451/69 of 8 December 1969 changing Council Regulation (EEC) 950/68 on the Common Customs Tariff, [1969] OJ L311/1–381.

[29] Bleihauer, in: Witte/Wolffgang (eds), 2012, p 378, para 1456; see also Art 9 para 1 TEEC.

[30] ECJ of 16 March 1983, Joined Cases 267/81, 268/81 and 269/81, *SPI and SAMI* [1983] ECR 801, summary paras, 1, 2.

[31] DBB, dbb-Europathemen Nr 21, April 2006, p 1.

long time after 1968,[32] various national rules and regulations concerning different sectors of customs law were applied, especially in the area of customs formalities.[33]

However, from the beginning, the standards of the Customs Union of the EU went beyond the definitions of both the WCO and the WTO. The creation of the Common Customs Tariff, and the assignment of the Common Trade Policy to the European level in Articles 110–16 TEEC, alone were insufficient for creating the European Customs Union,[34] because these meant primarily building only a customs tariff union without providing for an integrated market in the EU. Experience has shown that the simple harmonisation of custom duties for third country goods is insufficient if the proceedings for their imposition, suspension or exemption are regulated differently.[35] Differences between national regulations in various areas of customs law are sufficient to constrain the movement of goods. Therefore, it was also necessary to harmonise, or even unify, the customs law of the Member States to create a Common Market, in the meaning of Article 2 TEEC,[36] as circumscribed by the Court of Justice of the European Union (ECJ) through defining characteristics of the Single European Market of Article 14 TEC (now Article 26 TFEU).[37] Compared with the early attempts to create a Common Market, the new one seeking a single European market was to abolish internal frontiers not in a political sense, but with regard to the formalities and controls relating to the movement of goods between the Member States.[38]

This requirement was clear from the beginning of the EU in 1957, when Article 27 TEEC requested further harmonisation of the national administrative law of the Member States in the customs field. However, this legal norm allowed the European Commission only to make suggestions to the Member States. These were not legally binding and therefore could hardly lead to any harmonisation in national administrative law.[39] Furthermore, there were different opinions about how a harmonised customs law could or should be achieved.[40] After 1968, the European Community had tried to create more uniformity in customs law by enacting directives based on Article 100 TEEC and later Article 94 TEC (now Article 115 TFEU).[41] These related, in particular, to the harmonisation of provisions concerning customs treatment of goods entering the European Community,[42]

[32] Weerth, 2008 ZfZ 7, pp 178–85 (181).

[33] See Rüsken, in: Rüsken (ed), 2013, Vol I, Introduction CCC, paras 47, 48.

[34] Wolffgang, in: Witte/Wolffgang (eds), 2012, p 12, para 16; Rüsken, in: Rüsken (ed), 2013, Vol I, Introduction CCC, para 44; Lyons, 2008, p 65.

[35] Lux, 2008 AW-Prax 7, pp 283–86 (283).

[36] Rüsken, in: Rüsken (ed), 2013, Vol I, Introduction CCC, para 44.

[37] ECJ of 5 May 1982, Case 15/81, *Gaston Schul*, [1982] ECR 1409, para 33.

[38] Wolffgang, in: Witte/Wolffgang (eds), 2012, p 11, para 15.

[39] Rogmann, in: Kluth/Müller/Peilert (eds), 2008, pp 797–819 (799).

[40] Weerth, 2008 ZfZ 7, pp 178–85 (181).

[41] Lyons, 2008, p 100.

[42] Council Directive 68/312/EEC of 30 July 1968 on harmonisation of the provisions laid down by law, regulation or administrative action relation to: 1. customs treatment of goods entering the customs territory of the community; 2. temporary storage of such goods, [1968] OJ L194/13–16.

inward processing,[43] customs warehousing procedures,[44] free zones,[45] outward processing,[46] deferred payment of import or export duties,[47] standard exchange of goods exported for repair,[48] customs debt,[49] procedures for the release of goods for free circulation[50] and procedures for the export of Community goods.[51] However, those directives were only able to create an approximation of laws and not a legal unity, because like any directive, they were only binding regarding their target, whereas the Member States were free in choosing the form and instruments to reach said target, pursuant to Article 189 paragraph 3 TEEC (Article 249 paragraph 3 TEC, now Article 288 paragraph 3 TFEU). Therefore, they also proved to be insufficient for creating a legal unity in customs laws, and in time the European Community increasingly resorted to regulations, given their direct legal effect in the Member States.[52]

In the aftermath of this shift, many rules that were important for the proper operation of the Customs Union were issued, in particular regarding transit procedure,[53] remission and repayment[54] as well as post-clearance recovery of duties,[55] mutual assistance of the customs authorities,[56] temporary admission,[57]

[43] Council Directive 69/73/EEC of 4 March 1969 on the harmonisation of provisions laid down by law, regulation or administrative action in respect of inward processing, [1969] OJ L58/1–7.

[44] Council Directive 69/74/EEC of 4 March 1969 on the harmonisation of provisions laid down by law, regulation or administrative action relating to customs warehousing procedure, [1969] OJ L58/7–10.

[45] Council Directive 69/75/EEC of 4 March 1969 on the harmonisation of provisions laid down by law, regulation or administrative action relating to free zones, [1969] OJ L58/11–13.

[46] Council Directive 76/119/EEC of 18 December 1975 on the harmonisation of provisions laid down by law, regulation or administrative action in respect of outward processing, [1976] OJ L24/58–62.

[47] Council Directive 78/453/EEC of 22 May 1978 on the harmonisation of provisions laid down by law, regulation or administrative action concerning deferred payment of import duties or export duties, [1978] OJ L146/19–21.

[48] Council Directive 78/1018/EEC of 27 November 1978 on the harmonisation of provisions laid down by law, regulation or administrative action in respect of standard exchange of goods exported for repair, [1978] OJ L349/33–35.

[49] Council Directive 79/623/EEC of 25 June 1979 on the harmonisation of provisions laid down by law, regulation or administrative action relating to customs debt, [1979] OJ L179/31–35.

[50] Council Directive 79/695/EEC of 24 July 1979 on the harmonisation of procedures for the release of goods for free circulation, [1979] OJ L205/19–26.

[51] Council Directive 81/177/EEC of 24 February 1981 on the harmonisation of procedures for the export of Community goods, [1981] OJ L83/40–47.

[52] Hohrmann, in: Hübschmann/Hepp/Spitaler (eds), 2013, Vol XIV, Introduction CCC, paras 17, 18; Rogmann, in: Kluth/Müller/Peilert (eds), 2008, pp 797–819 (799).

[53] Council Regulation (EEC) 542/69 of 18 March 1969 on Community transit, [1969] OJ L77/1–48.

[54] Council Regulation (EEC) 1430/79 of 2 July 1979 on the repayment or remission of import or export duties, [1979] OJ L175/1–7.

[55] Council Regulation (EEC) 1697/79 of 24 July on the post-clearance recovery of import duties or export duties which have not been required of the person liable for payment on goods entered for a costumes procedure involving the obligation to pay such duties, [1979] OJ L197/1–3.

[56] Council Regulation (EEC) 1468/81 of 19 May 1981 on mutual assistance between the administrative authorities of the Member states and cooperation between the latter and the Commission to ensure the correct application of the law on customs or agricultural matters, [1981] OJ L144/1–5.

[57] Council Regulation (EEC) 3599/82 of 21 December 1982 on temporary importation arrangement, [1982] OJ L376/1–9.

relief from customs duties,[58] inward[59] and outward processing[60] and processing under customs control,[61] single administrative document,[62] the Combined Nomenclature[63] and the TARIC,[64] customs declarant[65] and customs debt[66] and customs debtor[67] as well as security to cover customs debt,[68] and eventually the binding tariff information (BTI).[69] The order of entry into force of these regulations illustrates the step-by-step approach taken in establishing the European Customs Union. As far as tariff matters were concerned, the legal basis of these acts was Article 28 TEEC (later Article 26 TEC, now Article 31 TFEU). For other subject matters the basis was, depending on the specific issue, either Article 113 TEEC (later Article 133 TEC, now Article 207 TFEU) regarding the implementation of the Common Trade Policy, Article 235 TEEC (later Article 308 TEC, now Article 352 TFEU) regarding measures necessary to ensure the functioning of the Community, or simply 'the treaty'. After the Single European Act[70] in 1987 the new Article 100a TEEC (later Article 95 TEC, now Article 114 TFEU) constituted an extensive legal basis for the necessary harmonisation of the administrative provisions regarding customs law in the Member States.[71]

The numerous regulations in European customs law have contributed to its extensive harmonisation, but they have also caused a fragmentation of the law through countless single regulations,[72] which additionally often stood in a difficult

[58] Council Regulation (EEC) 918/83 of 28 March 1983 setting up a Community system of reliefs from customs duty, [1983] OJ L105/1–37.

[59] Council Regulation (EEC) 1999/85 of 16 July 1985 on inward processing relief arrangements, [1985] OJ L188/1–9.

[60] Council Regulation (EEC) 2473/86 of 24 July 1986 on outward processing relief arrangements and the standard exchange system, [1986] OJ L212/1–6.

[61] Council Regulation (EEC) 2763/83 of 26 September 1983 on arrangements permitting goods to be processed under customs control before being put into free circulation, [1983] OJ L272/1–4.

[62] Council Regulation (EEC) 1900/85 of 8 July 1985 introducing Community export and import declaration forms, [1985] OJ L1979/4–5; see also Council Regulation (EEC) 717/91 of 21 March 1991 concerning the Single Administrative Document, [1991] OJ L78/1–3.

[63] Council Regulation (EEC) 2658/87 of 23 July 1987 on the tariff and statistical nomenclature and on the Common Customs Tariff, [1987] OJ L256/1–675.

[64] Commission Regulation (EC) 3057/94 of 14 December 1994 concerning the classification of certain goods in TARIC, [1994] OJ L323/12–13.

[65] Council Regulation (EEC) 3632/85 of 12 December 1985 defining the conditions under which a person may be permitted to make a customs declaration, [1985] OJ L350/1–3.

[66] Council Regulation (EEC) 2144/87 of 13 July 1987 on customs debt, [1987] OJ L201/15–20; Council Directive 79/623/EEC of 25 June 1979 on the harmonization of provisions laid down by law, regulation or administrative action relating to customs debt, [1979] OJ L179/31–35.

[67] Council Regulation (EEC) 1031/88 of 18 April 1988 determining the persons liable for payment of a customs debt, [1988] OJ L102/5–8.

[68] Council Regulation (EEC) 4046/89 of 21 December 1989 on the security to be given to ensure payment of a customs debt, [1989] OJ L388/24–27.

[69] Council Regulation (EEC) 1715/90 of 20 June 1990 on the information provided by the customs authorities of the Member States concerning the classification of goods in the customs nomenclature, [1990] OJ L160/1–5.

[70] [1987] OJ L169/1–28.

[71] See the preamble of the Community Customs Code.

[72] Lyons, 2008, p 24.

relation to the supplementary national law of the Member States.[73] In light of the Single European Market, realised on 1 January 1993, it was in the interest of both the economy and the administration to summarise those customs law provisions that were scattered throughout a multitude of Community regulations and directives.[74] An important point in the creation of the European Customs Union was therefore the creation of the Common Customs Code, the first uniform codified European customs law in procedural matters and the biggest codified body of laws of the EU so far. Coming into force on 1 January 1994 as a directly enforceable Council Regulation,[75] the Code was not only a systematisation of existing customs law, but also gave rise to changes in regard to content, making European customs law more coherent and simpler, as well as closing existing gaps.[76] At the same time, its implementing provisions became applicable also as a directly enforceable Commission Regulation.[77] Together they constituted the main sources of European customs law,[78] with its main focus on procedural law, and introduced new rules about customs law decisions and appeal proceedings in customs matters.[79] However, they did not and still do not regulate the Common Customs Tariff (CCT),[80] relief from customs duties,[81] preferential trade agreements (PTAs) and mutual assistance.[82] Nonetheless, the preliminary consolidation of European customs law

[73] Rüsken, in: Rüsken (ed), 2013, Vol I, Introduction CCC, para 48; Witte, in: Witte (ed), 2013, before Art 251 CCC, para 1.

[74] Wolffgang, in: Witte/Wolffgang (eds), 2012, p 13, para 17; Lyons, 2008, p 24.

[75] Council Regulation (EEC) 2913/92 of 12 October 1992 establishing the Community Customs Code, [1992] OJ L302/1–50, last amended by Council Regulation (EC) 1791/2006 of 20 November 2006, [2006] OJ L363/1–80.

[76] See the Second Recital of the Community Customs Code.

[77] Commission Regulation (EEC) 2454/93 of 2 July 1993 laying down provisions for the implementation of Council Regulation (EEC) 2913/92 establishing the Community Customs Code, [1993] OJ L253/1–766, last amended by Commission Implementing Regulation (EU) 58/2013 of 23 January 2013, [2013] OJ L21/19–21.

[78] Wolffgang, in: Witte/Wolffgang (eds), 2012, pp 12, 13, para 17.

[79] Lux, 2008 AW-Prax 7, pp 283–86 (283).

[80] Council Regulation (EEC) 950/68 of 28 June 1968 on the Common Customs Tariff, [1968] OJ L172/1–402, repealed by Council Regulation (EEC) 2658/87 of 23 July 1987 on the tariff and statistical nomenclature and on the Common Customs Tariff, [1987] OJ L256/1–675.

[81] Council Regulation (EEC) 918/83 of 28 March 1983 setting up a Community system of reliefs from customs duty, [1983] OJ L105/1–37, repealed by Council Regulation (EC) 1186/2009 of 16 November 2009, [2009] OJ L324/23–57.

[82] First Treaty of Naples I of 7 September 1967 as an international treaty between the Member States at that time and not a part of the European Community law, later Council Act 98/C 24/01 of 18 December 1997 drawing up, on the basis of Art K3 of the Treaty on European Union, the Convention on mutual assistance and cooperation between customs administrations ('Naples II'), [1998] OJ C24/2–22, last amended by Council Decision of 6 December 2007 concerning the accession of Bulgaria and Romania to the Convention of 18 December 1997, drawn up on the basis of Art K.3 of the Treaty on European Union, on mutual assistance and cooperation between customs administrations, [2008] OJ L9/21–22; and also Council Regulation (EC) 515/97 of 13 March 1997 on mutual assistance between the administrative authorities of the Member States and cooperation between the latter and the Commission to ensure the correct application of the law on customs and agricultural matters, [1997] OJ L82/1–16; last amended by Regulation (EC) 766/2088 of the European Parliament and of the Council of 9 July 2008 amending Council Regulation (EC) 515/97 on mutual assistance between the administrative authorities of the Member States and cooperation between the latter and the Commission to ensure the correct application of the law on customs and agricultural matters, [2008] OJ L218/48–59.

was completed and afterwards only selective modifications regarding the Community Customs Code and its implementing provisions were undertaken[83] until the Modernised Customs Code[84] was issued (but only partially enacted) in 2008 and the Union Customs Code[85] was proposed in 2012 and finally issued (but again only partially enacted) in 2013.

The historical background of EU customs law illustrates that the creation of the EU, and with it the Customs Union, was undertaken in several steps. The next important change will be the Union Customs Code, in which the legal obligation of using and networking electronic systems for all kinds of declarations will be a special characteristic.[86]

III. CURRENT LEGAL FRAMEWORK OF THE EU CUSTOMS UNION

EU customs law is shaped significantly by the Community Customs Code (CCC) of the European Union,[87] which regulates common customs procedural law. Yet the CCC is not the only relevant source of customs law;[88] it is complemented by other legal EU provisions. The most important provision is the CCC's Implementing Regulation (CCCIP),[89] but other key provisions include the regulation on the relief from customs duties,[90] preferential trade agreements (PTAs) and especially the Common Customs Tariff of the European Union (CCT),[91] which contains the common tariff customs law. Additionally, the national law of the EU Member States can have a supplementary or gap-filling function despite the intended all-encompassing EU customs regulations.[92] To some extent the Community Customs Code even explicitly leaves the regulation of certain single issues to the EU

[83] Lux, 2008 AW-Prax 7, pp 283–86 (283).

[84] Council Regulation (EC) 450/2008 of 23 April 2008 laying down the Community Customs Code (Modernised Customs Code), [2008] OJ L145/1–64.

[85] Regulation (EU) 952/2013 of the European Parliament and of the Council of 9 October 2013 laying down the Union Customs Code, [2013] OJ L269/1–88.

[86] Similar Lux, 2008 AW-Prax 7, pp 283–86 (283, 284) with reference to the Modernised Customs Code.

[87] Council Regulation (EEC) 2913/92 of 12 October 1992 establishing the Community Customs Code, [1992] OJ L302/1–50, last amended by Council Regulation (EC) 1791/2006 of 20 November 2006, [2006] OJ L363/1–80.

[88] Rüsken, in: Rüsken (ed), 2013, Vol I, Introduction CCC, para 56.

[89] Commission Regulation (EEC) 2454/93 of July 1993 laying down provisions for the implementation of Council Regulation (EEC) 2913/92 establishing the Community Customs Code, [1993] OJ L253/1–766, last amended by Commission Implementing Regulation (EU) 58/2013 of 23 January 2013, [2013] OJ L21/19–21.

[90] Council Regulation (EEC) 918/83 of 28 March 1983 setting up a Community system of reliefs from customs duty, [1983] OJ L105/1–37, repealed by Council Regulation (EC) 1186/2009 of 16 November 2009, [2009] OJ L324/23–57.

[91] Council Regulation (EEC) 950/68 of 28 June 1968 on the Common Customs Tariff, [1968] OJ L172/1–402, repealed by Council Regulation (EEC) 2658/87 of 23 July 1987 on the tariff and statistical nomenclature and on the Common Customs Tariff, [1987] OJ L256/1–675.

[92] The supplementary effectiveness of national law is discussed in detail in Chapter 6.I.A.1.

Member States,[93] for example Article 10 CCC, which provides for the invalidity of customs decisions based on national reasons unconnected with customs legislation, or Article 167 CCC, which allows EU Member States to determine the geographical scope of free customs zones. The supplementary effectiveness of national administrative law is often related to procedural law, as the Community Customs Code contains only a few rules for common administrative procedural law.[94] However, the jurisprudence of the ECJ requires that the EU Member States and their officials bear in mind the general principles of EU law when supplementing it with national procedural law.[95] Nevertheless, the Community Customs Code serves as a model for related law and shall apply uniformly throughout the customs territory of the EU, pursuant to Article 2 CCC. The issued, but only partially enacted, Modernised Customs Code (MCC)[96] was expected to have a similar effect from 2013 on, but now that role is to be taken over by the Union Customs Code (UCC)[97].

A. The Common Customs Tariff[98]

A customs tariff determines the duty rate on a concrete good at the time of its importation. In contrast to this, the substantive customs law in the Community Customs Code and the Implementing Regulation regulates the incurrence, recovery, extinction, repayment and remission of duties in the cross-border trade of goods. However, the larger part of customs duty law lies outside the Community Customs Code and its implementing provisions, as the former's Articles 20, 21 simply refer to the Common Customs Tariff regarding matters of the customs tariff and the classification of goods. Therefore, the tariff law is an important component of EU customs law and both sources of EU customs law—the Common Customs Tariff and the Community Customs Code—constitute an inseparable unity of substantive and procedural customs law in the EU.[99]

A customs tariff is a nomenclature for the classification of goods: a systematically edited catalogue of goods and the various tariff rates applicable.[100] The basis for the assessment of customs duties can be ad valorem duties, specific duties on

[93] Wolffgang, in: Witte/Wolffgang (eds), 2012, p 14, para 18.

[94] ibid; Lyons, 2008, p 98.

[95] See, inter alia, ECJ of 13 March 2008, Joined Cases C-383/06 to C-385/06, *Vereniging Nationaal Overlegorgaan Sociale Werkvoorziening*, [2008] ECR I-1561, paras 48, 49, 50; ECJ of 21 September 1983, Joined Cases 205 to 215/82, *Deutsche Milchkontor*, [1983] ECR 2633, para 17, and the case law cited.

[96] Council Regulation (EC) 450/2008 of 23 April 2008 laying down the Community Customs Code (Modernised Customs Code), [2008] OJ L145/1–64.

[97] Regulation (EU) 952/2013 of the European Parliament and of the Council of 9 October 2013 laying down the Union Customs Code (recast), [2013] OJ L269/1–101.

[98] For this section see also: Weiß, in: Grabitz/Hilf/Nettesheim (eds), 2013, Vol II, Art 207 TFEU, paras 127–34 and fn 226.

[99] Bleihauer, in: Witte/Wolffgang (eds), 2012, p 376, para 1452.

[100] ibid, p 376, para 1453; similar: Lyons, 2008, p 132.

a weight basis or a compound tariff. An ad valorem duty is assessed according to a pre-determined percentage of the customs value of the article in question; specific duties are assessed according to specific factor like weight, capacity etc.; and a compound tariff is a combination of both. Modern customs tariffs like the Common Customs Tariff of the EU contain primarily ad valorem duties.[101] The Common Customs Tariff was issued under the customs jurisdiction of the EU—mostly Article 31 TFEU for autonomous amendments and Article 207 TFEU for amendments concerning the Common Commercial Policy, but also Article 43 TFEU for amendments regarding the Common Agricultural Policy. Therefore its enactment and amendment is bound to certain procedural requirements.[102] This results from the fact that the Common Customs Tariff itself constitutes a legal act and even if its tariff codes differ from the structure of common legal norms there is a pressing need to handle those codes with juridical instruments.[103]

1. The Harmonised System

The development of the European customs tariff law is inseparably connected with the development of the EU and also with the development of the goods nomenclature.[104] In its first form, the Nomenclature of the Customs Cooperation Council, also called the Brussels tariff nomenclature, served as the tariff nomenclature.[105] On 1 January 1988, it was replaced with the Harmonised Commodity, Description and Coding System (HS), an international agreement for the harmonisation of national tariff nomenclatures for the purpose of trade facilitation. It was developed by the World Customs Organization (WCO), is administered with the assistance of the Harmonised System Committee and updated every four to six years. The Harmonised System is used by more than 200 states, areas, customs unions and economic unions, although one has to make a distinction between states that have formally joined the Harmonised System, and states that only accept and apply the Harmonised System.[106] The EU ratified the Harmonised

[101] Bleihauer, ibid, p 377, para 1454; Lyons, 2008, pp 136, 137; Gormley, 2009, p 37, para 2.07.

[102] Bleihauer, ibid, p 377, para 1454; Lux, in: Rüsken (ed) 2013, Vol III, Introduction CN Regulation, para 47.

[103] Bleihauer, ibid, pp 375, 376, paras 1451, 1452.

[104] Bleihauer, ibid, p 378, para 1455.

[105] Weerth, ZfZ 2008 7, pp 178–85 (180); Bleihauer, ibid, p 378, para 1456; Lyons, 2008, p 132.

[106] WCO, Harmonized System Convention–General Information, URL: www.wcoomd.org/en/topics/nomenclature/overview/what-is-the-harmonized-system.aspx and also URL: www.wcoomd.org/en/topics/nomenclature/overview.aspx; see also Wind, 2007 GTCJ (2), pp 79–86 (79). At the moment, 147 contracting parties and the EU apply the Harmonised System, see WCO, Harmonized System Convention—List of countries, territories or customs or economic unions applying the Harmonized System, URL: www.wcoomd.org/en/topics/nomenclature/~/media/WCO/Public/Global/PDF/Topics/Nomenclature/Overview/HS%20Contracting%20Parties/List%20of%20Countries/Countries_applying_HS.ashx (situation as of 2 July 2013).

System in 1987,[107] though it first had to be further specified for certain matters of the Common Customs Tariff under consideration of tariff aspects and matters of external trade statistics. Therefore, simultaneous to ratification, the Combined Nomenclature (CN) in the form of Regulation (EEC) 2658/87 of the Council of 23 July 1987 on the tariff and statistical nomenclature and on the Common Customs Tariff[108] was established, replacing the Nomenclature of Goods for the External Trade Statistics of the Community and Statistics of Trade between Member States (NIMEXE).[109] Since then, the EU and the EU Member States together represent a block of 28 contracting parties to the convention of the Harmonised System, as the convention constitutes a mixed agreement by both the EU and EU Member States.

In relation to the cross-border movement of goods, the term 'nomenclature' describes a catalogue of goods seeking to clearly classify all goods and products following systematic principles.[110] The nomenclature of the Harmonised System classifies over 98 per cent of the merchandise in international trade;[111] it is the basis of tariffs in more than 200 states and economic areas including the EU. It consists of four-digit HS-positions, six-digit HS-subdivisions, and legal notes referring to the 21 sections of the Harmonised System as well as also six general provisions, both of which are to assist in the interpretation of the Harmonised System.

2. *The Combined Nomenclature*

In the EU, the Harmonised System was transposed in April 1987 through the creation of the Combined Nomenclature, which added to the Harmonised System two genuine subdivisions, the seventh and eight position of the code. Because the Combined Nomenclature constitutes only a further itemisation of the Harmonised System, it follows the structural design of the latter and is divided into 21 sections, 97 chapters, 1224 positions and 5205 HS-subdivisions (as of 2013). It systemises the goods matter-of-factly after the manner of their production, following the so-called principle of production.[112] The Combined Nomenclature also entails introducing provisions and legal notes to the sections, chapters and

[107] Council Decision of 7 April 1987 concerning the conclusion of the International Convention on the Harmonized Commodity Description and Coding System and of the Protocol of Amendment thereto, [1987] OJ L198/3–10.

[108] [1987] OJ L256/1–675.

[109] Council Regulation (EEC) 1445/72 of 24 April 1972 concerning the nomenclature of goods for the external trade statistics of the Community and statistics of trade between Member States (NIMEXE), [1972] OJ L161/1–411, last amended by Commission Regulation (EEC) 3840/86 of 16 December 1986 amending the nomenclature of goods for the external trade statistics of the Community and statistics of trade between Member States (NIMEXE), [1986] OJ L368/1–588.

[110] Weerth, Witten 2007, p 121; Czakert, 1995, p 9.

[111] WCO, Harmonized System Convention–General Information, URL: www.wcoomd.org/en/topics/nomenclature/overview/what-is-the-harmonized-system.aspx and also URL: www.wcoomd.org/en/topics/nomenclature/overview.aspx; see also Lyons, 2008, p 133.

[112] Bleihauer, in: Witte/Wolffgang (eds), 2012, p 380, para 1460.

footnotes referring to the CN-subdivision. No later than 31 October of each year, the Combined Nomenclature is completely updated and issued as a regulation in the Official Journal of the EU together with the current tariff rates,[113] pursuant to Article 12 paragraph 1 CN.

3. *The TARIC*

Furthermore, pursuant to Article 2 CN the European Commission was authorised to create the Integrated Tariff of the Community (TARIC), which covers legal measures of the EU such as suspension of customs duties or tariff quotas. The creation of additional subdivisions and the incorporation of those in an integrated tariff of the EU were necessary because the itemisation of the Commodity Classification by the Combined Nomenclature cannot encompass the whole customs tariff of the EU in the meaning of Article 28 paragraph 1 TFEU.[114] Consequently, the purpose of the TARIC is to integrate and codify all EU measures concerning tariff, commercial and agricultural legislation, which leads to a further subdivision of a commodity name in the Combined Nomenclature.[115] Therefore, the TARIC is based on the Combined Nomenclature of the EU and expands this by two more subdivisions—the ninth and tenth digits of the code number. With the establishment of the TARIC, the European Commission seeks not only to provide economic operators with a clear view of all measures to be undertaken at the importation or exportation of goods and to collect EU-wide statistics on such activities, but moreover also seeks to secure the uniform application of those measures by the EU Member States.[116] For these purpose, the TARIC aims to guarantee immediate and correct information for the national customs administrations of the EU Member States through daily transmission of TARIC data via an electronic network.[117] The shifting of the collection, interpretation and integration of EU law from the EU Member States to the European Commission can indeed lead to a more uniform administration of EU law.[118]

The measures additionally covered by the TARIC in this way each have their legal basis within EU law, whereas the TARIC itself does not constitute a legal act

[113] See the customs tariff in 2013: Commission Implementing Regulation (EU) 927/2012 of 9 October 2012 amending Annex I to Council Regulation (EEC) 2658/87 on the tariff and statistical nomenclature and on the Common Customs Tariff, [2012] OJ L304/1–915; and the customs tariff for 2014: Commission Implementing Regulation (EU) 1001/2013 of 4 October 2013 amending Annex I to Council Regulation (EEC) 2658/87 on the tariff and statistical nomenclature and on the Common Customs Tariff, [2013] OJ L290/1–901.

[114] Alexander, in: Witte (ed), 2013, Art 20 CCC, para 14.

[115] Lux, in: Rüsken (eds), 2013, Vol III, Art 5 CN, para 2; Lyons, 2008, pp 134, 135, 145.

[116] See European Commission Directorate General TAXUD about the TARIC, URL: http://ec.europa.eu/taxation_customs/customs/customs_duties/tariff_aspects/customs_tariff/index_en.htm.

[117] See European Commission Directorate General TAXUD about the TARIC, URL: http://ec.europa.eu/taxation_customs/customs/customs_duties/tariff_aspects/customs_tariff/index_en.htm.

[118] See also Lux, in: Rüsken (ed) 2013, Vol III, Introduction CN Regulation, para 14.

and therefore has no legal status.[119] Nevertheless, with Article 5 CN the TARIC is to be granted the highest operational standard of binding force.[120] In this respect, Article 5 paragraph 2 CN can be seen as a legal basis for the mandatory application of the TARIC.[121] Therefore, the TARIC codes must be used for customs declarations in the EU as well as for statistical returns.[122] The reason for the complicated status of the TARIC results from the requirement that it be capable of reacting to changes in EU law in a fast and flexible way, including providing integrated solutions for overlapping legal acts and their quick transmission to the EU Member States.[123] A legally binding regulation with its corresponding procedural requirements cannot meet these demands. Therefore, the TARIC was issued as an announcement and effort to integrate its codes into single regulations continue to this day.[124] This fact makes the legal control of tariff measures often quite difficult, as considerable effort is often required to first find the legal basis of each single measure.[125]

Because of the fact that the trade code numbers and tariff rates change on a daily basis, the TARIC is no longer published in the Official Journal of the EU.[126] Today, the function of information sources is instead fulfilled by the website of the EU,[127] by the national working tariffs and tariff data files, as well as the relevant EU-regulations.[128] The TARIC itself is now a multilingual online customs tariff database[129] and its data are transmitted via an electronic network on a daily basis to the national administrations of the EU Member States, providing them with immediate and correct information that they then use mainly to feed into their national systems for customs clearance in order to maximise automatic customs clearance.[130] The responsibility for establishing, updating, managing and disseminating the TARIC lies with the European Commission pursuant to Article 6 CN. The European Commission was formerly assisted by the Committee on Tariff and Statistical Nomenclature, a role now fulfilled by the Customs Code Committee pursuant to Article 10 CN.[131] It is important to emphasise that a classification using only the TARIC is not possible, because the TARIC database is not a complete customs tariff, but rather an incomplete nomenclature.[132] Nevertheless,

[119] Bleihauer, in: Witte/Wolffgang (eds), 2012, p 379, para 1458; Lyons, 2008, p 145; Hofmann/Rowe/Türk, 2011, p 539.

[120] Lux, in: Rüsken (eds), 2013, Vol III, Art 5 CN, para 1.

[121] ibid, Vol III, Art 5 CN, para 7.

[122] Lyons, 2008, p 145; Hofmann/Rowe/Türk, 2011, p 539.

[123] Lux, in: Rüsken (eds), 2013, Vol III, Art 5 CN, para 2.

[124] ibid, Vol III, Art 5 CN, para 2.

[125] Alexander, in: Witte (ed), 2013, Art 20 CCC, para 14.

[126] Communication concerning TARIC (The integrated tariff of the European Communities), [2004] OJ C258/18.

[127] URL: http://ec.europa.eu/taxation_customs/index_en.htm.

[128] Lux, in: Rüsken (eds), 2013, Vol III, Art 5 CN, para 7.

[129] URL: http://ec.europa.eu/taxation_customs/dds2/taric/taric_consultation.jsp?Lang=en.

[130] European Parliament, Study 2012, IP/A/IMCO/ST/2011–11, PE 475.094, p 53.

[131] Lyons, 2008, p 146.

[132] Weerth, Witten 2007, p 129.

the TARIC, being a multilingual database containing measures relating to EU tariff, agricultural and trade defence legislation, supports the uniform application of those measures by making them available in a standardised manner and enables all economic operators and national customs authorities to have a clear overview of all the measures applicable to the import and export of goods.[133]

4. The National Working Tariffs

Lastly, the EU Member States can and sometimes do expand the 10-digit code by an eleventh digit, pursuant to Article 5 Paragraph 3 CN, in order to address national needs through a further refined differentiation. Germany, for example, is using its Electronic Customs Tariff[134] as the national working tariff, which consist of an 11-digit code as a rule.[135] National working tariffs are different from the Common Customs Tariff and the TARIC to the extent that they contain a national eleventh digit in the code number. Furthermore, the TARIC-information issued by the European Commission is often reformatted, and even sometimes edited manually, for national needs, with information about national consumption taxes and value-added taxes often being included.[136]

The provisions that must be considered with the importation and exportation of goods into or from the customs area of the EU do not all originate from EU law and, therefore, the TARIC is currently not an instrument that can supersede the national working tariffs.[137] The national tariff data files are used for automated customs handling and also cannot be replaced by the TARIC given that the TARIC does not contain a programme for the calculation of duties and taxes.[138] The national customs authorities instead simply use the daily data transmission from the TARIC to update their national systems for customs clearance and to improve automatic procedures.

Replacing the national working tariffs and the national tariff data files with a TARIC updated on a regular basis would be possible only if a complete harmonisation of the information covered by the national working tariffs and the national tariff data files, including national consumption taxes and value-added taxes, could be realised.[139] Until then, codification gaps can be closed by working tariffs and tariff data files.[140] Like the TARIC, working tariffs and tariff data files do not constitute legal acts. Rather, the legal basis of each customs administration

[133] European Parliament, Study 2012, IP/A/IMCO/ST/2011–11, PE 475.094, p 53.

[134] Elektronischer Zolltarif (EZT).

[135] Bleihauer, in: Witte/Wolffgang (eds), 2012, p 382, paras 1462, 1463.

[136] See for the German working tariff: Weerth, Witten 2007, p 131.

[137] Lux, in: Rüsken (eds), 2013, Vol III, Art 5 CN, para 12; Alexander, in: Witte (ed), 2013, Art 20 CCC, para 15.

[138] Lux, ibid, Vol III, Art 5 CN, para 12.

[139] ibid, Vol III, Art 5 CN, para 10.

[140] Alexander, in: Witte (ed), 2013, Art 20 CCC, para 15.

case rests on its own relevant legal provision.[141] Working tariffs and tariff data files of the EU Member States also must meet predetermined standards in their depiction of EU law, pursuant to Article 5 CN which supports the uniform application of EU law.[142] Those predetermined standards result from the fact that since the introduction of the TARIC, the function of collecting, interpreting and integrating common EU import and export law has been transferred from competent national authorities in the EU Member States—which worked individually—to the European Commission.[143] Therefore, the information about customs-related EU law and EU measures used in national working tariffs and tariff data files stems from a common EU basis—the TARIC—pursuant to Article 5 paragraphs 1 and 2 CN, thus enhancing the uniform application of EU customs tariff law.

Even though the regulation of the Combined Nomenclature allows only certain amendments and no alterations,[144] the EU Member States are to a large extent still free in determining the composition of their working tariffs and tariff data files.[145] This means that the EU Member States—apart from the restrictions of Article 5 CN—possess a certain degree of freedom of scope regarding the extent and composition of the working tariff, column headings as well as the terms for different types of revenue, the logical structure of the tariff data files, and the algorithms for the calculation of duties and taxes in automated procedures.[146]

However, it has to be emphasised that the tariff in the EU is based on EU law, and not on national law. Thus, national compilations of EU law do not constitute authoritative sources of law.[147] In fact, the ECJ has made it clear that national working tariffs, such as the German 'Gebrauchs-Zolltarif' (now called 'Elektronischer Zolltarif (EZT))[148] are only a kind of 'how-to manual' for customs clearance.[149]

B. The Community Customs Code: Main Regulatory Aspects of the Community Customs Code and its Implementing Provisions[150]

The Community Customs Code is the central legal act of EU customs law and is supplemented by implementing provisions on both the EU and EU Member

[141] ECJ of 20 November 2008, Case C-38/07 P, *Heuschen & Schrouff Oriëntal Foods Trading BV I* [2008] ECR I-8599, para 61; in particular ECJ of 12 July 1989, Case 161/88, *Friedrich Binder* [1989] ECR 2415, para 19; see for the German working tariff: Weerth, Witten 2007, p 131.

[142] Lux, in: Rüsken (eds), 2013, Vol III, Art 5 CN, para 13.

[143] ibid, Vol III, Art 5 CN, para 13.

[144] ibid, Vol III, Art 5 CN, para 8.

[145] ibid, Vol III, Art 5 CN, para 10.

[146] ibid, Vol III, Art 5 CN, para 10.

[147] Lyons, 2008, p 132.

[148] The German Electronic Customs Tariff.

[149] ECJ of 20 November 2008, Case C-38/07 P, *Heuschen & Schrouff Oriëntal Foods Trading BV I* [2008] ECR I-8599, para 61; in particular ECJ of 21 July 1989, Case 161/88, *Friedrich Binder* [1989] ECR 2415, para 19.

[150] For this section see also: Weiß, in: Grabitz/Hilf/Nettesheim (eds), 2013, Vol II, Art 207 TFEU, paras 135–42 and fn 226.

States level, see Article 1 paragraph 1 CCC. The Code encompasses the basic rules of EU customs law, while the details are found in the provisions of the Community Customs Code Implementing Regulation (CCCIP), whose articles and annexes are systematically ordered corresponding to the Code.[151] The Code thereby constitutes a major part of uniform EU customs law and sets out in Article 2 CCC the crucial principle that, unless otherwise provided, EU customs rules shall apply uniformly throughout the customs territory of the EU.[152]

Key aspects of both the Community Customs Code and its implementing provisions are general rules for the whole EU customs law, substantive law in the form of customs duty law, as well as procedural law, although the focus clearly lies on the latter.

In the Community Customs Code itself there are institutions and procedures for commerce in goods, namely the placing of goods under a customs procedure, Article 59 CCC et seq; the re-exportation, destruction and abandonment of goods, Article 182 CCC et seq; and provisions for free zones and free warehouses, Article 166 CCC et seq. The remainder of the Code contains primarily rules concerning customs duty law, especially incurrence of a customs debt, Article 201 CCC et seq, recovery of the amount of the customs debt, Article 217 CCC et seq, extinction of customs debt, Article 233 CCC et seq, and repayment and remission of a duty, Article 235 CCC et seq. However, it also contains rules concerning the factors on the basis of which import duties or export duties are applied, Title II CCC. For this, the Community Customs Code actually refers to the Common Customs Tariff regarding the customs tariff and the classification of goods, Articles 20 and 21 CCC, but it regulates the origin of goods, Article 22 CCC et seq, and the value of goods for customs purpose, Article 28 CCC et seq, by itself. With the help of these four bases of assessment, the rate of the customs debt payable at the import of goods can be determined. The fact leading to the recovery of the customs debt is not the importation itself, but the release of the goods for free circulation in the EU, for which one needs an import declaration. In principle, an export duty is also provided for in EU customs law. However, usually the export of goods to third countries and the resulting realisation of profits are in the interest of the EU. Therefore export duties are seldom charged, typically when the price level of a good in the EU is lower than that on the international market, resulting in the risk that goods needed for the supply of the EU Member States are exported instead.[153]

Together with the provisions of the Community Customs Code Implementing Regulation, which are necessary for the application of the Community Customs Code, EU customs law has an enormous and often overly detailed scope of provisions, yet at the same time there are still a multitude of unsolved problems

[151] Wolffgang, in: Witte/Wolffgang (eds), 2012, p 13, para 17.

[152] Lyons, 2008, p 100.

[153] Witte, in: Gabler Wirtschaftslexikon, Kurzerklärung 'Ausfuhrabgaben', URL: http://wirtschaftslexikon.gabler.de/Definition/ausfuhrabgaben.html.

concerning its interpretation and application.[154] Undefined legal terms and a partial lack of sufficient legal definitions, complicated and sometimes even confusing structures that do not always follow the procedural logic of a customs procedure, and references to the national law of EU Member States can make uniform interpretation and application of the Code and its implementing provisions difficult. However, the Community Customs Code and its Implementing Regulation constitute a far-reaching comprehensive body of rules and regulations that determines the fundamentals of EU customs law and especially EU customs procedural law, and which only in certain individual cases needs to be supplemented with national regulations.[155] Nevertheless, this basic framework is only complete with the addition of further legal acts on the EU as well as the national level, especially given that the EU is a supranational organisation without comprehensive governmental sovereignty and to a large extent lacks its own implementing administrative body.[156] Although the EU Customs Union is an exclusive competence of the EU pursuant to Article 3 paragraph 1 section (a) TFEU, implementing EU customs legislation is primarily the responsibility of the EU Member States.[157]

IV. THE NEED FOR A REFORM OF EU CUSTOMS LAW TO ENHANCE UNIFORM CUSTOMS ADMINISTRATION

The customs law as well as the external trade law of the EU is administered by the national administrations of the 28 EU Member States. Each of these 28 national customs administrations comes with its own organisation, structure, culture, administrative directives and IT systems. The legal structures of EU customs law provide only the foundation for a uniform administration that has to be created by national customs authorities.[158] EU customs administration automatically results in a balancing act between the decentralised administration and the simultaneous requirement for uniform implementation of EU customs.

A. The Requirement for Uniform Application of EU Customs Law

In EU customs law, Article 2 paragraph 1 CCC[159] establishes that EU customs rules shall apply uniformly throughout the customs territory of the EU. Furthermore, in EU primary law Article 197 paragraph 1 TFEU now explicitly emphasises the importance of effective implementation for the functioning of the EU, thus establishing the exigency of uniformity and its realisation in practice as guiding

[154] Rüsken, in: Rüsken (ed), 2013, Vol I, Introduction CCC, paras 59, 61; similar: Lyons, 2008, pp 97, 98.
[155] Rüsken, ibid, Vol I, Introduction CCC, para 56; similar: Lyons, 2008, p 98.
[156] Rüsken, ibid, Vol I, Introduction CCC, para 56; similar: Lyons, 2008, p 98.
[157] COM (2012) 791 final, p 3.
[158] Lyons, 2008, p 97.
[159] See also Art 1 para 1 subpara 2 UCC/former Art 1 para 1 subpara 2 MCC.

ideas of European administration.[160] In addition, Article 291 paragraph 2 TFEU governs the necessity for uniform conditions in the implementation of EU law,[161] as did the former Article 202 TEC.[162]

The importance of uniform customs administration derives originally from Article 4 paragraph 3 TEU, which contains the obligation for the well-regulated and loyal administrative implementation of EU law, given that the EU is to a large degree dependent upon national administrations for the enforcement of EU law.[163] Thus, the EU Member States and their administrations have to fulfil certain single obligations in order to realise the principle of loyalty expressed in Article 4 paragraph 3 TEU.[164] It is established case law that Article 4 paragraph 3 subparagraph 1 TEU imposes a general and reciprocal duty of genuine cooperation on the EU Member States and on the EU institutions. Pursuant to this principle of sincere cooperation, EU Member States are generally:

> to refrain from any measure which could jeopardise the attainment of the Union's objectives…[165] [and further] all the authorities of the Member States, including the administrative and judicial bodies, must ensure the observance of the rules of European Union law within the sphere of their competence.[166]

From the exigency to loyalty in Article 4 paragraph 3 TEU derives the obligation of EU Member States to realise the thorough, uniform and effective application and enforcement of EU law. In established case law, the ECJ emphasises the general need for the uniform application of EU law[167] and also the specific need in the context of EU customs law.[168] The ECJ has generally held:

> that, by virtue of the obligations arising from the FEU Treaty and assumed on ratification, Member States are under a duty not to obstruct the direct applicability inherent in regulations, given that the scrupulous observation of this duty is an indispensable requisite for the simultaneous and uniform application of European Union regulations throughout the Union.[169]

[160] Weiß, 2010, p 27; similar: Classen, in: Grabitz/Hilf/Nettesheim (eds), 2013, Vol II, Art 197 TFEU, para 10; Ruffert, in: Calliess/Ruffert, 2011, Art 197 TFEU, para 2.

[161] Weiß, 2010, p 42.

[162] ECJ of 18 January 2005, Case C-257/01, *Commission v Council*, [2005] ECR I-345, para 66.

[163] Hofmann/Rowe/Türk, 2011, p 134; Streinz, 2012, § 7, para 580; Kahl, in: Calliess/Ruffert (eds), 2011, Art 4 TEU, para 62.

[164] Hofmann/Rowe/Türk, 2011, pp 134, 136; Classen, in: Grabitz/Hilf/Nettesheim (eds), 2013, Vol II, Art 197 TFEU, paras 18, 20.

[165] See, inter alia, ECJ of 27 November 2012, Case C-370/12, *Thomas Pringle* [2012] ECR I-0, para 148 and the case law cited.

[166] See, inter alia, ECJ of 4 October 2012, Case C-249/11, *Hristo Byankov* [2012] ECR I-0, para 64, and the case law cited.

[167] See, inter alia, ECJ of 12 December 2013, Case C-486/12, *Gerechtshof te 's-Hertogenbosch* [2013] ECR I-0, para 19; ECJ of 5 December 2013, Case C-508/12, *Vapenik*, [2013] ECR I-0, para 23, and the case law cited.

[168] See, inter alia, ECJ of 12 December 2013, Case C-116/12, *Christodoulou* [2013] ECR I-0, para 34; ECJ of 12 December 2013, Case C-450/12, *HARK GmbH & Co KG* [2013] ECR I-0, para 37; ECJ of 18 April 2013, Case C-595/11, *Steinel Vertrieb GmbH* [2013] ECR I-0, para 34.

[169] See, inter alia, ECJ of 15 November 2012, Joined Cases C-539/10 P and C-550/10 P, *Stichting Al-Aqsa* ECR I-0, para 87, and the case law cited.

Indeed, the demand for uniform application and interpretation of EU law is not an end in itself but arises from the requirement of equal effectiveness of EU law throughout the EU. Therefore, the EU's interest in the uniform application and interpretation of EU law is regularly mentioned in the context of the general principle of equality,[170] but also with regard to the general need for effective application of EU law.[171] Such general principles regarding the implementation of EU law which the EU Member States have to obey[172] can be regarded as the legal foundation of EU administrative law, in that they provide a guide to the interpretation of EU law.[173]

With regard to the general principle of equality, also called 'principle of equal treatment',[174] the ECJ states that:

> the need for the uniform application of European Union law and the principle of equality require that the terms of a provision of European Union law which makes no express reference to the law of the Member States for the purpose of determining its meaning and scope must normally be given an autonomous and uniform interpretation throughout the European Union, which must take into account the context of that provision and the purpose of the legislation in question.[175]

Therefore, EU legal terms must have the same scope in all the EU Member States, one which cannot be altered by way of interpretation because:

> the direct applicability of a regulation precludes … the Member States from taking steps which are intended to alter the scope of the regulation itself.[176]

Indeed, from an early stage the ECJ has held that EU regulations

> can only fulfil their functions if the provisions to which they give rise are applied in a uniform manner in all the Member States.[177]

The Common Customs Tariff and the Customs Code,[178] both being directly applicable EU regulations, are clearly covered by the comprehensive claim of EU law for uniform application throughout the whole territory of the EU.

[170] See, inter alia, ECJ of 19 September 2013, Case C-140/12, *Pensionsversicherungsanstalt* [2013] ECR I-0, para 49; ECJ of 18 July 2013, Case C-515/11, *Deutsche Umwelthilfe eV* [2013] ECR I-0, para 21, and the case law cited.

[171] In this direction ECJ of 18 June 2013, Case C-681/11, *Schencker & Co. AG* [2013] ECR I-0, paras 47, 49.

[172] Hofmann/Rowe/Türk, 2011, p 144; Streinz, 2012, para 592; Classen, in: Grabitz/Hilf/Nettesheim (eds), 2013, Vol II, Art 197 TFEU, paras 18, 20.

[173] Hofmann/Rowe/Türk, 2011, p 144.

[174] Hofmann/Rowe/Türk, 2011, p 162.

[175] ECJ of 18 July 2013, Case C-515/11, *Deutsche Umwelthilfe eV* [2013] ECR I-0, para 21; see in the context of EU customs law ECJ of 15 November 2012, Case C-558/11, *SIA Kurcums Metal* [2012] ECR I-0, para 48.

[176] See, inter alia, ECJ of 15 November 2012, Joined Cases C-539/10 P and C-550/10 P, *Stichting Al-Aqsa* ECR I-0, para 86, and the case law cited.

[177] ECJ of 18 June 1970, Case 74–69, *Krohn* [1970] ECR 451, para 8.

[178] See Recital 7 of the Community Customs Code.

Furthermore, it is also established case law that the principle of equal treatment is infringed 'where comparable situations are treated differently or different situations are treated in the same way, unless such difference of treatment is objectively justified.'[179] In this context, the requirement of uniform administration in the practical implementation of EU law is necessary to avoid unequal treatment of economic operators in the EU and to secure the functioning of the European Internal Market. Therefore, uniform implementation is an important obligation especially in the administration of EU customs law, where it is required also by the EU's objectives to establish and realise a European Internal Market, pursuant to Article 3 paragraph 3 TEU and Article 26 TFEU, and to establish a system preventing any distortion of competition in the European Internal Market, pursuant to Article 3 paragraph 3 TEU and Article 101 TFEU.[180] Moreover, the Council has emphasised for some time that EU customs legislation 'must provide a framework for allowing economic operators in all the customs territory of the Community to benefit from equal conditions of competition.'[181]

With regard to the principle of effectiveness, the effective and uniform application of EU law must not be undermined. The general principle of effectiveness demands that the EU Member States take all measures required in order to give effect to EU law; mere formal implementation of EU law is not sufficient.[182] According to established case law of the ECJ, the principle of effectiveness, sometimes also referred to as 'practical effectiveness'[183] or 'effet utile',[184] requires that any measure under EU law taken by an EU Member State must be effective and must not 'render impossible in practice or excessively difficult the exercise of rights conferred by EU law.'[185] Any divergence in the application and administration of EU customs law by EU Member States has the potential to jeopardise its effectiveness, as non-uniform implementation can lead EU customs rules to have differing effects of varying intensity in different areas of the EU Customs Union.

In conclusion, uniformity in the EU Member States' administration of EU law is an instrument to achieve equal effectiveness of EU law. The effective implementation of EU law is of essential importance for the functioning of the EU, because a lack of effective implementation could be a negative location factor for businesses and thus could have negative effects on the competitiveness of the EU.[186] In the context of EU customs, the exigency of uniformity thus demands a degree of

[179] See, inter alia, ECJ of 5 December 2013, Case C-455/11 P, *Solvay SA* [2013] ECR I-0, para 77, and the case law cited.

[180] Rogmann, in: Kluth/Müller/Peilert (eds), 2008, pp 797–819 (802).

[181] Council Resolution of 30 May 2011 on a strategy for the Customs Union, [2001] OJ C171/1–3, p 3.

[182] Hofmann/Rowe/Türk, 2011, pp 154, 155.

[183] ECJ of 28 January 2010, Case C-456/08, *Commission v Ireland* [2010] ECR I-859, para 56.

[184] Hofmann/Rowe/Türk, 2011, p 144.

[185] See, inter alia, ECJ of 12 December 2013, Case C-362/12, *Test Claimants in the Franked Investment Income Group Litigation* [2013] ECR I-0, para 32, and case law cited.

[186] Classen, in: Grabitz/Hilf/Nettesheim (eds), 2013, Vol II, Art 197 TFEU, paras 4, 16.

uniformity that allows the administration of EU customs law, and especially customs controls, to be equally effective in every EU Member State regarding its main objectives of trade facilitation, security and recovery of the EU's own resources.

The institutions of the EU thus agree that the various national customs administrations of the EU Member States shall operate as if they were one customs administration, and shall achieve homogenous results at every location in the customs territory of the EU Customs Union.[187] This is to prevent disadvantages and additional costs for economic operators that could arise from the decentralised organisation and administration of the EU Customs Union, as well as to prevent the different application of EU customs law because of national rules of interpretation or national idiosyncrasies in customs procedures.[188]

B. Customs Specific Problems Regarding Uniform Implementation in EU Member States

The balancing act between the decentralised administration and the simultaneous requirement for uniform implementation of EU customs leads to many problems, in particular in the context of interpretation of the law and exercise of discretionary power by customs officials. EU customs law often contains undefined legal terms that need to be interpreted by customs officials, or contains a margin of discretion for customs officials when making customs decisions. Regularly, it is up to the EU Member State's courts to determine whether such discretion has been exercised properly by the national customs authorities.[189] Such judicial review can also be limited to ascertaining whether there was a manifest error of assessment or misuse of powers and whether the facts being relied on were accurate. Under such circumstances, the exercise of discretion when implementing EU customs law can hardly be completely uniform throughout the EU.[190]

Different administrative and legal cultures and traditions as well as differences in staff training and equipment between the customs administrations in the different EU Member States can thus have significant effects on EU customs administration.[191] This is the case not only with the Community Customs Code

[187] See, inter alia, European Commission, EU Customs strategy, URL: http://ec.europa.eu/taxation_customs/customs/policy_issues/customs_strategy/index_en.htm; COM (2001) 51 final, p 5; Customs 2013 Programme, Recital (2) and Art 4 para 1 section b) Decision No 624/2007/EC; European Court of Auditors, Special Report No 1/2010, [2010] OJ C149/8 and URL: http://eur-lex.europa.eu/LexUriServ/LexUriServ.do?uri=SRCA:2010:01:FIN:EN:PDF, para 34; European Court of Auditors, Special Report No 23/2000, [2001] OJ C84/1–18, summary p 3 and para 8; Council Resolution of 30 May 2001 on a strategy for the Customs Union, [2001] OJ C171/1–3, p 2; European Parliament, Resolution of 1 December 2011, (2001/2083(INI)), text adopted P7_TA(2011)0546, para 53.

[188] Lux, 2007 AW-Prax 7, pp 277–80 (277).

[189] Hofmann/Rowe/Türk, 2011, p 505.

[190] Hofmann/Rowe/Türk, 2011, p 505.

[191] Weerth, Witten 2007, p 79.

and its implementing provisions but also with the Common Customs Tariff, which like the former contains many terms that are open to interpretation: in the end, classification problems are often simply interpretation problems. Cultural traditions can be especially important causes of different opinions and mind-sets: EU Member States celebrate different festivities and public holidays on different occasions, and even common holidays such as Christmas or Easter are often celebrated with traditions and festive articles that are unknown in other EU Member States.[192] For example, Hallowe'en is not a traditional celebration in every EU Member State, and this has in the past led to different positions regarding the classification of articles related to this festivity. In Germany, from 2002 until 2007 products showing a grinning pumpkin had to be classified as festive articles under position 9505 CN, because of a national decree by the German Federal Ministry of Finance.[193] Other EU Member States classified them differently because the festivity of Hallowe'en was unknown. There existed no corresponding rule at the EU level for five years.[194] During this period, Hallowe'en pumpkins were not uniformly classified in the EU Customs Union. In 2007, the European Commission issued an explanatory note amending CN position 9505,[195] to the effect that Hallowe'en pumpkins had to be classified as festive articles from then on, leading again to the uniform classification of such articles in the EU Customs Union.[196]

The lack of common standards and criteria, as well as lack of mutual understanding and communication about working methods, increases the risk that customs procedures will differ significantly across the EU Member States. Although EU law provides some general principles regarding the handling of discretionary power – such as the principle of equality, the principle of legal certainty and the principle of legitimate expectations – the exercise of discretion by national customs authorities may vary greatly unless uniform standards are laid down by EU customs.[197] However, the numerous soft law acts the European Commission issues as a kind of interpretation assistance are not released in the Official Journal but are made public on the homepage of the European Commission, where they are often issued only in English rather than in all official EU languages. Thus, it cannot be guaranteed that every customs official can understand them.[198] Even if these acts are transformed into a national act, this transformation takes time and can slow down the distribution of useful information to customs officials.

Additionally, the many different official languages in the EU can complicate the communication of customs officials from different EU Member States, not only in day-to-day customs work but also when meeting in a committee, a working

[192] Blechschmidt, 2007 BDZ-Fachteil 1–2, F3–F5 (F5).

[193] German Federal Ministry of Finance, Decree of 24 July 2002–III B 5–ZT 0270–XI–45/01 III, Erl KN Pos 9505 (NEH), para 01.0.

[194] Weerth, 2007 AW-Prax 9, pp 357–58 (357).

[195] European Commission (2007/C164/02), [2007] OJ C164/3–4.

[196] Weerth, 2007 AW-Prax 9, pp 357–58 (357).

[197] Hofmann/Rowe/Türk, 2011, p 505.

[198] Lieber, 2007 AW-Prax 10, pp 424–26 (425).

group, or an expert group. Regularly, the primary language used is English, and although the national customs officials deployed on such occasions should be qualified in this regard, most of them are not native English speakers. Thus, to a certain degree a language barrier remains, while others are excluded from such possibilities for exchange in the first place. This was confirmed in an interview with a German customs official, who declared that English is still the main language used and that even at the operative level one should be able not only to follow but also to contribute to a discussion that is held in English.[199]

Furthermore, because of the transnational nature of many customs procedures and the transnational effect of customs decisions in the EU, the correct and uniform implementation of EU customs law depends also on the correct translation of documents. Especially in the area of customs classification, translation errors or errors in denotation can lead to problems regarding the correct classification,[200] as the Common Customs Tariff is based on the Harmonised System that was originally written in English and French. For example, until the ECJ decided on the correct interpretation,[201] the term 'textile flock', used in position 59.01 B I CN, was difficult to interpret because of the different kinds of terms used in the different official languages of the Common Customs Tariff in the EU.[202] Another clear example is the English term 'virgin [olive] oil', which caused significant problems in the context of tariff classification because the specific term contained in the English description of goods was unknown in Germany, leading to some confusion regarding the correct classification, until the translation issue was finally detected and clarified.[203]

[199] 'Und natürlich spielt da insofern die Sprache eine Rolle, weil man sollte schon sich in den Hauptsprachen bewegen können. Und man mag es drehen und wenden wie man will, man spricht nun einmal Englisch auf dieser Ebene. Französisch ist an sich auch schon wieder nur unter bestimmten Umständen. Deutsch ist wichtig geworden, aber hat noch nicht die Wichtigkeit erlangt wie Englisch. Also insofern, Fremdsprachenkenntnisse und dann auch Fachtermini sind natürlich insofern von Wichtigkeit, können aber auch gegebenenfalls durch Übersetzung aufgefangen werden. Deshalb … hängt immer davon ab wie hoch ist diese Sitzung angesetzt. Also je weiter Sie in das Operative kommen, umso mehr müssen Sie sich selbst helfen und sich selbst einschätzen, ob die sprachlichen Kenntnisse ausreichen um einer nur auf Englisch geführten Diskussion nicht nur folgen zu können, sondern auch Beiträge leisten zu können.' Interview of 20 May 2011 on file with author.

[200] Blechschmidt, 2007 BDZ-Fachteil 1–2, F3–F5 (F5); Schrömbges, 2009 ZfZ 8, pp 204–10 (204).

[201] ECJ of 16 October 1980, Case 816/79, *Klaus Mecke & Co* [1980] ECR 3029.

[202] Blechschmidt, 2007 BDZ-Fachteil 1–2, F3–F5 (F5); Lux, in: Rüsken (ed), 2011, Vol III, Introduction CN Regulation, para 150.

[203] In an interview with a German customs official I was told of this case where the English term 'virgin [olive] oil' had been wrongly translated into the German term 'Jungfernöl', instead of 'natives [Oliven-] Öl': 'Das fängt aber dann schon bei der Übersetzung an, dass da Unterschiede herauskommen. Und manchmal auch dummes Zeug. Ist halt so. Ich weiß, ich habe jahrelang gegen das sogenannte "Jungfernöl" im Zolltarif gekämpft. Jungfernöl. Sie wissen nicht was das ist? … Das ist Olivenöl, kaltgepresst. "Extra vergine". Und "vergine" ist nun eben die Jungfer. Und da hat irgendein Übersetzer aus diesem Olivenöl, kalt gepresst, Jungfernöl gemacht. Ja. Hat uns Jahre gebraucht, bis wir das heraus hatten. Erst bis wir das herausgefunden haben, was die Europäische Kommission uns mit diesem Ausdruck überhaupt sagen will, das hat schon etwas gedauert. Weil das machte für uns keinen Sinn. Und bis das dann draußen war, hat es dann noch einmal ein bisschen gedauert.' Interview of 10 May 2011 on file with author.

Additionally, many procedural issues of a general administrative nature are not contained in the Community Customs Code or its implementing provisions, but require recourse to national administrative law. For example, while annulment, revocation or amendment of favourable customs decisions are, at least basically, regulated in Articles 8 and 9 CCC, the Code contains no rule regarding the handling of wrongly issued unfavourable customs decisions.[204] Moreover, certain parts of the law have not yet been harmonised, for example appeal procedure, external audit and penalty for customs violation. Furthermore, in addition to provisions of EU customs law on the cross-border trade of goods, one also has to follow further provisions of both EU law and national law, especially regarding value added tax (VAT) and excise duty, as well as measures on agriculture policy, external trade policy, health care policy and environmental protection policy. These provisions, as well as the administrative action of the national authorities responsible for these matters, are often not completely synchronised, leaving some scope for national idiosyncrasies.[205] Finally, the aforementioned issues are all intensified by the use of different national IT solutions and even different scopes of IT system use in different Member States when administrating EU customs law. As the Community Customs Code and its implementing provisions were developed for a paper-based world, the use of IT solutions in national administrations is a national issue. To sum up, the conditions for uniform customs administration in the EU are difficult. The European Commission itself has already stated that 'while the legislation to be applied is the same, the outcome of its implementation is not.'[206]

C. Special Reports by the European Court of Auditors Regarding Uniform EU Customs Administration

The difficulties in the EU Customs Union with administering EU customs law in a uniform manner have also been noticed by the European Court of Auditors, which has criticised a lack of uniform implementation in several areas of EU customs.[207] In Special Report No 23/2000[208] concerning valuation of imported goods for customs purposes, the European Court of Auditors noted that it was hard for EU Member States to operate in a uniform manner within the EU Customs Union

[204] Alexander, in: Witte (ed), 2013, Before Art 8 CCC; para 1; Craig, in: Hübschmann/Hepp/Spitaler (eds), 2013, Vol XIV, Art 8 CCC, para 3.

[205] Lux, 2008 AW-Prax 7, pp 283–86 (284).

[206] COM (2012) 791 final, p 3.

[207] See European Court of Auditors, Special Report No 1/2010, [2010] OJ C149/8 and URL: http://eur-lex.europa.eu/LexUriServ/LexUriServ.do?uri=SRCA:2010:01:FIN:EN:PDF; European Court of Auditors Special Report No 2/2008, [2008] OJ C103/1–17; European Court of Auditors, Special Report No 11/2006, [2007] OJ C44/1–19; European Court of Auditors, Special Report No 1/2005, [2005] OJ C202/1–32; European Court of Auditors, Special Report No 23/2000, [2001] OJ C84/1–18; European Court of Auditors, Special Report No 8/1999, [2000] OJ C70/1–16; European Court of Auditors, Special Report No 13/1998, [1998] OJ C375/3–16.

[208] European Court of Auditors, Special Report No 23/2000, [2001] OJ C84/1–18.

and also identified the European Commission's difficulties in supervising and monitoring the national customs administrations.[209] The European Commission replied by pointing to the responsibility of the EU Member States to apply EU customs law in a uniform and correct manner and its own efforts to harmonise working methods by issuing soft law acts.[210] The European Commission also referred to the importance of uniform interpretation in cases where EU customs law leaves space for administrative discretion.[211] Also, Special Report No 11/2006[212] on the Community Transit System detected several deficiencies regarding the implementation of NCTS in its early stages.[213] This finding led to increasing monitoring by the European Commission.[214]

However, subsequent reports of the European Court of Auditors regarding the functioning of the EU Customs Union were more conciliatory and positive regarding the efforts of the EU Member States and especially of the European Commission to ensure uniform implementation of EU customs law throughout the EU. Special Report No 2/2008[215] concerning Binding Tariff Information (BTI) found the BTI system and the European Commission's management role in it to be well designed overall,[216] although various (not fundamental) shortcomings were noted in EU Member States.[217] A BTI establishes the correct classification of a given product, and the economic operator who receives it can rely on this classification being accepted by every customs authority in the EU, as a BTI is valid EU-wide for a specified period of time.[218] The main recommendations for improvement related to the prompt resolution of classification issues in situations of diverging BTIs, the European Commission's active role in the supervisory process, and the obligatory inclusion of BTIs in customs declarations by economic operators.[219] Nevertheless, overall the BTI system was found to promote 'uniform tariff classification within the EU, which is a WTO requirement and an essential part of the [EU] Customs Union.'[220]

Special Report No 1/2010[221] on the effective control of simplified procedures criticised the different and sometimes even deficient approaches of the EU Member States.[222] However, it also acknowledged the European Commission's sound approach for controls on simplified procedures and its newly developed

[209] ibid, summary p 3 and para 36.
[210] ibid, paras 42, 75.
[211] ibid, para 47.
[212] European Court of Auditors, Special Report No 11/2006, [2007] OJ C44/1–19.
[213] ibid, executive summary III p 3.
[214] ibid, paras 68, 69.
[215] European Court of Auditors Special Report No 2/2008, [2008] OJ C103/1–17.
[216] ibid, summary III p 4 and paras 13, 39.
[217] ibid, summary III lit (d) p 4 and para 14.
[218] A detailed analysis of Binding Tariff Information can be found in Chapter 10.I.E.
[219] European Court of Auditors Special Report No 2/2008, summary IV p 4 and paras 43–48.
[220] ibid, para 39.
[221] European Court of Auditors, Special Report No 1/2010, [2010] OJ C149/8 and URL: http://eur-lex.europa.eu/LexUriServ/LexUriServ.do?uri=SRCA:2010:01:FIN:EN:PDF.
[222] ibid, executive summary V p 9 and para 79.

regulatory framework supported by comprehensive guidelines that also took into account international standards,[223] recommending that the European Commission urge its application by EU Member States.[224] The European Commission also explained in response to this report the functioning of the Common Risk Management Framework,[225] under which the EU Member States are obliged to exchange and share risk-related information in electronic form and to use automated data processing techniques in the context of risk analysis.[226] The European Commission's role herein is a coordinating and supplementing one: facilitating the exchange of risk-related information via the provision of the electronic Community Risk Management System using Risk Information Forms and ensuring that appropriate information can be shared quickly and effectively between the appropriate risk management centres and customs control points in the EU Customs Union.[227] However, the EU Member States remain responsible for their own organisation of customs control activities for simplified procedures, including effective, risk-based, ex-post audits.[228] Nevertheless, the European Commission promised to investigate and examine the deficiencies in national customs administrations that the European Court of Auditors identified.[229]

Summing up, the special reports of the European Court of Auditors have criticised shortcomings in uniform customs administration, but simultaneously have contributed to the EU's efforts to ensure the uniform administration of EU customs law by screening the effectiveness of certain areas of customs policy and identifying possibilities for improvement. The reports are part of the EU's control mechanism for guaranteeing the principle of uniformity in the implementation of EU customs law.

D. Negative Consequences Resulting from Non-Uniform Customs Administration and the Need for a Reform of EU Customs

Non-uniform administration of EU customs law has negative consequences for the overall effectiveness of the EU Customs Union, producing inefficiencies, waste and mismatch of needs and resources, and leading to uneven service level as well as suboptimal overall protection of the EU's external borders.[230] Indeed, non-uniform customs administration causes many problems, with economic, fiscal, statistical and even legal effects and consequences, especially in the field

[223] ibid, executive summary IV p 8 and para 81.
[224] ibid, executive summary VII p 9 and para 91.
[225] A detailed analysis of risk management and risk analysis can be found in Chapter 4.I.
[226] European Court of Auditors, Special Report No 1/2010, reply of the European Commission, executive summary p 48 and paras 38, 50.
[227] ibid, executive summary p 51 and para 38.
[228] ibid, reply of the European Commission, executive summary p 49 and para 79.
[229] ibid, reply of the European Commission, paras 87, 88.
[230] COM (2012) 791 final, p 3.

of classification.[231] Non-uniform classification of goods impairs the statistical record of cross-border movement of goods, which in the worst case can lead to the incorrect economic and/or political conclusions, based on incorrect data.[232] Furthermore, non-uniform administration raises the risk of loss of revenue, as customs duties traditionally constitute an own resource of the EU. Disparities in the application of EU law in different EU Member States can even result in trade diversion and provoke a so-called 'customs arbitrage',[233] whereby economic operators purposefully exploit disparities in tariff rates caused by different classification practices and different customs procedure handling in different EU Member States. Moreover, non-uniform administration of EU customs law can produce expensive and tiresome legal proceedings for everyone involved: national customs administrations and economic operators when the latter fight against potential discrimination or allegedly wrong customs decisions; EU Member States in the event that the European Commission or another EU Member State makes a claim against an alleged infringement of the treaty; and the EU itself if there is an alleged violation of WTO obligations, as the dispute settlement *EC—Selected Customs Matters*[234] has already shown. Finally, non-uniform administration of EU customs law negatively affects the competitiveness of EU businesses: legal uncertainty, disparities in tariff rates, different practices in customs procedures (for example regarding duration, depth and extent of customs controls), or varying degrees of computerisation in national customs administrations can all have deterring effects on economic operators when deciding to do business with and within the EU. Moreover, non-uniform customs administration in the EU endangers not only the functioning of the EU Customs Union but even the safety and security of the cross-border movement of goods: not only economic operators could be tempted to exploit weak points (in the form of less or vague controls) in some EU Member States for their own interests, but also criminals and even terrorists.

In this situation, a harmonisation and standardisation of working methods is something to be aspired to.[235] By providing guidelines this can affect the interpretation of the law as well as the procedures at customs controls and in customs laboratories, the IT equipment used, organisation and processing, and also the training and retraining of the customs officials.[236] Amongst other things, this goal could be achieved by using common process mapping, common data and procedures regarding risk analysis, a common framework regarding the IT systems, common standards for quality, and monitoring and exchange of knowledge by way of so-called centres of excellence.[237]

231 Weerth, Witten 2007, p 13.
232 ibid, p 13.
233 Weerth, 2008 AW-Prax 1, pp 23–25; Weerth, 2008 AW-Prax 2, pp 68–72.
234 WT/DS/315.
235 Lux, 2008 AW-Prax 7, pp 283–86 (285); similar: Lyons, 2008, pp 24, 98.
236 Lux, 2012 AW-Prax 8, pp 257–62 (262).
237 Lux, 2008 AW-Prax 7, pp 283–86 (285).

In the WTO dispute settlement *EC—Selected Customs Matters*,[238] the decentralised administration system of the EU was challenged but the question of whether the practice of customs administration in the EU violated the requirements for a uniform administration in Article X:3(a) GATT 1994 was not answered clearly. For instance, the Panel criticised the fact that in Germany, national administrative provisions that do not exist in other EU Member States are of some importance in the field of classification.[239] Another criticism was that customs decisions concerning the classification of goods issued in other EU Member States were not considered by the German customs authorities.[240] The Appellate Body did not uphold the panel report in this respect and made some important clarifications. During this process, some of the claims of the United States in its complaint were dropped due to lack of proof, but this means that they could be picked up again one day, especially since the Appellate Body made it clear that the EU system of customs administration as a whole may be subject to review.[241] As was alluded to earlier, the criticism expressed after the WTO dispute settlement decision on the EU's system of customs administration[242] has to date received little unbiased reflection.[243] However, given the decentralised administration concept, the EU on its own is not able to fulfil the demands of WTO law and because of the structure of this Executive Federalism it relies to some extent on the support of the EU Member States.

V. CONCLUSION

In conclusion, it can be stated that the principle of uniformity in the implementation of EU law in general and EU customs law in particular is strongly anchored in EU law. Furthermore, the various institutions of the EU are aware of the special importance uniform implementation has for the functioning of the Internal Market and the EU Customs Union. Therefore, the EU and its Member States face the challenge of ensuring uniform application of EU customs law and equal implementing conditions throughout the EU. Yet given the decentralised implementation system, with 28 different EU Member States, manifold problems regarding uniform customs administration arise.

EU customs law is not above improvement, and uniformity in customs administration has been pointed out as a general or even core objective in reform processes[244] since about 2005; the temporal proximity here to the WTO dispute

[238] WT/DS/315.

[239] Panel Report, *EC–Selected Customs Matters*, WT/DS/315/R, paras 7.276, 7.380 et seq.

[240] Panel Report, *EC–Selected Customs Matters*, WT/DS/315/R, paras 7.276, 7.380 et seq.

[241] Appellate Body Report, *EC–Selected Customs Matters*, WT/DS/315/AB/R, para 172.

[242] See for example: Rogmann, 2008 ZfZ 3, pp 57–69; Rogmann, 2008 AW-Prax 5, pp 195–99; Weerth, 2008 AW-Prax 1, pp 23–25; Weerth, 2008 AW-Prax 2, pp 68–72; Dierksmeier, 2008 AW-Prax 5, pp 200–03; Niestedt/Stein, 2006 AW-Prax 12, pp 516–18.

[243] Weerth, 2008 ZfZ 7, pp 178–85 (182, 184).

[244] Lux, 2012 AW-Prax 8, pp 257–62 (258).

settlement in *EC—Selected Customs Matters* is too close to be merely coincidental. In fact, ever since the US complaint before the WTO, the uniform application of EU customs law and especially the Community Customs Code has become a codeword for any further development in the EU Customs Union.[245] On several occasions, the uniform application of EU customs law has been emphasised as an issue for European customs administration, indicating its importance for the functioning of the EU Customs Union.[246] Herein, the European Commission frequently demands that the national customs administrations of the EU Member States should work together as though they were one.[247]

In fact, the European Commission was aware of problems with the uniform application of EU customs law even before the aforementioned WTO dispute settlement case. In a communication of 2001 concerning a strategy for the Customs Union[248] the European Commission concluded that although EU customs law is considered to be well-established and uniform, this is not the case for customs operations throughout the EU.[249] Amongst other things, this communication announced some aspirations regarding reforms in this area, including improving control standards and practical cooperation between customs authorities and between customs and other authorities; increasing the use of risk analysis; reinforcing the fight against counterfeiting, piracy and false origin marking; and developing a new IT strategy.[250] However, in the context of the WTO dispute settlement case *EC—Selected Customs Matters*, the demands for a more uniform EU customs have increased in intensity. Therefore, the standards of WTO law with regard to uniform customs administration have to be considered further.

245 Hobbing, CEPS Papers No 39, June 2011, p 15.

246 See for example: Lux, 2012 AW-Prax 8, pp 257–62 (258).

247 See for example: European Commission, EU Customs strategy, URL: http://ec.europa.eu/taxation_customs/customs/policy_issues/customs_strategy/index_en.htm; COM (2012) 791 final, p 9; COM (2001) 51 final, p 5; Customs 2013 Programme, Recital (2) and Art 4 para 1 Section b) Decision No 624/2007/EC.

248 COM (2001) 51 final.

249 ibid, p 14.

250 ibid, pp 14, 15.

3

*Standards of WTO Law: Uniformity of the Administration of Law According to Article X:3(a) GATT 1994 and its Implications for EU Customs Law**

DUE TO INCREASING globalisation, worldwide harmonisation processes are affecting the EU customs administration system. The regulatory framework of customs administration in the EU is influenced by outside forces, especially the World Trade Organization (WTO), which has become a deep and extensive legal system. EU customs law is centrally constituted at the EU level, but implemented by the national customs authorities of the EU Member States. For such a system of indirect or decentralised administration, the legal system of the WTO prescribes in Article X:3(a) GATT 1994 the requirements for uniformity in the administration of customs law. Thus, coherence and uniformity of customs administration in the EU is demanded not only by EU self-interest in coherent administration of EU law, but also from exigencies stemming from the WTO.

I. EXIGENCIES OF UNIFORMITY IN ARTICLE X:3(a) GATT 1994

The essence of Article X GATT 1994 is transparency, as an important principle of the WTO and an essential requirement for open markets to contribute to the legal certainty and predictability of legal decisions that underlies all WTO law.[1] The due process theme underlying Article X GATT 1994 helps 'to ensure that traders are treated fairly and consistently when seeking to import from or export to a particular WTO member.'[2] The provision is also a great example of the far-reaching impact that WTO law, as international law, has on the domestic regulations of WTO members.[3]

* This chapter is an updated version of: Kathrin Przybilla, 'The "WTOisation" of the customs administration: Uniformity of the administration of law according to Article X:3 (a) GATT 1994 and its implications for EU customs law', 2010 FÖV Discussion Papers 58.

[1] Dierksmeier, 2007, pp 26 et seq.

[2] Panel Report, *EC—Selected Customs Matters*, WT/DS315/R, para 7.108; upheld by the Appellate Body, see Appellate Body Report, *EC—Selected Customs Matters*, WT/DS315/AB/R, paras 193, 220.

[3] Dierksmeier, 2007, p 27.

Paragraphs 1 and 2 of Article X GATT 1994 require the immediate publication of all domestic regulations of general application regarding international trade, so that administrations and economic operators can take notice of them before their application in particular cases.[4] Apart from creating transparency, Article X:3(a) GATT 1994 also prevents the indirect reintroduction of trade barriers through factually discriminatory trade regulations by helping to discipline the application of domestic trade regulations.[5] At the same time, the paragraph has to perform a balancing act between its aim of creating uniformity for traders in the shape of equal treatment of goods, on the one hand, and its quest to preserve the autonomy of WTO members in establishing and implementing their trade regulations that are compliant with the WTO, on the other hand.[6] Article X:3(a) GATT 1994 says: 'Each contracting party shall administer in a uniform, impartial and reasonable manner all its laws, regulations, decisions and rulings of the kind described in paragraph 1 of this Article.' Thereby, the obligations of uniformity, impartiality and reasonableness are not cumulative requirements but legally independent, with the WTO Members obliged to comply with all three of them.[7]

A. The Term 'Administration'

The injunction 'to administer ... laws, regulations, decisions and rulings of the kind described in paragraph 1 of this Article' defines the scope of Article X:3(a) GATT 1994. Article 31 paragraph 1 of the Vienna Convention, to which Article 3.2 DSU refers, specifies that a treaty provision has to be interpreted, on the one hand, in accordance with its ordinary meaning and, on the other hand, in its particular context. Apart from the context, its object and purpose also have to be considered. In doing so, there is also the jurisprudence of the Dispute Settlement Body of the WTO to be considered.

1. Ordinary Meaning

The ordinary meaning of the term 'administration' is defined as 'the process or activity of running a business, organization etc.'[8] The verb 'administer' therefore means to 'manage and be responsible for the running of (a business, organization, etc.) [or to] be responsible for the implementation or use of (law or resources)'.[9] The administration of trade regulations in the context of Article X:3(a) GATT

[4] Dierksmeier, 2007, p 26.

[5] Niestedt/Stein, 2006 AW-Prax 12, pp 516–18 (517).

[6] Niestedt/Stein, 2006 AW-Prax 12, pp 516–18 (517).

[7] Panel Report, *Argentina—Bovine Hides*, WT/DS155/R, para 11.86; Panel Report, *Dominican Republic—Cigarettes*, WT/DS302/R, para 7.383.

[8] Oxford Dictionary of English, 2005, p 21.

[9] Oxford Dictionary of English, 2005, p 21.

1994 is therefore related to the application of those regulations that, pursuant to paragraph 1 of Article X GATT 1994, are rules of general applicability and do not contain specific transactions.[10] This term also relates to the administrative process included in the application of a law, as it represents 'the series of steps, actions or events that are taken or occur in pursuance of what is required by the law in question.'[11] In *China—Raw Materials* the Panel further considered that such an administrative process should not necessarily be confined to a series of steps, actions or events, but could also consist of one step, one action or one event relating to the taking of an administrative decision.[12] However, the Appellate Body later dismissed the relevant claims in question as being outside the Panel's terms of reference, and declared any substantive findings to be moot and of no legal effect.[13] Furthermore, the term relates to the results of administrative processes as final manifestations of the application of a legal instrument in a particular case.[14]

However, expanding from the ordinary meaning of Article X:3(a) GATT 1994, the term can also encompass the laws and regulations themselves. While Article X:3(a) GATT 1994 basically contains no substantial requirements for laws and regulations, it does dictate the manner of their application, as the text clearly indicates that the requirements of uniformity, impartiality and reasonableness apply to the administration of those laws.[15] In *US—Corrosion-Resistant Steel Sunset Review* the Panel affirmed this opinion, deciding that the content of laws and regulations could be challenged under relevant provisions of the agreements covered.[16] Furthermore, in *EC—Selected Customs Matters* the Panel suggested that the term 'administer' refers to any action that puts into practical effect the relevant laws and regulations, but not the laws and regulations themselves, as they merely exist without effect until they are actually applied in practice.[17] Contrary to this opinion, in *Argentina—Bovine Hides* the Panel came to the conclusion that the substance of a measure can be challenged under Article X GATT 1994 as long as the substance of the measure is administrative in nature and has not been dealt with more directly under other provisions of the GATT 1994.[18] The different interpretation of the term by the Panel and the Appellate Body rests to some extent on the wording of the GATT 1994, as the English version is not the only official language of the text, the French and Spanish versions also being authoritative. However, the English term 'to administer' is much wider than the French term 'appliquer' or the Spanish

[10] Appellate Body Report, *EC—Poultry*, WT/DS69/AB/R, para 111.

[11] Panel Report, *EC—Selected Customs Matters*, WT/DS315/R, paras 7.105, 7.119; upheld by the Appellate Body, see Appellate Body Report, *EC—Selected Customs Matters*, WT/DS315/AB/R, para 227.

[12] Panel Report, *China—Raw Materials*, WT/DS394,395,398/R, para 7.690.

[13] Appellate Body Report, *China—Raw Materials*, WT/DS394,395,398/AB/R, paras 234, 235.

[14] Panel Report, *EC—Selected Customs Matters*, WT/DS315/R, paras 7.105, 7.119; uphold by the Appellate Body, see Appellate Body Report, *EC—Selected Customs Matters*, WT/DS315/AB/R, para 227.

[15] Appellate Body Report, *EC—Bananas*, WT/DS27/AB/R, para 201.

[16] Panel Report, *US—Corrosion-Resistant Steel Sunset Review*, WT/DS244/R, para 7.289.

[17] Panel Report, *EC—Selected Customs Matters*, WT/DS315/R, paras 7.104, 7.106.

[18] Panel Report, *Argentina—Bovine Hides*, WT/DS155/R, para 11.70.

term 'aplicar', which correspond more with 'to apply',[19] defined as to 'bring or put into operation or use.'[20]

2. Context

Any term—here 'administer'—must also be interpreted in the context of the provision. Any examination of the substantial content of laws and regulations cannot be deduced from the context of Article X:3(a) GATT 1994.[21] The Panel in *EC—Selected Customs Matters* suggested that the underlying theme of Article X GATT 1994 on due process relates to the application of laws and regulations, whereas any relation to laws and regulations as such was considered to be unclear.[22] Following the opinion in *EC—Bananas III*[23] (more restrictive than the wider approach in *Argentina—Bovine Hides*),[24] the Panel considered the text of Article X:3(a) GATT to require a distinction to be made between the instruments being administered and the acts of administration, and suggested overlooking:

> the possibility that laws and regulations can simultaneously qualify as laws ... of the kind described in Article X:1 GATT 1994 and as acts of administration within the meaning of Article X:3(a) GATT 1994.[25]

The Panel also discussed the view that the substantive content of laws and regulations may be subject to the obligation of uniform administration under Article X:3(a) GATT 1994 if these laws and regulations are administrative in nature or are tools of administration.[26] In its opinion this would render redundant either the term 'administer' or the reference to paragraph 1 and, therefore, is precluded by the principle of effective treaty interpretation, which requires all terms of a provision to be given effect.[27] Finally, the Panel saw no textual support in Article X:3(a) GATT 1994 for a difference to be made between laws and regulations examined to ensure administration in a uniform fashion and laws and regulations qualified as administrative in nature and therefore examined for their

[19] Dictionnaire Francais-Anglais and Spanish-English Dictionary at www.worldreference.com; see also Panel Report, *EC—Selected Customs Matters*, WT/DS315/R, para 7.109.

[20] Oxford Dictionary of English, 2005, p 75; see also Panel Report, *EC—Selected Customs Matters*, WT/DS315/R, para 7.109.

[21] Panel Report, *EC—Selected Customs Matters*, WT/DS315/R, para 7.108; Appellate Body Report, *EC—Bananas*, WT/DS27/AB/R, para 200.

[22] Panel Report, *EC—Selected Customs Matters*, WT/DS315/R, para 7.108.

[23] Appellate Body Report, *EC—Bananas*, WT/DS27/AB/R, para 200; see also Panel Report, *EC—Selected Customs Matters*, WT/DS315/R para 7.113, fn 255.

[24] Panel Report, *Argentina—Bovine Hides*, WT/DS155/R, paras 11.69–11.72; see also Panel Report, *EC—Selected Customs Matters*, WT/DS315/R para 7.114, fn 256.

[25] Panel Report, *EC—Selected Customs Matters*, WT/DS315/R, para 7.115; reversed by the Appellate Body, see Appellate Body Report, *EC—Selected Customs Matters*, WT/DS315/AB/R, para 217.

[26] A view relying upon comments made by the Panel in *Argentina—Bovine Hides*, paras 11.69–11.72 and put forward by the United States in this dispute.

[27] Panel Report, *EC—Selected Customs Matters*, WT/DS315/R, para 7.117; reversed by the Appellate Body, see Appellate Body Report, *EC—Selected Customs Matters*, WT/DS315/AB/R, para 217.

substantive content.[28] If one follows this restrictive opinion, the solution to the interpretation problem lies in the relationship between Article X:3(a) GATT 1994 and its reference to Paragraph 1, meaning it is therefore limited to the application of laws and regulations, whereas the substantial GATT conformity of those laws and regulations has to be examined under other GATT provisions.[29] At the same time, the practical relevance of this distinction is considered to be somewhat marginal, as laws 'administrative in nature' are expected to be regularly applied and this application can then be examined under Article X:3(a) GATT 1994.[30] Thus in the end it is always the concrete application that is relevant.[31]

The wider opinion also considers the relation between paragraph 1 and paragraph 3 in Article X GATT 1994, but leads to an extension of the scope of Article X:3(a) GATT 1994, so that the substantive content of laws and regulations can be examined if they are administrative in nature. The Panel in *Argentina—Bovine Hides* argued that the provision's own linkage to paragraph 1 would be contrary to a requirement that Article X:3(a) GATT 1994 apply only to unwritten rules of administration and 'would almost certainly require a review of a specific instance of abuse rather than the general rule applicable.'[32]

A similar approach was taken by the Appellate Body in *EC—Selected Customs Matters*. According to the Body's opinion, the distinction between laws and regulations of general application set out in Article X:1 GATT 1994 and the administration of those legal instruments does not exclude:

> the possibility of challenging under Article X:3(a) the substantive content of a legal instrument that regulates the administration of a legal instrument of the kind described in Article X:1.[33]

Only claims concerning the substantive content of legal instruments of the kind described in Article X:1 GATT 1994 fall outside the scope of Article X:3(a) GATT 1994, but this should not be a reason to overlook legal instruments that regulate the application or implementation of those paragraph 1 legal instruments under Article X:3(a) GATT 1994.[34] The Panel in *US—COOL* shared this view in its examination of an administrative authority's public letter whose issuance put into practical effect a certain regulation in the sense of Article X:1 GATT 1994 despite the absence of any specific instance of application.[35] However, the Appellate Body in *EC—Selected Customs Matters* simultaneously narrowed the scope of Article X:3(a) GATT 1994 by establishing additional requirements regarding the type of evidence for claims concerning the substantive content of legal

[28] Panel Report, *EC—Selected Customs Matters*, WT/DS315/R, para 7.118; reversed by the Appellate Body, see Appellate Body Report, *EC—Selected Customs Matters*, WT/DS315/AB/R, para 217.
[29] Niestedt/Stein, 2006 AW-Prax 12, pp 516–18 (517).
[30] ibid, pp 516–18 (517).
[31] Dierksmeier, 2007, p 54.
[32] Panel Report, *Argentina—Bovine Hides*, WT/DS155/R, para 11.71.
[33] Appellate Body Report, *EC—Selected Customs Matters*, WT/DS315/AB/R, paras 199, 200.
[34] ibid, paras 199, 200.
[35] Panel Report, *US—COOL*, WT/DS384, 386/R, paras 7.815, 7.821, 7.828, 7.829.

instruments regulating the administration of a legal instrument of the kind described in Article X:1 GATT 1994. Accordingly, the complainant has to prove that the challenged legal instrument necessarily leads to impermissible administration of the legal instrument of the kind described in Article X:1 GATT 1994.[36] The Panel in *China—Raw Materials* considered further that this requirement would be met if the identified features of the challenged administration posed a very real risk of non-uniform, partial and unreasonable administration,[37] though the Appellate Body later dismissed the relevant claims in question for being outside the Panel's terms of reference and declared any substantive findings to be moot and of no legal effect.[38]

3. *Conclusion*

The ordinary meaning of the term 'administer' and its context in Article X:3(a) GATT 1994 make clear that the administration of laws and regulations themselves is relevant and always requires reference to the application of a particular provision. This administration also encompasses the administrative process and its result, as well as laws and regulations regulating the administration of legal instruments of the kind described in Article X:1 GATT 1994. However, the violation of Article X:3(a) GATT 1994 lies not in the use of different administration tools but in impermissible administration through a lack of uniformity, impartiality or reasonableness. Even different administration tools can be used in such a manner that in practice their application still leads to uniform, impartial and reasonable results.[39] Thus, the examination of the substantive content of laws and regulations regulating the administration of other legal instruments is limited to contents that necessarily lead to non-uniform, partial or unreasonable administration.

In short, an infringement of Article X:3(a) GATT 1994 occurs either in the event that the administrative authorities actually apply legal instruments of the kind described in Article X:1 GATT in a non-uniform, partial or unreasonable manner or when differences in administrative processes used by the administrative authorities necessarily lead to non-uniform, partial or unreasonable results.

B. The Term 'Uniform'

The term 'in a uniform, impartial and reasonable manner' dictates the qualities administration must meet in order to be in compliance with Article X:3(a) GATT 1994. For the purpose of this book, which is concerned with the degree of uniformity in the European customs administration, only the term 'uniform' is of

[36] Appellate Body Report, *EC—Selected Customs Matters*, WT/DS315/AB/R, para 201.
[37] Panel Report, *China—Raw Materials*, WT/DS394, 395, 398/R, para 7.708.
[38] Appellate Body Report, *China—Raw Materials*, WT/DS394, 395, 398/AB/R, paras 234, 235.
[39] See also Dierksmeier, 2007, p 52.

relevance, whereas the terms 'impartial' and 'reasonable' can be set aside. Again, Articles 31 to 33 of the Vienna Convention have to be consulted for the purpose of interpretation. Therefore, the term 'uniform' has to be seen in the light of its ordinary meaning as well as in its context. Additionally, the jurisprudence of the Dispute Settlement Body of the WTO has to be considered.

1. *Ordinary Meaning*

The term 'uniform' is defined as 'remaining the same in all cases and at all times; unchanging in form or character';[40] the noun 'uniformity' therefore simply means 'the quality or state of being uniform.'[41]

The Panel in *Argentina—Bovine Hides* noted that the term 'uniformity' appears in the GATT 1994 only with respect to administration of customs laws.[42] It thus considered it evident that it was not a requirement for ensuring equal treatment with respect to WTO members, but between individual shippers and also with respect to the same person at different times and places.[43] At the same time Article X:3(a) GATT 1994 should not be read as a broad anti-discrimination provision for ensuring all products are treated equally, for it would not be an appropriate role for a Panel to judge the many variations in products that might require differential treatment.[44] Article X:3(a) GATT 1994 'focuses on the day-to-day application of Customs laws, rules and regulations.'[45] Therefore, the Panel interpreted the term to mean that customs laws should not vary, so that every trader would be able to expect the same treatment both over time and in different places and with respect to other persons.[46] Summing up, the term 'uniform' interpreted by the Panel in *Argentina—Bovine Hides* means that the laws have to be applied consistently and predictably.[47]

For the Panel in *EC—Selected Customs Matters*, the definition of the term 'uniform' requires geographic uniformity, as administration should be uniform in the whole territory of a WTO member.[48] Regarding the standard of uniformity, the Panel identified two possible interpretations: on the one hand, it could require absolute and instantaneous identical administration concerning the same facts; on the other hand, it could mean that simply the same rules should be applied but that these do not necessarily have to lead to identical results of administration.[49]

[40] Oxford Dictionary of English, 2005, p 1925.

[41] ibid, p 1925.

[42] Panel Report, *Argentina—Bovine Hides*, WT/DS155/R, para 11.81; this Panel Report was not appealed at the Appellate Body.

[43] ibid, para 11.83.

[44] ibid, para 11.84.

[45] ibid, para 11.84.

[46] ibid, para 11.83.

[47] ibid, para 11.83.

[48] Panel Report, *EC—Selected Customs Matters*, WT/DS315/R, para 7.123. The findings of the Panel regarding the interpretation of the term 'uniform' have not been changed by the Appellate Body; see Appellate Body Report, *EC—Selected Customs Matters*, WT/DS315/AB/R, para 212, fn 475.

[49] Panel Report, *EC—Selected Customs Matters*, WT/DS315/R, para 7.124.

2. Context

The first interpretation of the ordinary meaning suggests there is no requirement for absolute uniformity in each and every case where the facts are identical, as this would be a utopian demand, given the actual context of provision.[50] The reality of most systems of administration, which involve millions of acts of administration, and many administration officials every year, is that it is not viable to achieve such absolute uniformity.[51] Article X:3(a) GATT 1994 embodies an ideal, and the language of this provision cannot be interpreted literally. Rather it ought to be read as embodying an ideal type, because administration officials administer laws as human beings, and are unable to apply each law in each country at every time in an entirely uniform manner.[52] Therefore the real question is what is 'the permissible degree of variance among WTO Members from what is considered ideal.'[53]

For the same reasons, it seems unnecessary to impose an obligation of instantaneous uniformity in interpreting the provision. Although non-uniformity cannot persist for indefinite periods of time,[54] in following the principle of effective treaty interpretation, uniformity must be attained only within a reasonable period of time, depending upon the specific administration at issue, as well as the factual and legal complexity of a particular case.[55] Simultaneously, the measure at issue must have a significant impact on the overall administration of the law and affect administrative decisions on a regular basis, not simply on the outcome of a single case,[56] as individual cases of non-uniform administration can be reconciled later within a reasonable time.[57]

Looking at the immediate context of the term 'uniform' in Article X:3(a) GATT 1994, it is clear that this obligation is intrinsically tied to both the term 'administer' and the phrase 'laws, regulations, decisions and rulings of the kind described in paragraph 1 of this Article.'[58] Therefore, the Panel in *EC—Selected Customs Matters* considered it necessary 'to first clarify the administration that is being challenged in a particular case',[59] as the specific form, nature and scale of administration can vary from case to case and can concern a specific administrative process or the administration of an entire system. As a result, the term 'uniform' has to be interpreted in a flexible manner, considering the circumstances in a particular case, yet in all cases still entailing certain minimum standards of due process, such as notice, transparency, fairness and equity.[60] The narrower the challenge in

[50] ibid, para 7.131.
[51] ibid, para 7.131.
[52] Bhala, 2005, Chapter 16 Section III, 16-014, p 461.
[53] ibid, p 461.
[54] Panel Report, *EC—Selected Customs Matters*, WT/DS315/R, para 7.133.
[55] ibid, para 7.132.
[56] Panel Report, *US—Hot-Rolled Steel*, WT/DS184/R, para 7.268; affirming reference to this ruling was also made in Panel Report, *US—Corrosion-Resistant Steel Sunset Review*, WT/DS244/R, para 7.310.
[57] Panel Report, *EC—Selected Customs Matters*, WT/DS315/R, para 7.132.
[58] ibid, para 7.125.
[59] ibid, para 7.126.
[60] ibid, para 7.134.

a particular case with respect to the specific form of administration and the specific legal instruments alleged to be administered in a non-uniform manner, the stricter the requirement of uniformity will be, whilst a less exacting standard of uniformity will be demanded if the challenge in a particular case is broader and more wide-ranging.[61] Thus, the criterion for uniformity is not so strict in general, but becomes more so in cases with more concrete claims.

Finally, Article X:3(a) GATT 1994 entails no obligation on how to achieve uniform administration. This issue is rather the sovereign responsibility of the WTO members, to whom the provision vests discretion regarding both the nature and level of administrative authorities and the administrative tools for implementing the legal instruments of the kind described in Article X:1 GATT 1994.[62] Therefore, the provision does not require uniformity in administrative processes and such differences in themselves do not constitute a violation of Article X:3(a) GATT 1994.[63] Neither the processes leading to administrative decisions nor the tools that might be used in administration are required to be uniform, only the application of a legal instrument of the kind described in Article X:1 GATT 1994 must be so.[64] Furthermore, whether a WTO member has acted consistently with its own domestic legislation is not a Panel's task to consider, as this function is reserved for each member's domestic judicial system.[65] Lastly, an alleged departure from established policy also does not constitute a violation of Article X:3(a) GATT 1994.[66]

3. *Conclusion*

The key feature of the term 'uniform' is its flexibility. Article X:3(a) GATT 1994 provides no obligation of absolute uniformity, although this interpretation is one possibility when referring to the ordinary meaning of the term 'uniform'. Yet considering the context of the provision, namely the day-to-day administration of trade regulations, such a demand would be utopian and unreasonable. Uniformity in this context cannot be interpreted separately, but has to be considered in relation to the other terms of Article X:3(a) GATT 1994, specifically 'administer' and 'laws, regulations, decisions and rulings of the kind described in paragraph 1 of this Article'. Therefore, the criterion of uniformity depends to some extent on the circumstances of a particular case, taking into consideration the specific form of both the challenged administration and the legal instruments of the kind described in Article X:1 GATT 1994. Nonetheless, Article X:3(a) GATT 1994 establishes certain minimum standards for transparency and procedural fairness that administration of trade regulations must meet, and although the criterion

[61] ibid, para 7.129.
[62] ibid, para 7.141.
[63] Appellate Body Report, *EC—Selected Customs Matters*, WT/DS315/AB/R, para 224.
[64] ibid, para 224.
[65] Panel Report, *US—Hot-Rolled Steel*, WT/DS184/R, para 7.267.
[66] Panel Report, *US—Sheet/Plate from Korea*, WT/DS179/R, para 6.50.

for uniformity is not so strict in general, it becomes more strict in cases regarding concrete claims. Finally, one has to keep in mind that the provision does not prescribe how the WTO members have to achieve uniform administration. Simultaneously the measure at issue is not in violation of Article X:3(a) GATT if it is simply an outcome in an individual case with no impact on the administration of the law overall and which, therefore, does not affect administrative decisions on a regular basis.

II. RELEVANCE FOR THE ADMINISTRATION OF EU CUSTOMS LAW

The EU[67] is full signatory to the WTO Agreement pursuant to Article XI WTO Agreement and therefore is obliged under Article XVI:4 WTO Agreement to 'ensure the conformity of its laws, regulations and administrative procedures with its obligations as provided in the annexed Agreements.' Although each member state of the EU is also a signatory of this Agreement and can be addressed by WTO jurisprudence in the event of alleged violation of WTO law,[68] the EU maintains distinct and separate international obligations under the WTO treaties.[69] For this reason, the obligation entailed in Article X:3(a) GATT 1994 to administrate the legal instruments of the kind described in Article X:1 GATT 1994 in a uniform manner is binding on the EU, given that in creating the EU customs law, the EU took on a competence for which WTO law prescribes particular requirements.

A. Uniform Administration as Own Obligation of the European Union in the Area of Customs Administration

The obligation to uniform administration refers to legal instruments set out in Article X:1 GATT 1994 and therefore effects the execution of EU customs law, as this paragraph encompasses all laws and regulations of general application

> pertaining to the classification or the valuation of products for customs purposes, or to rates of duty, taxes or other charges, or to requirements, restrictions or prohibitions on imports or exports or on the transfer of payments therefore, or affecting their sale, distribution, transportation, insurance, warehousing inspection, exhibition, processing, mixing or other use.

[67] Since the Treaty of Lisbon came into force on 1 December 2009, the European Union (EU), as legal successor of the European Communities (EC), pursuant to Art 1 para 3 Treaty on European Union (hereinafter TEU), has its own legal personality pursuant to Art 47 TEU and can sign international agreements pursuant to Art 216 para 1 Treaty on the Functioning of the European Union (hereinafter TFEU). In this way, the EU legally succeeded the EC as member of the WTO. Under public international law, it is more important that no WTO member objected to the EU being the successor of the EC.

[68] Appellate Body Report, *EC—Computer Equipment*, WT/DS62/AB/R, WT/DS67/AB/R, WT/DS68/AB/R, para 1, fn 2.

[69] Erskine, (18) 2006 *Florida Journal of International Law* (2), pp 423–84 (454).

The laws and regulations of general application described in Article X:1 GATT 1994, which Article X:3(a) GATT 1994 refers to, are not limited in their scope of application, applying to a range of situations or cases.[70] The extensive enumeration in Article X:1 GATT 1994 makes clear that it covers not only the criteria of the bases for the taxation of cross-border traded products, but also encompasses the numerous forms of prohibitions and restrictions and all other trade regulations and decisions of general application.[71] In summary, it affects every regulation and decision of relevance for cross-border traded goods,[72] which are understood together as the legal framework for the whole supply chain, of which the customs law is part.

B. Specific Content of the Obligation to Uniform Administration with Regard to the EU System of Customs Administration

The obligation of uniform administration pursuant to Article X:3(a) GATT 1994 does not demand uniformity in legislation, but in application of laws, and although it allows a content-related examination when legal instruments are used for purposes of regulating administration, such administrative tools only constitute a violation of Article X:3(a) GATT 1994 when they necessarily lead to a lack of uniformity.[73]

A violation of Article X:3(a) GATT occurs when EU customs law as a legal instrument of the kind described in Article X:1 GATT 1994 is applied in a non-uniform manner by the customs authorities in the EU. Likewise, an infringement of the WTO obligation of uniform administration in WTO Member States occurs when differences in the administrative process or in the substantive content of legal instruments regulating the administration of rules and regulations of the kind described in Article X:1 GATT 1994 necessarily lead to non-uniform administration of the latter. Additionally, such measures of customs authorities in the EU must affect the overall administration of EU customs law and must not be only one-off results in individual cases[74] that can be reconciled later within reasonable time.[75]

In contrast, for non-uniform administration within the meaning of Article X:3(a) GATT 1994 to arise it is sufficient that EU customs law is applied differently in even just two EU Member States on a regular basis.[76] To constitute a structural

[70] Panel Report, *EC—Selected Customs Matters*, WT/DS315/R, para 7.116.

[71] Puth, in: Hilf/Oeter (eds), 2005, § 10 para 35; Rogmann, in: Kluth/Müller/Peilert (eds), 2008, pp 797–819 (803); Rogmann, 2008 ZfZ 3, pp 57–69 (59).

[72] Rogmann, in: Kluth/Müller/Peilert (eds), 2008, pp 797–819 (803); Rogmann, 2008 ZfZ 3, pp 57–69 (59).

[73] Appellate Body Report, *EC—Selected Customs Matters*, WT/DS315/AB/R, paras 201, 226.

[74] Panel Report, *US—Hot-Rolled Steel*, WT/DS184/R, para 7.268; affirming reference to this ruling was also made in Panel Report, *US—Corrosion-Resistant Steel Sunset Review*, WT/DS244/R, para 7.310.

[75] Panel Report, *EC—Selected Customs Matters*, WT/DS315/R, para 7.132.

[76] Dierksmeier, 2008 AW-Prax 5, pp 200–03 (201).

shortcoming of the EU system of customs administration in violation of Article X:3(a) GATT 1994 requires there be a lack of procedures, mechanisms and institutions that both prevent divergences in customs administrations and enable their removal should they occur anyhow.[77]

On the other hand, because the provision does not prescribe how to achieve uniform administration,[78] there is no obligation for the EU to build a centralised system of customs administration at the EU level. Therefore, the administration of EU customs law by 28 national customs authorities does not in itself constitute a breach of Article X:3(a) GATT.[79]

1. *Provisions of a Discretionary Nature*

EU customs law contains many provisions that provide customs authorities with some extent of flexibility in the application of the law. However, the existence and exercise of such discretion does not in itself create a violation of Article X:3(a) GATT 1994, as long as it neither has an improper effect on the provisions underlying due process nor leads to insecurity and unpredictability in the trading environment without justifiable reason.[80] The substantive content of such provisions regulating the administration of legal instruments of the kind described in Article X:1 GATT 1994 can be examined under Article X:3(a) GATT 1994.[81] Yet the ordinary meaning of the term 'uniform administration' does not indicate that Article X:3(a) GATT 1994 dictates that a provision regulating a particular matter of customs administration has to be drafted in prescriptive rather than discretionary terms.[82] Discretionary provisions by definition may be applied in different ways and may lead to different results, but at the same time they reflect a policy decision to provide administrations with a certain degree of freedom in the application of rules.[83]

Moreover, in many cases there is a plausible reason for allowing discretion, making it seem unlikely that it was the intention of the drafters of Article X:3(a) GATT 1994 to interpret such differences as an instance of non-uniform administration.[84] On the other hand, there are certain limits to the types of provisions that can be drafted in discretionary terms, and to the way discretion can be exercised in a particular case. Specifically the underlying due process principle of Article X:3(a) GATT 1994 as well as the security and predictability of the trading environment

[77] Rogmann, 2008 ZfZ 3, pp 57–69 (64); Rovetta/Lux, (2) 2007 GTCJ (5), pp 195–208 (207).

[78] Panel Report, *EC—Selected Customs Matters*, WT/DS315/R, para 7.141; Appellate Body Report, *EC—Selected Customs Matters*, WT/DS315/AB/R, para 224.

[79] Panel Report, *EC—Selected Customs Matters*, WT/DS315/R, para 7.141.

[80] ibid, para 7.434; upheld by the Appellate Body, see Appellate Body Report, *EC—Selected Customs Matters*, WT/DS315/AB/R, para 217.

[81] ibid, paras 200, 210.

[82] Panel Report, *EC—Selected Customs Matters*, WT/DS315/R, para 7.430.

[83] ibid, para 7.429.

[84] ibid, para 7.431.

must not be endangered without justifiable reason.[85] Indeed, the Panel in *China—Raw Materials* found that the lack of any definition, guidelines or standards on how a potentially critically criterion should be applied by administrative authorities could constitute evidence of non-uniform administration,[86] though as mentioned above, the Appellate Body later determined that the relevant claims in question were outside the Panel's terms of reference.[87]

In summary, one can say that the exercise of discretion may or may not constitute a violation of Article X:3(a) GATT 1994, and therefore has to be assessed based on its result.[88] It only constitutes an infringement when the process necessarily leads to an outcome of non-uniform administration.[89]

(a) Penalty Provisions and Customs Offences

One concrete issue that the Panel as well as the Appellate Body in *EC—Selected Customs Matters* examined was the existing differences in penalty provisions among the EU Member States, seeking to determine whether they constituted a violation of Article X:3(a) GATT 1994. Because of the absence of EU competence, there are no penalty provisions at the EU level; only the legislators of the EU Member States are empowered to set such provisions. In the absence of harmonised Union legislation that also includes customs offences, the national legislators are free to choose the appropriate penalties.[90] They are bound only by common principles to ensure penalties are effective, proportionate and dissuasive,[91] because otherwise the EU Member States would fail to fulfil their obligations under the EU Treaty, in particular Article 4 paragraph 3 subparagraph 2 TEU.[92]

However, the different national penalty provisions in the EU system of customs administration do not constitute an infringement of Article X:3(a) GATT 1994, as they do not necessarily lead to non-uniform administration.[93] Rather, different results may occur simply because of the exercise of discretion in the application of the penalty provisions in question and specific circumstances of a case.[94]

[85] ibid, para 7.431.

[86] Panel Report, *China—Raw Materials*, WT/DS394, 395, 398/R, para 7.751.

[87] Appellate Body Report, *China—Raw Materials*, WT/DS394, 395, 398/AB/R, paras 234, 235.

[88] Hoekmann/Mavroidis, (8) 2009 WTR (1), pp 31–44 (37).

[89] Appellate Body Report, *EC—Selected Customs Matters*, WT/DS315/AB/R, paras 201, 226.

[90] ECJ 7 December 2000, Case C-213/99, *Andrade* [2000] ECR I-11083, para 20.

[91] ECJ 21 September 1989, Case 68/88, *Commission v Greece* [1989] ECR 2965, paras 23–25; similarly, ECJ 7 December 2000, Case C-213/99, *Andrade* [2000] ECR I-11083, para 19; ECJ 26 October 1995, Case C-36/94, *Siesse* [1995] ECR I-3573, para 20; ECJ 10 July 1990, Case C-326/88, *Hansen* [1990] ECR I-2911, para 17; see also Council Resolution of 29 June 1995 on the effective and uniform application of Community law and on the penalties applicable for breaches of Community law in the internal market, [1995] OJ C188/1–3.

[92] ECJ 21 September 1989, Case 68/88, *Commission v Greece* [1989] ECR 2965, paras 23, 24, 25; the finding relates to Art 10 TEC, which is succeeded by Art 4 para 3 subpara 2 TEU in principle.

[93] Appellate Body Report, *EC—Selected Customs Matters*, WT/DS315/AB/R, para 211.

[94] ibid, para 213.

Therefore, a violation of Article X:3(a) GATT 1994 depends, on the one hand, on the degree of uniformity that is required, which in turn depends on the nature of the penalty provisions as well as the nature of the customs law to be enforced. On the other hand, it depends also on the impact of any differences between the penalty provisions in the enforcement of customs law.[95] This affirms that flexibility is the key feature of uniformity under Article X:3(a) GATT 1994, and that the requirements for uniform administration are not too strict until concrete claims are raised.

(b) Audit Procedures

A similar conclusion was made by both the Panel and Appellate Body in *EC—Selected Customs Matters* with respect to differences in audit procedures among the EU Member States.[96] Post-clearance audits are used to control economic operators through examination of their audits, accounts, systems and records. In this area, common EU law applicable throughout the EU does exist and is legally binding in the EU Member States. Additionally, in the course of the dispute the EC developed a non-binding guidance at EU level, the Community Customs Audit Guide, which assists the customs authorities of the EU Member States in implementing audit procedures and provides a practical basis for a common approach, setting out a framework for post-clearance and audit based controls. Nonetheless, the laws and guide still leave some discretion to the national customs authorities. Yet as was shown above, the mere existence of discretion is not a violation of uniform administration under Article X:3(a) GATT 1994. To constitute such, the result of the exercise of discretion must necessarily lead to non-uniform administration in a particular case.[97]

The concrete EU provision in question, namely Article 78 paragraph 2 CC, is drafted in discretionary terms (though it requires justifiable reason) because:

> a certain degree of uncertainty as to when and under what conditions an audit will be carried out is in the interest of sound customs administration and must be accepted by traders as part of a normal customs regime.[98]

Additionally, the Community Customs Audit Guide helps to ensure that traders are treated fairly and consistently.[99] As the existence and exercise of discretion in this provision neither unduly compromises the underlying due process principle of Article X:3(a) GATT 1994 nor creates insecurity and unpredictability in the trading environment without just cause, an infringement would require that the differences in audit procedures necessarily lead to non-uniform administration

[95] ibid, paras 211, 212.

[96] Panel Report, *EC—Selected Customs Matters*, WT/DS315/R, para 7.434; upheld by the Appellate Body, see Appellate Body Report, *EC—Selected Customs Matters*, WT/DS315/AB/R, para 217.

[97] Appellate Body Report, *EC—Selected Customs Matters*, WT/DS315/AB/R, paras 201, 226.

[98] ibid, para 215.

[99] Panel Report, *EC—Selected Customs Matters*, WT/DS315/R, para 7.432.

and do not stem from the exercise of discretion and the special circumstances of a concrete case.[100] Again, this reaffirms the flexible nature of uniformity under Article X:3(a) GATT 1994.

2. Undefined Legal Terms in EU Customs Law

The legal norms in EU customs law entail many undefined legal terms that need to be interpreted as a necessary part of the application of these provisions in customs administration. Assuming that every term in a legal norm is automatically a legal term, the character of such a term is undefined if its application is not possible with reference to a legally binding text, for example a legal definition, and therefore has to be interpreted under its ordinary meaning and systematic, historical and teleological context.[101] The application of a single provision is a form of administration, because such action puts legal norms into practical effect,[102] and since such a concrete act of administration is narrow in nature, a high degree of uniformity is therefore required given Article X:3(a) GATT 1994.[103] An infringement of Article X:3(a) GATT 1994 in such a case occurs if different customs authorities of the EU Member States interpret such undefined legal terms in legal norms of EU customs law differently and therefore apply them differently in cases with the same set of facts.[104]

Additionally, divergences in the substantive content of national legal instruments which regulate the application of legal instruments of the kind described in Article X:1 GATT 1994 by interpreting undefined legal terms in EU customs law can constitute a violation of Article X:3(a) GATT 1994 when those differences necessarily lead to non-uniform administration of a concrete legal norm in EU customs law.[105] The Panel in *China—Raw Materials* concluded that the lack of any guidance for administrative authorities regarding the interpretation and application of certain critical criterions could represent relevant evidence of non-uniform administration.[106] However, as mentioned above, the Appellate Body declared the relevant claims in question were outside the Panel's terms of reference.[107]

[100] Appellate Body Report, *EC—Selected Customs Matters*, WT/DS315/AB/R, para 216.

[101] Blechschmidt, 2006 BDZ-Fachteil 12, F89–F90 (F90).

[102] Panel Report, *EC—Selected Customs Matters*, WT/DS315/R, para 7.104; upheld by the Appellate Body, see Appellate Body Report, *EC—Selected Customs Matters*, WT/DS315/AB/R, para 224.

[103] Panel Report, *EC—Selected Customs Matters*, WT/DS315/R, para 7.153, see also paras 7.199, 7.214, 7.223, 7.247, 7.293, 7.361, 7.378, 7.392, 7.411, 7.458, 7.475; findings of the Panel regarding the interpretation of the term 'uniform' have not been changed by the Appellate Body, see Appellate Body Report, *EC—Selected Customs Matters*, WT/DS315/AB/R, para 212, fn 475.

[104] Panel Report, *EC—Selected Customs Matters*, WT/DS315/R, paras 7.293, 7.304, 7.305; upheld by the Appellate Body, see Appellate Body Report, *EC—Selected Customs Matters*, WT/DS315/AB/R, para 260.

[105] Appellate Body Report, *EC—Selected Customs Matters*, WT/DS315/AB/R, paras 239, 240, 241.

[106] Panel Report, *China—Raw Materials*, WT/DS394, 395, 398/R, para 7.751.

[107] Appellate Body Report, *China—Raw Materials*, WT/DS394, 395, 398/AB/R, paras 234, 235.

(a) Tariff Classification

In the customs area of tariff classification many legal norms take the form of positions in the headings and subheadings of the Combined Nomenclature as part of the Common Customs Tariff of the EU. To determine the proper tariff classification of a product, abstract terminology used to describe the goods must be interpreted so that it can be subsumed under those headings, subheadings and positions. The features of the goods prescribed therein are effectively matters of fact of these legal norms and the classification under a single position is a simple subsumption, with the tariff rate as legal consequence.[108] One can distinguish between collective terms encompassing a multiplicity of goods and single terms pertaining only to a specific product. The interpretation of the goods terminology can be very difficult and challenging, as to a great extent the terminology derives from the technical languages of a variety of fields, like the chemical or technological industry, and yet is not always used in its original specialised sense.[109]

Furthermore, there are 24 different official languages in the EU. However, the Combined Nomenclature of the EU is based on the Harmonised Commodity Description and Coding System of Tariff Nomenclature (HS).[110] This internationally standardised system of names and numbers for classifying traded products, developed and maintained by the World Customs Organization (WCO), is only authoritative in English or French, pursuant to Article 20 paragraph 3 HS. Therefore, some of the difficulties with interpretation in the area of tariff classification stem from translation difficulties or even mistranslation.[111]

Additionally, the EU Member States have different cultural backgrounds that can affect the interpretation of undefined legal terms. Different traditions regarding public holidays, for example, can include the use of single articles in a way that is unknown in other EU Member States but has to be considered in classification.[112]

In the meaning of Article X:3(a) GATT 1994, the tariff classification of a single product by the national customs authorities of the EU Member States constitutes an act of administration, for such action applies and puts into practical effect a legal instrument of the kind described in Article X:1 GATT 1994, namely the EU rules in the area of tariff classification.[113] Such an application of a tariff heading in the Common Customs Tariff is narrow in nature and thus requires a high

[108] Blechschmidt, 2006 BDZ-Fachteil 12, F89–F90 (F90).

[109] ibid, F89–F90 (F90).

[110] [1987] OJ L198/3–10.

[111] Blechschmidt, 2007 BDZ-Fachteil 1-2, F3–F5 (F5).

[112] ibid, F3–F5 (F5).

[113] Panel Report, *EC—Selected Customs Matters*, WT/DS315/R, para 7.104, see also paras 7.198, 7.213, 7.222, 7.246, 7.292; upheld by the Appellate Body, see Appellate Body Report, *EC—Selected Customs Matters*, WT/DS315/AB/R, para 224.

degree of uniformity.[114] Therefore, a violation of Article X:3(a) GATT 1994 occurs if different customs authorities apply the headings and subheadings of the Common Customs Tariff differently because of divergences in their interpretation of goods terminology.

To prove such an infringement it is not sufficient to demonstrate a different tariff classification of a single product in the past. Rather, it has to be shown that such an instance of non-uniform administration currently exists.[115] In this context, efforts to reconcile instances of non-uniform administration must be taken into consideration in order to determine whether a past violation still persists and continues to have effect.[116] The precise manner in which divergences in tariff classification should be resolved is not dictated by Article X:3(a) GATT 1994 as the provision does not prescribe how to achieve uniform administration, aside from stating that the measures should be effective.[117]

(1) Classification of Network Cards for Personal Computers

Because of these requirements the Panel in *EC—Selected Customs Matters* concluded that a non-uniform administration which had occurred more than 10 years earlier regarding the tariff classification of network cards for personal computers did not constitute a current violation of Article X:3(a) GATT 1994, due to a lack of evidence that the differences in tariff classification of this specific product continued to have effect at the time of the establishment of the Panel.[118] Furthermore, the Panel took the view that those differences in the past had been resolved through a preliminary ruling of the ECJ regarding two cases. Herein the court clarified the correct classification of network cards for personal computers.[119] Following this ruling there was no evidence of a persisting divergence in tariff classification of such products.[120]

Similarly, regarding the tariff classification of drip irrigation products, the Panel found that there was no evidence of non-uniform administration persisting to the time of the establishment of the Panel; in fact, they found the non-uniformity had occurred during a relatively short period of time in the past, with the differences having been resolved by the EC,[121] namely through the adoption of Commission Regulation (EC) 763/2002 of 3 March 2002.[122]

[114] Panel Report, *EC—Selected Customs Matters*, WT/DS315/R, paras 7.199, 7.214, 7.223, 7.247, 7.293; findings of the Panel regarding the interpretation of the term 'uniform' have not been changed by the Appellate Body, see Appellate Body Report, *EC—Selected Customs Matters*, WT/DS315/AB/R, para 212, fn 475.

[115] Panel Report, *EC—Selected Customs Matters*, WT/DS315/R, paras 7.206, 7.217.

[116] ibid, paras 7.202, 7.206.

[117] ibid, para 7.304.

[118] ibid, para 7.206.

[119] ECJ 10 May 2001, Case C-463/98, *Cabletron* [2001] ECR I-3495 and ECJ 19 October 2000, Case C-339/98 *Peacock* [2000] ECR I-8947.

[120] Panel Report, *EC—Selected Customs Matters*, WT/DS315/R, para 7.205.

[121] ibid, para 7.217.

[122] [2002] OJ L117/3–4.

(2) *Classification of LCD Flat Monitors with a Digital Video Interface*

However, in a third case, the Panel in *EC—Selected Customs Matters* adjudged the EC to have non-uniform tariff classification for LCD flat monitors with a digital video interface (hereinafter: LCD).[123] The Panel found that in 2004 and 2005 divergent tariff classification of such products did exist because of different interpretations of goods terminology regarding LCDs, a fact which was not disputed by the EC.[124] Indeed, the EC had taken action since 2004 to resolve those divergences, inter alia Council Regulation (EC) 493/2005 of 16 March 2005,[125] which provides the concerned importers with certainty about tariff treatment,[126] and Commission Regulation (EC) 634/2005 of 26 April 2005,[127] which regulates the classification of a particular type of LCD monitor.[128]

However, the Panel considered those measures to have been ineffective,[129] as some confusion among the national customs authorities of EU Member States on the tariff classification of such products apparently continued to exist.[130] Thus, it concluded that this confusion might still be causing different tariff classification in the present and be having an ongoing adverse impact on the trading environment.[131] Therefore, the Panel found a violation of Article X:3(a) GATT 1994,[132] even though the EC had inter alia issued Commission Regulation (EC) 2171/2005 of 23 December 2005[133] in the meantime, which in fact reconciled the divergences. However, these facts were not accepted as evidence by the Panel since they were submitted too late, after the interim review stage of the dispute settlement.[134]

Though the Panel's findings regarding the tariff classification of LCDs were subsequently upheld by the Appellate Body,[135] they have been criticised on several grounds. One point of criticism was that the Panel failed to take into account some of the evidence submitted by the EC, in particular Commission Regulation (EC) 2171/2005. However, the Appellate Body argued that the Panel did take the new EC regulation into account, but without giving it the weight the EC might have wished for, which was within its discretion.[136] This has been criticised as 'a weak argument for rejecting the appeal' because none of the features of the newly submitted regulation were discussed by the Panel, which was accused of having

[123] Panel Report, *EC—Selected Customs Matters*, WT/DS315/R, para 7.305.
[124] ibid, para 7.294.
[125] [2005] OJ L82/1–2.
[126] Panel Report, *EC—Selected Customs Matters*, WT/DS315/R, para 7.279.
[127] [2005] OJ L106/7–9.
[128] Panel Report, *EC—Selected Customs Matters*, WT/DS315/R, para 7.281.
[129] ibid, para 7.295.
[130] ibid, para 7.300.
[131] ibid, para 7.304.
[132] ibid, para 7.305.
[133] [2005] OJ L346/7–9.
[134] Panel Report, *EC—Selected Customs Matters*, WT/DS315/R, para 7.305, fn 580.
[135] Appellate Body Report, *EC—Selected Customs Matters*, WT/DS315/AB/R, para 260.
[136] ibid, para 258.

made an unsubstantiated assertion that the Appellate Body nonetheless considered to be sufficient.[137] Indeed, it is unclear on which point the Panel made an objective assessment of the facts with respect to Regulation (EC) 2171/2005, as it only mentioned its existence in a footnote. It seems doubtful that this approach met the requirement of an objective assessment of the facts within the meaning of Article 11 DSU.

Furthermore, the Panel relied on evidence that post-dated its establishment. Yet the Appellate Body decided this did mean the Panel had overstepped its terms of reference, arguing that a Panel could do so to the extent that such pre-dating or post-dating of evidence is relevant for the assessment of whether or not a violation of Article X:3(a) GATT 1994 existed at the time the Panel was established.[138] Therefore, both the Panel and the Appellate Body considered it to be sufficient evidence of an infringement of Article X:3(a) GATT 1994 that non-uniform administration with regard to tariff classification of LCDs had existed in the past—which was not disputed by the EC—regardless of the proof provided by the EC that this violation had been reconciled. This finding has been criticised as being:

> quite unintelligible, since the Appellate Body imposes a remarkable shift in the allocation of burden of proof: it is not for the EC to show that it is a good citizen; it is for the US to show that the EC is a bad citizen.[139]

The Panel had indeed already decided that it must be proven that violations in the past continue to have effect if they are to constitute appropriate evidence for the existence of an alleged non-uniform administration at the time of the establishment of the Panel.[140] It seems quite a different approach for the Panel, as well as for the Appellate Body in this case, to shift the burden of proof to the defendant (here the EC), which had to submit counter-evidence to prove that effective measures to resolve non-uniform administrations had been undertaken. However, there were differences in this case. The non-disputed divergence in tariff classification of LCDs did not date back very long, a mere two years compared to the 10 years in the case of the tariff classification of network cards for computers. Furthermore, there was some evidence that the measures undertaken by the EC did not solve the problem, unlike in the cases of tariff classification of both network cards for computers and drip irrigation products. Therefore, the Panel and the Appellate Body seem to have taken the view that non-uniform administration in the past can be prima facie evidence of a current violation of Article X:3(a) GATT 1994[141] if it does not date back a long time, for example a whole decade, and if no measures have been undertaken to resolve the infringement, or if they have not been effective.[142]

[137] Hoekmann/Mavroidis, (8) 2009 WTR (1), pp 31–44 (41).
[138] Appellate Body Report, *EC—Selected Customs Matters*, WT/DS315/AB/R, para 254.
[139] Hoekmann/Mavroidis, (8) 2009 WTR (1), pp 31–44 (41).
[140] Panel Report, *EC—Selected Customs Matters*, WT/DS315/R, paras 7.206, 7.217.
[141] Similar: Hoekmann/Mavroidis, (8) 2009 WTR (1), pp 31–44 (41).
[142] Similar: ibid, pp 31–44 (41).

Lastly, it has been criticised that the Panel did not explain which facts in the case of tariff classification of LCDs necessarily lead to non-uniform application.[143] However, in this regard one has to differentiate between the application of legal instruments of the kind described in Article X:1 GATT 1994, which have to be uniform, and the administrative process and the substantive content of legal instruments regulating the administration of those legal instruments of the kind described in Article X:1 GATT 1994, which do not have to be uniform in themselves, but must not necessarily lead to non-uniformity in the application of legal instruments of the kind described in Article X:1 GATT 1994. In the case of LCDs, the application of legal instruments of the kind described in Article X:1 GATT 1994, namely the EU rules in the area of tariff classification, had been challenged and therefore it was sufficient that this application was non-uniform for it to constitute a violation of Article X:3(a) GATT 1994, whereas the additional condition of 'necessarily leading' was not required.

(3) Classification of Blackout Drapery Lining

Indeed, the Appellate Body has reversed findings of a Panel regarding the administration of EU customs law in the area of tariff classification because it failed to explain how divergences in the substantive content of legal instruments—in the form of interpretative aids for undefined legal terms that are applicable only nationally—necessarily lead to non-uniform administration of particular legal norms of EU customs law. In the case of tariff classification of blackout drapery lining (BDL), the Panel in *EC—Selected Customs Matters* came to a contradictory result. On the one hand, it concluded that the divergent classification decisions of customs authorities in different EU Member States relied upon objectively justifiable reasons because it considered the products that had been the subject of classification not to be identical; therefore the Panel saw no non-uniform administration in violation of Article X:3(a) GATT 1994.[144]

On the other hand, it considered the administrative process leading to the tariff classification decision of BDL to, first, constitute an act of administration—within the meaning of Article X:3(a) GATT 1994[145]—and, secondly, to be non-uniform.[146] The Panel argued that the customs authorities in one EU Member State relied upon an interpretative aid for the purpose of classifying BDL that is applicable only nationally and, additionally, did not take into account the classification decisions of customs authorities in other EU Member States.[147] The Panel stated that:

> a system of customs administration which allows or at least does not prevent customs authorities from unilaterally relying upon interpretative aids in carrying out their functions, which are not provided for in the binding rules applicable to all customs

[143] Hoekmann/Mavroidis, (8) 2009 WTR (1), pp 31–44 (40).
[144] Panel Report, *EC—Selected Customs Matters*, WT/DS315/R, paras 7.264, 7.265.
[145] ibid, para 7.266.
[146] ibid, para 7.276.
[147] ibid, paras 7.267, 7.271, 7.272, 7.275.

> authorities, such as in the European Communities, could lead to non-uniform administration in violation of Article X:3(a) GATT 1994 in certain circumstances[148]

and that:

> a customs administration system which does not require reference by customs authorities to decisions taken by other customs authorities operating within the same system and/or cooperation between customs authorities before customs decisions are taken, such as in the European Communities, could lead to non-uniform administration in violation of Article X:3(a) GATT 1994 in certain circumstances.[149]

However, this was not the outcome in this specific case, because the outcome itself, the tariff classification of BDL, had not been considered to be objectionable by the Panel; thus it censured only the potential for a violation of Article X:3(a) GATT 1994, in that the administrative process could lead to GATT-inconsistent outcomes.

As has already been mentioned, the administrative process can be encompassed by the term 'administer' itself. However, such processes neither constitute an act of administration within the meaning of Article X:3(a) GATT 1994 nor do they require uniformity; it is rather the application of legal instruments of the kind described in Article X:1 GATT 1994 that must be uniform.[150] Divergences in the substantive content of legal instruments which are not of the kind described in Article X:1 GATT 1994, but which simply regulate their application, are permissible as long as they do not necessarily lead to different results of tariff classification on the same set of facts. Consequently, the findings of the Panel regarding the tariff classification of BDL were reversed by the Appellate Body, as the Panel failed to analyse whether the features of the administrative process in tariff classification of BDL, namely the use of a national interpretative aid in only a single EU Member State, necessarily lead to non-uniform administration of a legal instrument of the kind described in Article X:1 GATT 1994.[151] One has to agree with the Appellate Body's view that in a case such as the tariff classification of BDL, it seems impossible to come to such a conclusion, given the Panel's earlier finding that the result of the administrative process in this case was actually correct.[152]

(b) Customs Valuation

Within EU customs law the area of customs valuation also contains many undefined legal terms in legal norms that are interpreted and applied by the customs authorities of the EU Member States, and that constitutes acts of administration within the meaning of Article X:3(a) GATT 1994, given that such action puts

[148] ibid, para 7.267.

[149] ibid, para 7.272; emphasis in the original.

[150] Appellate Body Report, *EC—Selected Customs Matters*, WT/DS315/AB/R, para 224 and again with regard to BDL para 239.

[151] ibid, paras 240, 242.

[152] ibid, para 241.

into practical effect legal instruments of the kind described in Article X:1 GATT 1994,[153] specifically Chapter 3 of Title II of the Community Customs Code (Articles 28–36 CCC) and its Implementing Regulation (Title V, Articles 141–81a CCCIP) as the basic provisions on customs valuation. The administration of EU rules in the area of customs valuation is primarily the responsibility of the national customs authorities of the EU Member States, but there are a number of tools to ensure uniform administration, including amendments to EU rules regarding customs valuation, opinions of the Customs Code Committee and the Compendium of Customs Valuation texts.

With regard to the interpretation of undefined legal terms in the area of customs valuation, it is interesting to note that the European Commission has the option of amending the valuation rules contained in the Implementing Regulation, in accordance with the procedure of Article 247 CCC, if there is a need for more detailed rules on valuation, whereas the opinions of the Customs Code Committee and the Compendium of Customs Valuation texts are not legally binding. Furthermore, there are informal bilateral contacts among the national customs authorities of the EU Member States regarding the exchange of customs valuation information, but this system is not formalised.[154] Finally, Annex 23 of the Implementing Regulation contains interpretative notes that the national customs authorities must comply with when applying the provisions of the Community Customs Code (CCC) and its Implementing Regulation (CCCIP) regarding customs valuation pursuant to Article 141I CCCIP. Nevertheless, there remain plenty of undefined legal terms in the EU rules on customs valuation that have to be interpreted and applied in the day-to-day work of the national customs authorities of the EU Member States.

Relating to Article X:3(a) GATT 1994, customs valuation entails the application of a few provisions of EU customs law that are narrow in nature and thus requires a high degree of uniformity.[155] A violation of Article X:3(a) GATT 1994 occurs if different customs authorities apply single provisions of the Common Customs Code and its Implementing Regulation regarding customs valuation differently because of divergences in their interpretation of undefined legal terms in cases with the same set of facts. Additionally, it is not permissible under Article X:3(a) GATT 1994 for the administrative process and/or the substantive content of legal instruments regulating the administration of those legal instruments of the kind described in Article X:1 GATT 1994 to necessarily lead to non-uniformity in the application of the latter as regular result in particular cases.

[153] Panel Report, *EC—Selected Customs Matters*, WT/DS315/R, paras 7.360, 7.377, 7.391, 7.410.

[154] COM (2003) 672 final, p 25; similar COM (2008) 612 final, p 5.

[155] Panel Report, *EC—Selected Customs Matters*, WT/DS315/R, paras 7.361, 7.378, 7.392, 7.411; the findings of the Panel regarding the interpretation of the term 'uniform' have not been changed by the Appellate Body, see Appellate Body Report, *EC—Selected Customs Matters*, WT/DS315/AB/R, para 212, fn 475.

Regarding the interpretation of undefined legal terms in EU customs law, the Panel in *EC—Selected Customs Matters* was very strict in its requirement for substantial evidence proving that differences in administration by the national customs authorities lead to differences in outcome even in cases with the same set of facts. In one case regarding the treatment of royalty payments as part of the customs value under Article 32 paragraph 1 section c) CCC, the Panel came to the conclusion that the term 'royalties', in the context of forming part of the customs value, was actually applied differently by different customs authorities.[156] However, because of the lack of detailed information about the transaction in question, there was insufficient evidence that those divergences had occurred, despite the facts being the same, and therefore the Panel found no violation of Article X:3(a) GATT 1994.[157]

In the case of the deduction of vehicle repair costs covered by a seller's warranty from customs value, pursuant to Article 29 paragraph 3 section a) CCC, the Panel concluded that there had been non-uniform administration in the past, but found no evidence for such a violation of Article X:3(a) GATT 1994 at the present time, in light of an amendment of Article 145 CCCIP[158] that had removed this infringement in 2002.[159] This conclusion is in keeping with the Panel's findings also in the area of tariff classification. In both areas, any efforts to reconcile past instances of non-uniform administration must be taken into consideration in order to determine if a past violation still persists and continues to have effect.[160] Only if such continued effect exists in the present does it constitute a case of non-uniform administration.[161]

(c) Customs Procedures

The same requirements as in the area of tariff classification and customs valuation apply to customs procedures, which is one of the core areas in EU customs law. Customs procedures are regulated in the Common Customs Code and its Implementing Regulation, though some provisions refer to the domestic law of the EU Member States or have gaps that have to be closed by domestic law.[162] Simultaneously, the implementation of customs procedures is the responsibility of the EU Member States' authorities. Although Article 250 CCC provides that the decisions, measures and documents issued by one customs authority shall have the same legal effects in other EU Member States when the customs procedure is used in several EU Member States, there is no consulting obligation under EU

156 Panel Report, *EC—Selected Customs Matters*, WT/DS315/R, para 7.369.

157 ibid, paras 7.370, 7.371; not appealed on the Appellate Body.

158 Commission Regulation (EC) 444/2002 of 11 March 2002 amending Regulation (EEC) 2454/93 laying down provisions for the implementation of Council Regulation (EEC) 2913/92 establishing the Community Customs Code and Regulations (EC) 2787/2000 and (EC) 993/2001, [2002] OJ L68/11–17.

159 Panel Report, *EC—Selected Customs Matters*, WT/DS315/R, paras 7.401, 7.402, 7.403.

160 ibid, paras 7.202, 7.206.

161 ibid, paras 7.202, 7.206.

162 Wolffgang, in: Witte/Wolffgang (eds), 2012, p 27, para 32.

law when there is disagreement among the national customs authorities regarding customs procedures in a particular situation, though the customs authorities regularly exchange information.[163]

Such differences among customs authorities regarding customs procedures occur, inter alia, because, as in other areas, in the area of customs procedures the basic provisions in Title IV Chapter 2 of the Community Customs Code and in its Implementing Regulation contain many undefined legal terms that have to be interpreted by the national customs authorities of the EU Member States. If there is no legally binding text on the EU level, the national customs authorities often provide national guidance for the interpretation, implementation and administration of those provisions in EU customs law.

In *EC—Selected Customs Matters*, in the area of customs procedures the Panel examined inter alia the application of such different national guidance for processing under customs control by different national customs authorities. The Panel found neither substantive divergences in those legal instruments nor a non-uniform practice within the meaning of Article X:3(a) GATT 1994 in applying such guidance.[164] Although this case was not appealed to the Appellate Body, considering the Panel's general findings[165] one can say that neither divergences in the administrative process nor in national legal instruments regulating this process and the application of EU customs law are in themselves a violation of Article X:3(a) GATT 1994, provided they do not necessarily lead to non-uniform administration of concrete provisions of the kind described in Article X:1 GATT 1994.[166] This is only the case if the undefined legal terms in particular provisions are interpreted and applied differently to the same set of facts as a regular result of an administrative process or application of national guidance.

However, one has to keep in mind that such national guidance is issued by customs authorities themselves to regulate customs matters of importance in the day-to-day administration of EU customs law, and therefore often codifies customs practice.[167] Thus, substantive divergences in national guidance can indicate that concrete provisions in EU customs law are administered in a non-uniform manner, considering that the application of a single provision is an act of administration that is narrow in nature and requires a high degree of uniformity under Article X:3(a) GATT 1994.[168]

[163] Panel Report, *EC—Selected Customs Matters*, WT/DS315/R, European Communities' reply to Panel question No. 149, Annex B, pp B-37, B-38.

[164] ibid, para 7.464.

[165] Appellate Body Report, *EC—Selected Customs Matters*, WT/DS315/AB/R, paras 239, 240, 241.

[166] Dierksmeier, 2007, p 70.

[167] ibid, p 70.

[168] Panel Report, *EC—Selected Customs Matters*, WT/DS315/R, para 7.458; findings of the Panel regarding the interpretation of the term 'uniform' have not been changed by the Appellate Body, see Appellate Body Report, *EC—Selected Customs Matters*, WT/DS315/AB/R, para 212, fn 475.

(d) Summary

In the end, there are no differences between the different customs areas in EU customs law regarding the requirements of uniform administration under Article X:3(a) GATT 1994, as it pertains to the interpretation and application of undefined legal terms in legal norms of EU customs law by national customs authorities of the EU Member States. This means that undefined legal terms must not be interpreted differently on the same set of facts. It also means that the use of legal instruments that regulate the administration of EU customs law and are only applicable nationally must not necessarily lead to a different application of concrete legal norms in EU customs law as a regular result. The same holds true for differences in the substantive content of such national legal instruments that interpret undefined legal terms in EU customs law.

3. *Administrative Process and Administration Structure and Design*

As the Appellate Body in *EC—Selected Customs Matters* stated, the administrative process can be encompassed by the term 'administer' but does not itself constitute an act of administration within the meaning of Article X:3(a) GATT 1994 and therefore does not requires uniformity. Rather, it is the application of legal instruments of the kind described in Article X:1 GATT 1994 that must be uniform.[169] Although customs procedures are regulated in the Common Customs Code and its Implementing Regulation, general procedural law is regulated only in individual areas and gaps have to be closed by using the domestic law of the EU Member States.[170] Therefore, in the EU system of customs administration, the implementation of EU customs law, understood as the administrative process, is the responsibility of the EU Member States' authorities; thus it is often shaped by national administrative traditions.[171]

These circumstances have led critics to level the allegation that the EU Customs Union is merely a customs law union, and neither a process union nor an administration union.[172] Indeed, administrative sovereignty remains with the EU Member States and EU law in general does not include parameters for the distribution of competence or authority. Therefore, the particular organisation of customs authorities is regulated by the particular domestic law of the EU Member State.[173] The European Commission has no authority to issue orders to the national customs authorities of the EU Member States.[174] However, as already mentioned, the administration of EU customs law by 28 different national customs authorities

[169] Appellate Body Report, *EC—Selected Customs Matters*, WT/DS315/AB/R, para 224.
[170] Kunas, in: Bongartz (ed), 2000, pp 1–24 (7).
[171] ibid, pp 1–24 (21).
[172] See for example Weerth, 2008 ZfZ 7, pp 178–85 (181).
[173] Rogmann, 2008 ZfZ 3, pp 57–69 (58).
[174] ibid, pp 57–69 (67).

does not in itself constitute a breach of Article X:3(a) GATT, as WTO law does not prescribe how to achieve uniform administration[175] and therefore does not contain an obligation for the EU to build a centralised system of customs administration at the EU level.[176]

Nevertheless, the circumstances of administrative processes in the EU customs law system to some extent have the potential to lead to non-uniformity within the meaning of Article X:3(a) GATT 1994. The Panel in *EC—Selected Customs Matters* refused to review the structural aspects of the EU system of customs administration, as it considered this to be a matter outside its terms of reference;[177] therefore it only made statements regarding specific cases. Moreover, in those single cases the Panel *EC—Selected Customs Matters* criticised the EU system of customs administration.

One case was the treatment of amendments to explanatory notes by customs authorities in the area of tariff classification. The Panel stated that in its view:

> in the context of the EC system of customs administration, the absence of an obligation imposed upon the Member States to treat the explanatory note in the same way, could amount to an instance of non-uniform administration in violation of Article X:3(a) GATT 1994.[178]

The EU had been criticised regarding an amendment to an explanatory note for tariff classification of camcorders, that led the explanatory note to be treated as equivalent to a regulation and given prospective effect only in some EU Member States, whereas in other EU Member States the explanatory note had been treated as a mere clarification of the law and thus given retrospective effect.

In another case, the Panel in *EC—Selected Customs Matters* examined the administrative process regarding revocations of Binding Tariff Information (BTI) under Article 12 CCC by customs authorities of EU Member States. A BTI informs about the correct tariff classification of an individual product in the opinion of the issuing customs authority, can only be presented by the holder and has to be accepted by every customs authority throughout the EU, pursuant to Article 12 paragraph 2 CCC.[179] Every BTI issued by a national customs authority is introduced into the European Binding Tariff Information database (EBTI) developed and maintained by the European Commission.[180] The Panel criticised that the EU system of customs administration:

> does not provide for uniform withdrawal of revocations of BTI. Nor does the system impose an obligation on member State customs authorities to consult with and/or notify other customs authorities of decisions to withdraw revocations of BTI.[181]

175 Panel Report, *EC—Selected Customs Matters*, WT/DS315/R, para 7.141; Appellate Body Report, *EC—Selected Customs Matters*, WT/DS315/AB/R, para 224.

176 Panel Report, *EC—Selected Customs Matters*, WT/DS315/R, para 7.141.

177 ibid, para 7.63.

178 ibid, para 7.350; not appealed at the Appellate Body.

179 A detailed analysis of Binding Tariff Information can be found in Chapter 10.I.E.

180 A detailed analysis of the EBTI database can be found in Chapter 10.I.E.1.

181 Panel Report, *EC—Selected Customs Matters*, WT/DS315/R, para 7.340.

The Panel believed this issue could result in non-uniform administration of the Common Customs Tariff, in violation of Article X:3(a) GATT 1994.[182] Furthermore, it also criticised the lack of a provision in EU customs law which prescribes that the withdrawal of revocation of BTI be immediately binding on all the national customs authorities of EU Member States, as well as the lack of a specific EU customs law provision requiring the transmission of the withdrawal of revocation of BTI by national customs authorities of EU Member States to the European Commission.[183]

Although the Panel in *EC—Selected Customs Matters* took the view that it was outside its terms of reference to make any findings in relation to the design and structure of the EU system of customs administration, it did still discuss some institutional mechanisms, given their importance as context for the examination of particular instances of alleged violations of Article X:3(a) GATT 1994.[184] Therein, it noted that the customs authorities of the EU Member States are not obliged to consult with one another before making customs decisions or to consult the EBTI database when classifying a good.[185] In general, the Panel found the EU system of customs administration 'complicated and, at times, opaque and confusing.'[186]

The Appellate Body reversed the Panel's findings that the examination of the EU system of customs administration as a whole or overall and its design and structure was outside the Panels terms of reference,[187] but found itself unable to complete the analysis due to the lack of a sufficient foundation of factual findings upon which it could rely.[188] Nevertheless, the Appellate Body emphasised:

> Certainly, the Panel raised doubts about the effectiveness of these institutions and mechanisms in bringing about uniformity of administration of European Communities customs laws. However, the Panel did not find that these institutions and mechanisms are structurally flawed in such a way that the European Communities' system of customs administration would necessarily lead to non-uniform administration, in violation of Article X:3(a) of the GATT 1994.[189]

4. *Violation of EU Customs Law*

The implementation of EU customs law by national customs authorities is a case of indirect enforcement of EU law by the EU Member States. Therefore, the national customs officials have to base their customs decisions directly upon EU customs law.[190] If national customs officials interpret undefined and abstract legal terms of

182 ibid, para 7.340.
183 ibid, para 7.340, fn 624.
184 ibid, paras 7.155, 7.490.
185 ibid, paras 7.177, 7.180, 7.181, 7.187, 7.190.
186 ibid, para 7.191.
187 Appellate Body Report, *EC—Selected Customs Matters*, WT/DS315/AB/R, para 176.
188 ibid, paras 286, 287.
189 ibid, para 285.
190 Rogmann, 2008 ZfZ 3, pp 57–69 (58).

EU customs law in a manner that has no basis in EU law, or engage in a practice that is not followed by other customs authorities of EU Member States, this can be a violation of Article X:3(a) GATT 1994. It is not the task of a Panel to determine the consistency or otherwise of EU acts with EU customs law,[191] and therefore the infringement of EU customs law alone does not constitute a lack of uniformity within the meaning of Article X:3(a) GATT 1994. Rather, such behaviour has to lead to divergences in customs administration between different national customs authorities. If such an infringement only occurs in a single case that can subsequently be repealed, there is also no violation of the WTO law, because Article X:3(a) GATT 1994 does not impose instantaneous uniformity; rather uniformity must be attained within a reasonable period of time.[192] However, it becomes a problem if the infringement is part of the usual customs administration practice and there is no effective measure to end such behaviour by national customs authorities, resulting in a significant impact on the overall administration of the law and not simply on the outcome of an individual case.[193]

In *EC—Selected Customs Matters*, the Panel examined single cases of allegedly non-uniform administration in which the EC stated that the challenged administration did not have a legal basis in EU customs law. One case was the valuation of a good for customs purposes based on a basis other than the transaction of the last sale (hereinafter: 'successive sale'), in which the administration of Article 147 paragraph 1 CCCIP of some customs authorities was criticised for imposing a form of prior approval[194] that, according to the EC, had no legal basis in EU customs law.[195] The Panel found a violation of Article X:3(a) GATT 1994 because:

> the imposition of a requirement by member States, whether in practice and/or as a matter of law, that is not justified by the terms of EC law and which is not being applied in other member States ... necessarily falls foul of the obligation of uniform administration.[196]

This, however, was reversed by the Appellate Body because of a lack of evidence of actual non-uniform administration.[197]

In another case, the Panel in *EC—Selected Customs Matters* examined the attitude of customs authorities of EU Member States towards Binding Tariff Information (BTI) under Article 12 CCC. BTI is to be legally binding on the competent authorities of all EU Member States under the same conditions pursuant to

[191] Panel Report, *EC—Selected Customs Matters*, WT/DS315/R, para 7.320.

[192] ibid, paras 7.132, 7.133.

[193] Panel Report, *US—Hot-Rolled Steel*, WT/DS184/R, para 7.268; affirming reference to this ruling was also made in Panel Report, *US—Corrosion-Resistant Steel Sunset Review*, WT/DS244/R, para 7.310.

[194] US first written submission, Panel Report, *EC—Selected Customs Matters*, WT/DS315/R para 87; see also Panel Report, *EC—Selected Customs Matters*, WT/DS315/R, paras 4.19, 7.372.

[195] EC first written submission, *EC—Selected Customs Matters*, WT/DS315/R, para 395; see also Panel Report, *EC—Selected Customs Matters*, WT/DS315/R, para 7.373 and European Court of Auditors, Special Report No 23/2000, [2001] OJ C84/1-18, pp 16, 17.

[196] Panel Report, *EC—Selected Customs Matters*, WT/DS315/R, para 7.382.

[197] Appellate Body Report, *EC—Selected Customs Matters*, WT/DS315/AB/R, paras 269, 270.

Article 11 CCCIP. The Panel stated that when a BTI issued by one national EU customs authority is invoked by the holder and another EU customs authority fails to acknowledge and treat it as binding for an identical product, instead classifying the product differently, this will necessarily lead to non-uniform administration of the Common Customs Tariff in violation of Article X:3(a) GATT 1994.[198]

In conclusion, taking into account the general findings of the Appellate Body regarding the uniform administration obligation, one can say that the crucial issue is not so much inconsistency within EU law, but rather the differences in the application of EU customs law that arise as a consequence of an infringement of an individual EU customs provision by some, but not all, national customs authorities of the EU Member States. In this case, such behaviour necessarily leads to different customs decisions as a regular result, and not only in an individual case.

III. CONCLUSION

The relevance of Article X:3(a) GATT 1994 for the application of EU customs law is not to be underestimated. The degree of regulation in domestic law today is much higher than it was when the GATT was first created in 1947, as the implementation of laws and regulations is now codified to a great extent in other legal instruments.[199] Forgoing too formalistic a view, the Appellate Body in *EC—Selected Customs Matters* took a more sensitive approach to this issue than previous WTO jurisprudence. It considered the present reality in law and administration, explicitly taking into account such legal instruments that regulate the application of laws and regulations of the kind described in Article X:1 GATT 1994 in examination under Article X:3(a) GATT 1994.[200] Therefore, its findings have important implications for the scope of this provision and its impact on EU customs administration.

To some extent, the EU system of customs administration contains the risk of leading to non-uniformity within the meaning of Article X:3(a) GATT 1994. This is due to its decentralised character in the implementation of EU customs law. However, neither provisions of a discretionary nature nor the usage of undefined legal terms in EU customs law constitute a lack of uniformity in themselves; they do so only when necessarily leading to non-uniformity on a regular basis in concrete cases. Likewise, the infringement of EU customs law alone is not a violation of Article X:3(a) GATT 1994; to constitute as such it has to lead to divergent customs administration between different national customs authorities.

[198] Panel Report, *EC—Selected Customs Matters*, WT/DS315/R, para 7.320; not appealed to the Appellate Body.

[199] DSC, (WT/DS315/AB/R) / DSR 2006:IX, 3791, p 16.

[200] Similar: DSC, (WT/DS315/AB/R) / DSR 2006:IX, 3791, p 16.

Flexibility as the key feature of uniformity within the meaning of Article X:3(a) GATT 1994 seems to be the appropriate interpretation of this term in light of the administrative reality of today and also given the general character of the provision. Whilst the possibility of flexible application provides Article X:3(a) GATT 1994 with practical relevance for EU customs administration, it also leads to less predictability. This is because the emphasis on the flexible character of the provision creates the demand that its application always adjusts itself to the individual case.[201] These difficulties are a challenge not only for the EU, but for all systems of customs administration worldwide.

201 Dierksmeier, 2007, p 62.

Part III

The Great Reform of EU Customs

4

Modernised Customs Code, Electronic Customs Initiative and the Future Customs Initiative

THE COMMUNITY CUSTOMS Code was once the true foundation of the European Single Market, and together with its implementing provisions and the Common Customs Tariff it still constitutes the main legislation of the present EU customs environment. However, not all its original aspects are suited to contemporary conditions, to say nothing of the future, and since its introduction on 1 January 1993—especially in the last decade—the Community Customs Code (and the customs sector generally) has been repeatedly and substantially amended in order to address specific matters. Customs must contend not only with increasing international trade and evolving production and consumption patterns, but also global threats, such as terrorism and organised crime, as well as new hazards such as trade in dangerous goods and even climate change.[1] Therefore, the range of customs-related matters is expanding significantly beyond the traditional ambit of customs duties, to include aspects such as safety and security.

Furthermore, all the procedures contained in the Community Customs Code and its implementing provisions are based on the processing of paper documents, as was common at the time of their introduction, whereas today information technologies and communication technologies have become the rule. Therefore, the reform of EU customs has had to react to this new environment not only to maintain the competitiveness of EU business in global trade and ensure security and safety in the EU, but also to overcome the problems with regard to uniform administration of EU customs. Non-uniform customs administration and its negative consequences—such as, for instance, legal uncertainty, security risks, loss of revenue and trade diversion—are significant enough to undermine any and all reform efforts of the EU.

I. THE SECURITY AMENDMENT—A MINOR REFORM

In 2003, the European Commission issued a communication about a simple and paperless environment for customs and trade[2] (hereinafter: e-customs

[1] COM (2008) 169 final, p 2.
[2] COM (2003) 452 final.

Communication) that contained proposals for common information systems that would enable data exchange between customs authorities. Through a common framework shared by the European Commission and the EU Member States, the system would facilitate economic operators carrying out formalities, customs procedures such as centralised clearance and risk management. The Council Resolution of 5 December 2003 on creating a simple and paperless environment for customs and trade[3] (hereinafter: e-customs Resolution) picked up on these ideas, which then led to the so-called 'minor reform'[4] of the Community Customs Code in which Regulation (EC) 648/2005 of the European Parliament and of the Council of 13 April 2005[5] amended several provisions of the existing Community Customs Code, especially with regard to risk management, Article 4 Number 26 CCC and Article 13 CCC; the Authorised Economic Operator (AEO), Article 5a CCC; and the summary declaration before each import or export of goods in the EU customs territory, Article 36a CCC et seq and Article 182a CCC et seq respectively. All these amendments followed from ideas raised in the e-customs Communication, such as tightening security for the movement of goods across international frontiers by requiring economic operators to provide the customs authorities with detailed information on goods before their importation or exportation; the introduction of a basis for a one-stop-shop for importers and exporters, where different controls could be carried out at the same time and same place; simplifying trade by the introduction of the authorised economic operator (AEO); and requiring the EU Member States to use computerised risk-analysis methods.[6]

In order to adjust to new global-economic developments, risk management and risk analysis have become the guiding theme of the new Community Customs Code.[7] The main objective is that with the aid of a modern risk management the EU is to achieve the ability to identify risks at an early stage, which means before the importation or exportation of goods. Risk management constitutes a common technique for the systematic identification and implementation of all the measures necessary to limit the likelihood of risks occurring, utilising especially measures for collecting data and information, analysing and assessing risk, prescribing action and assessing the level of risk.[8] It provides for common and uniform working methods in customs administrations throughout the EU with regard to risk management and risk analysis in the field of customs controls.

In this context, the authorised economic operator (AEO) is a new status for economic operators combining procedural simplifications with aspects of safety and security,[9] facilitating easier customs handling. The AEO programme is to be of significant importance for determining the intensity of customs controls, as

[3] [2003] OJ C305/1–2.
[4] Weerth, Bundesanzeiger 2007, p 28.
[5] [2005] OJ L117/13–19.
[6] URL: http://europa.eu/legislation_summaries/other/l11010_en.htm.
[7] Weerth, Bundesanzeiger 2007, p 28.
[8] European Commission, Standardised Framework for Risk Management, p 3.
[9] Lux, 2012 AW-Prax 8, pp 257–62 (259).

AEOs will be granted procedural simplifications while other economic operators may have to face increased control measures. The EU grants AEO status only to economic operators that can fulfil the strict conditions laid down in Articles 14g, 14h, 14i, 14j, and 14k CCCIP, followed by a permanent monitoring pursuant to Article 14q CCCIP. This is to ensure that only trustworthy economic operators benefit from procedural simplifications including a lower level of customs control intensity. Therefore, the AEO certification is a kind of seal of quality, preceded by a comprehensive approval procedure.[10] The concrete advantages of the AEO status are specified in Article 14b CCCIP.

The European Commission and the EU Member States are also working together as partners in order to develop and implement a common risk management framework under the successive action programmes for customs.[11] Furthermore, the introduction of common EU guidelines for identifying risks for control purpose[12] to advance the effectiveness and efficiency of customs controls, indicating the importance of uniform application for ensuring the functioning of the EU common risk management system.

The EU's Security Amendment to the Community Customs Code mirrors the SAFE Framework of the World Customs Organization (WCO) and its four core elements,[13] which are: harmonising electronic cargo advance information requirements, employing a consistent risk management approach, performing inspection of high-risk containers, and granting benefits to business meeting certain security standards.[14] The minor reform also picks up the twofold approach of the WCO model regarding the customs-to-customs relations for risk management and the customs-to-business relations for pre-shipping notification and AEO.[15] It then refined these concepts to shape an EU supply chain mechanism that allows the supervision of national practices for security control to be managed with greater precision from at the central level.[16]

While the minor reform was certainly motivated to facilitate EU business and competitiveness, the changes the Security Amendment brought with it also served to provide greater coherence and uniformity in the administration of the EU Customs Union, as well to improve its visibility at a national level.[17] In this new risk management process, customs risk analysts assess the electronic output of electronic applications that are based on common risk criteria and standards for

[10] Witte, 2012 AW-Prax 5, pp 185–89 (187).

[11] European Commission, 'Standardised Framework for Risk Management in the customs administrations of the EU', URL: http://ec.europa.eu/taxation_customs/resources/documents/framework_doc.pdf.

[12] European Commission, 'Guidelines for import controls in the area of product safety and compliance', URL: http://ec.europa.eu/taxation_customs/resources/documents/common/publications/info_docs/customs/product_safety/guidelines_en.pdf.

[13] Hobbing, CEPS Papers No 39, June 2011, p 5.

[14] WCO, Safe Framework Standards, 2007, p 7.

[15] Hobbing, CEPS Papers No 39, June 2011, pp 5, 6.

[16] ibid, pp 5, 6.

[17] ibid, p 6.

security and safety risk analysis and that draw on multiple sources of information including information from other EU Member States.[18]

Common risk management thus contributes to uniform customs administration because it is based on methods for communication, exchange of and access to risk information as well as a common approach to the prioritisation of risk and associated customs action. It thus emphasises the importance of systematic cooperation between customs authorities. Standardisation, common working methods based on shared information, common guidelines and common standards are practical solutions to overcome differences in the day-to-day customs work in the EU. Indeed, EU common risk management can only be successful in guaranteeing security and safety if the national customs authorities implement measures related to risk management and risk analysis in a uniform manner based on a common foundation. The European Commission has explicitly expressed its opinion that 'there is a need for uniform enforcement of EU provisions for safety and compliance controls.'[19]

The management framework is operationally underpinned by the electronic EU Customs Risk Management System (CRMS), which constitutes a channel for wide-ranging communication and systematic risk information exchange between EU Member States.[20] Centrally managed on the EU level by the European Commission, the CRMS is available to the risk analysis centres of the EU Member States and to all external border control points.[21] Furthermore, guidelines are issued by the European Commission to assist EU Member States' customs authorities in improving cooperation methods and good administrative practice by making recommendations and focussing on the practical questions of performing customs controls.[22]

The Security Amendment is an example of a new pragmatism that is developing in the EU, whereby practical constraints in the management of the trade system can be addressed by pragmatic solutions that fall outside orthodox doctrines and do not formally challenge national autonomy in administrative organisation and implementation.[23] In order to enable national customs administrations to master the various challenges EU customs face today, this pragmatism has become a sort of political creed.[24] In this context, a pan-European electronic customs environment and soft law measures such as guidelines containing practical recommendations constitute an important part of the European Commission's system for ensuring EU-wide uniform customs administration despite the administrative autonomy of EU Member States.

[18] COM (2012) 793 final, p 5.
[19] European Commission, Import Control Guidelines, p 3.
[20] COM (2012) 793 final, p 4.
[21] ibid, p 4.
[22] European Commission, Import Control Guidelines, pp 3, 4.
[23] Hobbing, CEPS Papers No 39, June 2011, p 6.
[24] ibid, p 6.

The minor reform of the Community Customs Code was made in 2005 but came into force in three steps only at after the development of the necessary provisions for the Implementing Regulation.[25] The provisions of the Implementing Regulation set out the operational details in the customs processes for the implementation of the above-mentioned measures of the Security Amendment to the Community Customs Code. The common risk management framework to support improved risk-based controls by customs authorities had immediate effect; the provisions for the AEO programme entered into force on 1 January 2008, and finally on 1 July 2009 the electronic exchange of advance information between traders and customs authorities on all goods entering or leaving the EU was introduced.[26] The full implementation of all measures was scheduled for 2011.[27]

However, in the meantime gaps in the current approach have already been identified, as putting the EU common risk management framework into operation has proved difficult. Variances in development, capacity and technical capability of national electronic risk analysis systems have so far prevented the achievement of a common minimum standard of automated risk analysis for security and safety.[28] The burden of work also varies between EU Member States due to differences in the volume of trade to be risk-assessed. Most importantly, under currently operational methodologies and structures the risk-related information available has been criticised as insufficient, although operational coordination and exchange of information is essential for the functioning of the EU common risk framework.[29] The existing operational difficulties complicate the implementation of a uniform approach with regard to EU common risk management, and this lack represents a shortcoming of the EU.[30] Furthermore, the example of EU common risk management and its operational difficulties illustrate that uniform administration of EU customs law requires a combination of action at the EU Member State level as well as the EU level.

II. THE NEED FOR A GREAT REFORM: THE CHANGING ENVIRONMENT AND NEW ROLE FOR EU CUSTOMS

Although important steps have been made with the Security Amendment in the minor reform, the Community Customs Code is still out of date and is not sufficient for either present conditions or future developments. EU customs law needs extensive changes, such as streamlined customs procedures and processes and the adoption of common standards for IT systems, which in the opinion of the

[25] Commission Regulation (EC) 1875/2006 of 18 December 2006 amending Regulation (EEC) 2454/93 laying down provisions for the implementation of Council Regulation (EEC) 2913/92 establishing the Community Customs Code, [2006] OJ L360/64–125.

[26] European Commission, Press Release, 18 December 2006, IP/06/1821.

[27] COM (2012) 793 final, p 4.

[28] ibid, p 6.

[29] ibid, p 7.

[30] ibid, p 11.

European Commission cannot be achieved by further development of the existing Code but require its replacement by a new piece of legislation.[31] Thus the main reason for the proposal of the Modernised Community Customs Code in 2005[32] was the belief that the past amendments of the Community Customs Code had neither kept pace with the rapid growth in the use of information technology and the rise of electronic data, nor with other changes in the environment in which international trade is conducted, including the changing focus of the customs function.[33]

In the past, the customs authorities represented an oft-used barrier to international trade, used to protect national interests, but today their intervention in commercial transactions is accepted only when there is a demonstrably legitimate need based on identified risk.[34] At the beginning of the last decade, the EU had already noticed that one of the main challenges EU customs has to face is how to deal with divergent demands: applying a growing number of controls to protect the EU's interests in financial, social and business matters, whilst at the same time not creating unnecessary or cumbersome barriers to legitimate business.[35] Customs procedures have an impact on the competitiveness of EU business, with burdensome or inflexible procedures being a disadvantage. Therefore, the Commission has highlighted the need to improve customs in line also with the needs of economic operators.[36]

At the same time, the role of customs is shifting away from the collection of duties towards the application of non-tariff measures, especially those concerned with security and safety, and to the fight against fraud.[37] The advent of the global marketplace, the increasing complexity of international trade agreements and technological advances have not only revolutionised trade, but also have impacted the responsibilities of customs authorities.[38] This has entailed also a dramatic increase in customs authorities' workloads.[39]

Contributing further to such workloads, the current Community Customs Code is rather complex and still based on paper format customs procedures. Yet while there is no obligation under EU customs law to use computerised systems for the purpose of customs clearance, in fact electronic customs clearance is no longer the exception but the rule.[40]

However, at present there are no EU-wide IT applications for customs clearance. The national electronic systems of the EU Member States are not

[31] COM (2005) 608 final, p 3.
[32] ibid.
[33] ibid, p 2.
[34] European Parliament, Study 2012, IP/A/IMCO/ST/2011–11, PE 475.094, p 17.
[35] COM (2001) 51 final, p 11.
[36] ibid, p 8.
[37] COM (2005) 608 final, p 3.
[38] ibid, p 3.
[39] European Parliament, Study 2012, IP/A/IMCO/ST/2011–11, PE 475.094, p 17.
[40] COM (2005) 608 final, p 3.

interconnected, and each uses different IT solutions with different approaches to the implementation of customs procedures. The electronic communication between customs authorities differs as well and, furthermore, there are no common data requirements.[41] As a result, traders operating in several EU Member States have to comply with the requirements of different electronic customs systems, which jeopardises the competitiveness of European business and the functioning of the internal market.[42]

The Community Customs Code needs to be adapted to the governance requirements of the electronic environment of customs and trade. Its modernisation has to streamline customs procedures and processes and adopt common standards for IT systems. Trade facilitation also demands more efficient procedures and controls, which can be achieved by simplifying customs legislation at the EU level and making better use of electronic tools in customs procedures. A regulatory framework is required for simple, predictable, uniform customs controls and similar customs practices that place economic operators on an equal footing by reducing errors and increasing compliance.[43] A study of the European Parliament highlighted that this can only be achieved through a common EU framework to overcome problems linked to differences in national laws.[44] This demand emphasises that ensuring uniformity in European customs administration is indeed a part of the solution being pursued in the great reform to achieve effectiveness of customs administration.

Therefore, an ambitious reform is being undertaken to make sure that EU customs can continue to play its role as one of the pillars of the EU and the core of the European Single Market. First, the legal environment of EU customs is being modernised following the 'Better Regulation' Initiative,[45] as the current Community Customs Code is not a sufficient basis for such developments and thus needs a complete overhaul. Secondly, the Electronic Customs Initiative[46] is seeking to create an EU-wide electronic customs system by building a robust communication chain between all European customs authorities and also with other European authorities and traders. Finally, the Future Customs Initiative[47] has been created to address the future organisational and human dimension of customs administrations, including the modernisation of working methods, the development of staff-competences and the effective and efficient reallocation resources.[48]

The strategic framework for EU customs in this reform contains common objectives, similar to the objectives already proposed in the customs strategy of

[41] COM (2003) 452 final, p 5; European Parliament, Study 2012, IP/A/IMCO/ST/2011–11, PE 475.094, p 18; Lux, 2011 AW-Prax 8, pp 257–61 (257, 258).

[42] COM (2003) 452 final, p 5 et seq; European Parliament, Study 2012, IP/A/IMCO/ST/2011–11, PE 475.094, p 18.

[43] European Parliament, Study 2012, IP/A/IMCO/ST/2011–11, PE 475.094, pp 16, 17.

[44] European Parliament, Study 2012, IP/A/IMCO/ST/2011–11, PE 475.094, p 17.

[45] COM (2001) 726 final.

[46] Decision 70/2008/EC of the European Parliament and of the Council, [2008] OJ L23/21.

[47] COM (2008) 169 final.

[48] ibid, p 3.

2001, regarding the improvement of customs operations to ensure uniformity in customs administration.[49] These are: the protection of the society and the financial interests of the EU by developing effective risk management; the support of the competitiveness of European business by modernising customs working methods and developing new EU standards; trade facilitation by improving control systems and reducing administrative burden; control and management of the supply chain by enhancing effective risk information sharing; and, lastly, the development of cooperation between customs authorities as well as with other governmental agencies and economic agents.[50]

III. SIMPLIFYING LEGISLATION: THE 'BETTER REGULATION' INITIATIVE

The idea of facilitating trade by improving and simplifying legislation started with the 'Better Regulation' Initiative[51] in 2001, one of the commitments of the White Paper on European Governance.[52] Its aims are to simplify European legislation and provide a clear and effective regulatory framework in order to reduce the costs of doing business in Europe and increase legal certainty for citizens.[53] EU customs is a key area in this context, given its procedures are too complicated. The many variants of those procedures reflect a paper-based environment and relatively high duty rates that can no longer be justified.[54] In the context of EU customs, the 'Better Regulation' Initiative, with its aim of simplifying legislation regarding structure and legal terminology, is an important strategy to enhance uniform administration, as it can facilitate the application of EU customs law, improve the balance between the Customs Code and its implementing provisions, and simultaneously enable the adaption of detailed provisions to reduce margins of discretion.[55]

Furthermore, trade facilitation and the simplification of customs rules are part of the political agenda, both in the World Trade Organization (WTO) and the World Customs Organization (WCO). This international context of customs and customs cooperation has also been acknowledged by the European Parliament, including especially the participation of the EU in the WCO and the WTO. The European Parliament has encouraged the improvement of the security and effectiveness of EU customs by sharing standards and exchanging good practices within the WCO, thereby also contributing to joint standards and rules.[56]

[49] COM (2001) 51 final, pp 14, 15.

[50] URL: http://ec.europa.eu/taxation_customs/customs/policy_issues/customs_strategy/index_en.htm.

[51] COM (2001) 726 final.

[52] COM (2001) 428 final.

[53] COM (2001) 726 final, p 2.

[54] COM (2003) 452 final, p 6.

[55] Lux, 2012 AW-Prax 8, pp 257–62 (258).

[56] European Parliament Resolution of 1 December 2011 (2001/2083(INI)), text adopted P7_TA(2011)0546, paras 4, 75.

The European Parliament has also considered the regulatory role of the WTO and its agreements in enhancing open and free international trade and the vital importance of customs in this context, encouraging the European Commission to push for an agreement on trade facilitation as part of the ongoing Doha Round.[57]

The WTO Members are currently negotiating about trade facilitation in order to establish WTO rules in this area. Trade facilitation by reforming customs procedures was added to the WTO's agenda at its Ministerial Conference in Singapore in 1996, and the somewhat broad mandate was further specified in the Ministerial Declaration launching the Doha Round in 2001.[58] Important aims are the clarification and improvement of relevant aspects of Articles V, VIII and X GATT 1994, but also include enhanced technical assistance and support for capacity building. The term 'trade facilitation' thereby should be understood as 'the simplification and harmonization of international trade procedures, including activities, practices, and formalities involved in collecting, presenting, communicating, and processing data required for the movement of goods in international trade'.[59] The references to technical assistance and support for capacity building indicate that trade facilitation in a globalised world needs, to some extent, a modernised environment for cross-border procedures—a fact the EU is also aware of in its own customs reform agenda. In fact, the introduction to the WTO trade facilitation negotiations on the WTO's homepage[60] contains many of the same key issues that can be found in communications[61] and press releases[62] of the European Commission regarding the great reform of EU customs: enhancing technical assistance and capacity-building, but also improving effective cooperation and customs compliance issues. Therefore, compliance with common standards in EU customs is of importance for the EU to maintain a competitive position in global trade. Furthermore, by organising its own modern customs environment at an early stage, the EU will have the chance to exert stronger influence on the design of WTO standards for international trade facilitation by providing expert knowledge and own experience.

The WTO negotiations on trade facilitation began following the adoption of the 'July Package'[63] on 1 August 2004, which establishes the need to take into account the relevant work of the WCO[64] while aiming to develop provisions for effective cooperation between customs authorities or any other appropriate authorities.[65] The first draft of a consolidated negotiating text[66] was issued on 14 December 2009

[57] ibid, paras 10, 76.

[58] WTO, Doha Ministerial Declaration adopted on 14 November 2001, WT/MIN(01)/DEC/1, para 27.

[59] Bolhöfer, 2008 (2) WCJ (1), pp 31–40 (32).

[60] URL: www.wto.org/english/tratop_e/tradfa_e/tradfa_intro_e.htm.

[61] For example: COM (2008) 169 final.

[62] For example: European Commission, Press Release of 2 April 2008, IP/08/492.

[63] WTO, Doha Work Programme of 1 August 2004, WT/L/579.

[64] ibid, Annex D, para 1.

[65] WTO, Doha Work Programme of 1 August 2004, WT/L/579, Annex D, para 1.

[66] WTO, Negotiating Group on Trade Facilitation, Draft Consolidated Negotiating Text of 14 December 2009, TN/TF/W/165.

and has been continuously revised since.[67] With regard to Article X GATT 1994, the negotiations centre on issues that are also of great importance in the customs reform agenda of the EU Customs Union, for example the establishment of a single window concept.[68] Furthermore, case studies and implementation-related reports by WTO Members that cover trade facilitation, issued to share experiences, also contain many topics that are relevant to the reform process of the EU, such as authorised traders, customs cooperation, risk management, and transit.[69]

Therefore, in order to remain a key player in those organisations pushing for trade facilitation worldwide, the EU has to be at the forefront of the modernisation of customs administration.[70] The success of the Doha Development Agenda[71] is still heavily dependent on the ability of customs to achieve an effective balance between trade facilitation and regulatory intervention.[72] A successful reform process in EU customs would not only prevent the EU Customs Union from being left behind in international trade issues, weakening the competitiveness of EU businesses, but would also offer the opportunity for the EU to extend its own preferred solutions to other states (policy uploading).

In the minor reform of 2005, only some particularly important and urgent modernisation aspects were addressed, whereas the larger part was left for the great overhaul of the Community Customs Code. Aiming at the simplification of legislation and administration procedures, from the point of view of both customs authorities and traders, this project was undertaken to simplify the structure of the Community Customs Code.[73] In particular, it aimed to provide for more coherent terminology, with fewer provisions and simpler rules, and to undertake a radical reform of customs procedures by reducing their number and making it easier to keep track of goods, rationalising the customs guarantee system, and extending the use of single authorisations.[74] Such modernisation and simplification of the EU customs law would serve to meet the objectives of the 'Better Regulation' Initiative through reducing the costs for business as well as increasing legal certainty for citizens, provided that it is realised on the EU level and thus overcomes the problems linked to differences in national laws.[75]

[67] The last revision is document WTO, Negotiating Group on Trade Facilitation, Draft Consolidated Negotiating Text of 23 October 2013, TN/TF/W/165/Rev 18 (situation as of 2013).

[68] See, for example, the programme of the Seoul Symposium on Trade Facilitation and the Doha Development Agenda of 27–28 November 2012, which was focused on single window and risk management, URL: www.wto.org/english/tratop_e/tradfa_e/seoul_symp_nov12_e/seoul_symp_nov12_e.htm.

[69] WTO, Case Studies and Reports on Trade Facilitation implementation, URL: www.wto.org/english/tratop_e/tradfa_e/casestudies_reports_e.htm. A comprehensive summary of all the topics and procedures would go beyond the intended purpose of this analysis.

[70] COM (2003) 452 final, p 7.

[71] The current round of trade negotiations of the World Trade Organization (WTO).

[72] European Parliament, Study 2012, IP/A/IMCO/ST/2011–11, PE 475.094, p 18.

[73] COM (2005) 608 final; European Commission, Press Release on 30 November 2005, IP/05/1501.

[74] COM (2005) 608 final; European Commission, Press Release of 30 November 2005, IP/05/1501.

[75] European Parliament, Study 2012, IP/A/IMCO/ST/2011–11, PE 475.094, p 17.

A. The Modernised Customs Code (MCC)

In a great reform of EU customs law,[76] the whole Community Customs Code was rewritten as the Modernised Customs Code (MCC) in the form of Regulation (EC) 450/2008 of the European Parliament and of the Council of 23 April 2008.[77] Herein EU customs law was purged and simplified, with most references to national law removed and legal definitions increased. As a consequence, the application and interpretation of the Modernised Customs Code are much simpler compared to the Community Customs Code, reducing the likelihood of errors and differences.

The rationalisation of the regulatory framework left only three basic concepts of customs procedure: release for free circulation (Title VI MCC), export (Title VIII MCC) and the special procedures (Title VII MCC). The special procedures themselves were reduced to four processes: transit (Title VII Chapter 2 MCC), storage (Title VII Chapter 3 MCC), specific use (Title VII Chapter 4 MCC) and processing (Title VII Chapter 5 MCC). The structure of those titles and chapters was orientated on the process of the single procedures, and thus is highly coherent and intelligible. Furthermore, the electronic customs declaration became obligatory and, in so doing, simplifying the customs procedures. Additional databases for new applications were installed and the concepts of interface—the so-called One Stop Shop—and the Single Window concept were included, these being the most ambitious projects and regarded as very important for enhancing trade facilitation and the competitiveness of the EU Customs Union.

The concept of a 'One Stop Shop' calls for customs controls—or other controls and physical examinations for different international trade-related measures in respect to the same good—to be carried out at the same time and place as far as is possible, while the organisation of these controls and physical examinations remains structured and coordinated, irrespective of the administration involved.[78] The concept of a 'Single Window' allows standardised information and documents to be submitted to a single electronic entry point to fulfil all regulatory requirements related to import, export and transit, so individual data items need be submitted only once.[79] Furthermore, once this standardised information is electronically delivered to the single portal, it is made available to all relevant authorities.[80] In order to successfully introduce these important concepts into

[76] Weerth, Bundesanzeiger 2007, p 29.

[77] [2008] OJ L145/1–64.

[78] European Commission, Presentation, 'The Modernised Customs Code: why, how, what and when?', 1 November 2008, slide 13, URL: http://ec.europa.eu/taxation_customs/resources/documents/customs/procedural_aspects/general/community_code/pres_mccc_en.pdf; Lux, 2012 AW-Prax 8, pp 257–62 (259).

[79] European Commission, Presentation 'The Modernised Customs Code: why, how, what and when?', 1 November 2008, slide 13; Lux, 2012 AW-Prax 8, pp 257–62 (259).

[80] European Commission, Presentation 'The Modernised Customs Code: why, how, what and when?', 1 November 2008, slide 13; Lux, 2012 AW-Prax 8, pp 257–62 (259).

modernised customs administration, the reform also had to guarantee the interoperability of the national IT systems in the customs area.

All the above required that the Modernised Customs code made many changes to customs legislation.[81] In addition to rationalising the legal framework and streamlining definitions of customs rules and procedures, greater standardisation of customs rules and their implementation was also covered, especially regarding the rights and obligations of economic operators, decisions and guarantees. For example, national restrictions on customs representation were done away with and common criteria as well as possible conditions were laid down, see Title I Chapter 2 section 2 MCC. Common rules for all types of decisions by customs authorities including appeal procedures and principles for customs penalties were also laid down, Title I Chapter 2 section 4, 5, 6 MCC, while customs fees, charges and costs had to correspond to an actually rendered service or were forbidden, Article 30 MCC. Binding information, previously only existing in the areas of classification and origin, can now possibly be extended, Article 20 paragraph 9 MCC, and common rules on guarantees for customs liabilities covering all procedures were established, Title III Chapter 2 MCC. It included also streamlined rules and procedures allowing debtors to benefit from non-recovery or repayment/remission of duties in certain situations, Title III Chapter 3 MCC, and harmonised rules on time limits for customs to recover duties, Article 72 MCC.

Equally important were the intended simplifications of customs procedures through the use of information and communication technology and the computerisation of all declarations and data exchanges to include the interoperability of national electronic customs computer systems. Of particular importance was the newly established obligation to use electronic data processing techniques for all customs formalities and exchanges of data between operators and customs authorities, Article 107 MCC and Title IV Chapter 2 section 2 MCC, and the introduction of unified simplified customs procedures, Title V Chapter 2 section 3 MCC.

Another change worth highlighting was the introduction of a centralised customs clearance, in Article 106 MCC. This concept allows authorised operators to lodge their electronic customs declarations at the customs office of the place where they are established, irrespective of where their goods physically enter or leave the customs territory of the EU or where their forms need to be presented to European customs authorities.[82] This office will then carry out any documentary risk analysis and then provide the results to the border customs office where the goods are actually moved so that they can carry out any physical examinations that either of the offices involved deem necessary. The advantage of such a simplification is that the goods do not have to be moved between customs offices.

[81] European Commission, Presentation 'Implementation of the Modernised Customs Code (MCCIP)', 20 May 2010, slide 4, URL: http://ec.europa.eu/dgs/secretariat_general/admin_burden/docs/enterprise/administrative-burdens/high-level-group/files/2010_05_20_presentation_customs_en.pdf.

[82] Lux, 2012 AW-Prax 8, pp 257–62 (260).

Moreover, the Modernised Customs Code laid down the basis for new facilities like self-assessment by operators, Article 116 paragraph 2 section (d) MCC, and single interfaces, Article 26 MCC, the latter giving rise to the aforementioned concepts of 'Single Window' services and 'One Stop Shop' services as additional trade facilitations. Self-assessment introduces a kind of quasi-statutory work that the economic operator will be allowed to carry out instead of the customs authority, which enables further simplifications of customs formalities as well as customs controls.[83]

As already mentioned, the Modernised Customs Code was part of the European Commission's strategy for a great reform process that would ensure EU customs continued playing a crucial role in the challenging environment of increasing international trade and global threats. This crucial role of EU customs is to ensure at all times a balance is maintained between protecting society and facilitating trade through the control of the supply chain. Therefore, the main objective pursued with the Modernised Customs Code was to provide the necessary simplifications to make customs and trade work better, faster and cheaper.[84] It was also meant to ensure the equal treatment of traders, and in doing so also to enhance the uniform application of EU customs law, as simplification and standardisation are appropriate measures for avoiding errors in the implementation of customs procedures.

By enhancing the uniform administration of EU customs law, the EU is pursuing goals such as the continued competitiveness, safety and security of the EU Customs Union in the context of international trade and globalisation. Indeed, uniform customs administration in the EU can reduce and to some extent prevent trade diversion, loss of revenue and security risks in the cross-border movement of goods.

The sensitive character of the uniformity issue for the future of the EU Customs Union was highlighted by the provisions of the Modernised Customs Code,[85] with uniformity of application becoming a major principle in the operation of customs in the Modernised Customs Code through its inclusion in prominent places like Recital 5 MCC and Article 1 paragraph 1 MCC.[86] In this regard, centralised customs clearance as a new simplified customs procedure was considered to be the flagship of the Modernised Customs Code. It was to have become a standard procedure once the new Code was fully implemented, providing a genuine simplification that allowed multinational companies to conduct all of their EU business with a single customs office.[87] To take part in this procedure, the economic operators would have needed to obtain a Single Authorisation for Simplified Procedures (SASP), which would have ensured they were compliant and trusted traders. Thus,

[83] Henke, in: Witte/Henke/Kammerzell (eds), 2009, p 138.

[84] COM (2008) 169 final, p 5.

[85] Hobbing, CEPS Papers No 39, June 2011, p 26.

[86] ibid, p 15.

[87] URL: http://ec.europa.eu/taxation_customs/customs/procedural_aspects/general/centralised_clearance/index_en.htm.

it was expected that the frequency of inspections would be minimal, as such formally trusted traders would not be appropriate objectives for extensive controls.[88] Therefore, both formally trusted traders as well as customs administrations would have benefited from this programme.

Furthermore, the interoperability of national electronic customs systems envisaged in the Modernised Customs Code in Article 183 paragraph 1 MCC aimed to serve the dual objective of trade facilitation and protecting society by securing tight controls through common risk management and cooperation between European customs authorities. In particular, data exchange was intended to help ensure the uniform application of EU customs law, Article 26 paragraph 2 last sentence MCC.

B. The Modernised Implementing Provisions (MCCIP)

The Modernised Customs Code was issued on 24 June 2008, but only a small part of the provisions actually ever came into force. By far the bigger part required the enactment of corresponding implementing provisions in a Modernised Customs Code Implementing Regulation (MCCIP), see Article 188 paragraphs 1 and 2 sentence 1 MCC.

The reason for the suspension of the coming into force of its major part lay in the fact that the Modernised Customs Code is only the general framework of EU customs law, as is the case with the current Community Customs Code. Most of its provisions were not self-executive and needed implementing measures. Therefore, the European Parliament and the Council authorised the European Commission to draft and adopt a new Modernised Customs Code Implementing Regulation (MCCIP), Article 183 MCC. Its provisions are to contain the necessary details on the different customs rules and procedures of the new Code and follow the structure of the Modernised Customs Code. By defining the details for the application of the Customs Code, the European Commission intends to further reduce the room for national peculiarities in customs procedures throughout the EU as part of its strategy to enhance uniform customs administration.[89]

The European Commission is still preparing these implementing provisions,[90] which means there has never been an official draft or a proposal of the MCCIP. The most recent version is a working version, only available in English, which serves as a basis for further discussion by the Customs Code Committee, the EU Member States and relevant trade associations about possible substantive contents. This preliminary draft contains 579 Articles and 105 legal definitions upfront, which are significantly more than in the current CCCIP,[91] indicating that

[88] European Parliament, Study 2012, IP/A/IMCO/ST/2011–11, PE 475.094, p 22.

[89] Lux, 2012 AW-Prax 8, pp 257–62 (258).

[90] Last version of the unofficial preliminary draft of the MCCIP of 25 November 2011 (situation as of 2013): TAXUD/MCCIP/2010/100–3.

[91] Weerth, 2012 ZfZ 1, pp 8–14 (10).

the new implementing provisions intend to reduce undefined legal terms and interpretation problems, thereby enhancing uniform application of the provisions. Such reduction in margins of discretion through increasingly detailed EU customs law is an objective also of the great reform.[92]

However, the provisions are still under intense analysis, with special regard to their legal consistency, overall structure, unified and commonly agreed definitions, unified and consistent numbering of the Articles and proper references of the new Customs Code and its enacting provisions as well as proper cross-references within the implementing provisions themselves.[93] Their progress is being discussed with representatives of the EU Member States:[94] within the Customs Policy Group (CPG), where senior management representatives express their national positions;[95] within the General Customs Legislation Section (GEN) of the Customs Code Committee, where middle management representatives provide opinions on legal customs issues;[96] and within the Electronic Customs Group (ECG), where middle management representatives discuss issues of a legal, procedural, project management, operational, planning or technical nature.[97] Also important is the assistance being provided by trade representatives through trade and customs working groups, especially the Trade Contact Group (TCG),[98] wherein the main professional organisations running major customs operations are represented.[99]

An illustrative example of the ongoing difficult discussions about the substantive contents of the future implementing provisions and their possible impact on uniform customs administration can be seen in the area of customs valuation. European business organisations, together with the European Parliament and numerous EU Member States, have been concerned about an envisaged change in the area of customs valuation with the introduction of a last sale concept, which would have the potential to create legal uncertainty and, therefore, could also result in non-uniform customs administration. Customs officials of the Section for Customs Valuation in the United Kingdom have also been quite concerned about the plans to introduce the last sale concept:

> So the UK and a number of other Member States, quite some of the large ones as well, are arguing with the Commission saying that in a time of recession and high unemployment and whatever, it cannot be a good thing for the EU [to introduce the last sale concept],

[92] Lux, 2012 AW-Prax 8, pp 257–62 (258).

[93] Consolidated preliminary draft of the MCCIP of 25 November 2011, Document TAXUD/MCCIP/2010/100–3, Disclaimer, p 2.

[94] European Commission, Presentation 'Implementation of the Modernised Customs Code (MCCIP)', 20 May 2010, slide 7.

[95] Taxud a 3 (2013) 3651276 MASP Annex 3 Revision 12 v1.1, p 3.

[96] ibid, p 3.

[97] ibid, p 3.

[98] European Commission, Presentation 'Implementation of the Modernised Customs Code (MCCIP)', 20 May 2010, slide 7.

[99] European Commission, Customs Trade Consultations, URL: http://ec.europa.eu/taxation_customs/customs/policy_issues/customs_trade_consultations/index_en.htm.

particularly when certain other countries such as the United States are using still the earlier sale.[100]

The rules on customs valuation in the EU are based on the legally binding international WTO Customs Valuation Agreement (CVA)[101] which allows, inter alia, the customs valuation to be based on the transaction value provided there has been a sale for export to the importing country. In line with this agreement, EU customs law introduced the concept that the earlier sale for export in a chain of successive sales is a possible basis for customs valuation under certain conditions. However, the European Commission seems to no longer be willing to allow the use of an earlier sale but to oblige the use of the last sale, as the second sentence of Article 230-02(1) draft-MCCIP shows,[102] even though the current regime under the CVA does not even use a concept of last sale, and neither EU provisions nor international norms provide a definition of this concept.[103] Therefore, the introduction of this new concept would have the potential to endanger the uniformity of customs processes throughout the EU by raising the possibility of different interpretation due to the lack of a definition in the WTO CVA and in EU customs law.[104]

Even the European Parliament has called for the continuation of the current rules allowing an earlier sale to be used as a basis for customs valuation purposes, arguing that the last sale concept would not be in accordance with the legally binding GATT Customs Valuation Code[105] and may even violate the EU's obligations regarding the WTO CVA.[106] Similar concerns apply to envisaged changes with respect to the implementing provisions on royalties and licence fees.[107] Again, these concerns have been shared by customs officials of the Section for Customs Valuation in the United Kingdom: 'The other main issue for us is, there are proposals afoot, again in the implementing provisions, to change the text of royalties and the licence fees.'[108]

Furthermore, the implementation of the Modernised Customs Code required an important number of activities in different areas to be developed in parallel in order to reach the objectives of the reform. Business process models (BPMs) for the standardisation of EU customs, implemented through both legal provisions and IT systems, had to be created in the form of graphical representations

[100] Interview of 10 January 2012 on file with author.

[101] WTO, 'Agreement on Implementation of Article VII of the General Agreement on Tariffs and Trade 1994' of 15 April 1994, [1994] OJ L 336/119–37, and also URL: www.wto.org/english/docs_e/legal_e/20–val.pdf.

[102] Last version (situation as of 31.12.2013): TAXUD/MCCIP/2010/100–3.

[103] AmCham EU, Position Statement, 25 May 2012, pp 4, 5.

[104] ibid, 24 April 2012, p 2.

[105] European Parliament Resolution of 1 December 2011 (2001/2083(INI)), text adopted P7_TA(2011)0546, paras 40, 46.

[106] AmCham EU, Position Statement, 24 April 2012, p 2.

[107] European Parliament Resolution of 1 December 2011 (2001/2083(INI)), text adopted P7_TA(2011)0546, para 40; AmCham EU, Position Statement, 24 April 2012, p 2; AmCham EU, Position Statement, 25 May 2012, pp 4, 5.

[108] Interview of 10 January 2012 on file with author.

of respective sequences in customs procedures. Not only does the new Customs Code Implementing Regulation need to be developed, but so does legislation in the form of assisting instruments such as explanatory notes and even so-called 'soft laws' such as guidelines. Further, the development of necessary IT projects has to be continued, taking into account relevant BPMs, in cooperation with the European Commission and the EU Member States as well as economic actors. Lastly, new training, information and communications activities also had to be undertaken.

C. Dependency on Supporting IT Systems

Especially necessary instruments for the correct application of the Modernised Customs Code are provided for in the IT-supporting-programmes in the framework of the Electronic Customs Initiative.[109] The interdependence between the implementing provisions and the IT systems necessary for their application requires the development of a coherent plan for their integration.[110] Guiding principles in this regard are the development of efficient IT systems on the basis of legally binding provisions that define procedures as well as obligations and the design of legal provisions able to be translated into IT language. This was to result in legal provisions and supporting IT systems that use different languages but tell the same stories.[111]

To achieve this target while complying with these principles, the aforementioned concept of BPM was created, a standardised graphic notation (BPMN) that illustrates the sequences of necessary steps in the various customs procedures and processes and the flow of information that has to be exchanged.[112] These BPMs serve as the basis for the further development of IT systems in EU customs,[113] but also aid in the discovery of gaps in the legal provisions that must be closed.[114] Although such BPMs are not legally binding,[115] it is hoped that they will provide for a strong coherence between the legal provisions and the corresponding IT solutions; thereby, this kind of standardisation of customs procedures will prevent, or at least minimise, administrative errors while simultaneously enhancing uniform implementation.

The opinion that a strong coherence between the legal provisions and the corresponding IT solutions and overall standardisation of customs processes will solve

[109] A detailed analysis of the Electronic Customs Initiative follows in Chapter 4.IV.

[110] Grave, in: Gellert (ed), 2009, pp 13–25 (18); Zeilinger, in: Koszinowski (ed), 2013, pp 103–07 (104).

[111] Grave, in: Gellert (ed), 2009, pp 13–25 (18, 19).

[112] ibid, pp 13–25 (19); Zeilinger, in: Koszinowski (ed), 2013, pp 103–07 (104); Lux, 2012 AW-Prax 8, pp 257–62 (258).

[113] Zeilinger, in: Koszinowski (ed), 2013, pp 103–07 (104); Gellert, 2011 AW-Prax 4, pp 124–25 (125).

[114] Gellert, 2011 AW-Prax 4, pp 124–25 (125).

[115] Lux, 2012 AW-Prax 8, pp 257–62 (258).

many contemporary problems of uniform customs administration by reducing the possible rate of errors or the possibility for divergent conclusions has been repeatedly expressed by various customs officials at different levels in Germany.[116] In this context, it has been declared, with implementation in part already underway, that through the use of standardised codes throughout the whole EU, customs administration standardisation will allow for information exchange despite language barriers.[117]

Therefore, the development of the IT systems is taking place in parallel to and in accordance with the composition of the new implementing provisions—a fact that has made the ongoing reform process more difficult and considerably slower.[118] This is problematic because the remaining provisions of the Modernised Customs Code should have come into force automatically on 24 June 2013 at the latest—even without the corresponding implementing provisions pursuant to Article 188 paragraph 2 sentence 3 MCC. It was originally planned that the functioning of the IT programs and their compatibility with the implementing provisions would be secured by this time.[119] The establishment of a strong coherence between the implementing provisions and the IT systems is therefore one of the major challenges in the modernisation of EU customs law.

D. Progress on the 'Better Regulation' Initiative

Even while the reform process was in progress it was already clear that the deadline was highly ambitious, as progress was very slow.[120] Early time schedules had foreseen the finalisation of the draft MCCIP in mid-2009 and its adaption by the European Commission one year later in mid-2010.[121] In the meantime,

[116] 'Also ist sicherlich dem Ziel förderlich. Also, weil wenn ich das alles letztendlich elektronisch standardisiert habe, aber die Möglichkeiten auch da sind des Datenaustausches, umfassenden Datenaustausches, das verhindert schon wieder viele Möglichkeiten da irgendwie unterschiedliche Sachen zu realisieren.' Interview of 1 April 2011 on file with author; 'Das ist schon eine tolle Sache … Es geht weniger verloren.' Interview of 23 May 2011 on file with author.

[117] 'Grundsätzlich habe ich alle Informationen im System und das ist der große Vorteil, dass ich sie letztendlich nur noch, nur noch zu bewerten habe und sie nicht eingeben muss. Und das ich sagen muss, es ist sehr viel codiert und normiert, so dass ich über bestimmte Codefolgen ja auch sagen kann: Wenn ich diesen Code angebe, dann weiß auch der Kollege in Frankreich was es heißt. Und der Kollege in Slovenien weiß auch was es heißt. Und das ist eben sehr viel wert, dass ich insofern mich über Sprachgrenzen hinweg in einer kodierten Form austauschen kann und trotzdem jeder weiß, was gemeint ist.' Interview of 20 May 2011 on file with author.

[118] Grave, in: Gellert (ed), 2009, pp 13–25 (13); Zeilinger, in: Koszinowski (ed), 2013, pp 103–07 (104).

[119] Grave, in: Gellert (ed), 2009, pp 13–25 (17, 18).

[120] Zeilinger, in: Koszinowski (ed), 2013, pp 103–07 (104); Weerth, 2012 AW-Prax 1, pp 14–17 (15, 16); Weerth, 2012 ZfZ 1, pp 8–14 (12).

[121] European Commission, Presentation 'The Modernised Customs Code: why, how, what and when?', 1 November 2008, slide 18; European Commission, Presentation 'The Modernised Customs Code: Conditions and state of its implementation', 1 November 2008, slide 4, URL: http://ec.europa.eu/taxation_customs/resources/documents/customs/procedural_aspects/general/community_code/mcc_implement_en.pdf.

the monitoring of customs legislation had begun in 2008 with a pilot programme, followed by a first annual programme in 2009,[122] on binding tariff information and authorised economic operators, a tool that was planned also for the monitoring of the Modernised Customs Code and its implementing provisions once in force.[123] However, in mid-2010, the timeline for the adoption of the MCCIP Commission Regulation was postponed to the beginning or even end of 2011.[124]

Yet at the end of 2011, the European Parliament expressed concern that some essential implementing provisions were still under consideration.[125] Moreover, it criticised the lack of progress in the implementation of the centralised clearance concept, which needed to be streamlined,[126] as well as in bringing about the Single Window and One Stop Shop.[127] It further emphasised the importance of truly harmonised customs rules and customs control systems, as well as the need for the full commitment of the EU Member States for achieving consistency in the border management of the EU.[128] The European Parliament also stressed the simplification of customs controls as one of the key elements of European customs policy.[129] Further shortcomings were found in the procedure for applying for AEO status, with the necessary investments possibly constituting a serious obstacle for traders. It called for both the European Commission and the EU Member States to consider simplifications to the procedure and to propose additional concrete benefits to encourage traders to seek AEO status.[130] In its resolution, the European Parliament also reiterated that for the reform to be successful, it was necessary to have uniformity of customs controls and equal treatment of AEOs throughout the customs territory of the EU.[131] Thus the resolution made it clear that there was still much work to be done, and that important issues still had to be considered, which meant in turn that the *draft* MCCIP was not even near to being finalised, not to speak of its adoption.

In the meantime, the only provisions of the Modernised Customs Code that were applicable were those that authorised the European Commission to adopt implementing measures in the committee procedure. Another exception was Article 30 paragraph 1 MCC, which was one single article in respect of customs fees, charges and costs that had to be applied from 1 January 2011. Therefore,

[122] European Commission, Presentation 'The Modernised Customs Code: why, how, what and when?', 1 November 2008, slide 23; European Commission, Presentation 'The Modernised Customs Code: Conditions and state of its implementation', 1 November 2008, slide 7.

[123] Grave, in: Gellert (ed), 2009, pp 13–25 (22).

[124] European Commission, Presentation 'Implementation of the Modernised Customs Code (MCCIP)', 20 May 2010, slide 10.

[125] European Parliament Resolution of 1 December 2011 (2001/2083(INI)), text adopted P7_TA(2011)0546, para 19.

[126] ibid, paras 25, 66.

[127] ibid, paras 66, 67.

[128] ibid, paras 24, 26.

[129] ibid, para 55.

[130] ibid, paras 29, 30.

[131] ibid, para 33.

the Community Customs Code and its implementing regulation were not annulled and still provisionally applied.

IV. THE ELECTRONIC CUSTOMS INITIATIVE

The great reform of the Community Customs Code is supported and accompanied by Decision No 70/2008/EC of the European Parliament and of the Council of 15 January 2008 on a paperless environment for customs and trade,[132] a decision aimed at establishing electronic customs systems in the framework of the *e*Europe Action Plan and the eGovernment programme. The *e*Europe Action Plan,[133] initiated by the European Commission in 2002, aims to replace paper-based customs procedures and processes with pan-European electronic ones, thereby creating a more efficient and modern customs environment in order to make the EU the most competitive and dynamic knowledge-based economy.[134] The eGovernment programme[135] is defined as:

> the use of information and communication technologies in public administrations combined with organisational change and new skills in order to improve public services and democratic processes and strengthen support to public policies.[136]

The European Commission has expressed the opinion that the implementation of the larger part of the Modernised Customs Code requires not only further legal action, through drafting the implementing provisions, but also IT-related action on the European level.[137] Thus, the dual objective of the electronic customs project is the same as that of the Modernised Customs Code: to enhance security at the EU's external borders, and to facilitate trade,[138] while it is also a strategy to enhance uniform customs administration.[139] These are not contradictory goals, as the use of IT tools combined with modern risk management techniques is in fact the only adequate response to the developments in the customs environment.[140] Ensuring security in the movements of goods requires the real-time sharing of risk-related data between customs authorities of the EU Member States and other authorities concerned.[141] In addition, common risk management is to take into account the whole of the European Single Market, as the level of customs intervention must be the same throughout the EU Customs Union.[142]

132 [2008] OJ L23/21–26.
133 COM (2002) 263 final.
134 COM (2003) 452, final, p 7.
135 COM (2003) 567 final.
136 ibid, p 7.
137 European Parliament, Study 2012, IP/A/IMCO/ST/2011–11, PE 475.094, p 51.
138 European Commission, Press Release of 30 November 2005, IP/05/1501.
139 Lux, 2012 AW-Prax 8, pp 257–62 (258, 259).
140 COM (2003) 452 final, p 5.
141 European Parliament, Study 2012, IP/A/IMCO/ST/2011–11, PE 475.094, p 17.
142 COM (2003) 452 final, p 5.

This means that enhancing the uniform application of EU customs law is as much a part of the Electronic Customs Initiative as of the modernisation of the Customs Code and its implementing provisions. Indeed, the success of the Electronic Customs Initiative as part of the great reform depends to a high degree on its uniform implementation. The IT solutions aspired to can only be effective and match to the relevant implementing provisions when they support standardisation of customs processes by providing for equivalent conditions in the EU Member States.

A. Background of the Electronic Customs Initiative

In issuing the e-customs Communication in 2003, the European Commission took the opportunity to promote a simplified and paperless environment for trade, while creating an exemplar of eGovernment at the level of the Customs Union.[143] This step seemed only logical, and in the spirit of the EU Customs Union[144] played a pioneering role in the development of European administrative law. In fact, the first step towards the pan-European electronic exchange of customs declarations had been taken in 1997 with the New Computerised Transit System (NCTS), based on electronic declaration and processing, which was designed to replace the paper-based Community transit system in order to provide better management and control of transit matters. Since then, the NCTS has successfully demonstrated the feasibility of such systems and opened up new opportunities for similar applications in other customs regimes.[145]

However, while the *e*Europe Action Plan[146] of the European Commission made it a priority for EU Member States to work online and be accessible online by 2005, in the meantime the EU Member States, sharing the same legitimate concerns and goals, had developed their own national strategies for creating a paperless environment for customs and, in doing so, naturally took national practices and requirements into account.[147] This resulted in different IT solutions, raising the potential risk of different implementation of customs rules and procedures. Thus, old national barriers were maintained and new digital ones were introduced that could jeopardise the equivalent treatment of economic operators in the European Single Market.[148]

The European Commission considered these problems in the e-customs Communication,[149] demanding the EU Customs Union aim to create a simplified and paperless environment for customs and trade by ensuring the appropriate legal

143 COM (2003) 452 final.
144 ibid.
145 COM (2005) 608 final, p 3.
146 COM (2002) 263 final, pp 9 et seq.
147 COM (2003) 452 final, p 5.
148 ibid, p 5.
149 ibid.

and operational framework and interoperability between existing IT systems. To achieve this goal, the European Commission had to act as a 'catalyst', given that the EU Member States alone could not create the necessary legal and IT environment for ensuring the equal treatment of economic operators.[150] Thus it demanded that customs procedures not only be fully revised and radically simplified, but also that they be integrated with modern IT techniques; that customs work be organised in such a way that traders would benefit from the Single Market, irrespective of the place a customs procedure begins or ends; for customs interventions to ensure that no barriers, digital or otherwise, exist; for customs controls to be of equivalent intensity and reliability at the external borders of the EU as based on common risk management; and for customs IT systems operated by EU Member States to be fully inter-operational, offering the same facilities to traders everywhere.[151] Its strategic goals were endorsed by the e-customs Resolution of the Council,[152] which called for a Multi-Annual Strategic Plan (MASP)[153] to create an EU-wide electronic environment for customs consistent with operational and legislative developments. This plan, drafted and annually revised by the European Commission, sets out the vision and objectives, as well as the strategic framework and implementation milestones, of the Electronic Customs Initiative.

Along with the 2005 proposal of the Modernised Customs Code,[154] the European Commission also proposed a decision that would promote electronic customs.[155] This decision was an instrument for the implementation of interoperable and accessible automated customs systems and for coordinated services and processes, which was necessary to support the great reform of the Community Customs Code and make its implementation effective also regarding the necessary IT tools. It contained actions and deadlines for the EU Member States to make their electronic customs systems compatible with each other and for the creation of a single, shared computer portal to facilitate communication between traders and customs as well as to allow better and faster exchange of data and information between the European customs authorities.

For this reason, the decision suggested two measures. First was the setting up of an electronic 'Single Window', whereby traders of proven trustworthiness only have to deal with one customs authority instead of several frontier control bodies,

[150] ibid, p 5.

[151] ibid, p 6.

[152] Council Resolution of 5 December 2003 on creating a simple and paperless environment for customs and trade, [2003] OJ C 305/1–2.

[153] Latest version (situation as of 31.12.2013): Electronic Customs Multi-Annual Strategic Plan 2012 Revision—MASP Rev 11 Version 3.0, Taxud.a.3 ARES (2012) 1677638, 2012, URL: http://ec.europa.eu/taxation_customs/resources/documents/customs/policy_issues/e-customs_initiative/masp_strategic_plan_en.pdf; and also the new Electronic Customs Multi-Annual Strategic Plan 2013 Revision—MASP Rev 12 Version 1.2, Taxud.a.3 (2013) 3763373, 2013, URL: http://ec.europa.eu/taxation_customs/resources/documents/customs/policy_issues/e-customs_initiative/masp_strategic_plan_en.pdf, which has been available since 16 January 2014 and covers the strategic plan for 2014.

[154] COM (2005) 608 final.

[155] COM (2005) 609 final.

and need only send customs and other policy-related information once.[156] Second, it called for the concept of a 'One Stop Shop', whereby the goods are controlled at the same time and at the same place by customs authorities as well as all other necessary authorities such as police, border guards, veterinary and environmental authorities.[157] This proposal was accepted and resulted in Decision 70/2008/EC of the European Parliament and of the Council of 15 January 2008 on a paperless environment for customs and trade[158] (hereinafter: e-customs Decision).

B. The E-Customs Decision

The e-customs Decision sets out manifold and highly ambitious tasks for the European Commission and the EU Member States in regard to the Electronic Customs Initiative. To contribute to the success of the great reform of EU customs, the decision aims to introduce electronic data-processing techniques as an important aspect relating to the major part of the Modernised Customs Code. Indeed, it provides for the main IT systems that have to be developed or enhanced for the application of the new Code, as the implementation of certain key provisions of the Code depends on the availability of supporting IT systems.

The main obligation that the Code places on the European Commission is the establishment of an integrated tariff environment to facilitate the necessary connections between the electronic customs systems at both the national and the EU levels. The European Commission is also responsible for coordination activities concerning the implementation and operation of electronic customs systems, training requirements, and components for the synchronised implementation of projects. Furthermore, the EU has to provide and coordinate its own components for the EU-wide electronic customs systems, such as common functional and technical system specifications, common products, and common services, for example the Common Communications Network and Common Systems Interface (CCN/CSI). The CCN/CSI is a value-added network operated by DG TAXUD, which provides the technical infrastructure for the interoperability of IT systems in the policy fields of customs, indirect taxation and the fight against fraud on the EU level as well as the national level.[159] The network provides for the continuous exchange of relevant information through an agile, highly secure and seamless common service.[160]

The tasks for the EU Member States are comparably ambitious. These include the development of new IT systems and ensuring the interoperability of existing national electronic customs systems with the EU level systems as well as the establishment of a framework for single access points and electronic interfaces as tools

[156] European Commission, Press Release of 30 November 2005, IP/05/1501.

[157] ibid.

[158] [2008] OJ L23/21–26.

[159] Definition in: European Parliament, Study 2012, IP/A/IMCO/ST/2011–11, PE 475.094, p 54.

[160] European Parliament, Study 2012, IP/A/IMCO/ST/2011–11, PE 475.094, p 54.

for communication between independent national IT systems. Naturally they also have responsibility for the national components of the EU-wide electronic customs systems.

The ambitious targets of the e-customs Decision seem necessary for the success of the EU customs reform. For example, the supporting IT systems aim to provide reference tools for the purpose of further completing of customs formalities or controls such as, for example, customs decisions and common risk management.[161] One such system is the Economic Operators Registration and Identification System (EORI) for the identification and registration of economic operators that makes one registration sufficient for all interactions with customs authorities in the EU—the EORI number serving as the only identifier when fulfilling customs formalities. The EORI number also interoperates with the AEO system,[162] and replaced every national customs authorisation number. Since 1 July 2009, the use of the EORI number has been not only an obligation under Article 4k CCCIP but also a necessity for doing business with customs authorities in the EU, in particular when lodging a customs declaration or an Entry or Exit Summary Declaration.[163] Another IT system is the AEO full system for an authorisation procedure that includes information and consultation processes as well as registration and management of certificates in a data base accessible by all customs authorities in the EU.[164] Both systems are now integrated under the Economic Operator System (EOS).

The supporting IT systems are one of the three main blocks of the various European Information Systems (EIS) that are needed for the implementation of the Modernised Customs Code. Another one is transaction systems or trans-European IT systems that facilitate the completion of customs formalities or the performance of customs controls upon import, export or transit,[165] such as the already mentioned NCTS. Another example is the Import Control System (ICS), which is an electronic security declaration management system for the importation of goods into the customs territory of the EU[166] that is also part of a broader Automated Import System (AIS).[167] The Export Control System (ECS), as the first stage of a broader Automated Export System (AES), is another trans-European IT system. Both ICS and ECS are intended to enable the seamless flow of data between European customs authorities while also being interoperable with the system for transit.[168] The last of the three EIS blocks consist of information and communication systems for such things as business statistics.[169]

161 ibid, p 50 fn 65.
162 URL: www.eori.eu/eori-general-information/.
163 URL: http://ec.europa.eu/ecip/security_amendment/who_is_concerned/index_en.htm#eori.
164 Grave, in: Gellert (ed), 2009, pp 13–25 (19).
165 European Parliament, Study 2012, IP/A/IMCO/ST/2011–11, PE 475.094, p 53.
166 ibid, p 57.
167 Grave, in: Gellert (ed), 2009, pp 13–25 (20).
168 ibid, pp 13–25 (20).
169 European Parliament, Study 2012, IP/A/IMCO/ST/2011–11, PE 475.094, p 53.

The e-customs Decision illustrates clearly that the European Customs Union intends to properly modernise EU customs through the radical adoption of an electronic customs environment. Based on interoperable IT systems, EU customs is to be able to share information in real time, to have access to common data, and to operate within standardised customs processes. Such a radical change of European customs administration would facilitate trade and thus enhance the competitiveness of EU businesses. Economic operators would no longer have to adapt to different IT solutions in the different EU Member States or transfer relevant data to several customs administrations, or have to face several customs controls in different places, which naturally entails a certain amount of repetition. Furthermore, it would enhance EU-wide uniform customs administration by offering customs officials common data and common standardised customs processes in an interoperable electronic customs environment, thereby allowing them to make their customs decisions under equivalent conditions and with an equal amount of information.

C. Multi-Annual Strategic Plan (MASP)

In order to coordinate the implementation of the targets set in the e-customs Decision, a multi-annual strategic plan was issued and is continuously revised by the European Commission together with the EU Member States. The Multi-Annual Strategic Plan[170] (MASP) was created to govern the implementation of the e-customs Decision and follows the same agenda, but in more detail. It is an essential instrument for ensuring the overall coherence of all IT projects in the EU that relate to the Electronic Customs Initiative and providing for their effective management and coordination as well as for agreement on their implementation.[171]

The MASP provides for operational planning and the allocation of tasks.[172] Its various annexes contain detailed information about governance,[173]

[170] URL: http://ec.europa.eu/taxation_customs/resources/documents/customs/policy_issues/e-customs_initiative/masp_strategic_plan_en.pdf; earlier versions of this document, MASP 2008, TAXUD/477/2004 and its revisions, are no longer available. However, the MASP has undergone a major revision in 2012 from revision 9 to revision 11 and both versions of the MASP are still used for reporting progress by the EU Member States, see: 2012 E-Customs annual progress report, taxud.a.a (2013) 3213327, p 8. Therefore, the contents and objectives of the MASP are illustrated with reference to both versions, the current version MASP 2012 Revision (situation as of 31.12.2013) and the previous version MASP 2008 Revision 9 (manuscript in possession of the author). Also the new Electronic Customs Multi-Annual Strategic Plan 2013 Revision—MASP Rev 12 Version 1.2, Taxud.a.3 (2013) 3763373, 2013, URL: http://ec.europa.eu/taxation_customs/resources/documents/customs/policy_issues/e-customs_initiative/masp_strategic_plan_en.pdf, which first became available on 16 January 2014 and covers the time plan for 2014, will be referred to.

[171] MASP 2013 Revision, Taxud.a.3 (2013) 3763373, p 3; MASP 2012 Revision, TAXUD.a.3 ARES (2012) 1677638, p 3; similar MASP 2008, TAXUD/477/2004—Rev.9 –EN, p 4.

[172] 2012 E-Customs annual progress report, taxud.a.a (2013) 3213327, p 7.

[173] See Annex 3 on the governance scheme (2012), URL: http://ec.europa.eu/taxation_customs/resources/documents/customs/policy_issues/e-customs_initiative/annex_3_governance_scheme_en.pdf, and also Annex 3 on the governance scheme (2013), URL: http://ec.europa.eu/taxation_customs/resources/documents/customs/policy_issues/e-customs_initiative/masp_annex3_en.pdf.

policies[174] and strategies[175] as well as cooperation with economic operators.[176] The most important annexes are the detailed list of implementation actions[177] for both the European Commission and the EU Member States and the corresponding timetable[178] that has to be respected.[179] The time frame is to allow for each IT system to be tested for conformity to standards before entry into operation.

Therefore, the MASP constitutes the overall project management tool for the electronic customs project, while the e-customs Decision provides the general objectives, structure and allocation of tasks, and the Customs Code and its implementing provisions form the necessary legal basis for electronic customs.[180] The MASP is revised annually, as amendments are required in order to reflect progress made and align and update the planning of the respective IT projects.[181] Each update is drafted by the European Commission in partnership with the EU Member States in the Customs Policy Group (CPG) pursuant to Article 8 paragraph 2 Decision 70/2008/EC.

In the beginning, the MASP and its revisions covered the development and management of the trans-European IT systems and central IT systems known in 2008 when the first MASP was drafted.[182] The current MASP version contains all possible electronic customs projects whether related to the e-customs Decision or a specific customs policy area covered under the umbrella of European

[174] See Annex 5 on the BPM policy (2012), URL: http://ec.europa.eu/taxation_customs/resources/documents/customs/policy_issues/e-customs_initiative/annex_5_bpm_policy_en.pdf, and also Annex 4 on the BPM policy (2013), URL: http://ec.europa.eu/taxation_customs/resources/documents/customs/policy_issues/e-customs_initiative/masp_annex4_en.pdf.

[175] See Annex 6 on the IT strategy (2012), URL: http://ec.europa.eu/taxation_customs/resources/documents/customs/policy_issues/e-customs_initiative/annex_6_it_strategy_en.pdf, and also Annex 5 on the IT strategy (2013), URL: http://ec.europa.eu/taxation_customs/resources/documents/customs/policy_issues/e-customs_initiative/masp_annex5_en.pdf.

[176] See Annex 4 on the Trade Contact Group terms of reference (2008) no longer referred to under the MASP 2013, working document TAXUD/1426/2007 Revision 2, URL: http://ec.europa.eu/taxation_customs/resources/documents/customs/policy_issues/e-customs_initiative/annex_4_terms_reference_en.pdf.

[177] See Annex 2 on the consolidated project fiches (2012), URL: http://ec.europa.eu/taxation_customs/resources/documents/customs/policy_issues/e-customs_initiative/annex_2_consolidated_fiches_en.pdf, and also Annex 2 on the consolidated project fiches (2013), URL: http://ec.europa.eu/taxation_customs/resources/documents/customs/policy_issues/e-customs_initiative/masp_annex2_en.pdf.

[178] See Annex 1 on the detailed timetable (2012), URL: http://ec.europa.eu/taxation_customs/resources/documents/customs/policy_issues/e-customs_initiative/masp_timetable.pdf, and also Annex 1 on the detailed timetable (2013), URL: http://ec.europa.eu/taxation_customs/resources/documents/customs/policy_issues/e-customs_initiative/masp_annex1.pdf.

[179] MASP 2013 Revision, Taxud.a.3 (2013) 3763373, p 5; MASP 2012 Revision, TAXUD.a.3 ARES (2012) 1677638, p 6.

[180] 2012 E-Customs annual progress report, taxud.a.a (2013) 3213327, p 7; 2011 E-Customs progress report, Taxud.a.3 (2013) 1630576, p 6; 2010 E-customs progress report, Taxud.a.1 (2011) 806750, p 4; 2009 E-customs progress report, Taxud.a.1 (2010)364729, p 4; 2008 E-customs progress report, Taxud.c.1 (2009)172599, p 4.

[181] MASP 2013 Revision, Taxud.a.3 (2013) 3763373, pp 3, 13; MASP 2012 Revision, TAXUD.a.3 ARES (2012) 1677638, pp 4, 16; similar MASP 2008, TAXUD/477/2004—Rev.9 –EN, p 4.

[182] MASP 2013 Revision, Taxud.a.3 (2013) 3763373, p 4; MASP 2012 Revision, TAXUD.a.3 ARES (2012) 1677638, p 5; 2012 E-Customs annual progress report, taxud.a.a (2013) 3213327, p 6.

Information Systems (EIS).[183] To date, the main focus of the MASP has been the computerisation of customs processes to enhance effective risk analysis, monitor trade flows and make the appropriate selection of consignments to be checked, all of which are activities requiring interoperability between EU Member States and access to electronic customs for traders.[184]

Of great importance is the conversion of the legal changes and simplifications of EU customs law into an electronic customs environment that is also in accordance with the new implementing provisions. In this context, operational convergence is required to ensure the attainment of the objective of the Electronic Customs Initiative: the creation of an effective paperless customs environment. Therefore, the development of common guidelines and working methods for the efficient management of the EU Customs Union, reflecting both legal and IT aspects, is also part of the MASP.

Meanwhile, the new Business Process Management and the embedded Business Process Modelling (BPM) approach have received increasing attention, BPM having been identified as an important instrument for improving the functioning of the EU Customs Union and enhancing the standardisation of EU customs.[185] BPM aims to increase common understanding of customs process flows and the practical effects of their implementation.[186]

To meet the targets of the MASP, the European Commission and the EU Member States work together in several groups. Although the main responsibility for the governance of the implementation of electronic customs lies with the European Commission and the Customs Policy Group, these work also in close cooperation with the Electronic Customs Group (ECG), the Customs Code Committee (CCC), the Customs 2013 Committee, the Trade Contact Group (TCG), and also expert groups involved in the processes of the legal component of the customs reform.[187] This close coordination and consultation of the various groups involved in different parts in the reform process of EU customs is intended to ensure the overall coherence of all activities, the coordination of legal and operational aspects, the best and most efficient use of resources, and the respect of agreed upon deadlines.[188]

Furthermore, binding milestones have been established to ensure the respect for the agreed upon timetables and avoid extended periods of continued use of paper-based solutions in single EU Member States that were not able to meet deadlines.[189]

[183] MASP 2013 Revision, Taxud.a.3 (2013) 3763373, p 3; MASP 2012 Revision, TAXUD.a.3 ARES (2012) 1677638, p 3.

[184] MASP 2008, TAXUD/477/2004—Rev.9 –EN.

[185] MASP 2013 Revision, Taxud.a.3 (2013) 3763373, p 3; MASP 2012 Revision, TAXUD.a.3 ARES (2012) 1677638, p 3; similar MASP 2008, TAXUD/477/2004—Rev.9 –EN, pp 7, 8.

[186] 2012 E-Customs annual progress report, taxud.a.a (2013) 3213327, p 9.

[187] MASP 2013 Revision, Taxud.a.3 (2013) 3763373, p 10; MASP 2012 Revision, TAXUD.a.3 ARES (2012) 1677638, p 13.

[188] MASP 2013 Revision, Taxud.a.3 (2013) 3763373, p 10; MASP 2012 Revision, TAXUD.a.3 ARES (2012) 1677638, p 13.

[189] MASP 2013 Revision, Taxud.a.3 (2013) 3763373, pp 12, 13; MASP 2012 Revision, TAXUD.a.3 ARES (2012) 1677638, pp 15, 16.

Therefore, implementation of the MASP is to occur through a four-stage process, with each stage reflecting the development status of the IT projects contained therein.[190] This staged approach then contains the milestones and deadlines for the individual tasks that are assigned to both parties in the MASP, the European Commission and the EU Member States. The progress toward competition of the individual tasks allocated in the MASP has to be annually reported by the EU Member States and the European Commission pursuant to Article 12 Decision 70/2008/EC.

D. Progress on the Electronic Customs Initiative

In describing the current status of some IT systems, the European Commission has pointed to the success of the supporting system for the integrated tariff environment, which includes several databases[191] developed and operated in conjunction with the customs authorities of the EU Member States.[192] Indeed, many online business services are now provided to facilitate trade and make life easier for businesses, the TARIC[193] being just one of them.[194] Other online customs databases are: AEO (Authorised Economic Operators), EBTI (Binding Tariff Information), ECICS (European Customs Inventory of Chemical Substances), EORI (Economic Operators Identification and Registration number), EXPORT (tracking goods in export), QUOTA (tariff quotas), SURVEILLANCE (statistical monitoring of imports and exports), SUSPENSIONS (Autonomous Tariff Suspensions), Customs offices (offices where transit declarations can be made), and TRANSIT (Movement Reference Number (MRN) Follow-up Information).[195]

In particular TARIC[196] and QUOTA ensure fair and uniform treatment of economic operators. TARIC facilitates the daily transmission of TARIC data to the EU Member States via an electronic network, guaranteeing accurate and immediate information is available to national customs administrations.[197] QUOTA, a database for dealing with requests sent in by EU Member States' administrations, sends the allocation results of requests back to the EU Member Sates' administrations on a daily basis and, in addition, reports all developments in tariff quotas such as exhaustion, blocking, suspension, new balance, and so on.[198] These are also sent

[190] MASP 2013 Revision, Taxud.a.3 (2013) 3763373, p 12; MASP 2012 Revision, TAXUD.a.3 ARES (2012) 1677638, p 15.

[191] URL: http://ec.europa.eu/taxation_customs/common/databases/.

[192] European Parliament, Study 2012, IP/A/IMCO/ST/2011–11, PE 475.094, p 53.

[193] A detailed analysis of the TARIC can be found in Chapter 2.III.A.3.

[194] URL: http://ec.europa.eu/taxation_customs/resources/documents/common/dds2/material/flyer_taric_low_resolution_en.pdf.

[195] URL: http://ec.europa.eu/taxation_customs/common/databases/.

[196] A detailed analysis of the TARIC can be found in Chapter 2.III.A.3.

[197] European Parliament, Study 2012, IP/A/IMCO/ST/2011–11, PE 475.094, p 53.

[198] ibid, p 53.

daily via the TARIC transmission.[199] Such centrally managed IT systems are one of the most effective ways to ensure uniform customs administration.[200]

An impression of the progress made in the electronic customs project as part of the great reform can be gained from the reports issued every year of the European Commission pursuant to Article 12 Decision 70/2008/EC and based on national reports. So far, reports are available for 2008,[201] 2009,[202] 2010,[203] 2011[204] and 2012.[205]

The major task of the European Commission and the EU Member States during 2008, 2009, and 2010 was to implement the IT systems related to the Safety and Security Amendment to the Community Customs Code[206] as required by the corresponding implementing provisions.[207] Enhancing the stability of these IT systems has been one of the main focuses of the EU Member States' efforts in 2011[208] and 2012.[209] Their completion was intended for 1 July 2009 and was only a first step in the electronic customs project.[210] The reports state the European Commission fulfilled their tasks mainly by preparing the centrally developed functional and technical specification for the safety and security systems and by supporting the EU Member States in the conformance tests of those systems.[211]

However, although all safety and security systems, such as the Import Control System (ICS), the Export Control System (ECS), the EORI and AEO Economic Operators Systems (EOS), and the Customs Risk Management System

[199] ibid, p 53.

[200] Lux, 2012 AW-Prax 8, pp 257–62 (258).

[201] URL: http://ec.europa.eu/taxation_customs/resources/documents/customs/policy_issues/e-customs_initiative/2008_progress_report_after_ecg_en.pdf.

[202] URL: http://ec.europa.eu/taxation_customs/resources/documents/customs/policy_issues/e-customs_initiative/2009_progress_report_en.pdf.

[203] URL: http://ec.europa.eu/taxation_customs/resources/documents/customs/policy_issues/e-customs_initiative/2010_progress_report_en.pdf.

[204] URL: http://ec.europa.eu/taxation_customs/resources/documents/customs/policy_issues/e-customs_initiative/2011_progress_report_en.pdf.

[205] URL: http://ec.europa.eu/taxation_customs/resources/documents/customs/policy_issues/e-customs_initiative/2012_progress_report.pdf. Situation as of 31.12.2013.

[206] Regulation (EC) 648/2005 of the European Parliament and of the Council of 13 April 2005 amending Council Regulation (EEC) 2913/92 establishing the Community Customs Code, [2005] OJ L117/13–19.

[207] Commission Regulation (EC) 1875/2006 of 18 December 2006 amending Regulation (EEC) 2454/93 laying down provisions for the implementation of Council Regulation (EEC) 2913/92 establishing the Community Customs Code, [2006] OJ L360/64–125. 2008 E-customs progress report, Taxud.c.1 (2009) 172599, pp 3, 4; 2009 E-customs progress report, Taxud.a.1 (2010) 364729, pp 3, 4, 5; 2010 E-customs progress report, Taxud.a.1 (2011) 806750, pp 3, 5.

[208] 2011 E-Customs progress report, Taxud.a.3 (2013) 1630576, pp 5, 7.

[209] 2012 E-Customs annual progress report, taxud.a.a (2013) 3213327, p 8.

[210] 2011 E-Customs progress report, Taxud.a.3 (2013) 1630576, p 7; 2010 E-customs progress report, Taxud.a.1 (2011) 806750, p 5; 2009 E-customs progress report, Taxud.a.1 (2010)364729, p 4; 2008 E-customs progress report, Taxud.c.1 (2009)172599, p 4.

[211] 2012 E-Customs annual progress report, taxud.a.a(2013) 3213327, p 8; 2011 E-Customs progress report, Taxud.a.3 (2013) 1630576, p 7; 2010 E-customs progress report, Taxud.a.1 (2011) 806750, p 6; 2009 E-customs progress report, Taxud.a.1(2010)364729, p 6; 2008 E-customs progress report, Taxud.c.1(2009)172599, p 5.

(CRMS), attained operational status,[212] there was in almost every area a delay in their deployment in the EU Member States.[213] Other IT systems required by the e-customs Decision and the Modernised Customs Code got their implementation dates generally postponed from 2011 to 2014.[214] The MASP was not updated until 11 December 2012, with no revisions in 2009, 2010 or 2011.[215]

The yearly MASP update as a general rule is intended to reflect the work progress and upcoming tasks,[216] so its suspension led to the conclusion that there had been no significant progress in the Electronic Customs Initiative that would justify a useful update. Indeed, the progress reports of 2010, 2011 and 2012 are characterised by a lack of an overall IT implementation plan.[217] Without an agreed upon IT architecture and implementation strategy,[218] the EU Member States could not report as much progress as originally hoped for.

The experience with the deployment of the safety and security systems in time-challenging conditions, similar to that of the Modernised Customs Code, has resulted in an ongoing discussion between the European Commission and the EU Member States to define a realistic scope for the IT systems to be operational by June 2013.[219] Yet conclusions on the necessary IT requirements—in particular legislation and BPM[220]—are still pending.[221] Even at the end of the year 2012, it was said that an overall IT Implementation plan might be a 'too ambitious goal at this stage.'[222]

The European Parliament has expressed its concern about the lack of progress in the electronic customs project, in particular the fact that strategic decisions on the IT architecture of the EU Customs Union have not been taken yet.[223] It has

[212] A current list of the trans-European IT systems and central IT systems operational to date can be found in: MASP 2013 Revision, Taxud.a.3 (2013) 3763373, p 4; MASP 2012 Revision, TAXUD.a.3 ARES (2012) 1677638, p 5.

[213] 2009 E-customs progress report, Taxud.a.1(2010)364729, p 6, see also 2010 E-customs progress report, Taxud.a.1 (2011) 806750, p 10.

[214] 2009 E-customs progress report, Taxud.a.1(2010)364729, p 4; 2008 E-customs progress report, Taxud.c.1(2009)172599, p 4.

[215] 2012 E-Customs annual progress report, taxud.a.a(2013) 3213327, p 6; 2011 E-Customs progress report, Taxud.a.3 (2013) 1630576, p 7.

[216] 2011 E-Customs progress report, Taxud.a.3 (2013) 1630576, p 7; 2010 E-customs progress report, Taxud.a.1 (2011) 806750, p 6; 2009 E-customs progress report, Taxud.a.1(2010) 364729, p 5.

[217] MASP 2013 Revision, Taxud.a.3 (2013) 3763373, p 13; MASP 2012 Revision, TAXUD.a.3 ARES (2012) 1677638, p 16.

[218] MASP 2013 Revision, Taxud.a.3 (2013) 3763373, p 13; MASP 2012 Revision, TAXUD.a.3 ARES (2012) 1677638, p 16.

[219] 2010 E-customs progress report, Taxud.a.1 (2011) 806750, p 6; 2009 E-customs progress report, Taxud.a.1(2010) 364729, p 5.

[220] MASP 2013 Revision, Taxud.a.3 (2013) 3763373, p 13; MASP 2012 Revision, TAXUD.a.3 ARES (2012) 1677638, p 16.

[221] 2010 E-customs progress report, Taxud.a.1 (2011) 806750, p 6; 2009 E-customs progress report, Taxud.a.1 (2010)364729, p 5; similar: 2011 E-Customs progress report, Taxud.a.3 (2013) 1630576, p 7.

[222] MASP 2013 Revision, Taxud.a.3 (2013) 3763373, p 13; MASP 2012 Revision, TAXUD.a.3 ARES (2012) 1677638, p 16.

[223] European Parliament Resolution of 1 December 2011 (2001/2083(INI)), text adopted P7_TA (2011) 0546, para 19.

criticised the very slow progress in this regard, the more so as it simultaneously has emphasised the importance of electronic customs systems for uniform customs administration,[224] which in turn is important for the functioning of the EU Customs Union.

V. THE FUTURE CUSTOMS INITIATIVE

To enable customs administration in the EU to adapt to a changing and challenging environment, the European Customs Union is looking beyond the modernisation and simplification of customs' legal and technical environment. The new Customs Code and its new implementing provisions, as well as the e-customs Decision and its Multi-Annual Strategic Plan, are important legal and technological steps, aimed to equip customs administrations for the immediate future as well as the medium term.[225] However, for the overarching goal of customs reform in the EU, a new strategic framework on the future organisation and human dimension has to be considered. The main objective of such reform is to maintain the pivotal role and position of the customs authorities in the EU in fulfilling their dual task of collecting duties and taxes while simultaneously acting as a guardian of the safety, security and health of EU citizens.[226] Thus, EU customs needs to be a modern and responsive partner for the private trade-based sector, has to cooperate closely with other governmental authorities and must be able to respond to crises as well as new public policy demands,[227] whilst the national customs administrations are expected to act as if they were a single entity.[228]

A uniform customs administration can only be achieved by taking into account the relevant stakeholders in the customs authorities: the customs officials responsible for day-to-day customs work, including consideration of their skills and competences, training, equipment and working conditions. The effectiveness of the great reform requires that developments proceed in a harmonised and synchronised way throughout the EU.[229] The use of IT systems in an electronic customs environment does not relieve customs administrations of the need to be staffed with competent customs officials and optimise customs process flows.[230] Therefore, the human dimension and organisational aspects of the reform project must not be neglected and the promotion of cooperation among national customs administrations and also with the European Commission is an important strategy for enhancing the functioning and uniformity of the EU Customs Union.[231]

[224] European Parliament Resolution of 1 December 2011 (2001/2083(INI)), text adopted P7_TA(2011)0546, para 53.

[225] COM (2008) 169 final, p 5.

[226] ibid, p 5.

[227] ibid, p 5.

[228] COM (2012) 791 final, p 9.

[229] COM (2008) 169 final, p 7.

[230] Lux, 2012 AW-Prax 8, pp 257–62 (257).

[231] ibid, pp 257–62 (259).

In the Future Role of Customs (FRoC) project, the European Commission together with the EU Member States reviewed the role and work of EU customs in order to prepare for a great overhaul to ensure its consistent development in the longer term.[232] The FroC led to the Future Customs Initiative (FCI), a strategic framework for improving working methods and cooperation as well as for assessing the overall functioning of the EU Customs Union and the requirements of EU Member States for resources, training and equipment.[233] The development and implementation of the EU Customs Union is supported by the Customs Policy Group (CPG), the overall policy coordination group overseeing a wide set of project groups, steering groups and actions on the EU level.[234] The CPG is comprised of the Directors General of the EU Member States' customs administrations and is chaired by the European Commission.[235]

A. Background of the Future Customs Initiative

To complete the reform process, the European Commission issued a communication about a new strategy for the evolution of the Customs Union.[236] This communication concerned the comprehensive long-term development of EU customs based on renewed common strategic objectives such as protection, competitiveness, facilitation, control and cooperation. It also pressed for the political support of the EU Member States in adopting a common approach for developing new working methods and staff competences and reallocating resources in an effective and efficient manner to achieve all the objectives of the great reform.[237]

Endorsing these suggestions, the European Parliament adopted a resolution on the fortieth anniversary of the Customs Union.[238] It requested that the European Commission survey and monitor the uniform application of EU customs law in the EU Member States and continuously inform the European Parliament about the results,[239] underlining again the importance uniform administration holds in the EU customs strategy.

In the context of uniform customs administration, the European Parliament welcomed the establishment of a European customs laboratories' network,[240] pointing out the significance of uniform interpretation of new EU technical standards, and signalling its support for any other initiative serving the purpose

232 COM (2011) 922 final, p 3.
233 ibid, p 3.
234 COM (2012) 791 final, p 11.
235 ibid, p 11.
236 COM (2008) 169 final.
237 ibid, p 7.
238 European Parliament Resolution of 19 June 2008, Text adopted P6_TA(2008)0305.
239 ibid, para 21.
240 URL: http://ec.europa.eu/taxation_customs/customs/customs_controls/custom_laboratories/group_ecl/index_en.htm.

of uniform application of EU customs law.[241] Being the scientific arm of customs, the 80 or so customs laboratories in the EU[242] are an important tool for customs authorities as well as an essential element in ensuring the integrity of the EU's borders.[243] They support customs authorities in addressing the changes in the trade environment by providing scientific expertise and advice.[244] The Group of European Customs Laboratories (GCL) provides a platform for their cross-border coordination under the overarching guidance of the European Commission. Better exchange of scientific expertise, and development of common and uniform work processes are to be developed through a Common Quality Policy for all custom laboratories in the EU.[245] The resolution of the European Parliament thus has been regarded as an important sign of political support for tackling the ambitious goal of an integrated network of European customs laboratories.[246]

The common strategic objectives and the new role of customs regarding the trade, financial, fiscal, safety and security interests of the EU were also approved by the Council of the EU.[247] In particular, they invited the development of a single comprehensive implementation plan. Like the MASP for the Electronic Customs Initiative, this plan is to contain a similarly detailed strategy for a coordinated and common implementation of the objectives, and to provide a basis for the effective planning of the use of the individual resources of all the actors involved, such as European Commission, EU Member States and economic operators.[248]

Therefore, a plan for harmonised and synchronised progress and investment in the skills, competences and resources of customs throughout all EU Member States, operated continuously and in a strategic manner, was to be designed by the European Commission in close cooperation with the EU Member States in the Customs Policy Group.[249] The Council invited the European Commission to draft such a plan by the end of 2009, providing a clear orientation for customs in the 2013 to 2019 period and to report on its progress by 2011. This strategic framework for a common approach to modernised working methods and competences has since been in development.[250] Its progress so far is reported in the European Commission's Report on Progress in the Strategy[251] and also in its communication on the state of the EU Customs Union.[252] However, up to now the Future Customs Initiative implementation plan seems to be largely a report, without visible impact at the national level.[253]

241 European Parliament Resolution of 19 June 2008, Text adopted P6_TA(2008)0305, para 19.
242 European Commission, Brochure on the European Customs Laboratories, 2010, p 5.
243 ibid, p 4.
244 ibid, p 6.
245 ibid, p 18.
246 ibid, p 17.
247 ECOFIN Council Conclusions of 14 May 2008, 8850/08 (Presse 113), pp 24–25.
248 COM (2008) 169 final, p 7.
249 ECOFIN Council Conclusions of 14 May 2008, 8850/08 (Presse 113), p 25.
250 COM (2011) 922 final, p 4.
251 ibid.
252 COM (2012) 791 final.
253 The Evaluation Partnership, Mid-Term Evaluation—Annex II, June 2011, p 17.

B. Progress on the Future Customs Initiative

The progress report of December 2011, covering the developments pertaining to the strategy for the evolution of the European Customs Union for 2008 to 2013, again points out that a uniform and efficient European Customs Union is the overarching goal of the reform process.[254] This goal is to be achieved by applying efficient and effective control and cooperation within customs administrations as well as with other authorities, businesses and international partners.[255] Thereby the EU can ensure two main strategic objectives, the protection of the EU and the support of EU competitiveness.

However, since the adoption of the EU customs strategy in 2008[256] significant events have taken place that are bound to influence the operation of customs in the EU,[257] in particular the financial and economic crisis but also the European Commission's Europe 2020 strategy[258] and its Single Market Act[259] to support growth. The financial and economic crisis has negatively affected progress in the Future Customs Initiative, as it requires significant investment in human and material capital that is no longer available due to financial limitations.[260] Moreover, the slow modernisation process in both legislation and IT development has also slowed down the Future Customs Initiative, as a common approach for improved working methods, training and cooperation depends to a large extent on the legal and IT environment that must first be created.

1. *Strategic Discussions*

Although a number of strategic discussions about improving the performance of EU customs in terms of effectiveness and uniformity as well as efficiency have taken place in the top management of EU customs services,[261] an implementation plan is still missing.[262] Indeed, in its most recent conclusions on the progress of the Future Customs Initiative,[263] the Council once again invited the European Commission 'to take measures, together with the Member States administrations, on implementing the strategy.'[264]

To address more structural issues, a self-assessment study[265] identifying key points and evaluating a number of options for improving the functioning of the

[254] COM (2011) 922 final, p 4.
[255] ibid, p 4.
[256] COM (2008) 169 final.
[257] COM (2011) 922 final, pp 4, 5.
[258] COM (2010) 2020 final.
[259] COM (2011) 206 final.
[260] COM (2012) 791 final, p 11.
[261] COM (2011) 922 final, p 13.
[262] The Evaluation Partnership, Mid-Term Evaluation—Annex II, June 2011, p 17.
[263] Council of the European Union, Customs Union Strategy Conclusions of 10 and 11 December 2012.
[264] ibid, p 4.
[265] Deloitte, Final Report on Task 2.3, TAXUD/R3/VDL D (2010) 433216, 2011.

EU Customs Union has been launched and since 2011 has been under discussion by the European Commission and the EU Member States, who are exploring the options' potential implementation and follow up.[266] Almost all areas identified as needing improvement are directly or indirectly related to enhancing uniform customs administration.

Further strategic discussions by the European Commission and national customs administrations on reinforcement of the uniform, effective and efficient performance of the EU Customs Union are thus concentrating on the following areas: working more closely, seeking synergies, and improving governance as well as quality of outputs.[267] Working more closely together as a customs union requires the spread of common modern working methods through innovations in enabling mechanisms at the operational level and in working areas with scarce resources.[268] Furthermore, in areas where human input is of special importance for EU-wide uniform outcomes, closer cooperation in training of people has to be made a special priority.[269] The need for better, regular and adequate training of customs officers has also been stressed by the European Parliament in its resolution on the modernisation of customs.[270] Common modern working methods and close cooperation in training customs officers are thereby appropriate methods for improving uniform implementation of EU customs law.

Seeking synergies requires the adoption of a strategic approach for cooperation within a growing number of policy areas interacting with customs work to ensure matching and producing synergies of legal requirements, working methods and business processes.[271] Again, a similar demand has already been made by the European Parliament in calling for the establishment of operational platforms common to all EU Member States and the European Commission, as well as the combination of knowledge and expertise of all relevant stakeholders in their respective fields.[272] Additionally, close cooperation and exchange of expertise with regard to business process serves not only to create or maximise synergies but also to enhance uniform customs administration.

Improving governance requires the revision of working methods, focusing especially on already identified challenges in the complex coordination structure within and between European institutions, including operational activities.[273] In this context, business process modelling (BPM) has become important.[274]

[266] COM (2011) 922 final, p 13; COM (2011) 376 final, p 12.
[267] COM (2011) 922 final, pp 14, 15.
[268] ibid, p 14.
[269] ibid, p 14.
[270] European Parliament Resolution of 1 December 2011 (2001/2083(INI)), text adopted P7_TA(2011)0546, paras 47 and 68, 69.
[271] COM (2011) 922 final, p 14.
[272] European Parliament Resolution of 1 December 2011 (2001/2083(INI)), text adopted P7_TA(2011)0546, paras 64, 69.
[273] COM (2011) 922 final, p 14.
[274] ibid, p 15.

Systematic business process modelling (BPM) has been introduced in order to prevent differences in the interpretation and implementation of the law in the future and to ensure newly developed processes are not incompatible with IT developments and that deadlines are achievable.[275] Furthermore, the possibility of a coherent system of performance management within the EU Customs Union is being examined by a newly established project group of experts.[276] Moreover, as the European Parliament has requested the monitoring of the uniform application of EU customs law in the EU Member States and that it be continuously informed of the findings,[277] further detailed gap analyses have been carried out in critical areas, such as, for example, risk management, while even more are planned.[278]

All these statements lead to the conclusion that many working fields in the modernisation process of EU customs have been identified. However, the modernisation of the structure and architecture of European customs administration is still being discussed. There thus remains a need for a clear, concrete and common strategy and approach for achieving optimal performance and outcomes that thereby ensure uniform implementation of EU customs law.

2. *Summary*

The slow progress in the Future Customs Initiative has to be viewed in a critical light, with the challenges that confront EU customs requiring significant progress in all parts of the reform. Possible insufficiencies or inadequacies of customs authorities in the EU in carrying out their tasks—managing trade while protecting the EU—have been criticised on several occasions by the European Court of Auditors.[279] Moreover, the media and public have recently also grown more interested in the issue, due to some highly publicised incidents regarding the security of the supply chain.[280] The European Parliament has also debated the reality of modernisation, expressing particular concerns about national differences in

[275] ibid, p 7.

[276] ibid, p 15.

[277] European Parliament Resolution of 19 June 2008, text adopted P6_TA(2008)0305, para 21.

[278] COM (2012) 791 final, p 12.

[279] See European Court of Auditors, Special Report No 1/2010, [2010] OJ C149/8 and URL: http://eur-lex.europa.eu/LexUriServ/LexUriServ.do?uri=SRCA:2010:01:FIN:EN:PDF; European Court of Auditors, Special Report No 2/2008, [2008] OJ C103/1–17; European Court of Auditors, Special Report No 11/2006, [2007] OJ C44/1–19; European Court of Auditors, Special Report No 1/2005, [2005] OJ C202/1–32; European Court of Auditors, Special Report No 23/2000, [2001] OJ C84/1–18; European Court of Auditors, Special Report No 8/1999, [1998] OJ C375/3–16; European Court of Auditors, Special Report No 13/1998, [1998] OJ C 375/3–16. For a detailed analysis see Chapter 2.IV.C.

[280] For example the 'Yemen incident' of October 2010, where a bomb hidden in a printer cartridge—probably by al-Qaeda—and destined for a Jewish institution in the US was detected in the UK after it had transited the German airport of Cologne; detection in the UK occurred after a tip-off by a former al-Qaeda member, rather than through systematic checks by the border authorities; for details see BBC, 'Q&A: Air freight bomb plot', BBC.co.uk, 2 November 2010, URL: www.bbc.co.uk/news/11658452; Matt Zuvela, 'Authorities review airport security after failed bomb plot', de-world.de, 1 November 2010, URL: www.dw-world.de/dw/article/0,,6178554,00.html; Dave Graham/Myra MacDonald, Reuters news article 'Freight stopped from Yemen after bomb scare—Germany', Reuters.

the interpretation of EU customs law.[281] Therefore, they have called for the EU Member States to fully commit to the modernisation process, and particularly to uniform customs administration, while pressing the European Commission to take all necessary actions without delay to secure the smooth and harmonised administration of EU customs law throughout the EU.[282]

C. Future Actions

The strategic objectives of the Future Customs Initiative are as valid and relevant today as they were in 2008. The priorities for the EU Customs Union thus remain a broader strategic approach to cooperation, improving working methods and structures of governance; sharing and pooling of capacities and capabilities in EU customs; and developing a coherent system of performance management by defining a basis for measuring outputs and outcomes, thereby being able to identify weaknesses and gaps.[283] The European Commission will continue to provide the main support mechanisms for the EU Member States through adequate development work and through the Customs Action Programme,[284] which in the future[285] is to be strengthened in terms of tools and funding.[286] In this context, the European Parliament has already called for a follow-up programme to the current Customs Action Programme 2013. The follow-up is particularly intended to support the uniform administration of EU customs law and a balanced approach to enhancing European competitiveness while simultaneously ensuring safety and security.[287]

Regarding future actions, the European Commission has identified three key elements for the evolution of the EU Customs Union that directly relate

com, 31 October 2010, URL: http://in.reuters.com/article/2010/10/31/idINIndia-52573720101031; or the 'Italy incident', another and possibly more serious affair with a suspected 'dirty bomb', which was in a cargo container in the docks of the Italian port of Naples in February 2011; for details see Felicity Landon, '"Dirty bomb" fears over radioactive container at Italian port', lloydsloadinglist.com, 18 February 2011, URL: www.lloydsloadinglist.com/freight-directory/searcharticle.htm?articleID=20017850492&highlight=true&keywords=&phrase.

[281] European Parliament Resolution of 1 December 2011 (2001/2083(INI)), text adopted P7_TA(2011)0546, para 7.

[282] ibid, para 7.

[283] COM (2011) 922 final, p 15.

[284] Current programme (situation as of 31.12.2013): Customs 2013, see Decision 624/2007/EC of the European Parliament and of the Council of 23 May 2007 establishing an action programme for customs in the Community (Customs 2013), [2007] OJ L154/25–31. For a detailed analysis of the benefits the Customs Action Programme provides for uniform customs administration, see Chapter 7.IV.

[285] Future programme (situation as of 31.12.2013): Regulation (EU) 1294/2013 of the European Parliament and of the Council of 11 December 2013 establishing an action programme for customs in the European Union for the period 2014–2020 (Customs 2020) and repealing Decision 624/2007/EC, [2013] OJ L347/209–2/20.

[286] COM (2011) 922 final, p 13.

[287] European Parliament Resolution of 1 December 2011 (2001/2083(INI)), text adopted P7_TA(2011)0546, para 72.

to the improvement of uniform customs administration. One is the completion of the legal and IT modernisation process, a necessary basis for operational modernisation.[288] Furthermore, the gap analyses, which have recently been done or are currently being carried out in order to identify weak points in the functioning of the EU Customs Union, have to be completed so that priorities for further development and improvement can be set.[289] Finally, and most interestingly regarding the improvement of uniform customs administration, the European Commission hope to see a reform of the governance and management structures of the EU Customs Union. Problems with the current decentralised system of implementation such as duplication, inconsistency, and mismatch of resources, are seen to have limited its effectiveness and efficiency.[290]

Therefore, the reform of the governance of implementation is to provide for increased operational coordination and joint action, definition of operational objectives and of quality of service including a joint monitoring system, and a mechanism for identifying needs and priorities, one which is also able to transfer capacities where required.[291] Indeed, the overall objective of the reform of governance to provide consistently high-quality service right across the EU demands nothing less than the improvement of uniform customs administration. This is in accordance with the European Parliament's resolution on the modernisation of customs, which also demands further action by both the European Commission and EU Member States for the modernisation of EU customs and even recites the European Commission's own objective, 'to make national customs administrations act as if they were one, ensuring controls with equivalent results at every point of the Union's customs territory'.[292]

VI. CONCLUSION

The manifold activities in the context of the Future Customs Initiative, as well as in the Electronic Customs Initiative and the 'Better Regulation' Initiative, clearly demonstrate that the uniform application of EU customs law is indeed a priority in the evolution of the EU Customs Union. Being aware of its political and practical importance for protection and effectiveness—the main tasks of EU customs—the European Commission and the EU Member States' customs administrations have undertaken some actions to improve the performance of EU customs.

[288] COM (2012) 791 final, pp 13, 14.

[289] ibid, pp 13, 14.

[290] ibid, p 15.

[291] ibid, p 16.

[292] European Parliament Resolution of 1 December 2011 (2001/2083(INI)), text adopted P7_TA(2011)0546, para 53.

However, even more progress is needed, as can be seen by the ambitious agenda for future reform. Unfortunately, further progress in the evolution of EU customs will be troubled by problems in the ongoing reform process, specifically regarding the drafting of the implementation provisions of the Modernised Customs Code and the simultaneous development of IT solutions, combined also with severe and challenging deadlines that have already been extended on several occasions. Because of the fact that the great reform of EU customs consists of three interconnected parts connected, these troubles affect the whole evolution of EU customs.

5

Recast of the Great Reform: The Union Customs Code and European IT Strategy

WHEN THE GREAT reform of EU customs was launched in 2008, the deadline for the application of the Modernised Customs Code of 24 June 2013 indicated a clear timeframe for the reform process and also expressed the determination of the European Commission as well as the European Parliament and the Council to complete the modernisation of EU customs by that date.[1] The initial plan also envisaged the implementing provisions—necessary for the application of the Modernised Customs Code—being published and brought into force sufficiently in advance of the expiry of the final deadline. Thus, there would have been enough time for monitoring and evaluation to ensure their compatibility with the necessary supporting IT systems,[2] as well as to give EU businesses the opportunity to adjust to the changes introduced. However, even this initial plan, which was very optimistic in regard to its time frame, did admit that the reform of EU customs would be a highly complicated process, due to the need to develop implementing provisions and supporting IT systems in parallel.

The modernisation of EU customs does of course involve more than simply the adoption of new implementing provisions. It requires a whole series of coordinated actions, including the adaption of IT support systems, the drafting of guidelines, the training of customs officials, and communication with economic actors.[3] These coordinated actions are required to ensure that information on the new customs legislation is widely available, as well as that its application is effective and uniform and enables easy day-to-day management.[4] Given the lessons from the implementation of new security systems introduced in the minor reform of the Community Customs Code—that it can take approximately six years for such customs IT systems to be fully implemented in the EU—it should have been clear that the deadline was an impossible target.[5]

Nonetheless, the statement in Article 5 MCC regarding the wide use of electronic data processing techniques in EU customs was highly ambitious.[6] Yet delays

[1] European Parliament, Study 2012, IP/A/IMCO/ST/2011–11, PE 475.094, p 24.
[2] ibid, p 25; Grave, in: Gellert (ed.), 2009, pp 13–25 (17, 18).
[3] European Parliament, Study 2012, IP/A/IMCO/ST/2011–11, PE 475.094, p 25.
[4] ibid, p 25.
[5] ibid, p 25; AmCham EU, Information Paper, 5 August 2011, p 4.
[6] AmCham EU, Information Paper, 5 August 2011, p 2.

in the implementation of the new security systems in the minor reform had already slowed down the drafting of the Modernised Customs Code implementing provisions,[7] and ongoing delays in the development of new IT systems, as well as in the upgrading of existing IT systems, had hindered their implementation as of June 2013.[8]

It had already been admitted by the European Commission as well as the EU Member States' national customs administrations that even in the best case only a very limited number of new IT systems would be operational by June 2013.[9] In particular, the concept of centralised customs clearance, which is of special importance for the modernisation of EU customs and its need for uniform customs administration, depends on a wide range of IT systems that have yet to be defined and developed by the European Commission, national customs administrations and economic operators.[10] Therefore, the final deadline of 24 June 2013 was not met for a large number of the activities related to the implementation of the Modernised Customs Code, because of new developments and due to specific technical and practical reasons, especially the difficulties in adapting the necessary IT systems before the new computerised customs procedures could become operational.

In May 2011, EU Commissioner Algirdas Šemeta announced a recast of the Modernised Customs Code by the end of the year, with the primary goal of postponing the deadline for its application.[11] Furthermore, the recast is also to align the Code with the requirements of the Lisbon Treaty and correct a limited number of provisions that were either no longer in line with changes introduced to EU legislation since the adoption of the Modernised Customs Code in 2008, or had turned out to be difficult, impossible or simply impractical to implement.[12] The proposal for a re-cast Union Custom Code was finally presented on 20 February 2012[13] after some delay in the drafting of the announced amendments of the Modernised Customs Code.[14]

The date of application of the Modernised Customs Code was postponed to 1 November 2013, from the original planned date of 24 June 2013. The Union

[7] ibid, p 4.

[8] See the statements of DG TAXUD in: European Parliament, Study 2012, IP/A/IMCO/ST/2011–11, PE 475.094, p 51; also Algirdas Šemeta, EU Commissioner, Speech of 25 May 2011, p 3.

[9] COM (2012) 64 final, p 2; European Commission, Presentation 'Union Customs Code (recast)', 26 April 2012, slide 3, URL: www.europarl.europa.eu/document/activities/cont/201205/20120521ATT45426/20120521ATT45426EN.pdf; also European Parliament, Study 2012, IP/A/IMCO/ST/2011–11, PE 475.094, p 83.

[10] European Parliament, Study 2012, IP/A/IMCO/ST/2011–11, PE 475.094, p 25; also European Parliament Resolution of 1 December 2011 (2001/2083(INI)), text adopted P7_TA(2011)0546, paras 25, 26.

[11] Algirdas Šemeta, EU Commissioner, Speech of 19 May 2011; Algirdas Šemeta, EU Commissioner, Speech of 25 May 2011, p 3.

[12] Algirdas Šemeta, EU Commissioner, Speech of 19 May 2011; Algirdas Šemeta, EU Commissioner, Speech of 25 May 2011, p 3.

[13] COM (2012) 64 final.

[14] European Parliament, Study 2012, IP/A/IMCO/ST/2011–11, PE 475.094, p 44.

Customs Code was finally adopted on 9 October 2013,[15] although the major part of its provisions – similar to the now repealed Modernised Customs Code – will apply only from 1 June 2016, pursuant to Article 288 paragraph 2 UCC. This deferral of application is to allow adequate time for national administrations and economic operators in the EU to undertake necessary investments as well as to further provide for a realistic, step-by-step implementation of electronic processes.[16]

The European Parliament had already criticised the Modernised Customs Code as being highly ambitious in terms of deadlines, and had expressed its expectation that the new Union Customs Code would improve the current situation and bring clear added value for economic operators in the EU.[17] It had also demanded that when setting a new deadline for the application of the Union Customs Code, this time the technical and financial capabilities of both national administrations and economic operators to deploy new systems should be taken into account.[18] The European Commission has promised to work together with all stakeholders on making the new electronic processing environment operational by 31 December 2020 at the latest.[19]

As announced, the Union Customs Code repeals and replaces the Community Customs Code as well as the Modernised Customs Code[20] and aims to take account of the new institutional framework of the EU as well as to introduce necessary amendments that were revealed in business process analyses undertaken during the drafting process of the implementing provisions.[21] However, although postponing the deadline and recasting the Modernised Customs Code, the European Commission has made it clear that the new Union Customs Code preserves the objectives of the Modernised Customs Code, because these objectives are still required to conform with the existing policies and objectives of the EU customs strategy.[22]

Therefore, the objectives of the Union Customs Code remain the same as in the Modernised Customs Code and are still consistent with the overall objective of the reform process, which is to improve customs services in order to protect the EU and to promote the competitiveness of EU businesses by enhancing efficiency, effectiveness and uniformity. Indeed, the improvement of uniform customs administration by 2020 in particular remains a principal target of the reform process.[23]

[15] Regulation (EU) 952/2013 of the European Parliament and of the Council of 9 October 2013 laying down the Union Customs Code, [2013] OJ L269/1–88.

[16] COM (2012) 64 final, p 3.

[17] European Parliament Resolution of 1 December 2011 (2001/2083(INI)), text adopted P7_TA(2011)0546, para 1.

[18] ibid, para 21.

[19] COM (2012) 64 final, p 3.

[20] ibid, p 4.

[21] COM (2011) 922 final, p 8; Lux, 2012 AW-Prax 8, pp 257–62 (260).

[22] COM (2012) 64 final, p 4.

[23] Lux, 2012 AW-Prax 8, pp 257–62 (258, 259).

I. LEGAL ASPECTS

The Union Customs Code aims to align the provisions of the Modernised Customs Code to the evolution of EU customs and other relevant legislation, especially to adjust the new Code to requirements resulting from the Treaty of Lisbon.

A. The Impact of the Lisbon Treaty

The Treaty of Lisbon,[24] which entered into force on 1 December 2009, has had a major impact on the Customs Code, as it refined the powers and competences with regard to implementation and delegated legislation of the Council, the European Parliament and the European Commission in its Articles 290 and 291 TFEU. Pursuant to this redefinition, the European Commission has been granted delegated and implementing powers. However, there is also scrutiny of the European Commission's exercise of these powers. In fact, the new distinction between these two categories of acts, and their corresponding empowerments, establishes a clear line between acts of a 'quasi-legislative' nature, adopted by the European Commission acting in its delegated capacity and controlled by the Council and the European Parliament in their capacity as EU institutions, and acts of an executive nature, implemented by the European Commission and controlled by the EU Member States with no intervention of the Council or the European Parliament afterwards.[25]

The delegated powers of the European Commission are provided for in Article 290 TFEU, which allows the European Parliament and the Council to delegate to the European Commission power for amending or supplementing certain non-essential elements of legislative acts. Such adopted acts are of general application but a non-legislative nature, and thus are very similar to the type of 'quasi-legislative' measures[26] that were formerly adopted under the regulatory procedure with scrutiny that was introduced by the Council through Council Decision 2006/512/EC[27] amending Council Decision 1999/468/EC[28] (hereinafter: Comitology Decision).

The implementing powers of the European Commission are provided for in Article 291 TFEU, whereby pursuant to paragraph 2, the European Commission

[24] Treaty of Lisbon amending the Treaty on European Union and the Treaty establishing the European Community, signed at Lisbon, 13 December 2007, [2007] OJ C306/1–271.

[25] Grave, (5) 2010 GTCJ (3), pp 95–111 (109, 110).

[26] Grave, (5) 2010 GTCJ (3), pp 95–111 (110).

[27] Council Decision 2006/512/EC of 17 July 2006 amending Council Decision 1999/468/EC laying down the procedures for the exercise of implementing powers conferred on the Commission, [2006] OJ L200/11–13.

[28] Council Decision 1999/468/EC of 28 June 1999 laying down the procedures for the exercise of implementing powers conferred on the Commission, [1999] OJ L184/23–26, and Council Decision 2006/512/EC of 17 July 2006 amending Council Decision 1999/468/EC laying down the procedures for the exercise of implementing powers conferred on the Commission, [2006] OJ L200/11–13.

can adopt implementing acts when they are necessary to ensure uniform conditions for the implementation of legally binding EU acts in the EU Member States. This takes account of the European Commission's need for corresponding implementing powers when obliged to ensure the uniform implementation of EU law.[29]

This important distinction between delegated acts and implementing acts impacts the European Commission's capacity to adopt measures in the future. To implement the Modernised Customs Code after its application deadline had expired, the European Commission would have had to exercise its delegated or implementing powers in accordance with Articles 290 and 291 TFEU and with Regulation (EU) 182/2011[30] (hereinafter: Comitology Regulation), which replaced the Comitology Decision. This is all the more important as the European Commission is still responsible for the pending adaption of necessary implementing provisions to make the new Code applicable. Therefore, the European Commission cannot ignore the new distribution between delegated acts and implementing acts introduced by the Treaty of Lisbon: although the scope of application of Article 290 TFEU versus Article 291 TFEU is quite a controversially debated issue, it is clear that they constitute different kinds of acts, with different control mechanisms and requirements, and thus cannot be mixed.[31]

1. *Differentiation Between Articles 290 and 291 TFEU*

The distinction between legislative and implementing measures can be characterised as determining what should happen in principle, or determining how implementation of the principles will in fact take place.[32] Delegated law-making in the sense of Article 290 TFEU applies to legal acts of the European Commission supplementing or amending legislative acts in a generally applicable way, and thus is a form of substantial tertiary law-making.[33] Implementing acts pursuant to Article 291 TFEU concern the administrative implementation measures that give effect to EU law, in particular the application or enforcement of legal acts, but are not themselves legislative acts pursuant to Article 289 paragraph 3 TFEU.[34] Delegated acts, on the other hand, are formally not legislative acts in the sense of Article 289 paragraph 3 TFEU but will often be legislative in nature.[35] Thus

[29] Grave, (5) 2010 GTCJ (3), pp 95–111 (110).

[30] Regulation (EU) 182/2011 of the European Parliament and of the Council of 16 February 2011 laying down the rules and general principles concerning mechanisms for control by Member States of the Commission's exercise of implementing powers, [2011] OJ L55/13–18.

[31] A detailed analysis of the European Commissions' competences pursuant to Articles 290, 291 TFEU, including control mechanisms and the role of the European Parliament, the Council, and the EU Member States in these mechanisms can be found in Chapter 8.I.B (delegated acts) and Chapter 6.II.A.2 and Chapter 8.II.B (implementing acts).

[32] Hofmann, 2009 ELJ (15), pp 482–505 (490).

[33] Nettesheim, in: Grabitz/Hilf/Nettesheim (eds), 2013, Vol III, Article 290 TFEU, para 19.

[34] Weiß, (2) 2011 JECLAP (5), pp 441–51 (449); Weiß, 2010, p 57; Nettesheim, in: Grabitz/Hilf/Nettesheim (eds), 2013, Vol III, Article 290 TFEU, para 19.

[35] Craig, in: Griller/Ziller (eds), 2008, pp 109–34 (113); Craig, 2010, pp 263, 264.

in hierarchical terms they are more than simple implementing acts, in the sense of Article 291 TFEU.[36] While implementing acts are not a part of EU legislation, delegated acts constitute a new type of delegated law-making without precedent in the former TEC, although its scope of application matches that of the former regulatory procedure with scrutiny pursuant to Article 5a Comitology Decision.[37] Therefore, the Lisbon Treaty now differentiates clearly between, on the one hand, administrative implementing acts pursuant to Article 291 TFEU and, on the other hand, delegated acts pursuant to Article 290 TFEU that constitute a kind of executive EU law-making or 'quasi-legislative'[38] power.[39]

Delegated law-making pursuant to Article 290 TFEU facilitates the modification of legal acts by delegation of non-essential elements to the European Commission, whereas Article 291 TFEU provides implementing competences to the European Commission in light of the necessity for uniform conditions for the correct implementation of EU legal acts.[40] While Article 290 TFEU constitutes a shifting of competences from the EU legislator—the European Parliament and the Council—to the European Commission, Article 291 TFEU constitutes a shifting of competences from the EU Member States to the European Commission, which adopts implementing measures that replace national measures.[41]

Therefore, the European Commission's exercise of its delegated competences as part of EU law-making is politically controlled by the European Parliament and the Council as the EU's legislative organs, whereas the European Commission's competences regarding executive implementation measures underlay the control of the EU Member States, which are normally responsible for the implementation of the EU's legally binding acts. It lies within the discretion of the EU legislator whether to regulate a particular field of action in EU law only partially and delegate to the European Commission the responsibility for supplementation or amendment pursuant to Article 290 TFEU, or whether to enact comprehensive legal acts and entrust the European Commission, where necessary, to ensure their uniform implementation through implementing acts pursuant to Article 291 TFEU.[42]

The functional differentiation between executive law-making pursuant to Article 290 TFEU and administrative implementation measures pursuant to Article 291 TFEU calls for the demarcation of their respective scopes of application.[43] Delegated acts are defined by their scope and consequences, being

[36] Weiß, (2) 2011 JECLAP (5), pp 441–51 (449); Hofmann, 2009 ELJ (15), pp 482–505 (491).

[37] Weiß, 2010, p 57, Hofmann, 2009 ELJ (15), pp 482–505 (494).

[38] COM (2009) 673 final, p 3; Grave, (5) 2010 GTCJ (3), pp 95–111 (110).

[39] Weiß, 2010, pp 57, 58; Bast, 2012 CMLRev (49), pp 885–927 (917).

[40] Weiß, 2010, pp 58, 59.

[41] Stelkens, 2012 EuR 5, pp 511–45 (512).

[42] COM (2009) 673 final, p 4; Weiß, 2010, p 60; Bast, 2012 CMLRev (49), pp 885–927 (921); contra: Hofmann/Türk, 2012 ZG, pp 105–37 (113, 114), who deny a margin of discretion with regard to the choice of the correctly applicable legal basis as the principles regarding the forming of a political will are determined in the Lisbon Treaty.

[43] COM (2009) 673 final, p 3; Bast, 2012 CMLRev (49), pp 885–927 (921); Craig, 2010, p 275.

generally applicable legal acts supplementing or amending a legislative act, whereas implementing acts are determined by the legal requirement for uniform implementation conditions.[44] Furthermore, the European Commission's power to adopt delegated acts pursuant to Article 290 TFEU is of a discretionary nature because it constitutes a 'quasi-legislative' power carried out in the interest of efficiency.[45] Conversely, the European Commission's implementation powers are purely executive and have to be exercised when the conditions of Article 291 TFEU are fulfilled.[46]

However, such a clear differentiation without any overlap is still troublesome, at least when based on pure formal factors, because the European Commission can also issue implementing regulations pursuant to Article 291 TFEU.[47] Indeed, Article 291 TFEU authorises the European Commission either to use measures of an individual nature or to adopt implementing acts of general application, whereas the wording of Article 290 TFEU does not allow the enactment of a delegated act relating to an individual measure.[48]

For a better differentiation between the scope of Article 290 TFEU and Article 291 TFEU, in particular when it comes to a differentiation between a supplementing measure and an implementing measure, the European Commission suggests that the EU legislator should assess whether the future measure will add non-essential rules that change the framework of the basic legislative act and leave a margin of discretion to the European Commission—which would call for a delegation—or if the future measure should only give effect to the existing rules of a legal act—which would call for an implementing act.[49] Implementing powers often concern fields of typical executive nature, such as the concretisation of uncertain legal terms or regulatory structures, while delegated law-making can update, adjust and even to some extent change legal norms.[50] A division of the terrain between delegated and implementing acts, by deciding on whether the measure in question supplements the basic legislative act by adding any new non-essential elements, has also been suggested.[51]

Therefore, it is for the EU legislator, which is the European Parliament and the Council, to decide on the competences of the European Commission to adopt delegated acts or implementing acts, and to lay these competences down in the basic legal act—which in EU customs law is the Customs Code. The different scopes of application of Articles 290 and 291 TFEU require a clear distinction.

[44] ibid, p 3.
[45] ibid, p 3.
[46] ibid, p 3.
[47] Weiß, 2010, pp 59, 60.
[48] COM (2009) 673 final, p 4.
[49] ibid, p 4.
[50] Nettesheim, in: Grabitz/Hilf/Nettesheim (eds), 2013, Vol III, Article 291 TFEU, para 40.
[51] Craig, 2011 ELRev (36), pp 671–87 (673).

2. Need for an Alignment of the Modernised Customs Code

With the adoption of the Comitology Regulation,[52] the pre-existing comitology regime has finally gone.[53] This is of special importance in EU customs law, where the 'Better Regulation' Initiative has led to a simplification of the Customs Code, reducing it to the essential rules of customs legislation. Less important and non-essential elements are to be regulated by the European Commission in separate provisions as required to make the Customs Code's application and implementation possible. Therefore, the new Customs Code is in special need of the delegation of powers pursuant to Article 290 TFEU and for the conferral of implementing powers pursuant to Article 291 TFEU.

However, the Modernised Customs Code, adopted in 2008, did not formally provide for delegated acts but only for implementing measures—see Article 183 MCC. In this context, the Modernised Customs Code instead further referred to the Comitology Decision[54] and its procedures—see Article 184 MCC, which has since been overtaken by the Comitology Regulation. This new Comitology Regulation is only relevant with regard to implementing acts in the sense of Article 291 TFEU, and has no relevance for delegated acts pursuant to Article 290 TFEU—see Article 291 paragraph 3 TFEU. Therefore, the Modernised Customs Code did not distinguish between delegation of powers and conferral of implementing powers but only between implementing measures to be adopted in accordance with the regulatory procedure with scrutiny—see Article 183 paragraph 2 MCC, and other implementing measures—see Article 183 paragraph 1 MCC.

The Customs Code needed to be aligned with the procedural changes in the Lisbon Treaty regarding delegated and implementing powers,[55] contrary to older opinions assessing an alignment of the existing EU customs legislation as unnecessary due to the lack of retroactive effect of the Lisbon Treaty.[56] Although the legal nature of acts adopted under the regulatory procedure with scrutiny pursuant to Article 5a Council Decision 1999/468/EC is similar to the 'quasi-legislative' nature of delegated acts,[57] the former comitology regime cannot be regarded as precedent for the new distinction between delegated and implementing acts.[58] The legal

[52] Regulation (EU) 182/2011 of the European Parliament and of the Council of 16 February 2011 laying down the rules and general principles concerning mechanisms for control by Member States of the Commission's exercise of implementing powers, [2011] OJ L55/13–18.

[53] Craig, 2011 ELRev (36), pp 671–87 (671).

[54] Council Decision 1999/468/EC of 28 June 1999 laying down the procedures for the exercise of implementing powers conferred on the Commission, [1999] OJ L184/23–26, and Council Decision 2006/512/EC of 17 July 2006 amending Council Decision 1999/468/EC laying down the procedures for the exercise of implementing powers conferred on the Commission, [2006] OJ L200/11–13.

[55] Grave, (5) 2010 GTCJ (3), pp 95–111 (110); Reuter, 2012 ZfZ 6, pp 147–50 (150); Lux, 2012 AW-Prax 8, pp 257–62 (260).

[56] Fuchs, 2011 ZfZ 11, pp 281–88 (284).

[57] Grave, (5) 2010 GTCJ (3), pp 95–111 (110).

[58] European Parliament, 'Alignment of legal acts to the new Comitology Decision', P6_TA(2008)0424, European Parliament resolution of 23 September 2008 with recommendations to the Commission on the alignment of legal acts to the new Comitology Decision (2008/2096(INI)) (2010/C 8 E/05), [2010] OJ C8E/22–25, p 23; Craig, 2011 ELRev (36), pp 671–87 (676).

requirements for a basic legislative act, in the sense of Article 290 TFEU, require an explicit delegation of competence.[59] In the end, the divide between delegated and implementing acts is even more significant as the divide between regulatory procedures with scrutiny and other comitology procedures. It is now embodied in primary EU law and thus also has constitutional significance.[60]

As a consequence, the Modernised Customs Code did not fulfil the requirements of a basic legislative act in the sense of Article 290 TFEU, and the provisions in the Modernised Customs Code referring to the regulatory procedure with scrutiny could not be reinterpreted into a delegation of powers. Therefore, the European Commission would have been unable to adopt the necessary delegated acts based on the Modernised Customs Code as the basic legal act in the sense of Article 290 TFEU.

The European Parliament has indeed already expressed its high opinion of the new procedural changes, pointing out that the new system of delegation powers and granting of implementation powers is representative of a newly established balance between itself and the Council.[61] It has therefore welcomed the alignment of the provisions of the Modernised Customs Code with the Treaty of Lisbon.[62]

Thus, the Modernised Customs Code had to be updated to refer to the new system of delegated and implementing acts, although the Comitology Regulation maintained the effects of the regulatory procedure with scrutiny for affected legal acts adopted before the entry into force of the Lisbon Treaty,[63] see Article 12 Regulation (EU) 182/2011. The needs that governed the new alignment were: the provision of exhaustive empowerments in terms of delegated and implementing powers, because general provisions such as Article 143 MCC did not meet the requirements of Articles 290 and 291 TFEU; the provision of coherent types of empowerments for the setting of delegated and implementing acts; and the introduction of new provisions for a complete framework of empowerments because delegations have to refer to substantive provisions.[64]

The necessary alignments with regard to delegation of power in the sense of Article 290 TFEU have led to 39 additional articles in the Union Customs Code. Even more provisions were added were added concerning the conferral of implementing powers in the sense of Article 291 TFEU. This extensive reference to conferral of implementing powers that can be seen in Recital (5) UCC and the corresponding 48 articles in the Union Customs Code clearly show that the European Commission will be able to ensure uniform implementing conditions in the administration of EU customs. The underlying strategy herein is to use

[59] Hofmann/Rowe/Türk, 2011, p 524.

[60] Craig, 2011 ELRev (36), pp 671–87 (677).

[61] European Parliament Resolution of 1 December 2011 (2001/2083(INI)), text adopted P7_TA(2011)0546, para 22.

[62] ibid, para 22.

[63] Craig, 2011 ELRev (36), pp 671–87 (675).

[64] European Commission, Presentation 'Union Customs Code (recast)', 26 April 2012, slide 6.

increasingly detailed provisions in EU customs law as an instrument to limit margins of discretion in order to enhance uniform customs administration.[65]

3. *Impact of the Lisbon Treaty on the Modernised Customs Code Implementing Provisions*

The new rules also have consequences for the drafting of the Modernised Customs Code Implementing Regulation, because those implementing provisions still have to be adopted by the European Commission and thus have to be directly linked to the new Union Customs Code. However, due to the major differences between the adoption procedures for delegated acts after Article 290 TFEU and implementing acts after Article 291 TFEU together with the Comitology Regulation, the grouping of their provisions in a single instrument such as the MCCIP is excluded.[66]

Therefore, as a further consequence of the Lisbon Treaty, the draft MCCIP of the European Commission has to be split into two acts depending on the kind of powers exercised by the European Commission when adopting it: one delegated act and one implementing act.[67] This requires the identification of the implementing provisions' legal nature, whether they result in either an implementing act or delegated act as determined by the defined empowerments in the Union Customs Code.[68] As a basis for the implementing and delegated acts, the European Commission has already decided to use a completed draft of the preliminary MCCIP.[69]

B. Other Changes in the Union Customs Code

Besides the alignment with the Lisbon Treaty and postponing the deadline for application, there was also a need to align some provisions of the Modernised Customs Code with changes in EU legislation following its coming into force in 2008 in order to take into account the evolution of legislation in other policy fields such as transport safety and security.[70] Furthermore, anticipated relevant developments had to be considered in adjusting the Customs Code to possible future amendments in given policy fields, such as aviation security.[71]

Moreover, the Modernised Customs Code needed to be aligned to the results of the work being carried out while drafting the implementing provisions and

[65] Lux, 2012 AW-Prax 8, pp 257–62 (258).

[66] Grave, (5) 2010 GTCJ (3), pp 95–111 (111); Reuter, 2012 ZfZ 6, pp 147–50 (149).

[67] See the announcement of the 'splitting exercise' in the current preliminary draft, last version (situation as of 31.12.2013): Consolidated preliminary draft of the MCCIP of 25 November 2011, Document TAXUD/MCCIP/2010/100–3, p 3 'legal follow-up'.

[68] See the statements of DG TAXUD in: European Parliament, Study 2012, IP/A/IMCO/ST/2011–11, PE 475.094, p 45.

[69] See the statements of DG TAXUD in: ibid, p 46.

[70] COM (2012) 64 final, p 3.

[71] ibid, p 6.

establishing the Business Process Models. This work had revealed a lack of compatibility between the text of some Modernised Customs Code provisions and the actual functioning of customs procedures in certain customs areas,[72] such as temporary storage or invalidating entry and exit summary declarations.[73] According to the European Commission, attempts were made to limit such alignments to those absolute necessary for streamlining or for ensuring consistency between EU customs law and operational processes.[74] These corrections were introduced in the Union Customs Code in order to allow the phased, binding and realistic implementation of the new electronic-based customs processes.

Additionally, some editorial changes to the wording of the Modernised Customs Code were needed, sometimes to correct simple typing errors but also to fix incorrect references as well as updating of references due to the Lisbon Treaty and other legislative acts, relocate incorrectly placed provisions, and resolve the inconsistent use of terms.[75] The European Commission also proposed some substantive changes with regard to single provisions,[76] though in most of its parts the Union Customs Code mirrors the Modernised Customs Code with regard to its substantive contents.

Material problems had been discovered in the area of security, while some doubt was cast on whether the concepts of centralised customs clearance[77] as well as self-assessment[78] would actually facilitate trade, as customs controls must still be guaranteed in order to protect the EU and its citizens.[79] In this context, European business organisations were concerned about the modifications in Article 138 of the UCC proposal regarding the concept of centralised customs clearance.[80] These modifications indicated a lack of willingness to further harmonise customs procedures and customs controls as required, as they introduced a two-step clearance procedure[81] that would have forced economic operators to

[72] ibid, p 3; Zeilinger, in: Koszinowski (ed.), 2013, pp 103–07 (143).

[73] COM (2012) 64 final, p 6; European Commission, Presentation 'Union Customs Code (recast)', 26 April 2012, slide 7; Zeilinger, in: Koszinowski (ed), 2013, pp 103–07 (143).

[74] COM (2012) 64 final, p 6.

[75] ibid, p 6; Zeilinger, in: Koszinowski (ed), 2013, pp 103–07 (143); Lux, 2012 AW-Prax 8, pp 257–62 (260).

[76] Zeilinger, in: Koszinowski (ed.), 2013, pp 103–07 (143).

[77] The concept of 'centralised customs clearance' allows authorised operators to lodge their electronic customs declarations at the customs office of the place where they are established, irrespective of where their goods physically enter or leave the customs territory of the EU or where their forms need to be presented to European customs authorities; see: Lux, AW-Prax 8, pp 257–62 (260).

[78] 'Self-assessment' introduces a kind of quasi-statutory work that the economic operator will be allowed to carry out instead of the customs authority, which enables further simplifications of customs formalities as well as customs controls; see: Henke, in: Witte/Henke/Kammerzell (eds), 2009, p 138.

[79] See the statements of national customs authorities in: European Parliament, Study 2012, IP/A/IMCO/ST/2011–11, PE 475.094, p 46.

[80] Trade Contact Group, Statement, 30 May 2012, p 1.

[81] AmCham EU, Position Statement, 25 May 2012, p 6; for the main changes in the concept of centralised customs clearance see also European Commission, Presentation 'Union Customs Code (recast)', 26 April 2012, slide 8.

send the required customs clearance information to multiple customs authorities in different EU Member States. This would have taken away one of the biggest advantages for EU businesses as foreseen in the Modernised Customs Code, resulting in increased complexity in business operations and reducing efficiency through duplication of entry processing and customs controls, possible delays and the need for representation in two places.[82]

However, the European Parliament has called on the EU Member States to adhere fully to the concept of centralised customs clearance, in view of its importance for consistency in the management of the EU's external borders and the harmonisation of customs control systems.[83] It further pointed out the special importance of the concept of centralised customs clearance, with its corresponding information exchange systems and data formats, in the modernisation process of EU customs.[84] Therefore, it demanded a return to the original concept of Article 106 MCC, wherein the supervising customs office at which the customs declaration is lodged was authorised to decide about the release of goods, and the presentation office at which the goods are presented would carry out only security and safety inspections.[85] The final Article 179 UCC once again meets these requirements.

Nevertheless, the concept of centralised customs clearance requires further elaboration,[86] especially in the context of other fields of taxation such as value added tax. This is required to provide more benefits for trade through the development towards the concept of the Single Window[87] – a proposition which is also suggested and supported by the European Parliament.[88] However, the complexity of the aspirational combination of centralised customs clearance and VAT will make its implementation difficult, even by the year 2020.[89]

Altogether, European business organisations still support the modernisation of the EU customs legal framework,[90] in particular the creation of a paperless environment for customs and trade. Furthermore, they stress the following conditions

[82] AmCham EU, Position Statement, 25 May 2012, p 6.

[83] European Parliament Resolution of 1 December 2011 (2001/2083(INI)), text adopted P7_TA(2011)0546, paras 24, 26; Lux, AW-Prax 8, pp 257–62 (260).

[84] European Parliament Resolution of 1 December 2011 (2001/2083(INI)), text adopted P7_TA(2011)0546, paras 24–28.

[85] European Parliament, First Reading Report of 26 February 2013, A7–0006/2013, Amendments 90, 91, 92, pp 62, 63, 63.

[86] Lux, 2012 AW-Prax 8, pp 257–62 (260).

[87] The concept of a 'Single Window' allows standardised information and documents to be submitted to a single electronic entry point to fulfil all regulatory requirements related to import, export and transit, so individual data items need be submitted only once; once this standardised information is electronically delivered to the single portal it is made available to all relevant authorities; see: Lux, 2012 AW-Prax 8, pp 257–62 (259).

[88] European Parliament Resolution of 1 December 2011 (2001/2083(INI)), text adopted P7_TA(2011)0546, paras 25, 27, 66; see also European Parliament, Study 2012, IP/A/IMCO/ST/2011–11, PE 475.094, p 42.

[89] Lux, 2012 AW-Prax 8, pp 257–62 (260).

[90] Trade Contact Group, Statement, 30 May 2012, p 1.

to ensure trade facilitation: the streamlining of common procedures, the introduction of a comprehensive single guarantee for all procedures, the simplification of customs clearance procedures, the concept of authorised economic operator,[91] the maintenance of the possibility for customs representation, and the promotion of computerisation of information exchange, of facilitation through a trusted operator programme, and of the validity of customs decisions throughout the EU.[92]

C. New Timing for the Legal Reform

Unfortunately, there are still legal issues that could prevent the timely adoption of the implementing provisions and the application of the Union Customs Code, as well as hinder the effectiveness of the legal overhaul of the Customs Code and its implementing provisions.

The European Commission does not think that splitting the Modernised Customs Code implementing provisions into a delegated act and an implementing act will be time-consuming once the implementing provisions are finally drafted. Indeed, in their opinion, such preparation could be completed within six month to one year after the adoption of the new Union Customs Code.[93] However, no final version of the draft MCCIP is yet available.[94] A European Parliament study of February 2012 came to the conclusion that the drafting of the final legal texts alone would, in the best case scenario, be completed in December 2013, while in the worst case completion being envisioned for 2017.[95]

Customs officials in the United Kingdom have expressed concern about the slow progress with the drafting of the implementing provisions:

> So we are at the moment a little bit sitting in no-man's land. There is absolutely no clear guidance, because realistically that date [24 June 2013] is not achievable and I think everybody would admit that, but there is nothing physically coming out from the whole package saying 'right this is now going to be the date – 2015, 2014,' because they are looking at options as to whether they can introduce parts of the implementing regulations but leave out some of the IT issues, the difficult pieces, which should have been taken in time, or whether they should delay the entire package … So they are really in, well, like caught up in a mess really.[96]

[91] 'Authorised economic operator' (AEO) is a new status for economic operators combining procedural simplifications with aspects of safety and security, facilitating easier customs handling because the AEO programme is to be of significant importance for determining the intensity of customs controls; see: Lux, 2012 AW-Prax 8, pp 257–62 (259).

[92] See the statements of European business organisations in: European Parliament, Study 2012, IP/A/IMCO/ST/2011–11, PE 475.094, pp 47, 48.

[93] See the statements of DG TAXUD in: European Parliament, Study 2012, IP/A/IMCO/ST/2011–11, PE 475.094, p 46.

[94] Situation as of 31.12.2013.

[95] European Parliament, Study 2012, IP/A/IMCO/ST/2011–11, PE 475.094, p 10, figure 1.

[96] Interview of 10 January 2012 on file with author.

Furthermore, because there is a lack of information on the final text of the new implementing provisions, it is unknown what changes might be needed to national legislation. Indeed, customs officials of the German customs administration have been quite concerned about this lack of information.[97] Although the Union Customs Code and its implementing provisions will be regulations of the EU, and therefore directly applicable in EU Member States, certain aspects still need to be further specified in national legislation for their implementation, including issues such as direct representation, administrative fines and penalties, or the organisation of the national customs administration in the EU Member States.[98]

In addition to the lack of the delegated and implementing act of the Union Customs Code's implementing provisions, there is also still the need for agreed upon Business Process Models and technical EU IT specifications.[99] Indeed, in the opinion of some EU Member States' national customs authorities, the ongoing work on the development and adjustment of the necessary IT systems is the main reason for the delay in implementing the reform.[100] Unfortunately, it seems the implementation of the European IT architecture will not be completed even by 2020.[101]

Moreover, questions have also been raised regarding the legal reform of EU customs law effectiveness in simplifying procedures.[102] A European Parliament study has revealed EU Member States' national customs authorities are concerned about processes provided for in the Modernised Customs Code and the preliminary draft of its implementing provisions, in particular regarding the communication between EU Member States authorities.[103] At the same time, the European Parliament had stressed the importance of formal mechanisms being installed in all EU Member States for transparent dialogue between customs administrations and the private sector.[104] It has further called for the identification and promotion of best

[97] 'Das Problem ist natürlich, dass die Durchführungsverordnung noch nicht existiert, wir noch nicht einmal genau wissen: Wie wird dieser Antrag aussehen? Wie lange werden die Felder sein? Können elektronische Dokumente und Bilder mit geschickt werden in dem Antrag? Auch viele Rechtsnormen sind einfach noch nicht umgesetzt, wo wir noch nicht entscheiden können wie machen wir das.'; interview of 13 April 2011 on file with author.

[98] See the statements of national customs authorities in: European Parliament, Study 2012, IP/A/IMCO/ST/2011–11, PE 475.094, p 46.

[99] MASP 2013 Revision, Taxud.a.3 (2013) 3763373, p 13; MASP 2012 Revision, TAXUD.a.3 ARES (2012) 1677638, p 16; see also the statements of national customs authorities in: European Parliament, Study 2012, IP/A/IMCO/ST/2011–11, PE 475.094, p 46; MASP 2013 Revision, Taxud.a.3 (2013) 3763373, p 12; MASP 2012 Revision, TAXUD.a.3 ARES (2012) 1677638, p 15.

[100] See the statements of national customs authorities in: European Parliament, Study 2012, IP/A/IMCO/ST/2011–11, PE 475.094, p 46.

[101] Lux, 2012 AW-Prax 8, pp 257–62 (260).

[102] Trade Contact Group, Statement, 30 May 2012, p 1.

[103] See the statements of national customs authorities in: European Parliament, Study 2012, IP/A/IMCO/ST/2011–11, PE 475.094, p 46.

[104] European Parliament Resolution of 1 December 2011 (2001/2083(INI)), text adopted P7_TA(2011)0546, paras 65, 69, 71, 73.

practices for cooperation also within customs and the establishment of common operational platforms, as well as improvement in the organisation of customs procedures at the EU's external borders.[105]

D. Conclusion

In conclusion, the success of the legal reform cannot yet be evaluated because it depends on the success of its implementation process, in particular the final implementing provisions of the Union Customs Code as well as effective Business Process Models and the necessary IT systems.

Nevertheless, the importance of the modernisation of EU customs argues against delaying the legal implementation until all the required IT systems come into operation.[106] The modernisation of EU customs is too important to put off legal implementation until all the IT systems are ready, which in the worst case could mean delaying the application of the Union Customs Code until 2020 or even later. Therefore, a phased implementation with simultaneous work streams for legal, IT and operational aspects has been considered in order to realise the gradual implementation of the Union Customs Code.[107] The European Commission has stated that such a phased implementation would require transitional measures during the development of the necessary supporting IT systems, as most provisions involve the use of data processing techniques pursuant to the basic principle in Article 6 paragraph 1 UCC.[108] Indeed Article 278 UCC does now provide, until 31 December 2020, for the possibility of such arrangements for a transitional period in the event that necessary IT systems are not operational in a timely manner. The European Commission has already indicated that the implementation will presumably start once significant parts of the necessary IT support systems are available.[109]

However, the Union Customs Code can only achieve its maximum potential once it is fully supported by properly developed and sophisticated IT systems, as required by the great reform of EU customs.[110] The main articles totally dependent on new IT systems before coming into operation are Article 6 paragraph 1 UCC, on the exchange and storage of data, Article 16 paragraph 1 UCC, on electronic systems, and Article 179 UCC, on centralised customs clearance.[111] Article 109 MCC on the different types of customs declarations and their strong dependence of electronic processing techniques has not been brought into the

[105] ibid, paras 65, 69, 71, 73.

[106] European Parliament, Study 2012, IP/A/IMCO/ST/2011–11, PE 475.094, p 75.

[107] ibid, p 10.

[108] See the statements of DG TAXUD in: European Parliament, Study 2012, IP/A/IMCO/ST/2011–11, PE 475.094, p 48.

[109] See the statements of DG TAXUD in: ibid, p 49.

[110] European Parliament Resolution of 1 December 2011 (2001/2083(INI)), text adopted P7_TA(2011)0546, para 20.

[111] European Parliament, Study 2012, IP/A/IMCO/ST/2011–11, PE 475.094, p 74.

Union Customs Code. Furthermore, transitional solutions require a mix of automated and manual customs processes, adding financial burdens, and therefore are not in favour of either European businesses or EU Member States' customs administrations.[112] Therefore, the actual benefit of a phased implementation of the Union Customs Code has to be carefully calculated given the potentially expensive interim solutions.

II. IT ASPECTS

A major challenge for the implementation of the Union Custom Code is the overall introduction of electronic data-processing techniques, as required by the e-customs Decision. The European Commission now has plans for an update of the e-customs Decision in order to align it with the Lisbon Treaty,[113] just as it updated the Modernised Customs Code earlier.

The e-customs Decision and the Union Customs Code are linked pursuant to Article 16 UCC regarding electronic systems in the customs administration, and pursuant to Article 6 paragraph 1 UCC regarding electronic data exchange and the setting up of IT systems on whose support certain key provisions of modern EU customs law strongly depend.[114] This aspect relates to the majority of the Union Customs Code, as was the case with the Modernised Customs Code: the implementation of more than half of the chapters of the Modernised Customs Code needed IT-related action on the EU level.[115] The Union Customs Code does not renounce this strong IT dependence, given its major benefits, not least the arrangement of a proper balance between security and trade considerations through a truly modern customs environment that improves uniform customs administration.

The European Commission has indeed ensured that the Union Customs Code avoids introducing fundamental changes to the Modernised Customs Code. Changes made are limited to those required by the Lisbon Treaty, as well as some necessary but minor corrections.[116] Thereby the European commission is not throwing away all the past work invested in drafting customs legislation that matches the reality of both the economic operators and the customs administrations in the EU.[117]

[112] AmCham EU, Information Paper, 5 August 2011, p 4.

[113] DG Taxation and Customs Union Management Plan 2012, p 27; DG Taxation and Customs Union Management Plan 2013, p 35. The latest version of the MASP 2013 Revision is still referring to the e-customs Decision of 2008, see MASP 2013 Revision, Taxud.a.3 (2013) 3763373, p 5.

[114] European Parliament, Study 2012, IP/A/IMCO/ST/2011–11, PE 475.094, p 50.

[115] See the statements of DG TAXUD in: European Parliament, Study 2012, IP/A/IMCO/ST/2011–11, PE 475.094, p 51.

[116] COM (2012) 64 final, p 6; AmCham EU, Position Statement, 25 May 2012, p 2.

[117] Algirdas Šemeta, EU Commissioner, Speech of 19 May 2011; Algirdas Šemeta, EU Commissioner, Speech of 25 May 2011, p 3; see also European Commission, Presentation 'Union Customs Code (recast)', 26 April 2012, slide 4.

However, the newly introduced Article 6 paragraph 4 UCC allows for derogation from the previously unconditional basic principle of electronic data exchange, which is not without problems. The former Article 5 MCC was highly ambitious in constituting an underpinning principle that introduced the mandatory and unconditional use of electronic data exchange between customs authorities and economic operators for various processes.[118] Nevertheless, the provision was also considered to be vital for the modernisation process of EU customs in its creation of an unambiguous operating environment with clear procedures in terms of customs processes based on electronic exchange; therefore it was highly welcomed by customs administrations as well as economic operators.[119] Article 6 paragraph 4 UCC undermines the broad goal of EU customs modernisation, as well as one of the basic principles of contemporary EU customs law, to create a modern and paperless environment for customs processes in the EU. It also constitutes a potential risk to uniform customs administration throughout the EU by allowing the customs administrations of the EU Customs Union to potentially work at different speeds even though their customs authorities are mandated to act as if they were one.[120]

Furthermore, the provision introduces an obstacle to the concept of centralised customs clearance[121] in the EU, resulting in a decentralisation of centralised customs clearance despite its importance in the modernisation of EU customs.[122] Thus, it maintains the need for economic operators to have duplicate processes in place, paper-based procedures as well as electronic-based ones, which not only works against trade facilitation but also constitutes a disadvantage for the competitiveness of the EU Customs Union vis-á-vis other important trade blocs such as the United States or China.[123] By enabling the European Commission to exclude one or more EU Member States from the standardisation of customs IT systems if the European Commission is convinced such need exists, Article 6 paragraph 4 UCC overthrows one of the basic pillars of the Modernised Customs Code.[124] Yet in this context, the European Parliament has expressed its conviction that a modern EU customs law can reach its full potential only if supported by proper IT systems.[125]

[118] AmCham EU, Position Statement, 25 May 2012, p 12.
[119] ibid, p 12.
[120] ibid, p 12.
[121] The concept of 'centralised customs clearance' allows authorised operators to lodge their electronic customs declarations at the customs office of the place where they are established, irrespective of where their goods physically enter or leave the customs territory of the EU or where their forms need to be presented to European customs authorities; see: Lux, 2012 AW-Prax 8, pp 257–62 (260).
[122] Trade Contact Group, Statement, 30 May 2012, p 1.
[123] AmCham EU, Position Statement, 25 May 2012, p 13.
[124] ibid, p 2.
[125] European Parliament Resolution of 1 December 2011 (2001/2083(INI)), text adopted P7_TA(2011)0546, paras 6, 20.

A. Centralised IT Approach

One of the most challenging technical aspects remains the concern that differences between EU Member States' national IT solutions could lead to non-uniform output. Because of this, business organisations have called for an overall EU approach with one platform for uniform IT implementation.[126] Yet currently the IT solutions for external communication with economic operators and for the operation of controls are the national responsibility of the EU Member States. For this reason, even minor IT changes often need to be installed in the 28 different IT systems of 28 different customs administrations, with even the lead-time of such an action taking up to two years. This results in IT implementation in EU customs progressing at different paces in different EU Member States and customs administrations not always being able to realise time-savings, cost-savings and—most importantly—to ensure the uniform administration of EU customs law throughout the EU.[127]

Therefore, the European Commission is considering a more centralised approach regarding the electronic customs environment, with more human and financial resources on the EU level, as well as further harmonisation in technical requirements.[128] Possible centralisation solutions range from having one centralised IT system on the EU level, to the sharing of existing national or new IT systems between several EU Member States.[129] These are to be developed in an evolutionary process, leading to reductions in lead-time and cost for the implementation of the IT changes.[130] Once established, these will allow economic operators to use one system-interface that is identical in all EU Member States.[131] On the national level, such an EU centralised IT system will at least require interfacing software to connect them with economic operators.[132]

However, the feasibility of a centralised IT approach has been questioned by specialists of IT companies.[133] The centralisation of customs IT solutions will not necessarily lead to equal treatment and identical outcomes throughout the EU: enhancing efficiency, effectiveness and uniformity in the administration of EU customs law is complicated at any rate, as the situations of small and large EU Member States differ greatly. Therefore one IT solution may perhaps not fit them all.[134]

[126] See the statements of European and national business organisations in: European Parliament, Study 2012, IP/A/IMCO/ST/2011–11, PE 475.094, pp 52 and 53.

[127] European Parliament, Study 2012, IP/A/IMCO/ST/2011–11, PE 475.094, p 76.

[128] See the statements of DG TAXUD in: European Parliament, Study 2012, IP/A/IMCO/ST/2011–11, PE 475.094, p 55.

[129] European Parliament, Study 2012, IP/A/IMCO/ST/2011–11, PE 475.094, p 76.

[130] ibid, p 76.

[131] ibid, p 76.

[132] ibid, p 77.

[133] ibid, p 76.

[134] See the statements of IT specialists in: ibid, p 56.

Furthermore, the European Commission admits has neither the resources nor the expertise to manage and operate such a centralised approach. The technology certainly exists, but the implementation of an EU centralised IT system would require significant harmonisation of standardised procedures, data elements and interfaces, and especially national IT implementing measures;[135] it follows that an EU centralised IT system is currently not a viable option.

At the very least, the harmonisation and standardisation of interfaces is considered to be a crucial step for uniform customs administration.[136] The harmonisation of interfaces for communication between the IT systems of EU economic operators and national customs would dispense with the need for traders to provide connections with different specifications in several EU Member States.[137] However, the goal of a universal system to solve all problems has again been criticised by IT specialists, who warn of its impossibility and thus failure, and therefore suggest an alignment of interfaces focusing on interoperability and standardisation.[138] It has also been emphasised that such standardisation should not constitute a restriction to a single standard, but should offer a variety of options for electronic data transfers with European customs IT systems.[139]

Indeed, the improvement of existing IT systems and their interoperability has been given a high priority by the European Commission, which plans thereby to ensure the quality of customs operations as a shared responsibility with the EU Member States.[140] There are plans to integrate a new division of responsibilities between the EU Member States and the European Commission in an update of the e-customs Decision. This plan is to facilitate further harmonisation in future developments by building systems with a unique interface for economic operators enhancing collaboration between groups of EU Member States to the maximum level possible.[141]

B. IT Strategy for Trans-European Networks

Regarding the development and implementation of the necessary trans-European IT systems, the only systems existing at present are the New Computerised Transit Systems (NCTS and NCTS-TIR-RU) and the Export Control System (ECS)

[135] See the statements of DG TAXUD in: ibid, p 57.

[136] Lux, 2012 AW-Prax 8, pp 257—262 (259); similar European Parliament, Study 2012, IP/A/IMCO/ST/2011–11, PE 475.094, p 78.

[137] See the statements of DG TAXUD and European Business in: European Parliament, Study 2012, IP/A/IMCO/ST/2011–11, PE 475.094, p 59, see also p 60, figure 12.

[138] See the statements of IT specialists in: ibid, p 60.

[139] European Parliament, Study 2012, IP/A/IMCO/ST/2011–11, PE 475.094, p 78 and the statements of IT specialists in: ibid, p 60.

[140] See the statements of DGTAXUD in: ibid, p 62.

[141] DG Taxation and Customs Union Management Plan 2012, p 27; DG Taxation and Customs Union Management Plan 2013, p 35.

as well as the Import Control System (ICS).[142] These systems were adapted for the national level in implementing the Security Amendment of the Community Customs Code of 2005 over a timespan of almost six years. The implementation of other trans-European IT systems will most likely take a similar timespan of several years. However, to develop new trans-European IT systems on a national level, the national customs administrations need sufficient information about the Business Process Models and technical specifications as well as user requirements and a clear IT strategy.[143] Therefore, the expectations of being able to introduce even one new IT system by 2020 are low.[144]

An agreed IT strategy, laying down the future IT architecture and technical IT implementation as well as the harmonisation and standardisation of interfaces, is indeed of high importance for the success of the Electronic Customs Initiative and the implementation of the Union Customs Code.[145] Therefore, the European Commission is obliged to adopt a work programme for the IT aspects of the implementation of the modernisation process, in particular the development and deployment of the necessary electronic customs systems by 1 May 2014, pursuant to Article 280 UCC. This work programme is to be based on an IT Master plan[146] that the European Commission is developing in three iterations,[147] yet a final draft is still missing.[148] The further development and implementation of trans-European IT systems will also be supported in the customs 2020 programme.[149]

Past IT implementation projects have made it clear that robust timing is essential. Serious problems had been reported when relying on simply making up time for delays in the early stages by reducing the time for later implementation stages.[150] Such an approach does not work for meeting the original timeline and therefore cannot be the solution for implementation problems.[151] Furthermore, the more IT systems need to be developed or adapted, and the higher their

[142] MASP 2013 Revision, Taxud.a.3 (2013) 3763373, p 4; MASP 2012 Revision, TAXUD.a.3 ARES (2012) 1677638, p 5.

[143] See the statements of customs authorities in: European Parliament, Study 2012, IP/A/IMCO/ST/2011–11, PE 475.094, p 57.

[144] Lux, 2012 AW-Prax 8, pp 257–62 (260).

[145] European Parliament, Study 2012, IP/A/IMCO/ST/2011–11, PE 475.094, pp 9, 50, 75, 95, 98 and see also the statements of DG TAXUD and national customs authorities at pp 52, 53.

[146] European Commission, Presentation 'Union Customs Code (recast)', 26 April 2012, slides 5 and 10.

[147] See the statements of DG TAXUD in: European Parliament, Study 2012, IP/A/IMCO/ST/2011–11, PE 475.094, p 51; also DG Taxation and Customs Union Management Plan 2012, p 4, and DG Taxation and Customs Union Management Plan 2013, p 5.

[148] MASP 2013 Revision, Taxud.a.3 (2013) 3763373, p 13; MASP 2012 Revision, TAXUD.a.3 ARES (2012) 1677638, p 16.

[149] Future programme (situation as of 31.12.2013): Regulation (EU) 1294/2013 of the European Parliament and of the Council of 11 December 2013 establishing an action programme for customs in the European Union for the period 2014–2020 (Customs 2020) and repealing Decision 624/2007/EC, [2013] OJ L347/209–20. For a detailed analysis of the benefits the Customs Action Programme provides for uniform customs administration, see Chapter 7.IV.

[150] European Parliament, Study 2012, IP/A/IMCO/ST/2011–11, PE 475.094, p 83.

[151] ibid, p 83.

complexity, the more time is required for achieving full IT implementation.[152] Therefore, the IT implementation of the Union Customs Code will be a bigger challenge and more time-consuming than former projects, because the IT systems implemented in the Security Amendment of the Community Customs Code only targeted specific customs areas, while the IT systems required for the application of the Union Customs Code deal with the whole administration of EU customs.[153] The estimated timing in this respect ranges from December 2017 in the best case, to March 2030 in the worst case.[154]

C. Conclusion

In conclusion, the implementation of the Union Customs Code still depends on supporting IT solutions, but not as strongly as the Modernised Customs Code did. Article 6 paragraph 1 UCC clearly communicates the spirit of the e-customs Decision by dictating the use of electronic data processing techniques, and the ongoing work of the European Commission on an overall IT strategy as well as their plans for an alignment of the e-customs Decision with the Lisbon Treaty prove the importance of IT technical matters for the great reform process and its implementation. The timing for the full implementation of Article 6 paragraph 1 UCC depends on important strategic decisions about the IT policy of the EU, including the envisaged IT architecture. Therefore, the determination of a common IT strategy is the fundamental requirement for creating a coherent IT approach for the European Customs Union in the spirit of the e-customs Decision and to implement the Union Customs Code in the full meaning of Article 6 paragraph 1 UCC.

III. OPERATIONAL ASPECTS

The implementation of the Union Customs Code depends greatly on the completion of the necessary legal and IT related aspects, but not exclusively so. Operational requirements also have to be taken into account in order to achieve full and uniform application of the new Customs Code;[155] they make an essential contribution to the overall goal of the reform to ensure protection of the EU while enhancing the competitiveness of EU businesses through efficient, effective and uniform customs administrations.[156] The realisation of these benefits is essential for the acceptance of the new Customs Code by economic operators, who must not only be fully aware of its expected impact, but also expect to benefit from it.[157]

[152] ibid, p 87.
[153] ibid, p 87.
[154] ibid, p 87, figure 17.
[155] ibid, p 79; Lux, 2012 AW-Prax 8, pp 257–62 (257).
[156] European Parliament, Study 2012, IP/A/IMCO/ST/2011–11, PE 475.094, p 79.
[157] ibid, p 80.

Regarding the uniform administration of the Union Customs Code in all EU Member States, it is of utmost importance to provide for correct, timely and sufficient information and communication with all stakeholders as well as for guidelines to align national working instructions and training of relevant staff.[158] Indeed, the scope of operational implementation of the Union Customs Code consists mainly of training people and providing information, whereas the main responsibility of the European Commission is to ensure that all stakeholders get the required information in sufficient time to be able to provide for the application of the new Customs Code.[159] The operational part of such actions will again to a large extent consist of training people, which in the EU is a main responsibility of the national customs administrations that have almost all operational power in EU customs. The operational implementation of the Union Customs Code and in particular the timing of such a process greatly depends on the legal and IT aspects of the reform, because in order to adapt and take the required actions, the national customs administrations and economic operators need information about the final version of the legal and technical aspects of the implementing provisions, Business Process Models, supporting IT systems, and so on.[160]

According to the European Court of Auditors, the minimum requirements for the implementation of the Union Customs Code are the preparation of the customs officials that have to use the new systems, the certification of economic operators and the realisation of the change in the paradigm of customs.[161] Certification of economic operators means the application of a system to grant the status of authorised economic operator,[162] while the change in customs paradigm means the shifting towards fewer controls during clearance and more post-clearance controls.[163] The required operational action on the level of national customs authorities will involve a certain amount of training, including e-learning, but will also consist of adjusting pre-printed forms and official instructions, change of working procedures and alignment of the current authorisations with the new EU customs legislation, and even organisational changes in the competences of national customs authorities.[164] The European Commission's responsibility lies in the preparation of guidelines for the national customs authorities that are to be incorporated into national working instructions, the monitoring and maintenance of IT systems, and communications with all stakeholders.[165]

158 ibid, p 80.

159 ibid, p 66.

160 ibid, p 66.

161 See the statements of the European Court of Auditors in: ibid, p 69.

162 'Authorised economic operator' (AEO) is a new status for economic operators combining procedural simplifications with aspects of safety and security, facilitating easier customs handling because the AEO programme is to be of significant importance for determining the intensity of customs controls; see: Lux, 2012 AW-Prax 8, pp 257–62 (259).

163 See the statements of the European Court of Auditors in: European Parliament, Study 2012, IP/A/IMCO/ST/2011–11, PE 475.094, p 69, fn 96.

164 See the statements of customs authorities in: ibid, p 67.

165 See the statements of DG TAXUD in: ibid, p 67.

However, it seems that the lack of sufficient information is the main issue for operational implementation of the Union Customs Code. Because a major part of the operational implementation on the national level depends on information about the legal and technical aspects of the reform, the national customs administrations of the EU Member States are currently unable to develop and invest in the necessary IT systems or align their national working procedures.[166]

Furthermore, clear and transparent communication is required not only with national customs authorities but also with economic operators. This will contribute to the competitiveness of European businesses by giving them a chance to inform others about their own experiences of the reform and opinions on additional required action.[167] Furthermore, the European Parliament has urged the European Commission to publish all the relevant information and documentation on expert meetings as soon as they are available, thus giving a wider audience access to customs-related issues.[168] Moreover, the midterm evaluation report for the Customs Action Programme 2013 suggested more intensive involvement of economic operators in the operational implementation process, appropriate transparency in the selection and invitation of trade representatives for participation in joint actions, and communication of the results of the Future Customs Initiative to a wider audience.[169] At the same time, the national customs authorities support for economic operators seems to be working rather smoothly.[170]

Another problem for the timely operational implementation of the reform is the limited resources, financial and otherwise, available in times of economic austerity, which affects all stakeholders. Therefore, the creation of the IT environment and the new timetable for its application has to consider the technical as well as the financial capabilities of the EU, the EU Member States, and the economic operators.[171]

In conclusion, the operational implementation crucial for the achievement of uniform administration of EU customs law across the EU depends on the finalisation of the legal texts and the clear definition of the IT environment of EU customs, as well as the timely provision of sufficient information to all stakeholders about both the legal and IT aspects. Therefore, the timing of the operational implementation of the Union Customs Code can only be very vaguely estimated at the moment, varying from September 2017 to March 2033.[172]

[166] ibid, p 80.

[167] ibid, p 80.

[168] European Parliament Resolution of 1 December 2011 (2001/2083(INI)), text adopted P7_TA(2011)0546, para 63.

[169] COM (2011) 537 final, pp 5, 6.

[170] See the statements of business organisations in: European Parliament, Study 2012, IP/A/IMCO/ST/2011–11, PE 475.094, p 68 and p 69 figure 15.

[171] European Parliament Resolution of 1 December 2011 (2001/2083(INI)), Text adopted P7_TA(2011)0546, para 21.

[172] European Parliament, Study 2012, IP/A/IMCO/ST/2011–11, PE 475.094, p 68 and p 88, figure 18.

IV. CONCLUSION

The legal, IT and operational aspects of the great reform cannot be implemented independently from each other given the interdependences that exist among those three processes. Therefore, certain steps of one implementation process need to be finalised before the other processes can begin.[173] In particular, the legal texts for the delegated and implementing powers set out in the Code's implementing provisions have to be finalised in order for further IT implementation. Once the IT development is completed at both the EU and national levels, staff training can be organised and guidelines issued, both which are pivotal for the uniform application of EU customs law.[174] Only the operational aspect of information and communication has to be conducted simultaneously with the other implementation steps and processes, while the content of such communication will evolve and alter with the progress made in the implementation process,[175] thereby ensuring coordinated implementation and uniform operation in the evolution of EU customs.

In this context, it is highly important to decide on the future IT strategy of EU customs and design an overarching and integrated Union Customs Code implementation action plan. The development of such an implementation plan for the Union Customs Code is part of an integrated implementation plan for the customs strategy, which must also take account of an overall IT plan and other plans originating from different customs-related areas.[176] Based on reasonable time estimates as well as experience from the implementation of the minor reform and its IT projects the achievement of full implementation of the Union Customs Code can be expected in 2020.[177]

From the beginning, the modernisation of customs has aimed to protect society and the financial interests of the EU and the EU Member States, as well as to support the competitiveness of the European economy, while maintaining a proper balance between customs controls and trade facilitation. To meet those objectives, the modernisation of EU customs is to enable customs authorities to work more efficiently, effectively and uniformly. Also in the context of the recast Modernised Customs Code, the European Commission made it clear that one of the main priorities in the management of the EU Customs Union remains 'further increasing the uniform effectiveness and efficiency of the Customs Union.'[178]

Therefore, the general objectives of EU customs remain the modernisation and streamlining of the functioning of the EU Customs Union and ensuring its effective management by developing high quality, uniformly applied customs

[173] ibid, p 88.

[174] ibid, p 89.

[175] ibid, p 88.

[176] DG Taxation and Customs Union Management Plan 2012, p 30; DG Taxation and Customs Union Management Plan 2013, p 38.

[177] European Parliament, Study 2012, IP/A/IMCO/ST/2011–11, PE 475.094, p 89; Lux, 2012 AW-Prax 8, pp 257–62 (259, 260).

[178] DG Taxation and Customs Union Management Plan 2012, p 5; similar: DG Taxation and Customs Union Management Plan 2013, p 5.

legislation and IT systems.[179] Once the Union Customs Code is fully implemented and all these expectations met, it is hoped that customs duties and customs-related taxes will be paid more correctly.[180] Customs controls would be automated and based on the extensive use of electronic risk-based assessments in order to target illegal trade more efficiently, while facilitations would be available for reliable trade partners, in particular traders with the status of an authorised economic operator.[181]

Furthermore, the new concepts of centralised customs clearance[182] and Single Window[183] have the potential to radically reduce and simplify customs formalities, lightening the administrative burden on both customs authorities and economic operators. The shift to an electronic customs environment should enable customs authorities in the EU to further ensure the safety and security of the EU's society and legal trade, while enhancing the competitiveness of European businesses.

In summary, the application of the Union Customs Code promises many benefits that currently cannot yet be fully and definitively evaluated, as much will depend on the successful completion of the implementation process. Furthermore, to assess the possible improvement of the management of the EU Customs Union, it is necessary to further analyse the system of customs administration in the EU and the challenges and opportunities in enforcing EU customs law in a uniform manner.

[179] DG Taxation and Customs Union Management Plan 2012, p 8; DG Taxation and Customs Union Management Plan 2013, p 9.

[180] European Parliament, Study 2012, IP/A/IMCO/ST/2011–11, PE 475.094, p 90.

[181] 'Authorised economic operator' (AEO) is a new status for economic operators combining procedural simplifications with aspects of safety and security, facilitating easier customs handling because the AEO programme is to be of significant importance for determining the intensity of customs controls; see: Lux, 2012 AW-Prax 8, pp 257–62 (259).

[182] The concept of 'centralised customs clearance' allows authorised operators to lodge their electronic customs declarations at the customs office of the place where they are established, irrespective of where their goods physically enter or leave the customs territory of the EU or where their forms need to be presented to European customs authorities; see: Lux, 2012 AW-Prax 8, pp 257–62 (260).

[183] The concept of a 'Single Window' allows standardised information and documents to be submitted to a single electronic entry point to fulfil all regulatory requirements related to import, export and transit, so individual data items need be submitted only once; once this standardised information is electronically delivered to the single portal it is made available to all relevant authorities; see: Lux, 2012 AW-Prax 8, pp 257–62 (259).

Part IV

Implementation of the European Union's Customs Law and Strategies for Enhancing Uniform Administration

6

The System of Decentralised Implementation in EU Customs Administration

EVEN AFTER THE entry into force of the Treaty of Lisbon, the EU is still a supranational organisation without comprehensive governmental sovereignty and to a large extent lacking its own administrative executive body. Thus it has a system of indirect implementation for EU law. This kind of implementation system follows the rule that – unless the EU takes direct action – the implementation of EU law is the duty of the EU Member States following from their membership in the EU and pursuant to Article 4 paragraph 1 and Article 5 paragraph 1 sentence 2 TEU.

The EU has no comprehensive competence for the administration of EU law because the principle of attributed powers pursuant to Article 5 TEU as well as the limited institutional resources of the EU itself considerably restrain the possibility of direct administration.[1] Therefore, the EU itself is only responsible for the direct implementation of EU law when there is a clear legal basis conferring administrative functions to its institutions or other authorities of the EU as such,[2] pursuant to the principle of conferral, Article 5 paragraph 2 TEU.

Furthermore, Article 291 paragraph 1 TFEU now emphasises that due to the lack of special EU provisions on administration, the implementation of EU law falls under national law.[3] Article 197 TFEU also emphasises the systemic principle of the EU Member States' responsibility for the implementation of EU law provided no special EU provisions are relevant. Thus, the EU Member States' responsibility for the implementation of EU law in principle is explicitly confirmed by EU primary law and therefore is the predominant mode of implementation.[4]

Although Article 298 TFEU outlines a European administration and Article 17 paragraph 1 TEU acknowledges the administrative function of the European Commission,[5] these general attributions of the EU's executive functions do not

[1] Weiß, 2010, p 37; Hofmann/Rowe/Türk, 2011, p 260.

[2] Hofmann/Rowe/Türk, 2011, pp 11, 12.

[3] ibid, p 13.

[4] Kahl, in: Calliess/Ruffert (eds), 2011, Art 4 TEU, paras 60, 61; Weiß, 2010, p 13; similar Hofmann/Rowe/Türk, 2011, p 260.

[5] Weiß, 2010, pp 13, 14.

specify concrete administrative competences. Article 17 paragraph 1 TEU contains only the traditional and general tasking of the European Commission, while Article 298 paragraph 1 TFEU requires certain missions of the EU be anchored in EU primary law in the form of an administrative task.[6] Thus, Article 298 TFEU refers to the European institution's execution of tasks, and not to the EU as a whole.[7] Therefore, those legal norms in EU primary law only confirm the possibility of administrative functions on the EU level, without establishing any administrative competences of the EU.[8]

Pursuant to EU primary law, the EU has only a few implementation competences.[9] Thus, the enforcement of EU law through EU Member States is the rule not only in areas where the EU is working on the approximation of laws, but also in areas of directly applicable EU law such as EU customs.[10] Indeed, because of the lack of a specific legal conferral of implementing power on the EU in the area of EU customs law, its implementation falls under the responsibility of the EU Member States, and their national customs administrations make up for the missing sub-construction of the EU. Moreover, Article 33 TFEU rather implies the national responsibility for customs administration by referring to the strengthening of customs cooperation between EU Member States and between the latter and the European Commission.

Therefore, the centralised legislative competences of the EU in EU customs are paired with decentralised competences of the EU Member States at the implementation level, pursuant to the principle of conferral in Article 5 paragraph 2 TEU in conjunction with the obligation of the EU Member States to implement legally binding Union acts pursuant to Article 4 paragraph 3 TEU, and now also explicitly stated in Article 291 paragraph 1 TFEU.[11] This decentralised concept of customs administration in the EU is the so-called 'Executive Federalism'.[12]

In this Executive Federalism, the indirect implementation of directly applicable EU law is based on the distinction between EU and EU Member State administrations.[13] This clear distinction is further based on the principle of organisational and institutional autonomy of the EU Member States,[14] which means that EU law is executed not by delegation of the EU's authority but by

[6] Weiß, 2010, p 37.

[7] Classen, in: Grabitz/Hilf/Nettesheim (eds), 2013, Vol II, Art 298 TFEU, para 10.

[8] Weiß, 2010, p 38.

[9] Kahl, in: Calliess/Ruffert (eds), 2011, Art 4 TEU, para 61; Hofmann/Rowe/Türk, 2011, p 260.

[10] Nettesheim, in: Oppermann/Classen/Nettesheim (eds), 2011, § 12, para 23; Hofmann/Rowe/Türk, 2011, p 13.

[11] Hobbing, CEPS Papers No 39, June 2011, p 15; Hofmann/Rowe/Türk, 2011, p 13.

[12] Hofmann/Rowe/Türk, 2011, p 13.

[13] ibid, p 13.

[14] Similar ECJ of 6 October 2010, Case C-389/08, *Base NV and Others* [2010] ECR I-9073, paras 3, 26 with regard to the establishment of a regulatory authority; see also Hofmann/Rowe/Türk, 2011, p 260; Kadelbach, in: Joerges/Dehousse (eds), 2003, pp 167–206 (170); Nettesheim, in: Oppermann/Classen/Nettesheim (eds), 2011, § 12, para 25; Kahl, in: Calliess/Ruffert (eds), 2011, Art 4 TEU, para 2.

national authority in their own name and under their own responsibility.[15] According to this principle of institutional and organisational autonomy, it is for the EU Member States to decide, within the framework of national sovereignty, how to organise the exercise of their rights and powers, including internal hierarchy and competence structures.[16] The administrative organisation of the EU Member States is not a matter over which the EU has any power.[17] The EU does not have competence to interfere directly in domestic administrative organisation and institution-building, and the design of national customs authorities has to be organised nationally, as EU law in principle sets no parameters regarding competences and functions of national authorities.[18]

This institutional and organisational autonomy in national administration not only involves administrative organisation but also administrative procedures and administrative jurisdiction,[19] because in the absence of any explicit requirements in EU law, the EU Member States make use of their already existing organisational and procedural forms.[20] Only in single specific cases does EU law determine such specific requirements and have a direct impact on the organisational autonomy of the EU Member States.[21]

However, in any case EU Member States' administrations have to comply with the principles of equivalence and effectiveness[22] and are subject to general principles of EU law when implementing it, which thus constitutes some general limitations on the EU Member States' autonomy.[23] Indeed, the growing focus on effective and uniform implementation of EU law in general has led to a catalogue of general principles to be observed by EU Member States when implementing EU law created by the ECJ in its settled case law.[24]

Furthermore, today, the strict distinction between central direct enforcement and decentralised indirect implementation of EU law does not match exactly the reality of European administrative execution, because of the manifold and intertwined exercise of sovereignty.[25] The guidance of the European Commission for the correct implementation is of major importance for national customs administrations and the uniform implementation of EU customs law. Indeed, the

[15] Similar ECJ of 16 July 2009, Case C-428/07, *Horvath* [2009] ECR I-6355, para 49; ECJ of 15 December 1971, Joined Cases 51 to 54-71, *International Fruit Company NV and Others* [1971] ECR 1107, para 4.

[16] ECJ of 16 July 2009, Case C-428/07, *Horvath* [2009] ECR I-6355, para 49; ECJ of 19 February 2002, Case C-309/99, *Wouters and Others* [2002] ECR I-1577, paras 54, 67.

[17] ECJ of 13 June 2013, Case C-386/11, *Piepenbrock Dienstleistungen GmbH & Co. KG* [2013] ECR I-0, para 23.

[18] Streinz, 2012, § 7, para 580; similar Kadelbach, in: Joerges/Dehousse (eds), 2003, pp 167–206 (171).

[19] Kahl, in: Calliess/Ruffert (eds), 2011, Art 4 TEU, para 61; Hofmann/Rowe/Türk, 2011, p 260.

[20] Hofmann/Rowe/Türk, 2011, p 260.

[21] ibid, p 261; Kadelbach, in: Joerges/Dehousse (eds), 2003, pp 167–206 (172).

[22] See, inter alia, ECJ of 12 July 2012, Joined Cases C-608/10, C-10/11 and C-23/11, *Südzucker AG and Others* [2012] ECR I-0, para 62, and the case law cited.

[23] Hofmann/Rowe/Türk, 2011, pp 10, 12.

[24] ibid, p 10.

[25] Weiß, 2010, pp 13, 15.

need for effective administration of EU customs has led to vertical and horizontal relations between and among national customs authorities of different EU Member States and also with the European Commission, resulting in a sort of network structure.[26]

Cooperation and exchange of information between actors at the national level of different EU Member States as well as with actors on the EU level are important in EU customs, with customs procedures regularly involving cross-border aspects and impacts. Such 'transterritorial'[27] effects of administrative activity, as can be found in the implementation of EU customs, have been seen as the emergence of a European integrated administration, in which the distinction between direct and indirect administration has become increasingly blurred.[28] Such elements of cooperation and interdependence with rights of information and participation, as can be found in the implementation of EU customs, are representative of a new kind of integrated European administration.[29] Intense networks of interdependence in an integrated administration can to some extent even come close to resembling a functional uniform administration.[30]

Nevertheless, the interaction of EU institutions and national administrations in the indirect implementation of EU law is governed by the important fact that they do not constitute a hierarchically organised administration[31] in which the EU institutions can manage the actions of national authorities through individual instructions, take over an administrative process, or declare a national administrative decision invalid.[32] However, this model of decentralised administration entails some danger for the uniform application of EU law.[33] Thus, its procedural and organisational aspects require further analysis.

I. STATUS QUO AND DEVELOPMENT REGARDING AN EU CUSTOMS PROCEDURE UNION

Lacking a structured and codified European administrative procedural law, the EU Customs Union under the current Community Customs Code has been criticised for not being a customs procedure union.[34] Although EU customs law is centrally enacted at the level of the EU, and therefore supranationalised, its implementation is chiefly the responsibility of the EU Member States.[35] In the absence of an EU

[26] Hofmann/Türk, 2007 ELJ (13), pp 253–71 (259).
[27] Hofmann/Türk, 2007 ELJ (13), pp 253–71 (259).
[28] Hofmann/Türk, 2007 ELJ (13), pp 253–71 (254, 259).
[29] Weiß, 2010, p 16; Hofmann/Türk, 2007 ELJ (13), pp 253–271 (254).
[30] Weiß, 2010, p 18.
[31] Kadelbach, in: Joerges/Dehousse (eds), 2003, pp 167–206 (170); Hofmann/Rowe/Türk, 2011, p 572.
[32] Similar: Hofmann/Rowe/Türk, 2011, p 573.
[33] Hofmann/Rowe/Türk, 2011, p 260.
[34] Weerth, 2008 ZfZ 7, pp 178–85 (181, 182).
[35] Hobbing, CEPS Papers No 39, June 2011, p 15; Anaboli, (5) 2010 GTCJ (9), pp 389–93 (389).

customs service, the national customs administrations and even to some extent the national law of the EU Member States are crucial for the functioning of the EU Customs Union.[36] Nevertheless, the Community Customs Code and its implementing provisions determine the customs procedures in the EU and are a quite an exhaustive codification of customs administration law and customs duty law in principle.[37] Therefore, in the administration by EU Member States, the national customs officials have to base their decisions directly on EU regulations, and not on national implementing acts.[38]

However, in the decentralised administration arrangements of the EU Customs Union, the Community Customs Code as the central body of EU customs law determines the types of customs procedures, but regulates only single areas of common administrative procedural law, whereas in the absence of a European provision, the national procedural law continues to have supplementary effect. Indications of non-exhaustive provisions where there is room for national specifications are frequently provisions that clearly set only a minimal standard in EU law, because of the differing legal structures and traditions of the various EU Member States.[39] For example, the establishment of an appeal procedure as a minimal standard is laid down in Article 245 CCC (Articles 43 and 44 paragraphs 2 and 4 UCC/former Articles 22 and 23 paragraphs 2 and 4 MCC), but the provisions for its implementation are to be determined by the EU Member States.

However, the Union Customs Code (as well as the former Modernised Customs Code) leaves a much narrower margin of discretion of regulatory power to the EU Member States, and instead sets further standards, at least for appeal decisions not taken by a judicial authority.[40] In particular, Article 44 paragraph 4 UCC (former Article 23 paragraph 4 MCC) makes clear that in this regard the EU Member States can only adopt national procedural provisions where EU customs law contains no specific rule.[41] The extent of national law's supplementary use in the implementation of EU customs law by EU Member States allows us to draw conclusions regarding the uniform administration of EU customs.

A. Regulation of EU Customs Procedures in the Community Customs Code

In numerous provisions of the Community Customs Code, the national customs administrations are authorised to regulate certain details by themselves, such as invalidation of customs decisions for reasons unconnected with customs legislation pursuant to Article 10 CCC (Article 23 paragraph 3 UCC/former Article 16

[36] Lyons, 2008, p 120.

[37] Rüsken, in: Rüsken (ed), 2013, Vol I, Introduction CCC, para 77.

[38] Rogmann, in: Kluth/Müller/Peilert (eds), 2008, pp 797–819 (800).

[39] Alexander, in: Witte (ed), 2013, Art 6 CCC, para 15; Weymüller, in: Rüsken (ed), 2013, Vol I, Art 6 CCC, para 1.

[40] Lux, 2009 ZfZ Special Vol 1, pp 1–36 (14).

[41] Alexander, in: Witte (ed), 2013, Art 245 CCC, para 3.

paragraph 6 MCC), establishment of free zones or free warehouses pursuant to Article 167 CCC (Articles 243 and 244 UCC/former Articles 155 and 156 MCC), entry into accounts pursuant to Article 217 paragraph 2 CCC (Article 104 paragraph 3 UCC/former Article 69 paragraph 2 MCC), or payment facilities pursuant to Article 229 CCC (Article 112 UCC/former Article 77 MCC).

In some provisions, the Community Customs Code refers explicitly to national procedural law, as for example in Article 10 CCC (Article 23 paragraph 3 UCC/former Article 16 paragraph 6 MCC) regarding the invalidation of administrative decisions for reasons unconnected with customs legislation. In other cases, the provisions contain regulatory gaps and have to be complemented by national law. For example, Articles 8 and 9 CCC (Articles 27 and 28 UCC/former Articles 18 and 19 MCC) regulate the annulment or revocation of favourable administrative decisions, but contain no rules for a burdensome administrative decision. Therefore, in those cases recourse to national administrative procedural law is demanded.[42]

Regulation deficits in a wider sense also occur in cases where the Community Customs Code picks up on a subject but regulates it only fragmentarily, without the denseness of regulation in the EU Member States. In such cases, it has to be analysed whether this fragmentary regularisation exists on purpose, providing no room for supplementary recourse to national law, or whether the intention behind it is to establish a principle or regulate only parts, thus allowing for supplementary application of national law to secure an equal denseness of regulation between national and EU law.[43]

However, one has to keep in mind that in principle, undefined legal terms in EU law cannot be interpreted or defined by national law, because this would endanger the uniform application of EU customs law throughout the EU.[44] Therefore, each individual case has to be analysed to see if there is indeed a gap in the regulation of the Community Customs Code which has to be closed by supplementary application of national law for reasons of legal certainty and in order to create an equal regularisation level.[45] For example, Article 213 CCC (Article 84 UCC/former Article 51 MCC) establishes the joint liability of several debtors for a customs debt without giving a definition in the Community Customs Code or its implementing provisions. Nevertheless, the ECJ has decided that the undefined legal term of joint liability allows no recourse to national law or national principles.[46]

Reservations of regulation in favour of national rules or the exclusion of certain regulation areas, such as rules of administrative enforcement, rules of administrative offences or of penal law, lead to the supplementary application of national

[42] ibid, before Art 8 CCC, para 1.

[43] Wolffgang, in: Witte/Wolffgang (eds), 2012, p 27 para 32.

[44] Craig, in: Hübschmann/Hepp/Spitaler (eds), 2013, Vol XIV, Art 6 CCC, para 14.

[45] Wolffgang, in: Witte/Wolffgang (eds), 2012, p 27 para 32; Rüsken, in: Rüsken (ed), 2013, Vol I, Introduction CCC, para 78.

[46] ECJ of 17 February 2011, Case C-78/10, *Marc Berel and Others* [2011] ECR I-717, paras 41, 66.

law.[47] This grants national customs administrations a wide scope of discretion by not only allowing them to make customs decisions in concrete cases, but also to regulate whole areas of administrative procedural law independently.[48] The reason behind this attitude is respect for the different national law systems and law traditions of the EU Member States. Therefore, the Community Customs Code does not regulate some administrative issues and instead leaves the solution of certain questions explicitly to the EU Member States.[49] Indeed, regarding common administrative procedural law, the Community Customs Code and its implementing provisions constitute only a rudimentary rather than a comprehensive codification.[50]

However, it remains a fact that the Community Customs Code and its implementing provisions tend in principle toward being an exhaustive regulation whose uniform administration in the EU is non-negotiable. In the area of EU customs, the EU has exclusive competence to adopt legal acts, pursuant to Article 3 paragraph 1 section (a) TFEU in conjunction with Article 2 paragraph 1 TFEU. Therefore, the supplementary application of EU Member States' national law has to be limited to what is absolutely necessary for the reasonable administration of EU customs in the EU Member States.[51] The difficult assessment as to whether an exhaustive regulation of a specific matter in the provisions of the Community Customs Code exists requires differentiation and identification of the various possibilities for the application of national administrative procedural law.

1. Supplementary Effectiveness of National Administrative Procedural Law

The application of national law is unproblematic if the facts of the case in question are not covered by EU customs law in the sense of Article 1 sentence 1 CCC (Article 1 paragraph 1 sentence 1 UCC/former Article 1 paragraph 1 sentence 1 MCC),[52] such as, for example, granting of export refunds, which is not part of the provisions in the Community Customs Code and therefore falls under national law.[53] Whether or not the facts of the case are covered by EU customs law has to be examined not only based on the wording of the provision in question, but also through a teleological interpretation.[54]

[47] Rüsken, in: Rüsken (ed), 2013, Vol I, Introduction CCC, para 78; Witte, in: Witte (ed) 2013, before Art 1 CCC, para 16.

[48] Dierksmeier, 2007, p 196.

[49] Rüsken, in: Rüsken (ed), 2013, Vol I, Introduction CCC, para 76.

[50] Alexander, in: Witte (ed), 2013, before Art 8 CCC, para 1.

[51] ECJ of 17 February 2011, Case C-78/10, *Marc Berel and Others* [2011] ECR I-717, para 47, and the case law cited.

[52] Alexander, in: Witte (ed), 2013, Art 6 CCC, para 5; Craig, in: Hübschmann/Hepp/Spitaler (eds), 2011, Vol XIV, Art 6 CCC, para 7.

[53] ECJ of 17 July 1997, Case C-334/95, *Krüger* [1997] ECR I-4517, paras 36 et seq.

[54] ECJ of 17 February 2011, Case C-78/10, *Marc Berel and Others* [2011] ECR I-717, para 49.

(a) References to Domestic Law

National law occasionally refers to the Community Customs Code, which, for example, is the case in Germany for certain tax procedures regarding the import of excisable goods like § 19 EnergieStG[55] or § 21 TabStG.[56] Explicit references in the Community Customs Code to national law, which allow recourse to it, also facilitate the differentiation.[57] As mentioned above, this is the case in various Articles of the Community Customs Code such as Article 10, 182 paragraph 1, or Article 201 paragraph 3 subparagraph 2 CCC – though those direct references can no longer be found in the new Code, see Article 23 paragraph 3 UCC/former Article 16 paragraph 6 MCC replacing Article 10 CCC, Article 270 paragraph 1 UCC/former Article 179 paragraph 1 MCC replacing Article 182 paragraph 1 CCC, and Article 77 paragraph 3 subparagraph 2 UCC/former Article 44 paragraph 3 subparagraph 2 MCC replacing Article 201 paragraph 3 subparagraph 2 CCC. The same applies when EU Member States are authorised to regulate details, as for example in Article 60 CCC (Articles 159 and 43, 44 paragraphs 2 and 4 UCC/former Articles 105 and 22, 23 paragraphs 2 and 4 MCC).

In contrast, references in the Community Customs Code to 'provisions in force' in the sense of Article 4 Number 23 CCC – a definition that can no longer be found in the Union Customs Code or the Modernised Customs Code – are problematic. In such a case, national law is only applicable if there is no exhaustive regulation on the EU level, because 'provision in force' refers to both the national law and the EU law, with primacy in application given to the latter.[58]

Sometimes the Community Customs Code even allows customs authorities to lay down specific practical details. Such references can be found, for example, in Article 38 paragraph 1 CCC and Article 229 CCC (Article 135 paragraph 1, and Article 112 UCC/former Article 92 paragraph 1, and Article 77 MCC). By allowing customs authorities to define specific details, such references also allows national legislators as well as superior national customs authorities to define the specific practical details for its subordinated national customs authorities.[59]

Although the right of EU Member States' national legislators and superior national customs authorities to make a corresponding provision by law, order or

[55] The German Energy Tax Law: Gesetz zur Neuregelung der Besteuerung von Energieerzeugnissen und zur Änderung des Stromsteuergesetzes vom 15 Juli 2006.

[56] The German Tobacco Duty Act: Viertes Gesetz zur Änderung von Verbrauchsteuergesetzen vom 15 Juli 2009, Artikel 1 Tabaksteuergesetz, BGBl. I p 1870; last amended 22.12.2011, BGBl. I p 3044.

Alexander, in: Witte (ed), 2013, Art 6 CCC, para 6; Craig, in: Hübschmann/Hepp/Spitaler (eds), 2011, Vol XIV, Art 6 CCC, para 8.

[57] Alexander, in: Witte (ed), 2013, Art 6 CCC, para 7; Craig, in: Hübschmann/Hepp/Spitaler (eds), 2011, Vol XIV, Art 6 CCC, para 10.

[58] Witte, in: Witte (ed), 2013, before Art 1 CCC, para 12; Alexander, in: Witte (ed), 2013, Art 6 CCC, para 8; Craig, in: Hübschmann/Hepp/Spitaler (eds), 2013, Vol XIV, Art 6 CCC, para 12.

[59] Witte, in: Witte (ed), 2013, before Art 1 CCC, para 13; Alexander, in: Witte (ed), 2013, Art 6 CCC, para 9.

instruction is partially questioned,[60] it remains unclear why the action of national customs authorities could not be specified by their national legislator. Allegations that the national legislator cannot be subsumed under the term 'customs authorities' and that the Customs Code does not intend to create a norm-setting competence in such a case is not convincing because, in practice, such references in the Community Customs Code have already been specified by national legislators. For example, the above-mentioned Article 38 paragraph 1 CCC (Article 135 paragraph 1 UCC/former Article 92 paragraph 1 MCC), which explicitly refers to customs authorities in specifying the import route and linked instructions, is given full particulars by national law in Germany, particularly §§ 2, 3 ZollVG,[61] and yet has not raised any objection from the EU level.[62] Nevertheless, such action is limited to the adoption of measures necessary for the reasonable application of the Customs Code and its implementing provisions given the exclusive competence of the EU to adopt legal acts in the area of EU customs, pursuant to Article 3 paragraph 1 section (a) TFEU in conjunction with Article 2 paragraph 1 TFEU.

(b) Margins of Discretion

The provisions in which the Community Customs Code or its implementing provisions grant margins of discretion regarding administrative decisions are also problematic. However, not every provision containing the term 'can' is a grant of discretionary power. Rather, the provision in question has to provide different decision-making possibilities to really grant the customs authorities discretionary power, like for example in Article 110 paragraph 7 CCCIP. With regard to the 'EUR 1' movement certificate, Article 110 paragraph 7 CCCIP allows customs authorities to call for any documentary evidence or to carry out any check which they consider appropriate to decide whether the conditions for issuing such a certificate are met or not. Therefore, it is for the competent customs authority to decide which documents or checks are necessary in every single case.

Furthermore, it is questionable whether the exercise of such an administrative margin of discretion could be co-determined through national administrative law. In the area of EU customs legislation, the EU has exclusive competence to adopt legal acts, pursuant to Article 3 paragraph 1 section (a) TFEU in conjunction with Article 2 paragraph 1 TFEU. However, in the decentralised administration concept of the EU Customs Union, the main responsibility for the implementation of EU customs law lies with the EU Member States. Therefore, the ECJ has held that EU Member States:

> retain the possibility of adopting measures to contribute effectively to the implementation of the objectives of the customs legislation … and may thus, in compliance with

[60] Craig, in: Hübschmann/Hepp/Spitaler (eds), 2013, Vol XIV, Art 6 CCC, para 12.

[61] The German Customs Administration Law: Zollrechtsänderungsgesetz vom 21. Dezember 1992, Artikel 1 Zollverwaltungsgesetz, BGBl I p 2125; 1993 I p 2493; last amended 21.07.2012, BGBl I p 1566.

[62] Witte, in: Witte (ed), 2013, before Art 1 CCC, para 13.

> those objectives and in accordance with the principle of proportionality, prescribe if appropriate rules specifying the conditions of application of the provisions laid down in that legislation.[63]

However, the complementary application of national rules requires a genuine gap in the EU legislation, and the lack of perfection in EU customs legislation does not automatically constitute such a gap.[64] Allowing recourse to national rules regarding the exercise of discretion could raise the risk of non-uniform application.[65] Therefore, the Community Customs Code has to be interpreted generally by itself and with consultation of the case law of the ECJ.[66] Furthermore, in the event that a provision lays down conditions that have to be fulfilled, the ECJ interprets the term 'can' to grant customs authorities only a non-discretionary power when taking a customs decision.[67]

(c) Undefined Legal Terms

The use of undefined legal terms in the Community Customs Code is also causing application problems. As mentioned above, undefined legal terms in the Community Customs Code cannot, in principle, be provided by national law,[68] as is the case for the entirety of EU law. Therefore, for example, the terms 'acquiring' or 'receiving' in Articles 202 paragraph 3 subdivision 3, and 203 paragraph 3 subdivision 3 CCC (Article 79 paragraph 3 section (c) UCC/former Article 46 paragraph 3 section (c) MCC) cannot be interpreted by recourse to the meaning of those terms in national law, such as in the German §§ 854 et seq BGB.[69] However, in cases where the legal term refers to 'provisions in force', an exception is to be made. For example, Article 221 paragraph 1 CCC refers to 'appropriate procedures' with regard to the procedure for communication of the customs debt to the debtor. Thus, the provision is open for the application of national law.[70]

[63] ECJ of 17 February 2011, Case C-78/10, *Marc Ber el and Others* [2011] ECR I-717, para 47, and the case law cited there.

[64] Rüsken, in: Rüsken (ed), 2013, Vol I, Introduction CCC, para 78; Witte, in: Witte (ed), 2013, before Art 1, para 16.

[65] Craig, in: Hübschmann/Hepp/Spitaler (eds), 2013, Vol XIV, Art 6 CCC, para 13; Witte, in: Witte (ed), 2013, Art 4 CCC, para 2, keyword 'Entscheidung'.

[66] See for example the interpretation of Art 454 CCCIP in: ECJ of 23 March 2000, Joined Cases C-310/98 and C-406/98, *Labis* [2000] ECR I-1797, paras 44–47.

[67] General Court of 5 June 2013, Case T-65/11, *Recombined Dairy System* [2013] ECR II-0, para 23; General Court of 19 March 2013, Case T-324/10, *Léon van Parys* [2013] ECR II-0, para 34; ECJ of 18 October 2007, Case C-173/06, *Agrover* [2007] ECR I-8783, para 30; ECJ of 14 November 2002, Case C-251/00, *Ilumitrónica* [2002] ECR I-10433, para 37; ECJ of 19 October 2000, Case C-15/99, *Sommer* [2000] ECR I-8989, para 35; ECJ of 27 June 1991, Case C-348/89, *Mecanarte* [1991] ECR I-3277, para 14.

[68] Alexander, in: Witte (ed), 2013, Art 6 CCC, para 11; Craig, in: Hübschmann/Hepp/Spitaler (eds), 2011, Vol XIV, Art 6 CCC, para 14.

[69] The German Civil Code: Bekanntmachung der Neufassung des Bürgerlichen Gesetzbuches vom 2 Januar 2002, BGBl I p 42, 2909; 2003 I p 738; last amended 01.10.2013, BGBl I p 3719.

[70] ECJ of 23 February 2006, Case C-201/04, *Molenbergnatie NV* [2006] ECR I-2049, paras 51, 52, 53, 54.

Insofar, the new Code contains no changes but modifications: Article 102 paragraph 1 subparagraph 1 UCC (former Article 67 paragraph 1 subparagraph 1 MCC) refers to Article 87 UCC (former Article 75 MCC), meaning that the national law applicable now follows from the place where the customs debt was incurred.[71] Article 221 paragraph 4 CCC refers to the 'provisions in force' with regard to the extinction of a customs debt through the passage of time when the customs debt arose as a result of a criminal act and thus also allows the complementary use of national law in this regard.[72] In contrast, the new Code in Article 103 paragraph 2 UCC (former Article 68 paragraph 2 MCC) contains no such reference but determines the time limits itself in such cases.

(d) Summary

There is no easy solution for identifying gaps in EU customs law that allow for the supplementary application of national administrative procedural law. Rather, the Community Customs Code requires a detailed analysis as to whether a regulation in the Community Customs Code is exhaustive or if the provision constitutes only parts or principles or minimum standards.[73] In general, one has to differentiate between substantive customs provisions and procedural customs provisions: substantive customs provisions on the EU level generally intend to be exhaustive because of the exclusive competence of the EU to adopt legal acts for EU customs, pursuant to Article 3 paragraph 1 section (a) TFEU in conjunction with Article 2 paragraph 1 TFEU.

However, with regard to administrative procedural law, the EU Member States are allowed to contribute effectively to the implementation of EU customs law and, in this regard, to adopt national measures specifying the necessary conditions of application of EU customs provisions. Although currently a structured and codified European administrative procedural law does not exist, an overly hasty recourse to national law is not advisable, as a lack of perfection in the Community Customs Code or its implementing provisions does not automatically constitute a regulatory gap in the European legislation.[74] Moreover, such action would negatively affect the uniform application of EU customs law throughout the EU.[75] Therefore, where blanket solutions are not adequate for the question of supplementary applicability of national law in the administration of EU customs, one has to choose the interpretation which allows for the greatest effect on the European character of EU customs law, and especially its uniform administration.[76]

[71] Alexander, in: Witte (ed) 2013, Art 221, para 14.
[72] ECJ of 17 June 2010, Case C-75/09, *Agra Srl* [2010] ECR I-5595, paras 33, 34, 35, 36.
[73] Alexander, in: Witte (ed), 2013, Art 6 CCC, paras 12, 13, 15.
[74] Witte, in: Witte (ed), 2013, before Art 1 CCC, para 16.
[75] ibid, before Art 1 CCC, para 16.
[76] Craig, in: Hübschmann/Hepp/Spitaler (eds), 2011, Vol XIV, Art 6 CCC, para 15.

2. *Minimum Standard of General Principles in EU Customs Procedures*

Nevertheless, where EU customs law has to be supplemented by national administrative procedural law, the general principles of Union law have to be followed.[77] To a large extent, those general principles, such as, for example, legal certainty or proportionality, have been developed by the ECJ over many years through many administrative legal disputes. In the event that they conflict with national procedural law, the latter must give way to these general principles of EU law.[78] Indeed, EU law contains principles of specific application to the administration as such, and these are important legal foundations of EU administrative law.[79] Those general principles of EU administrative law include, for example, the principle of data protection, of acting within power, and of reasonableness.[80] They provide guidance in the interpretation of EU administrative law and thus are the basis for uniform administrative decision-making.[81]

Regarding EU customs law in particular, an EU-wide common minimum standard of general principles is established in Article 6 CCC (Article 22 paragraphs 1, 2, 3 and 6 UCC/former Article 16 paragraphs 1, 2, and 4 subparagraph 2 MCC), including for example demanded principle on the reasoning of customs decisions. The stating of reasons for an administrative decision is not a common practice in every EU Member State and therefore, the provision sets minimum standards in this regard.[82] Further common minimum standards in Article 6 CCC are the principle to supply information, time limits for decisions and extension of those time limits, announcement of decisions as well as an obligation for substantiation of decisions.

However, the minimum standard of procedural administrative law in the Community Customs Code is not sufficient for aligning the standard of EU customs administration with the common administrative standard in the EU Member States – even taking into account the general principles of EU administrative law and consulting the case law of the ECJ. Therefore, recourse to national procedural law has to be made when the minimum standards in EU customs law, along with the general principles of EU law, are not sufficient for a reasonable application of EU customs legislation.[83]

[77] See, inter alia, ECJ of 20 June 2013, Case C-568/11, *Agroferm A/S* [2013] ECR I-0, para 47, and the case law cited; in particular ECJ of 21 September 1983, Joined Cases 205 to 215/82, *Deutsche Milchkontor* [1983] ECR 2633, para 17.

[78] Hofmann/Rowe/Türk, 2011, p 144.

[79] ibid, pp 143, 144.

[80] ibid, p 144.

[81] ibid, pp 143, 144.

[82] Alexander, in: Witte (ed), 2013, Art 6 CCC, para 15.

[83] See, inter alia, ECJ of 23 February 2006, Case C-201/04, *Molenbergnatie NV* [2006] ECR I-2049, para 52, and the case law cited.

3. Conclusion

In conclusion, out of respect for the different national law systems and legal traditions of the EU Member States, the Community Customs Code sometimes leaves certain issues and procedural aspects of administration to the EU Member States. Thus it does not constitute an exhaustive regulation but instead determines a minimum standard.[84] This can especially be seen in Article 6 CCC (Article 22 paragraphs 1, 2, 3 and 6 UCC/former Article 16 paragraphs 1, 2 and 4 subparagraph 2 MCC). In the past, further harmonisation has failed due to the opposition of the EU Member States.[85]

However, the numerous aforementioned possibilities in the Community Customs Code for national customs authorities to apply national administrative procedural law when administering EU customs have the potential to endanger the uniform administration of EU customs. Under these conditions it could be difficult to secure the uniform administration of such complex areas as the Common Customs Tariff, the Customs Code and its implementing provisions throughout the EU.[86]

B. Development Towards a Stronger EU Customs Procedure Union and Strategies for Enhancing Uniform Application Under the Union Customs Code

The Union Customs Code implements the strategies of the EU for enhancing uniform application of EU customs law, and in doing so contributes to the development of a stronger EU Customs Procedure Union. Those strategies specifically related to procedural aspects are the establishment of electronic customs in the Customs Code, reduction and simplification of customs procedures, simplifying legal terminology, ensuring Union-wide validity of customs decisions, and reduction of references to domestic law. Even in the customs areas of appeal procedures and customs debt, in which the EU Member States have extensive regulatory power left by the current Community Customs Code, further harmonisation is aspired to. Therefore, the Union Customs Code points towards a stronger emphasis on the supranational character of EU customs law.

1. Establishment of Electronic Customs

The criticism of the numerous non-uniform aspects of customs procedures under the current Community Customs Code explicitly refers to customs declarations operated electronically and carried out through different national IT systems

[84] Rüsken, in: Rüsken (ed), 2013, Vol I, Introduction CCC, para 76, Alexander, in: Witte (ed), 2013, Art 6 CCC, para 15.

[85] Wolffgang, in: Witte/Wolffgang (eds), 2012, p 27, para 33.

[86] Weerth, 2008 ZfZ 7, pp 178–85 (181).

often with different national customs tariff databases, which is for example the case with Germany's electronic customs tariff, the 'Elektronischer Zolltarif'.[87]

The Union Customs Code will introduce obligatory IT technical procedures in order to avoid grey zones in the future interpretation of EU customs procedural law through the use of electronic data processing techniques with precisely laid out working steps, see Articles 6 to 17 UCC (former Articles 5 to 10 MCC). These will not only lead to the advantage of swifter and more efficient handling of customs procedures, but also contribute to the more uniform application of EU customs law.[88] There are great expectations especially for the new electronic working environment for EU customs to promote the simpler and more uniform administration of EU customs, and therefore it is a major and important part of the ongoing reform.[89]

In fact, the changes introduced in the Union Customs Code are necessary to pave the way for interoperable electronic customs systems in the EU. Without the simplification and further harmonisation of the customs provisions and procedures, including the deletion of numerous references to national law, the advantages of the computerisation of EU customs would be very limited, and the aspired-to centralisation of customs clearance[90] endangered, despite its importance to the modernisation process.[91] As mentioned before, details have to be set out in the as yet still in progress implementing provisions and delegated acts, but the real challenge is the introduction of transnational and interoperable IT systems in the EU Customs Union. Therefore, only if the electronic customs project is finally implemented will the reform of EU customs take a huge step towards a true EU Customs Procedure Union.

2. *Reduction of Customs Procedures and More Coherent Structure of the Code*

A fundamental contribution to a more uniform interpretation and application of EU customs law by national customs authorities lies in the reduction of the number of customs procedures and the simplification of the legal terminology in the Union Customs Code (as well as in the former Modernised Customs Code). The new Customs Code reduces the current number of more than 10 customs procedures to three basic concepts: release for free circulation (Title VI UCC/former MCC), export (Title VIII UCC/former MCC) and special procedures (Title VII

[87] ibid, pp 178–85 (181, 182).

[88] Lux, 2009 ZfZ Special Vol 1, pp 1–36 (3).

[89] The importance of the IT technical aspects of the great reform in EU customs is analysed above in Chapter 4.IV and Chapter 5.II.

[90] The concept of 'centralised customs clearance' allows authorised operators to lodge their electronic customs declarations at the customs office of the place where they are established, irrespective of where their goods physically enter or leave the customs territory of the EU, or where their forms need to be presented to European customs authorities; see: Lux, 2012 AW-Prax 8, pp 257–62 (260).

[91] Lux/Larrieu, 2006 ZfZ 11, pp 329–41 (340).

UCC/former MCC). The latter is divided into four groups of customs procedures: transit (Title VII Chapter 2 UCC/former MCC), storage (Title VII Chapter 3 UCC/former MCC), specific use (Title VII Chapter 4 UCC/former MCC), and processing (Title VII Chapter 5 UCC/former MCC). Thus, the Union Customs Code (as well as the former Modernised Customs Code) subordinates similar customs procedures under common provisions more clearly than the current Community Customs Code.

In this regard, the new Customs Code has been said to be 'procedure-oriented', integrating similar procedures into common provisions with little exceptions, and thereby making the application of the new Customs Code much simpler.[92] The simplified declaration procedure, centralised customs handling[93] and stronger anchoring of self-assessment[94] in the Union Customs Code contribute to the simplification and harmonisation of customs procedures throughout the EU,[95] as well as bolstering the common framework for risk analysis and data exchange between customs authorities.[96] The simplified structure of the new Customs Code describes customs handling from an administrative point of view, in contrast to the Community Customs Code, and is now directed at the process of importation or exportation and the needs of the economic operators.[97] The more balanced and comprehensible structure of the provisions better accommodates the work flow in customs handling and facilitates analysis for organisational purposes, the introduction of electronic systems and data exchange, all which improve the functioning of EU-transnational customs procedures.[98]

Altogether, the Union Customs Code has resulted in a more balanced distribution between regulations in the Customs Code and its implementing provisions through relocation of technical details in the current Community Customs Code to the implementing provisions and shifting of basic rules of the current implementing provisions into the new Customs Code.[99] For example, Article 153 UCC (former Article 101 MCC) now contains basic rules with regard to the presumption of customs status of Union goods; an equivalent cannot be found in the Community Customs Code, but in Article 313 CCCIP.

Although the Union Customs Code contains 288 Articles, it also includes 39 provisions regarding delegation of power to the European Commission, as well

[92] Lux, 2009 ZfZ Special Vol 1, pp 1–36 (3).

[93] The concept of 'centralised customs clearance' allows authorised operators to lodge their electronic customs declarations at the customs office of the place where they are established, irrespective of where their goods physically enter or leave the customs territory of the EU or where their forms need to be presented to European customs authorities; see: Lux, 2012 AW-Prax 8, pp 257–62 (260).

[94] 'Self-assessment' introduces a kind of quasi-statutory work that the economic operator will be allowed to carry out instead of the customs authority, which enables further simplifications of customs formalities as well as customs controls; see: Henke, in: Witte/Henke/Kammerzell (eds), 2009, p 138.

[95] Lux, 2007 AW-Prax 7, pp 277–80 (279).

[96] Lux/Larrieu, 2006 ZfZ 11, pp 329–41 (332).

[97] Lux/Larrieu, 2006 ZfZ 10, pp 301–06 (305).

[98] Lux/Larrieu, 2006 ZfZ 10, pp 301–06 (305).

[99] Lux/Larrieu, 2006 ZfZ 11, pp 329–41 (336).

as 48 provisions regarding the conferral of implementing powers to the European Commission. The current Community Customs Code contains no such provisions but nevertheless comprises 255 Articles. Therefore, the number of substantive customs provisions in the Union Customs Code has been significantly reduced in comparison to the Community Customs Code, with many less important or technical details now to be regulated in delegated acts and in implementing provisions.

3. *Simplified Legal Terminology*

To modernise EU customs law, the reform of the Community Customs Code has also created provisions which have been called 'customer-oriented', that they use generally understandable definitions for activities.[100] In fact, the Union Customs Code contains 41 definitions of terms—the former MCC contained 33 definitions—while the Community Customs Code contains only 26 definitions.

One improvement in terminology is the elimination in the Community Customs Code of the term 'customs-approved treatment or use of goods', defined in Article 4 Number 15 CCC, as compared to 'customs procedures', defined in Article 4 Number 16 CCC. Even both definitions together do not encompass all possible customs procedures, and therefore have led to some confusion.[101] In the Union Customs Code, only the term 'customs procedure' will be maintained, in realisation of the modernisation aim to use terms in their ordinary meaning;[102] see Article 5 Number 16 UCC (former Article 4 Number 12 MCC).

Another contribution to a better and more uniform interpretation and application of EU customs law is the definition of 'customs legislation' in Article 5 Number 2 UCC (former Article 4 Number 2 MCC), which integrates as part of EU customs law not only the Customs Code and its implementing provisions but also the Common Customs Tariff, international agreements, as well as the provisions on the system of reliefs from customs duties.

Furthermore, more uniform terminology is also used regarding decisions, binding information and similar activities of customs authorities. These are now brought together under the generic term 'decisions relating to the application of customs legislation' with largely common provisions in Title I Chapter 2 section 3 UCC (former Title I Chapter 2 section 4 MCC). Compared to the Union Customs Code, the Community Customs Code in Article 4 Number 5 CCC also integrates binding information, but this definition is not followed by general provisions for all customs decisions. The Community Customs Code contains rather widespread and less clearly arranged provisions regarding various kinds of customs decisions. In this regard, the new terminology and especially the common provisions in the Union Customs Code will facilitate the application of the law regarding customs decisions.

100 Lux, 2009 ZfZ Special Vol 1, pp 1–36 (3).
101 Lux/Larrieu, 2006 ZfZ 11, pp 329–41 (330).
102 Lux/Larrieu, 2006 ZfZ 11, pp 329–41 (330).

In the course of the reform, the term 'decision' was temporarily not defined in the new Customs Code, as is currently the case with the Community Customs Code in Article 4 Number 5 CCC. This seemed surprising, given that the modernisation of EU customs law aims to enhance its EU-wide uniform application by introducing clear definitions and avoiding undefined legal terms where possible. The term 'decision' is not that clear because similar acts by the customs authorities in different EU Member States often have different legal forms, such as the German 'Allgemeinverfügung', which is regarded to be a decision, and the similar Austrian 'Allgemeinverfügung', which is regarded to be a regulation. Thus, the latter is subject to national judicial review and not to the provisions on administrative appeal in the new Customs Code.[103] Recital 12 MCC contained a similar description of the term 'decision' and thus suggested that a change in the legal situation was not intended by the deletion of the definition in the Modernised Customs Code.[104]

However, this recital was changed in the proposal for the Union Customs Code in such a way that even the remainder of the definition in Article 4 Number 5 CCC no longer could be found, see Recital 20 of the UCC proposal. At this time, only the latest preliminary draft of the MCCIP[105] still contains a definition of the term 'decision' in Article 110-01 Number 43 *draft* MCCIP, which essentially corresponded to Article 4 Number 5 CCC. Although the placing of such a basic rule in the implementing provisions seemed to be without reason and in contradiction to the conceptual design of the relationship between the new Customs Code and its implementing provisions,[106] the maintenance of the definition in the implementing provisions seems preferable to its complete deletion for reasons of legal certainty and uniform application of EU customs law. However, the final adopted Union Customs Code again contains the definition of the term 'decision', see Article 5 Number 39 UCC.

4. *Union-Wide Validity of Customs Decisions*

One of the most important improvements regarding uniform application, and which contributes greatly to the development of a customs procedure union, is the establishment of Union-wide validity of decisions in Article 26 UCC (former Article 17 MCC). Although Article 250 CCC already establishes the equal footing of customs decisions in the EU Member States, it also limits this rule to the handling of EU-transnational customs procedure.[107] The Union Customs Code does not contain such a restriction, and its general application therefore provides

[103] Reuter/Fuchs, 2008, pp 56, 57.

[104] ibid, p 57.

[105] Last version (situation as of 31.12.2013): consolidated preliminary draft of the MCCIP of 25 November 2011, Document TAXUD/MCCIP/2010/100-3.

[106] Reuter/Fuchs, 2008, p 56.

[107] Witte/Henke, in: Witte/Henke/Kammerzell (eds), 2009, p 54.

customs authorities and economic operators with more legal certainty.[108] Customs decisions will thus be valid Union-wide, unless the effects of a decision are explicitly limited to one or several EU Member States.

Under the current Community Customs Code, only decisions of the ECJ have EU-wide validity, apart from in the area of EU-transnational customs procedures, pursuant to Article 250 CCC, and the areas of binding information pursuant to Article 12 CCC and Article 11 CCCIP. However, judgements of the ECJ do not affect every customs decision. Therefore, those features of the current Community Customs Code can damage its coherence and uniform application.[109]

For these reasons, the altered form of the regulation in the Union Customs Code is an important step towards a stronger customs procedure union in the EU. In such a customs union, it should and must make no difference at which place and by which customs authority a decision is made, provided they are within the customs territory. Thus, the great advantages of the Union-wide validity of customs decisions outweigh the practical challenges such as translation problems.[110]

5. *Reduction of References to Domestic Law*

On the whole, the national procedural simplifications and references to domestic law found in the Community Customs Code are widely avoided in the Union Customs Code (as they were in the former Modernised Customs Code).[111] The approach of the Union Customs Code is to allow the application of national law only in the areas of appeals and the practical organisation of the customs authorities' work.[112] For example, the possibility for national simplifications and additional national simple customs procedures in the area of Community transit procedures that was provided for in Article 97 paragraph 2 CCC are not present in the Union Customs Code (or in the former Modernised Customs Code).

Although the potential for national idiosyncrasies in customs procedures is not entirely eliminated, the potential for non-uniform administration in EU customs will be reduced with the Union Customs Code. In fact, the term 'provisions in force' in Article 4 Number 23 CCC is deleted in the Union Customs Code (as well as in the former Modernised Customs Code)—as has already been alluded to.[113] Instead, national implementing provisions are defined as a subset of 'customs legislation' in Article 5 Number 2 section (a) UCC (former Article 4 Number 2 section (a) MCC). The new definition points to the importance of uniform application of

[108] ibid, p 54.

[109] Lux/Larrieu, 2006 ZfZ 10, pp 301–06 (303).

[110] Witte/Henke, in: Witte/Henke/Kammerzell (eds), 2009, p 54.

[111] Lux, 2009 ZfZ Special Vol 1, pp 1–36 (6).

[112] Lux/Larrieu, 2006 ZfZ 11, pp 329–41 (332), Lux, 2009 ZfZ Special Vol 1, pp 1–36 (4); Witte, in: Witte/Henke/Kammerzell (eds), 2009, p 39.

[113] See Chapter 6.I.A.1(a).

EU customs law throughout the EU, while simultaneously all the authorisations for nationally determined specifications have been removed, except in the areas of appeal and administrative organisation.[114]

Further, the possibility in certain EU Member States to adopt additional requirements for customs agents with regard to customs declarations was particularly criticised for hampering wider procedural harmonisation.[115] Article 5 paragraph 2 subparagraph 2 CCC allows EU Member States to restrict the right to make customs declarations by representation to local customs agents. In the past, attempts to introduce harmonisation in the area of customs agents have failed,[116] but the Union Customs Code no longer permits EU Member States to restrict direct or indirect representation to local customs agents, see Article 18 paragraphs 2, 3 UCC (former Article 11 paragraph 2 MCC). In the future, every economic operator meeting the conditions set out in Article 39 sections (a) to (d) UCC (former Article 14 sections (a) to (d) MCC) can act as a customs representative in any other EU Member State. Special national conditions will only be allowed under Directive 2006/123/EC of the European Parliament and of the Council of 12 December 2006 on services in the Internal Market[117] in the EU Member State where the economic operator is domiciled.[118] The new general rules in the Union Customs Code with regard to customs agents will thus reduce national idiosyncrasies in customs procedures throughout the EU.

In the area of customs debt, references to national law have also been avoided in the new Customs Code and a further harmonisation of the rules has been undertaken, resulting in an improvement in the functioning of the Internal Market and thus also in a stronger customs procedure union.[119] For example, the reference to domestic law in Article 201 paragraph 3 subparagraph 2 CCC has not been transferred to Article 77 paragraph 3 subparagraph 2 UCC (former Article 44 paragraph 3 subparagraph 2 MCC). Also, the reference in Article 221 paragraph 4 CCC has not been transferred to Article 103 paragraph 2 UCC (former Article 68 paragraph 2 MCC) and instead a uniform limitation period for a customs debt has been provided for. The stronger emphasis on the supranational character of EU customs law in the Union Customs Code is to be welcomed, because the broad application of national provisions in customs procedures has the potential to lead to non-uniform administration of EU customs law and makes it difficult to provide equal conditions for economic operators throughout the customs territory of the whole EU.[120]

[114] Witte, in: Witte/Henke/Kammerzell (eds), 2009, p 39.
[115] Weerth, 2008 ZfZ 7, pp 178–85 (181).
[116] Witte, in: Witte (ed) 2013, Art 5 CCC, para 3.
[117] [2006] OJ L376/36–68.
[118] Witte/Henke, in: Witte/Henke/Kammerzell (eds), 2009, p 46.
[119] Lux, 2009 ZfZ Special Vol 1, pp 1–36 (17, 18); Lux/Larrieu, 2006 ZfZ 11, pp 329–41 (337).
[120] Lux, 2009 ZfZ Special Vol 1, pp 1–36 (6).

6. *First Steps Towards Harmonisation of Administrative Penalties and Further Harmonisation in Customs Appeal Procedures*

Furthermore, the new Customs Code initiates the first preliminary stages for a harmonisation of administrative penalties for the violation of customs rules in the EU Customs Union. In the EU Customs Union, the EU Member States are exclusively competent to pursue any customs violation in their territory. Thus, application of penalties is based on national provisions, which can be of a criminal as well as an administrative nature, as determined by the relevant domestic law.[121]

Up to now, there has been a lack of harmonisation of administrative penalties in EU customs law, especially in the current Community Customs Code and its implementing provisions. Indeed, there are great differences between the EU Member States, which is troublesome for a customs union and not acceptable for the Internal Market, as divergent customs penalties can cause distortions.[122] The existence of 28 national penalty regimes in the area of EU customs has been called inconsistent with the unity that is implicit in a customs union.[123] Indeed, the unity of the EU Customs Union can be violated if differences generate additional costs for economic operators and thus lead to 'penalty-shopping', which might even lead to loss of revenue for some EU Member States.[124]

In this respect, the ECJ has routinely noticed in case law that if penalties are essential to combat serious offences against EU law, then the EU is not prevented from taking measures that relate to the criminal law of the EU Member States.[125] Of particular importance are the statements of the ECJ regarding a case on EU environmental law,[126] which are considered to be of general nature, meaning the findings can be transferred to other areas of EU law provided the conditions are similar.[127] Therefore, the EU's competence for taking measures of a penal character is recognised when it is necessary for the full effectiveness of EU law.[128]

In the light of this case law, the new Customs Code will dictate general principles for administrative penalties, obliging EU Member States to provide for penalties for failure to comply with customs legislation, and which are effective, proportionate and dissuasive, see Article 42 paragraph 1 UCC (former Article 21 paragraph 1 MCC). The Code even provides a non-exhaustive list of possible administrative penalties in Article 42 paragraph 2 UCC (former Article 21 paragraph 2 MCC). The new provision essentially repeats the case law of the ECJ, which has determined the procedural and substantive conditions for the penalisation of violations

[121] Anaboli, (5) 2010 GTCJ (9), pp 389–93 (389).

[122] Lux/Larrieu, 2006 ZfZ 11, pp 329–41 (334), Anaboli, (5) 2010 GTCJ (9), pp 389–93 (389).

[123] Lyons, 2008, p 123.

[124] Anaboli, (5) 2010 GTCJ (9), pp 389–93 (393); Weerth, (8) 2013 GTCJ (2), pp 42–52 (47).

[125] ECJ of 16 October 2003, Case C-91/02, *Hannl + Hofstetter Internationale Spedition GmbH* [2003] ECR I-12077, para 17; ECJ of 7 December 2000, Case C-213/99, *Andrade* [2000] ECR I-11083, para 19.

[126] ECJ of 13 September 2005, Case C-176/03, *Commission v Council* [2005] ECR I-7879, para 48.

[127] Lux/Larrieu, 2006 ZfZ 11, pp 329–41 (333).

[128] Lux/Larrieu, 2006 ZfZ 11, pp 329–41 (334).

of EU law.[129] In several more recent judgements, the ECJ has taken the opportunity to reiterate the obligation of EU Member States to properly and adequately enforce EU law, while acknowledging also that choices on the nature of the penalties remain within the discretion of the EU Member States.[130]

The new provision is expected to lead to a review and perhaps in part even to an intensification of the current systems of administrative penalties and sanctions in the EU Member States, as some do not yet even have a proper system in this regard.[131] Indeed, the future streamlining of customs procedures within an electronic environment and the EU-wide activities of authorised economic operators will lead to an increase of shared responsibilities between EU Member States, making it necessary to ensure a proper level of sanctions throughout the customs territory of the EU, see Recital (23) UCC (former Recital (14) MCC). The fact that customs offences very often involve more than one EU Member State and that, in any case, the penalties can have an impact on the whole customs territory of the EU – especially now, through the introduction of electronic customs systems – is leading to a pragmatic 'de facto Europeanisation' of provisions regarding customs violations.[132]

Furthermore, the Treaty of Lisbon provides legal possibilities to act in the field of customs offences and penalties in Article 83 paragraph 2 TFEU.[133] According to this provision, minimum standards for the definition of criminal offences and sanctions can be established in areas with a high degree of harmonisation if the approximation of national provisions regarding penalties is considered to be essential for the effective implementation of the Union policy in question.[134] Some even favour following a more pragmatic and result-oriented approach by using Article 83 paragraph 2 TFEU as the exclusive legal basis for the approximation of all kind of penalties in the area of EU customs. This approach is advocated over the separate harmonisation of non-criminal violations and penalties because there are no clear boundaries between criminal and non-criminal offences when comparing the legal systems of EU Member States.[135] Thus, the diversity of the national legal systems could make a harmonisation of only administrative penalties difficult.[136]

[129] The first case was ECJ of 15 December 1976, Case 41-76, *Donckerwolcke/Schou* [1976] ECR 1921, para 38; see also, inter alia, ECJ of 16 October 2003, Case C-91/02, *Hannl + Hofstetter Internationale Spedition GmbH* [2003] ECR I-12077, para 17; ECJ of 7 December 2000, Case C-213/99, *Andrade* [2000] ECR I-11083, para 19; ECJ of 16 December 1992, Case C-210/91, *Commission v Greece* [1992] ECR I-6735, paras 19, 20, and the case law cited there.

[130] See, inter alia, ECJ of 16 December 1992, Case C-210/91, *Commission v Greece* [1992] ECR I-6735, paras 19, 20, and the case law cited, in particular ECJ of 21 September 1989, Case 68/88, *Commission v Greece* [1989] ECR I-2965, paras 23, 24, 25.

[131] Witte/Henke, in: Witte/Henke/Kammerzell (eds), 2009, p 57.

[132] Anaboli, (5) 2010 GTCJ (9), pp 389–93 (391).

[133] Weerth, (8) 2013 GTCJ (2), pp 42–52 (48).

[134] Anaboli, (5) 2010 GTCJ (9), pp 389–93 (392).

[135] ibid, pp 389–393 (393); Hobbing, CEPS Papers No 39, June 2011, p 16; Grave, (5) 2010 GTCJ (3), pp 95–111 (105).

[136] Anaboli, (5) 2010 GTCJ (9), pp 389–93 (393).

Others object to a pragmatic solution and are of the opinion that the harmonisation of administrative penalties in the context of EU customs should be based on Article 33 TFEU.[137] Some consider Article 325 TFEU – regarding necessary measures for combatting fraud affecting the financial interests of the EU – to have the potential to become the core of a new European penal law that covers also infringements of EU customs law.[138] Indeed, customs duties are traditionally own resources of the EU, and thus criminal action in the field of EU customs affects the financial interests of the EU.[139] Despite the lack of a distinction between administrative and criminal penalties in some EU Member States,[140] the possibility of further harmonisation of criminal customs sanctions has been considered.[141]

Indeed, the European Commission has already proposed such a directive based on Article 325 paragraph 4 TFEU.[142] This proposal contains a definition of the EU's financial interests, which comprises all revenues and expenditures covered by, acquired through, or due to the Union budget (see Article 2 of the proposal), and thus also covers customs duties.[143] The proposal further sets out specific criminal offences affecting the EU's financial interests in Articles 3 and 4 of the proposal. It also lays down general provisions for sanctions and penalties against these criminal offences including jurisdiction and statutes of limitations, Articles 5 et seq of the proposal. Thus, this directive could become an important step towards a harmonisation of criminal offences in the context of EU customs, though it does still allow EU Member States a certain degree of flexibility.

Although the development of a EU framework for criminal law provisions in the field of the EU's financial interests including customs duties is being undertaken outside the Union Customs Code, the intention is to be welcomed. Also, the newly introduced provision of Article 42 UCC (former Article 21 MCC) is a positive signal of more harmonisation and therefore of a stronger customs procedure union in the future.[144] This is especially the case for Article 42 paragraph 3 UCC (former Article 21 paragraph 3 MCC), which obliges the EU Member States to notify the European Commission of relevant provisions in force. The European Commission will use this reporting obligation as an indication as to whether a common and uniform practice of administrative penalties in the EU Member States exists.[145]

Also in the area of appeal procedures, a further – even if slight – harmonisation is underway. In contrast to Article 245 CCC, Article 44 UCC (former Article 23 MCC) no longer stipulates the clear priority of national law regarding appeal procedures in the area of EU customs. Instead, Article 44 paragraphs 2 and 4 UCC

137 Weerth, (8) 2013 GTCJ (2), pp 42–52 (49).
138 Möller, 2011 ZfZ 2, pp 39–42 (41).
139 Möller, 2011 ZfZ 2, pp 39–42 (40); Retemeyer/Möller, 2013 ZfZ 2, pp 29–32 (30).
140 Hobbing, CEPS Papers No 39, June 2011, p 16; Grave, (5) 2010 GTCJ (3), pp 95–111 (105).
141 COM (2005) 608 final, p 9.
142 COM (2012) 363 final.
143 Retemeyer/Möller, 2013 ZfZ 2, pp 29–32 (30).
144 Lux/Larrieu, 2006 ZfZ 11, pp 329–41 (334).
145 Witte/Henke, in: Witte/Henke/Kammerzell (eds), 2009, p 58.

(former Article 23 paragraphs 2 and 4 MCC) states that EU Member States have to regulate what is not covered by the Union Customs Code, wherein some principles regarding the filing of an appeal are now provided for. These provisions constrain the general authorisation of EU Member States to determine the details of appeals through national law.[146] However, judicial court decisions remain completely within the competence of the EU Member States and thus under national law, Article 43 UCC (former Article 22 MCC).

C. Conclusion

In conclusion, the Union Customs Code does indeed facilitate a stronger customs procedure union by further harmonising procedural law in EU customs. The establishment of electronic customs through the obligation to use IT technical procedures with electronic data-processing techniques will simplify customs procedures and avoid grey zones in the interpretation of the law, thereby enhancing uniform application of EU customs law. The reduction and simplification of customs procedures and the more coherent structure of the Union Customs Code facilitate its application and will improve the functioning of EU-transnational customs procedures. The simplified legal terminology of the Union Customs Code will contribute to a better and more uniform interpretation and application of EU customs law. The EU-wide validity of customs decisions is an important step because in the EU Customs Union it must make no difference at which place and by which customs authority a customs decision is made. The reduction of references to domestic law will avoid national idiosyncrasies in customs procedures throughout the EU. Even though the Union Customs Code still does not constitute an exhaustive codification of customs procedure law, together with the electronic environment for EU customs – for which the Union Customs Code constitutes the legal framework – it will allow a more simple, quick and uniform functioning of the EU Customs Union.

II. STATUS QUO AND DEVELOPMENT REGARDING AN EU CUSTOMS ADMINISTRATION UNION

While there are developments towards a stronger customs procedure union with uniform administrative procedural law, the EU Customs Union has also been criticised for being not a customs administration union with a uniform administrative organisation given that EU customs law is administered by the national

[146] Alexander, in: Witte (ed), 2013, Art 245 CCC, para 3; Lux/Larrieu, 2006 ZfZ 11, pp 329–41 (334); Lux, 2009 ZfZ Special Vol 1, pp 1–36 (14); Witte/Henke, in: Witte/Henke/Kammerzell (eds), 2009, pp 59, 60.

customs administrations of the 28 EU Member States.[147] This accusation is based on the assumption that the centralised administration of EU customs is a necessary requirement for a customs administration union. Indeed, strict institutional and organisational autonomy of EU Member States would hardly be compatible with the expectations of such a customs administration union. To a certain degree, a kind of 'patchwork situation', with 28 national infrastructures applying EU customs law in their own way, can be seen in the area of EU customs.[148]

However, the decentralised concept of customs administration in the EU does not necessarily preclude the existence of an EU Customs Administration Union per se: the institutional and organisational autonomy of the EU Member States is affected by EU law in various ways,[149] also in the area of EU customs. Therefore, the functional unity of European administration and cooperation between the EU Member States' administrations, as well as between the latter and the European Commission, has to be considered in order to capture the reality of European administration.[150] In this sense, approaches for an EU Customs Administration Union do exist despite the decentralised organisation of customs administration in the EU.[151] Nevertheless, the absence of a centralised administration for the EU Customs Union could be problematic for the uniform implementation of EU customs law.[152] Therefore, the legal possibility for a centralised customs administration on the EU's level has to be analysed further.

A. The Legal Possibility for Direct Implementation in EU Customs Administration

The EU Member States' organisational autonomy in national administration has to be respected in regard to the indirect implementation of EU law; correspondingly, every exercise of competences by the EU needs a legal basis.[153] The doctrine of implied powers can constitute such a legal basis for administrative competences on the EU level as an annex competence linked to a corresponding legislative competence of the EU in a certain area. The concept of implied powers is known in the EU legal system[154] and has also been acknowledged by the ECJ.[155]

[147] Weerth, 2008 ZfZ 7, pp 178–85 (181).

[148] Hobbing, CEPS Papers No 39, June 2011, p 15.

[149] Nettesheim, in: Oppermann/Classen/Nettesheim (eds), 2011, § 12, para 29; Hofmann/Rowe/Türk, 2011, p 262.

[150] Hofmann/Rowe/Türk, 2011, p 262.

[151] See Chapter 6.I.

[152] Hofmann/Rowe/Türk, 2011, p 260.

[153] See Chapter 6.I.

[154] Craig, 2012, p 371.

[155] See, inter alia, ECJ of 13 September 2005, Case C-176/03, *Commission v Council* [2005] ECR I-7879, paras 44, 47, 48, and the case law cited; see also General Court of 17 November 2009, Case T-143/06, *MTZ Polyfilms Ltd* [2009] ECR II-4133, para 47, and the case law cited.

However, the EU's legislative competences are typically aimed at a certain objective and, therefore, administrative competences relating to procedural or organisational regulations require special substantiation.[156] The doctrine of implied powers itself cannot constitute a special right for administrative competences because such competences based on the doctrine of implied powers can only exist if there are corresponding legislative competences of the EU in a certain area.[157] Therefore, the doctrine of implied powers has to abide by the general limitations for EU competences, such as the principles of subsidiarity, Article 5 paragraph 1 sentence 1 and paragraph 3 TEU, and proportionality, Article 5 paragraph 4 TEU.[158]

1. *The Principle of Subsidiarity*

The principle of subsidiarity is a rule to decide whether and how competences shall be exercised on the EU's level.[159] Nevertheless, the ECJ has also decided that administrative competences of the EU for direct implementation of EU law can indeed be established by EU secondary law provided that, first, the EU has a corresponding legislative competence regarding the area in question, and, secondly, that existing limitations of the legislative competence in question were respected when creating a corresponding annex competence for EU administration. For example, if the legal act in question was based on Article 114 TFEU (former Article 95 TEC), the creation of an annexe competence based on the doctrine of implied powers would also have to aim to improve the functioning of the Internal Market by facilitating the uniform implementation and application of the legal act in question.[160]

However, the specific requirements for the existence of implicit powers are contested.[161] While the ECJ seems to take a wide view of the concept of implied powers,[162] the General Court takes a narrower approach following the example of earlier judgments of the ECJ, which hold that implicit powers are only recognised when they are necessary to ensure the practical effectiveness of EU law.[163] Furthermore, Article 197 paragraph 1 TFEU now constitutes an objective legitimation for the establishment of regulations to ensure the uniform implementation of

[156] Classen, in: Grabitz/Hilf/Nettesheim (eds), 2013, Vol II, Art 197 TFEU, para 12.

[157] Weiß, 2010, pp 38, 39; Stelkens, 2012 EuR 5, pp 511–45 (522).

[158] Weiß, 2010, pp 38, 39; Stelkens, 2012 EuR 5, pp 511–45 (522).

[159] Weiß, 2010, p 37, fn 49.

[160] ECJ of 2 May 2006, Case C-217/04, *ENISA* [2006] ECR I-3771, paras 42, 44; ECJ of 6 December 2005, Case C-66/04, *United Kingdom v Parliament and Council* [2005] ECR I-10553, para 44; ECJ of 9 August 1994, Case C-359/92, *Germany v Council* [1994] ECR I-3681, para 37.

[161] Craig, 2012, p 371.

[162] ECJ of 13 September 2005, Case C-176/03, *Commission v Council* [2005] ECR I-7879, paras 47, 48.

[163] General Court of 17 November 2009, Case T-143/06, *MTZ Polyfilms Ltd* [2009] ECR II-4133, para 47, and the ECJ's case law cited.

EU law.[164] Also, Article 291 paragraph 2 TFEU explicitly requires uniform implementing conditions when conferring implementing powers on the European Commission.[165]

In the area of EU customs, the EU has the legal power to replace the indirect implementation by the EU Member States in EU customs administration with a direct application on the EU level by installing administrative competences for EU bodies in EU secondary law based on the doctrine of implied powers, which is a sufficient legal basis given its comprehensive legislative competences in the area of EU customs. Moreover, the EU would not have to obey the principle of subsidiarity here, because this principle does not apply to areas where the EU has exclusive legislative competences, pursuant to Article 5 paragraph 3 TEU – which is the case in EU customs pursuant to Article 3 TFEU. Although Article 3 TFEU does not constitute exclusive competences which have to be further concretised in EU primary law,[166] it refers to Articles 28, 31, 32, 33 TFEU and therefore to the competences for the regulation of the EU Customs Union.[167] Consequently, the enactment of the central piece of EU customs law, namely the Customs Code, falls under the exclusive competence of the EU and does not fall under the principle of subsidiarity, as was expressly noted in the proposals of the Modernised Customs Code as well as of the Union Customs Code.[168] In this context, the administrative power of the EU Member States in the area of EU customs has been said to be simply an arrangement between the EU and the EU Member States in order to ensure EU customs law is administered at the appropriate level.[169]

However, the Customs Code is based inter alia on Article 114 TFEU/former Article 95 TEC,[170] the general competence for the harmonisation of regulatory areas with relevance for the Internal Market. Indeed, Article 2 paragraph 1 TFEU clearly states that only legislative competences are exclusive, while responsibility for implementation remains with the EU Member States. Thus, Article 114 TFEU's limitations have to be respected if the EU intended to gain new administrative competences based on the doctrine of implied powers.[171] Therefore, the requirements for an annexe competence of the EU for the direct implementation of EU customs law by the EU itself are not low and should not be underestimated. A mere finding of disparities between EU Member States would be insufficient to trigger recourse to Article 114 TFEU (former Article 95 TEC),[172] though the

[164] Classen, in: Grabitz/Hilf/Nettesheim (eds), 2013, Vol II, Art 197 TFEU, para 1.

[165] Hofmann/Rowe/Türk, 2011, p 120.

[166] Classen, in: Grabitz/Hilf/Nettesheim (eds), 2013, Vol I, Art 3 TFEU, para 1.

[167] Calliess, in: Calliess/Ruffert (eds), 2011, Art 3 TFEU, para 5; Nettesheim, in: Grabitz/Hilf/Nettesheim (eds), 2013, Vol I, Art 3 TFEU, para 10.

[168] COM (2005) 608 final, p 7; COM (2012) 64 final, p 9.

[169] Grave, (5) 2010 GTCJ (3), pp 95–111 (97).

[170] COM (2005) 608 final, p 7; COM (2012) 64 final, p 8.

[171] Weiß, 2010, p 39.

[172] See, inter alia, ECJ of 12 December 2006, Case C-380/03, *Germany v Parliament and Council*, [2006] ECR I-11573, para 37 and the case law cited.

high standards once applied by the ECJ[173] have been mitigated in subsequent case law.[174] Thus, a central competence of the EU for the direct implementation of EU customs law could only be in accordance with EU primary law if non-uniform implementation of EU customs law in the decentralised administration would endanger the functioning of the Internal Market and its aim of legal unity in a concrete way.[175]

However, the system of indirect implementation in the administration of EU customs is consistent with the actual distribution of administrative capacities and places administration in closer proximity to citizens as well as to the policy being governed.[176] It thus also serves to protect national sovereignty and promote the acceptance of EU law in the EU Member States.[177] Furthermore, though a centralised EU customs administration could perhaps improve the uniform implementation of EU customs law, it is also likely that such an overarching administrative organisation would face problems such as excessive complexity, inefficiency and lengthy decision-making processes.[178]

Furthermore, in the event that the European Commission seeks to transfer its administrative competences to a newly established European agency acting as a central customs authority on the EU level, it would have to respect additional requirements the ECJ first laid out in its *Meroni* decision[179] and which in principle continue to be valid.[180] On the other hand, if an EU regulation were to establish an EU agency with new competences and functions that were not previously executed by the European Commission, the *Meroni* doctrine may not be applicable to its full extent because the transfer of competences in question would mainly affect the vertical relationship between the EU and its EU Member States.[181] Therefore, the requirements of EU law for a conferral of implementing powers to the European Commission, pursuant to Article 291 paragraph 2 TFEU, have to be analysed further, as do developments in EU customs law regarding a more centralised approach to customs administration.

[173] High standards for legislative competences pursuant to Art 114 TFEU/former Art 95 TEC have been thoroughly discussed in: ECJ of 5 October 2000, Case C-376/98, *Tobacco Advertising Directive* [2000] ECR I-8419.

[174] See, inter alia, ECJ of 22 January 2014, Case C-270/12, *United Kingdom v Parliament and Council* [2014] ECR I-0, paras 113–17; ECJ of 12 December 2006, Case C-380/03, *Germany v Parliament and Council*, [2006] ECR I-11573, paras 37, 38, 39, and the case law cited.

[175] ECJ of 22 January 2014, Case C-270/12, *United Kingdom v Parliament and Council* [2014] ECR I-0, paras 104, 107, 108; ECJ of 2 May 2006, Case C-217/04, *ENISA* [2006] ECR I-3771, para 44.

[176] Weiß, 2010, p 37.

[177] ibid, p 37.

[178] ibid, p 37.

[179] ECJ of 13 June 1958, Case 9-56, *Meroni* [1958] ECR English Special Edition 133 et seq (151, 152).

[180] See, inter alia, ECJ of 22 January 2014, Case C-270/12, *United Kingdom v Parliament and Council* [2014] ECR I-0, para 41 et seq. The *Meroni* doctrine was inducted into Council Regulation (EC Euratom) 1605/2002 of 25 June 2002 on the Financial Regulation applicable to the general budget of the European Communities, [2002] OJ L248/1–86.

[181] Weiß, in: Hofmann/Weaver (eds), 2011, pp 221–50 (226, fn 16); Ohler, 2006 EuZW 12, pp 369–74 (373); critically Dehousse, in: Joerges/Dehousse (eds), 2003, pp 207–29 (220–23).

2. *Criteria for the Need of Uniform Implementing Conditions Pursuant to Article 291 Paragraph 2 TFEU*

Article 291 paragraph 2 TFEU allows the EU legislator to empower the European Commission to adopt implementing acts and thus allows for the possibility of a centralisation of administrative action under certain conditions. To bring Article 291 paragraph 2 TFEU in line with the adoption of individual acts by the European Commission, this provision has to be interpreted in the light of the principle of subsidiarity, pursuant to Article 5 paragraph 3 TFEU.[182] The need for uniform implementation conditions substantiating the transfer of executive competence from the EU Member States to the European Commission has to correspond to the intensity of the EU level's intervention in the implementation of EU law.

The adoption of individual acts regarding the implementation of legally binding EU law requires strong substantiation, as such centralisation of administrative implementation interferes with the basic distribution of competences in the EU.[183] Individual acts can possibly reduce any scope of discretion for the national authorities in a concrete case of administrative action. Therefore, the legitimate interest for uniform implementing conditions alone is an inadequate reason for a central implementation competence.[184] Rather, an additional benefit from the centralisation of the administrative implementation is required, especially in the sense of better achievement of the objectives of the legal act in question, pursuant to Article 5 paragraph 3 TFEU.[185]

The criteria required to substantiate the need for a conferral of implementing powers to the EU level are undefined.[186] To some extent it is preferred to assess the degree of effectiveness of national implementation compared to a more centralised administration on the EU level and to then decide about the additional benefit in the concrete case.[187] Yet it has been adumbrated that expectations regarding the restraints on a conferral of implementing powers are limited, despite the new conditions introduced by Article 291 paragraph 2 TFEU, because the EU legislator still has wide discretion regarding the need for uniform implementing conditions.[188] The conferrals of implementing powers in the Union Customs Code seem to confirm this assessment.

The need to ensure the uniform application of EU law is of special importance in EU customs law because of the requirement of the WTO to administer customs law uniformly pursuant to Article X:3(a) GATT 1994. Experience from the

[182] Weiß, 2010, p 42; Ruffert, in: Calliess/Ruffert (eds), 2011, Art 291 TFEU, para 6; similar Hofmann/Rowe/Türk, 2011, p 530.

[183] Weiß, 2010, p 41.

[184] ibid, p 41.

[185] ibid, p 42; Ruffert, in: Calliess/Ruffert (eds), 2011, Art 291 TFEU, para 6.

[186] Hofmann/Rowe/Türk, 2011, p 530.

[187] Nettesheim, in: Grabitz/Hilf/Nettesheim (eds), 2013, Vol III, Art 291 TFEU, para 23.

[188] ibid, Vo III, Art 291 TFEU, para 24; similar Hofmann/Rowe/Türk, 2011, p 530.

dispute settlement *EC—Selected Customs Matters*[189] has shown the importance of ensuring on the EU level that EU customs legislation is implemented under uniform conditions. The European Commission's request for more authority, more competence in and more influence on the regulation of the indirect implementation of EU customs law is therefore understandable. However, the special importance of a uniform customs administration in the EU does not release the EU legislator from its obligation pursuant to Article 291 paragraph 2 TFEU. The EU legislator is obliged to substantiate the additional benefit of an authorisation of the European Commission while also proving the insufficient effectiveness of the indirect implementation of EU customs law.

Recital (5) UCC contains a summary of the manifold areas in which implementing powers should be conferred to the European Commission in order to ensure uniform conditions for the implementation of the Union Customs Code. However, there is no specific reason provided to clarify the need for a conferral of implementing powers in the sense of Article 291 paragraph 2 TFEU. Recital (5) UCC simply determines that any conferral of implementing powers to the European Commission in the Union Customs Code has been laid down to ensure uniform implementing conditions. This superficial reference in Recital (5) UCC is more a simple recitation of the wording of Article 291 paragraph 2 TFEU than an adequate reason for the alleged need for implementation by the European Commission.

Most of the provisions conferring implementing powers to the European Commission contain no reference to the need to provide uniform implementing conditions at the EU level as required by Article 291 paragraph 2 TFEU. Article 50 UCC at least refers to this condition in authorising the European Commission to adopt measures to ensure the uniform application of customs controls and risk management, but such reference does not constitute a substantiation of an additional benefit in the sense of Article 291 paragraph 2 TFEU. The Union Customs Code thus fails to substantiate the additional benefit of a more centralised approach with regard to uniform implementing conditions and instead seems to request a more centralised administration of EU customs by simply referring to the interest in the uniform application of EU customs legislation.

3. *Conclusion*

The possibility to administer EU customs by direct implementation through a genuine European administrative organisation, for example an EU customs agency, has not yet been realised. With regard to the conferral of implementing powers to the European Commission in the administration of EU customs, the Union Customs Code does not seem to have introduced a new era in the European Commission's exercise of implementing powers, as so far there is no indication

[189] WT/DS/315.

of the application of an additional executive subsidiarity test in favour of the EU Member States concurrent implementing powers. This is consistent with the general estimation about the European Commission's adaption of its day-to-day law-making practice to the Lisbon Treaty, which entails simply the routine issuing of acts entitled 'implementing acts'.[190]

The absence of any substantiation in the Union Customs Code regarding the requirements of Article 291 paragraph 2 TFEU could indicate that the institutions of the EU indeed claim an extensive scope of legislative leeway regarding the need for uniform implementing conditions.[191] Therefore, any expectations regarding the affirmation and guarantee of EU Member States' competence for the implementation of EU law by introducing new conditions in Article 291 paragraph 2 TFEU may not be met.[192] However, although a stronger position for the European Commission might be desirable to ensure the uniform implementation of EU customs law, which is indeed essential for the functioning of the EU Customs Union, the conditions set out in Article 291 paragraph 2 TFEU should still be respected to avoid a lack of credibility with regard to the EU's democratic legitimacy. At the very least the European Commission should substantiate the reasons for its implementing action when adopting an implementing act, even though this does not exactly meet the requirements of Article 291 paragraph 2 TFEU. It is for the EU legislator, namely the Council and the European Parliament, to decide whether the conditions of Article 291 paragraph 2 TFEU are met or not.[193]

As long as the EU administers its EU custom law by national customs administrations through indirect implementation, the organisational autonomy of the EU Member States has to be respected. Nevertheless, in single and especially strongly supranationalised areas, EU secondary law has some influence on the structure of the national administrations and substantial EU law can to some extent contain certain requirements for domestic administrative organisation that the EU Member States have to obey and to implement correctly given the primacy of EU law over coextensive national law.[194] EU customs law constitutes such a strongly supranationalised area.

B. Special Provisions in EU Customs Law Regarding Administrative Organisation

The administration of EU customs requires a clear and coherent allocation of tasks and responsibilities between the different customs authorities in the EU Customs Union. However, in EU customs law, the current Community Customs Code and

[190] Bast, 2012 CMLRev (49), pp 885–927 (909).

[191] Nettesheim, in: Grabitz/Hilf/Nettesheim (eds), 2013 Vol III, Art 291 TFEU, para 24.

[192] ibid, Art 291 TFEU, para 24.

[193] Craig, 2010, p 281.

[194] Streinz, 2012, § 7, paras 583, 584, 589; Hofmann/Rowe/Türk, 2011, p 261; Kadelbach, in: Joerges/Dehousse (eds), 2003, pp 167–206 (171).

its implementing provisions contain only a few specific provisions regarding the allocation of functions between competent customs offices in the administration of EU customs.

1. Community Customs Code

Article 60 CCC (Article 159 UCC/former Article 105 MCC) is of special importance because, despite its systemic position, it contains basic rules regarding the competent national customs office for the execution of tasks in a customs procedure or in other fields of customs administration, rules that apply for the whole scope of the Community Customs Code.[195] Simultaneously, the provision constitutes a catch-all provision for national rules on the determination of the competent customs office for a customs procedure or other fields of customs administration.[196] According to this, the EU Member States are to determine the competent customs offices situated in their territory when the customs legislation of the EU does not lay down any specific rules on the matter. In doing so, the EU Member States are obliged to take account of the nature of the goods in question and the customs procedure under which they are to be placed.

Even if the proposition that Article 60 CCC (Article 159 UCC/former Article 105 MCC) has application beyond Title IV Chapter 2 of the Community Customs Code were to be rejected,[197] the unwritten principle of the primacy of EU customs law regarding the regulation of competences in EU customs administration would have to be obeyed.[198] Therefore, the EU Member States would still be able to adopt rules on the competent customs offices situated in their territory when EU customs law contains no specific provisions in this regard.[199] Thus, a more limited scope of application of Article 60 CCC (Article 159 UCC/former Article 105 MCC), narrowed down to placing goods under a customs procedure, would not result in practical differences.

For the rest, only sporadic provisions on the competent customs office for the execution of tasks in a customs procedure exist in EU customs law. These include: Article 92 paragraph 1 CCC (Article 196 paragraph 2, Article 185 paragraph 2 UCC/former Article 146 paragraph 2 MCC) for the finalisation of transit procedures, Article 161 paragraph 5 (Article 271 UCC/former Article 180 MCC) for export declaration, and Article 500 paragraph 2 CCCIP for single authorisation. Albeit of lesser importance, further regulations on competent customs authorities

[195] Henke, in: Witte (ed), 2013, Art 60 CCC, para 1; contra Weymüller, in: Rüsken (ed), 2013, Vol I, Art 60 CCC, para 1.

[196] Stüwe, in: Hübschmann/Hepp/Spitaler (eds), 2013, Vol XIV, Art 60 CCC, para 3; Henke, in: Witte (ed), 2013, Art 60 CCC, paras 1, 4; contra Weymüller, in: Rüsken (ed), 2013, Vol I, Art 60 CCC, para 1.

[197] Weymüller is of this opinion, in: Rüsken (ed), 2013, Vol I, Art 60 CCC, para 1.

[198] ibid, Art 60 CCC, para 1.

[199] ibid, Art 60 CCC, para 1.

in a customs procedure can be found, for example, in Article 38 paragraph 1 section (a) CCC (Article 135 paragraph 1 UCC/former Article 92 paragraph 1 MCC) and Article 40 CCC (Article 139 paragraph 1 UCC/former Article 95 paragraph 1 MCC) as well as Article 201 paragraph 1, Article 359, Article 496 and Article 498 CCCIP.

The sporadic rules on the competent customs offices regarding the execution of tasks in customs administration are focused on the provisions regarding customs procedures, but there exists also allocation of tasks in other customs administration areas. However, to a large extent EU customs law leaves the determination of the competent customs offices regarding the execution of tasks in these customs administration areas to the EU Member States' own devices.[200] Those customs administration areas are, for example, decisions relating to binding information, Article 12 CCC (Article 33 UCC/former Article 20 MCC); customs controls, Article 13 CCC (Article 46 UCC/former Article 25 MCC); determination of origin, Title II Chapter 2 CCC (Title II Chapter 2 UCC/former MCC); determination of customs value, Title II Chapter 3 CCC (Title II Chapter 3 UCC/former MCC); and customs debt, Title VII CCC (Title III UCC/former MCC).

2. *Union Customs Code*

In the new Customs Code, the common mission of the customs authorities in the EU Customs Union was laid down for the first time in Article 2 MCC, now Article 3 UCC: customs authorities shall be primarily responsible for the supervision of the EU's international trade, thereby contributing to fair and open trade; to the implementation of the external aspects of the Internal Market, of the common trade policy and of the other common Union policies having a bearing on trade; and to overall supply chain security. Although the European Commission will be bound by the objectives of Article 3 UCC, former Article 2 MCC, when developing implementing provisions and other customs related action, there are no rules regarding the organisation of customs administrations in the new Customs Code. The mere description of the mission of customs administrations in the EU cannot change the fact that organisational power and sovereignty in the administration of EU customs remains with the EU Member States.[201]

In the Union Customs Code, Article 159 UCC (former Article 105 MCC) deals with the determination of the competent customs office. While the EU Member States still can determine the locations and competences in their national customs administrations, the new Code explicitly emphasises the primacy of EU law. Moreover, as a novelty, the EU Member States are now also expressly obliged to ensure their customs offices provide appropriate and reasonable opening hours, Article 159 paragraph 2 UCC (former Article 105 paragraph 1 subparagraph 2 MCC). Furthermore, the European Commission is authorised and empowered to

[200] ibid, Art 60 CCC, para 15.

[201] Lux/Larrieu, 2006 ZfZ 11, pp 329–41 (335).

adopt implementing provisions – and also delegated acts – in order to determine the various tasks and responsibilities of the competent customs offices, Articles 160, 161 UCC (former Article 105 paragraph 2 MCC).

Therefore, details of a new distribution of tasks between inland customs offices and frontier customs offices are being developed in the modernised implementing provisions. In these provisions, the European Commission aspires to a differentiated solution that focuses inland customs officers on fiscal and trade policy related tasks with economic objectives, while frontier customs officers will operate security controls.[202] Indeed, the preliminary draft of the Modernised Customs Code implementing provisions contains for the first time general rules on the competent customs offices and authorisations for all customs procedures in Title V, Chapter 2, section 1, subsection 1 draft-MCCIP.[203] These provisions regulate the competence for lodging a customs declaration, Article 521-1-01 draft-MCCIP; as well as application and authorisation, Article 521-1-02 draft-MCCIP; conditions for authorisation, Article 521-1-03 draft-MCCIP; and time-limits, Article 521-1-04 draft-MCCIP. It also provides for a consultation procedure between competent customs authorities when needed to reach agreement on authorisation, as well as outlining its possible simplifications, Articles 521-1-05 and 521-1-06 draft-MCCIP.

Furthermore, Title 1, Chapter 1, Article 110-01, Numbers 29 to 41, 68, 95 draft MCCIP introduces another novelty by providing 15 definitions for various kinds of competent customs offices with different tasks, including occasionally excessively detailed descriptions, such as 'customs office of exit' (Numbers 33 and 34), 'customs office of import' (Number 37), 'customs office of presentation' (Number 40), 'customs office of transit' (Number 41), or even 'monitoring customs office' (Number 68) and 'supervising customs office' (Number 95). These various definitions indicate that the European Commission has taken seriously its responsibility to arrange the various tasks of the competent customs offices in implementing provisions – and delegated acts – pursuant to Articles 160, 161 UCC (former Article 105 paragraph 2 MCC). They also imply that the new Customs Code implementing provisions will indeed contain more detailed rules with a predetermined assignment of tasks for the different customs offices in the implementation of EU customs law, which has also the potential to influence the national allocation of competences in customs administration. Although the EU Member States still have organisational autonomy in the administration of EU customs, the provisions in the new Customs Code and presumably in the new implementing provisions set certain general preconditions on the allocation of competences by determining the various tasks and responsibilities of customs offices in customs procedures.

[202] Lux/Larrieu, 2006 ZfZ 11, pp 329–341 (331).

[203] Last version (situation as of 31.12.2013): Consolidated preliminary draft of the MCCIP of 25 November 2011, Document TAXUD/MCCIP/2010/100-3.

C. Conclusion

The EU Member States do not possess limitless organisational autonomy in the administration of EU customs. Furthermore, the Union Customs Code provides for the manifold conferral of implementing powers to the European Commission, while the new conditions introduced by Article 291 paragraph 2 TFEU are not reflected in the Union Customs Code, indicating the stronger position of the European Commission in the EU customs administration than previously was the case. Nevertheless, the EU has not yet realised a centralised EU customs administration at the EU level. Therefore, the organisational autonomy of the EU Member States in the indirect implementation of EU customs law still has to be respected. The Community Customs Code as well as the Union Customs Code contain only a few general rules regarding administrative organisation and sporadic rules for some specific customs procedures.

However, horizontal forms of cooperation and interdependences between national administrations and also vertically with the European Commission could be sufficient to replace the outdated structure of indirect implementation with a new kind of integrated European administration that also has elements of a functional uniform administration.[204] In this spirit, the European Customs Union could come close to an EU Customs Administration Union without requiring the central implementation of EU customs law. Therefore, forms of cooperation in the system of indirect implementation of EU customs, as well as the role and competences of the European Commission, have to be analysed further.

[204] Hofmann/Rowe/Türk, 2011, pp 14, 262; Weiß, 2010, pp 16, 18.

7

Administrative Cooperation as a Strategy for Enhancing Uniform Customs Administration

ALTHOUGH THE EU is not an administration union in the sense of a centrally organised administrative body, the principle of the institutional autonomy of the individual EU Member States is gradually receding with the increasing cooperation between national administrations.[1] This development can also be observed in the area of EU customs. This chapter considers the importance of administrative cooperation for the uniform functioning of the EU Customs Union.

Enhancing cooperation is a strategy used by the EU to ensure uniform application of EU customs law throughout the EU Customs Union.[2] The decentralised system of customs administration in the EU requires close cooperation between the EU Member States and between them and the European Commission.[3] Cooperation is an instrument to improve the functioning of EU customs administration; its promotion is part of the Future Customs Initiative.

Generally, cooperation in the administration of EU law can be realised through vertical cooperation between EU Member States and institutions of the EU as well as through horizontal cooperation among the EU Member States themselves.[4] Both forms of cooperation have their general legal basis in EU law, and in both forms of cooperation the administrative acts of national authorities are national acts irrespective of their legal basis, even if they affect legal relationships in other EU Member States.[5] There also exist mixed forms of vertical and horizontal cooperation, in which EU institutions are often involved in developing and distributing information in order to facilitate the horizontal cooperation of the EU Member States.[6]

[1] Nettesheim, in: Oppermann/Classen/Nettesheim (eds), 2011, § 13, para 33 and even more clearly in the 4th edn 2009, see: Nettesheim, in: Oppermann/Classen/Nettesheim (eds), 2009, § 13, para 33.
[2] Lux, 2012 AW-Prax 8, pp 257–62 (259).
[3] Lux, in: Lenz/Borchardt (eds), 2013, Art 33 TFEU, para 1.
[4] Hatje, 1998, p 128.
[5] Schmidt-Aßmann, 1996 EuR 3, pp 270–301 (273).
[6] Hofmann/Rowe/Türk, 2011, pp 16, 17; Schmidt-Aßmann, 1996 EuR 3, pp 270–301 (273, 274).

Indeed, cooperation in the area of EU customs represents a combination of both vertical and horizontal cooperation, in which also the European Commission has some influence.[7] The cooperation between EU Member States and the European Commission focuses on ensuring the correct application of EU customs law, because the protection of the financial interests of the EU places high demands on the national customs administrations of the EU Member States.[8] Especially in the context of mutual assistance in matters of customs infringements by economic operators, the cooperation amongst the EU Member States has been described as an exemplar of comprehensive horizontal cooperation.[9]

There are various possibilities for customs cooperation in the EU. On the political level, the EU Member States can consult each other in order to coordinate their operations in the Council of Ministers of the EU, and the Council of Ministers can issue statements of common positions on operations in the EU.[10] More interestingly, there are possibilities for administrative operational cooperation regarding implementation issues. The securing of uniform customs administration requires, most notably, the cooperation of national customs authorities for guaranteeing the uniform application of EU customs law, smooth operation of cross-border customs procedures, interoperability of national IT systems among the EU Member States and between them and the European Commission, exchange of information, and also effective measures for the fight against fraud.[11] Therefore, EU law allows for intensive cooperation in the field of EU customs, including operational cooperation of customs authorities with police and other governmental authorities for the purpose of investigating customs infringements, but also cooperation in training as well as exchange of customs officials and of best practices.[12]

However, customs cooperation in the EU finds itself also in a special situation as a result of the former three-pillar structure of the EU introduced with the Treaty of Maastricht in 1993.[13] This three-pillar structure consisted of the European Communities (EC) (the first pillar), the Common Foreign and Security Policy (CFSP) (the second pillar), and Police and Judicial Co-operation in Criminal Matters (PJCC) (the third pillar). This structure split customs cooperation between first pillar action and third pillar action and distributed the performance of customs tasks on the European level to three departments:[14] political tasks in the first pillar are located in the European Commission DG TAXUD;[15] operational tasks regarding the fight against fraud as administrative prevention and investigation of customs infringements are situated in the European Anti-Fraud Office (OLAF);

[7] Dietrich, 2005, p 5; Waldhoff, in: Calliess/Ruffert, 2011, Art 33 TFEU, para 8.
[8] Kunas, in: Bongartz (ed), 2000, pp 1–24 (11).
[9] von Bogdandy, in: Hoffmann-Riem/Schmidt-Aßmann (eds), 2000, pp 133–94 (184).
[10] Kunas, in: Bongartz (ed), 2000, pp 1–24 (9).
[11] Herrmann, in: Grabitz/Hilf/Nettesheim (eds), 2013, Vol I, Art 33 TFEU, para 1.
[12] Kunas, in: Bongartz (ed), 2000, pp 1–24 (9, 10).
[13] Treaty on European Union, signed at Maastricht on 7 February 1992, [1992] OJ C191/1–112.
[14] Hobbing, CEPS Papers No 39, June 2011, p 8.
[15] European Commission, Directorate General Taxation and Customs Union (DG TAXUD).

functions of the former Article 29 TEU (now Article 67 TFEU) in the third pillar, specifically police cooperation with customs authorities in matters regarding the prosecution and penalisation of customs infringements, were transferred to the European Commission's DG HA.[16] The former Article 135 TEC (now Article 33 TFEU) explicitly excluded its application in the fields of national criminal law and national administration of justice, while former Articles 29 and 30 TEU (now Articles 67 and 87 TFEU) contained references to customs authorities with regard to cooperation in the area of freedom, security, and justice. This split has often been criticised because customs cooperation in the third pillar contains important first pillar elements:[17] besides the infringement element, case specifics in third pillar customs cooperation regularly stem from the normal day-to-day customs operations, which is the administration of EU customs legislation as a first pillar element.[18] Thus, a close link between third pillar customs cooperation and first pillar customs cooperation is required.[19]

Nevertheless, a certain degree of duplication of competences with regard to cooperation in EU customs has remained even since the entry into force of the Lisbon Treaty on 1 December 2009 and the dissolution of the three-pillar structure.[20] Under the Lisbon Treaty, several areas of EU competence involve customs cooperation. Thus, customs cooperation is still divided into cooperation in the context of the EU Customs Union, pursuant to Article 33 TFEU, and cooperation in the context of Justice and Home Affairs, pursuant to Articles 82, 83 on judicial cooperation in criminal matters and to Article 87 TFEU on police cooperation.[21]

Because of this divided competence, vertical customs coordination has been called – in a political context – a 'currently vacant function'.[22] At the EU level, various preparatory bodies in the Council deal with customs matters from different points of view and that involve, in a haphazard manner, either DG TAXUD, OLAF, or DG HA: for example, the Working Party on Own Resources of the Economic and Financial Affairs Council, the Customs Cooperation Working Party of the Justice and Home Affairs Council, and the Working Party on Customs Union of the Internal Market, Industry, Research and Space Council.[23] Moreover, there is a lack of regulation regarding administrative cooperation in day-to-day customs operations. OLAF deals only with administrative cooperation in the area of EU customs law infringements by economic operators. Combating customs law offences also

[16] European Commission, Directorate General for Home Affairs (DG HA); Hobbing, CEPS Papers No. 39, June 2011, p 8.

[17] COM (2004) 376 final, p 31; Hobbing, CEPS Papers No 39, June 2011, p 9.

[18] Hobbing, CEPS Papers No 39, June 2011, pp 8, 9.

[19] COM (2004) 376 final, p 34.

[20] Lux, in: Lenz/Borchardt (eds), 2013, Art 33 TFEU, para 5; Waldhoff, in: Calliess/Ruffert (eds), 2011, Art 33 TFEU, para 7.

[21] Grave, (5) 2010 GTCJ (3), pp 95–111 (102–06).

[22] Hobbing, CEPS Papers No 39, June 2011, p 17.

[23] Council of the European Union, General Secretariat (2013), List of Council Preparatory Bodies, Doc 12111/1/13 REV 1, pp 8, 9, 12.

constitutes the main objective of police cooperation with customs authorities in criminal matters.

This lack of general coordination of national implementation deficits has led to criticism of the effectiveness of cooperation in improving uniform customs administration.[24] There is no obligation for national customs administrations to consult the customs administrations of other EU Member States or the European Commission in the event that differing administrative practices in customs matters between the EU Member States' customs authorities have been discovered.[25] A further criticism was that, as a consequence, national customs administrations could keep their administrative practices even if they diverge from other EU Member States, while the European Commission's role of central coordination is limited because of its lack of authority to give instructions to national customs authorities.[26]

Therefore, the legal basis for customs cooperation as well as the established rules and possibilities for administrative cooperation have to be further analysed in order to draw conclusions on the contribution of cooperation to uniform customs administration.

I. LEGAL BASIS FOR CUSTOMS COOPERATION

Legal obligations for customs cooperation can be found in both EU primary law and EU secondary law. Article 4 paragraph 3 TEU contains the principle of sincere cooperation and thus constitutes the general legal basis for administrative cooperation not only in the vertical line between institutions of the EU and administrative bodies of the EU Member States, but also for horizontal cooperation between national administrations of different EU Member States.[27]

Article 33 TFEU contains the legal basis for legal acts regarding cooperation in the area of EU customs, and constitutes in this field the legal basis for concrete measures to fulfil the obligation for sincere cooperation as laid out in Article 4 paragraph 3 TEU.[28] However, Article 33 TFEU does not define the term 'customs cooperation' and provides only a limited basis to take measures for strengthening cooperation between EU Member States and between EU Member States and the European Commission in the area of EU customs.[29] Therefore, Article 33 TFEU is in competition with several other legal provisions that also provide a legal basis for cooperation.[30]

[24] Rogmann, 2008 AW-Prax 5, pp 195–99 (199).
[25] ibid, pp 195–99 (199).
[26] ibid, pp 195–99 (199).
[27] Schmidt-Aßmann, 1996 EuR 3, pp 270–301 (294).
[28] Herrmann, in: Grabitz/Hilf/Nettesheim (eds), 2013, Vol I, Art 33 TFEU, para 1.
[29] Grave, (5) 2010 GTCJ (3), pp 95–111 (106).
[30] Lux, in Lenz/Borchardt (eds), 2013, Art 33 TFEU, para 1.

In the structure of the TFEU, Article 33 TFEU follows immediately after the provisions on the EU Customs Union that can be found in Articles 30 et seq TFEU, suggesting a reference to activities of national customs authorities and the European Commission in application of EU customs law.[31] In EU customs law, the EU has exclusive competence pursuant to Article 3 paragraph 1 section (a) TFEU. EU customs legislation comprises the Customs Code and its implementing provisions, the Common Customs Tariff, the Council Regulation on exemption from Customs Duty,[32] and provisions about money laundering, counterfeiting and piracy, as well as cultural endowments that are directly addressed to customs authorities.[33] However, cooperation that mainly concerns aspects other than customs matters should be based on other relevant provisions in EU primary law.[34]

Differentiation between the various legal bases for cooperation involving customs matters can be difficult.[35] In particular, the legal basis for customs cooperation in the area of freedom, security, and justice, which is an area of shared competence between the EU and the EU Member States pursuant to Article 4 paragraph 2 section (j) TFEU, seems problematic. While the former Article 135 TEC expressly excluded customs cooperation from interfering with cooperation in this field, Article 33 TFEU contains no such exclusion. Furthermore, in Article 67 TFEU (former Article 29 TEU), which contains general provisions about the area of freedom, security and justice, there is no longer a reference to customs authorities. Only Article 87 TFEU (former Article 30 TEU) still contains a reference to customs authorities with regard to police cooperation. Therefore, it has been suggested to base cooperation in criminal matters among custom authorities on Article 33 TFEU, while Article 87 TFEU would provide the legal basis for operative police cooperation between customs authorities and other authorities.[36] Others, however, emphasise the position of Article 33 TFEU in proximity to the provisions on the EU Customs Union, saying this implies its separation from criminal matters pertaining to the area of freedom, security, and justice.[37]

Indeed, the legal basis for customs cooperation should depend on the legal nature of the action customs authorities are involved in and not depend on the authorities involved in the cooperative action. In addition to EU customs

[31] ibid, Art 33 TFEU, para 6; Herrmann, in: Grabitz/Hilf/Nettesheim (eds), 2013, Vol I, Art 33 TFEU, para 11.

[32] Council Regulation (EC) 1186/2009 of 16 November 2009 setting up a Community system of reliefs from customs duty, [2009] OJ L324/23–57.

[33] Lux, in Lenz/Borchardt (eds), 2013, Art 33 TFEU, para 20.

[34] ibid, Art 33 TFEU, paras 1, 6; Grave, (5) 2010 GTCJ (3), pp 95–111 (102).

[35] Lux, in Lenz/Borchardt (eds), 2013, Art 33 TFEU, para 8.

[36] Waldhoff, in: Calliess/Ruffert (eds), 2011, Art 33 TFEU, para 8; similar Herrmann, in: Grabitz/Hilf/Nettesheim (eds), 2013, Vol I, Art 33 TFEU, para 12.

[37] Grave, (5) 2010 GTCJ (3), pp 95–111 (105, 106); in this context, Grave also indicates that a possible recycle of the Naples II Convention, which regards mutual assistance and cooperation between customs administrations in criminal matters and is discussed later in this chapter, into secondary EU law would have its proper legal basis either in the chapter on judicial cooperation or in the chapter on police cooperation, see Grave, (5) 2010 GTCJ (3), pp 95–111 (104).

law, national customs authorities often carry out different tasks in different EU Member States depending on the allocation of tasks in national customs administrations.[38] For example, national customs authorities in Germany carry out some tax-related actions. The provisions of the Lisbon Treaty enabling cooperation between national authorities focus not on the nature of the national authorities involved, but on the field of law that is applied by national authorities.[39]

Therefore, customs cooperation under Article 33 TFEU does not interfere with customs cooperation in the area of freedom, security and justice and has to respect the boundaries of Articles 82 and 83 TFEU on judicial cooperation in criminal matters and of Article 87 TFEU on police cooperation.[40] Articles 82 and 83 TFEU constitute a special legal basis for the approximation of the laws regarding criminal offences and sanctions in customs matters, and thus any prosecution activity of customs authorities in this regard has to be based on those provisions.[41] Cooperation in prevention, investigation, and detection of criminal offences in the area of EU customs falls under police cooperation pursuant to Article 87 TFEU.[42] Measures regarding cooperation in combating fraud affecting the EU's financial interests have to be legally based on Article 325 TFEU (former 280 TEC), this being a special legal basis.[43] However, the prevention, detection and prosecution of administrative offences in the area of EU customs have no special legal basis in EU primary law and thus can be based on Article 33 TFEU.[44] Article 43 TFEU provides a special legal basis for cooperation in the area of agricultural policy and fisheries policy,[45] while the general provision on administrative cooperation in Article 197 TFEU is subsidiary to Article 33 TFEU in EU customs matters.[46]

Thus, Article 33 TFEU amends the other provisions on administrative cooperation in EU primary law that have no explicit reference to EU customs, and authorises the EU to enact legal provisions – regulations, directives or decisions in the sense of Article 288 TFEU – in order to strengthen cooperation in EU customs matters.[47] With further regard to its content, Article 33 TFEU thus constitutes the legal basis for rules on mutual acceptance, mutual assistance, exchange of information, human resource development, and exchange of officials in the EU-transnational administration of EU customs.[48]

[38] Lux, in Lenz/Borchardt (eds), 2013, Art 33 TFEU, para 1.

[39] ibid, Art 33 TFEU, para 1.

[40] Grave, (5) 2010 GTCJ (3), pp 95–111 (106); Lux, in Lenz/Borchardt (eds), 2013, Art 33 TFEU, paras 17, 20.

[41] Grave, (5) 2010 GTCJ (3), pp 95–111 (105); Lux, in Lenz/Borchardt (eds), 2013, Art 33 TFEU, paras 5, 8.

[42] Lux, in Lenz/Borchardt (eds), 2013, Art 33 TFEU, paras 14, 20.

[43] Grave, (5) 2010 GTCJ (3), pp 95–111 (102); Lux, in Lenz/Borchardt (eds), 2013, Art 33 TFEU, paras 5, 8.

[44] Lux, in Lenz/Borchardt (eds), 2013, Art 33 TFEU, para 20.

[45] ibid, Art 33 TFEU, para 9.

[46] ibid, Art 33 TFEU, para 1; Herrmann, in: Grabitz/Hilf/Nettesheim (eds), 2013, Vol I, Art 33 TFEU, para 4.

[47] Herrmann, in: Grabitz/Hilf/Nettesheim (eds), 2013, Vol I, Art 33 TFEU, para 1.

[48] ibid, Vol I, Art 33 TFEU, para 12.

II. RULES FOR MUTUAL ASSISTANCE OF ADMINISTRATIVE BODIES IN EU CUSTOMS LAW

Explicit rules for administrative cooperation in EU law are often not systematic and refer only to a single sector or specific aspects, single phases of administrative procedures, or consequences of cooperative action.[49] This is also true for EU customs, where rules for administrative cooperation can be found in several legal acts of the EU, but which typically do not systematically address daily compliance issues in order to enhance the uniform application of EU customs law by the customs authorities throughout the EU. Instead, they more frequently concern the prevention, investigation and prosecution of customs infringements by economic operators.[50]

The current Community Customs Code, as well as the Union Customs Code (and the former Modernised Customs Code), establish cooperation in many customs procedures, especially transnational customs procedures, but provide provisions on the mutual assistance of customs authorities only for specific points of specific customs procedures.[51] For example, with regard to transit procedures, Article 92 paragraph 2 CCC (Article 233 paragraph 2 UCC/former Article 146 paragraph 2 MCC) requires the data available to the office of departure and those available to the office of destination be compared, but does not go into any further detail. Additionally, the implementing provisions contain only specific rules about mutual assistance in single sectors,[52] as for example: Article 97s CCCIP (Article 222-2-53 draft-MCCIP) on methods of administrative cooperation regarding certificates of origin 'Form A'; Article 121 CCCIP (Article 222-3-27 draft-MCCIP) on methods of administrative cooperation regarding 'EUR 1' movement certificates in the customs area of origin; and Article 365 et seq CCCIP (Article 722-23 et seq draft-MCCIP) on cooperation in an enquiry procedure in community transit. Because of such selective rules on cooperation in the Customs Code, the Modernised Customs Code was legally based also on Article 135 TEC,[53] which is now Article 33 TFEU. Article 33 TFEU has now become one of the legal bases of the Union Customs Code.

More systematic rules on mutual assistance can be found outside the Customs Code and its implementing provisions, especially in Council Regulation (EC) 515/97 of 13 March 1997 on mutual assistance between the administrative authorities of the Member States and cooperation between the latter and the Commission to ensure the correct application of the law on customs and agricultural matters (hereinafter: Mutual Assistance Regulation);[54] and in the Naples II Convention on

[49] Schmidt-Aßmann, 1996 EuR 3, pp 270–301 (275).

[50] See, inter alia, Council Resolution of 13 December 2011, [2012] OJ C5/1–3.

[51] Herrmann, in: Grabitz/Hilf/Nettesheim (eds), 2013, Vol I, Art 33 TFEU, para 8.

[52] Dietrich, 2005, pp 41, 42.

[53] Herrmann, in: Grabitz/Hilf/Nettesheim (eds), 2013, Vol I, Art 33 TFEU, para 9.

[54] [1997] OJ L82/1–16; last amended by Regulation (EC) 766/2088 of the European Parliament and of the Council of 9 July 2008 amending Council Regulation (EC) 515/97 on mutual assistance between the administrative authorities of the Member States and cooperation between the latter and the Commission to ensure the correct application of the law on customs and agricultural matters, [2008] OJ L218/48–59.

mutual assistance and cooperation between customs administrations of 1997[55] regarding intergovernmental cooperation in criminal matters (hereinafter: Naples II Convention). The Mutual Assistance Regulation concerns administrative assistance in the administration of EU customs law with a focus on breaches of EU customs legislation on the level of administrative offences.[56] The regulation is based on Article 135 TEC in conjunction with Article 280 TEC, and thus now falls within the scope of Article 33 TFEU in conjunction with Article 325 TFEU,[57] the area of the EU Customs Union being an area of exclusive EU competence, pursuant to Article 3 paragraph 1 section (a) TFEU. The Naples II Convention concerns legal cooperation in customs offences on the level of criminal offences and is considered to be an element of judicial cooperation in criminal matters that now falls within the scope of Article 82 TFEU or Article 83 TFEU.[58] Thus, it addresses matters relating to the area of freedom, security and justice, which is an area of shared competence, pursuant to Article 4 paragraph 2 section (j) TFEU.

One of the most interesting concerns raised regarding the uniform implementation of EU customs law is its seeming incompleteness in the areas of customs cooperation because of the emphasis on security matters, with a corresponding neglect of regulatory and facilitation aspects.[59] Thus, customs cooperation does not always aim to improve the day-to-day application of EU customs law and its enforcement by national customs authorities.[60] Indeed, the most important aim of customs cooperation is the fight against infringements by economic operators in the area of EU customs, and only after this does customs cooperation aim to secure the correct charging of customs duties.[61] The Council emphasised the importance of customs cooperation in safeguarding an area of freedom, security, and justice in its resolution on the future of customs law enforcement cooperation.[62] The improvement of customs cooperation thus is mainly considered with regard to its contribution to the fight against cross-border crime rather than to the improvement of uniform administration in day-to-day customs work.

Therefore, in some areas customs cooperation does not seem to contribute significantly to enhancing uniform customs administration. However, in aiming to secure a comparative level of checks and customs controls in order to fight against infringements, customs cooperation also aims to secure the application

[55] Convention drawn up on the basis of Art K3 of the Treaty on European Union, on mutual assistance and cooperation between customs administrations ('Naples II') of 18 December 1997, [1998] OJ C24/1, last amended by Council Decision of 6 December 2007 concerning the accession of Bulgaria and Romania to the Convention of 18 December 1997, drawn up on the basis of Art K3 of the Treaty on European Union, on mutual assistance and cooperation between customs administrations, [2008] OJ L9/21–22.

[56] Dietrich, 2005, p 59.

[57] Grave, (5) 2010 GTCJ (3), pp 95–111 (102, 106).

[58] ibid, pp 95–111 (104).

[59] Hobbing, CEPS Papers No 39, June 2011, p 24.

[60] Grave, (5) 2010 GTCJ (3), pp 95–111 (106); Hobbing, CEPS Papers No 39, June 2011, p 24.

[61] Dietrich, 2005, pp 16, 17.

[62] Council Resolution of 13 December 2011, [2012] OJ C5/1–3, especially p 1 number 1, p 2 numbers 4 and 5, p 3 number 1 section (e).

of equivalent control measures. Thus, customs cooperation focused on customs infringements by economic operators can contribute also to the enhancement of the uniform application of EU customs law throughout the EU and especially at every point of the EU's external borders, guaranteeing mutual trust and equal conditions of competition.[63]

A. Mutual Assistance Regulation

In the area of mutual assistance in EU customs matters, the most important legal basis in EU secondary law is Council Regulation (EC) 515/97 of 13 March 1997 on mutual assistance between the administrative authorities of the Member States, and cooperation between the latter and the Commission to ensure the correct application of the law on customs and agricultural matters.[64] The Mutual Assistance Regulation has been called a role model for extensive horizontal cooperation.[65] It constitutes basic rules for cross-national mutual assistance between EU Member States and between the latter and the European Commission in administrative procedures.[66]

As already alluded to,[67] the Mutual Assistance Regulation covers only administrative assistance in administrative procedures with regard to breaches of EU customs law and thus falls under Article 33 TFEU, while cooperation in the area of criminal customs offences falls under Articles 82 or 83 TFEU, or Article 87 TFEU. Furthermore, national procedural law is supplementary effective and is to enable the reasonable application and implementation of the Mutual Assistance Regulation.[68] In this context, however, the Mutual Assistance Regulation contains a special embodiment of the general principle of equivalence, which in accordance with settled case law[69] demands that national procedural law applied with regard to the implementation of EU law be not less favourable than national provisions governing similar domestic actions. In two places, the Mutual Assistance Regulation explicitly requires that the applicable customs authority operate in the same way and with the same intensity when managing a transnational request for administrative assistance as it would in the case of a national matter, see Article 4 paragraph 2 and Article 9 paragraph 1 Regulation (EC) 515/97. As a consequence, the

[63] Moussis, 2011, p 77.

[64] [1997] OJ L82/1–16; last amended by Regulation (EC) 766/2088 of the European Parliament and of the Council of 9 July 2008 amending Council Regulation (EC) 515/97 on mutual assistance between the administrative authorities of the Member States and cooperation between the latter and the Commission to ensure the correct application of the law on customs and agricultural matters, [2008] OJ L218/48–59. As the analysis focuses on EU customs matters, agricultural matters will not be further mentioned in this section, though the regulation covers them as well.

[65] von Bogdandy, in: Hoffmann-Riem/Schmidt-Aßmann (eds), 2000, pp 133–94 (184).

[66] Dietrich, 2005, p 39.

[67] See Chapter 7.II.

[68] Dietrich, 2005, p 65.

[69] See, inter alia, ECJ of 12 July 2012, Joined Cases C-608/10, C-10/11 and C-23/11, *Südzucker AG and Others* [2012] ECR I-0, para 62, and the case law cited.

applicable authority is not allowed to differentiate between domestic authorities and national authorities of other EU Member States, an indication of the intensity of administrative cooperation in the supranationalised area of EU customs.[70]

The Mutual Assistance Regulation provides for various forms of administrative assistance and, in particular, for the establishment of a common automated information system, but it does not deal with the recovery of duties.[71] Its provisions address the European Commission and competent national authorities, see Article 1 paragraph 1 Regulation (EC) 515/97. Each EU Member State independently appoints those authorities competent for applying the Mutual Assistance Regulation and has to communicate a list of those authorities, see Article 2 paragraph 2 Regulation (EC) 515/97. Therefore, not every national customs authority is a competent authority in the meaning of Article 1 paragraph 1 Regulation (EC) 515/97. In Germany, for example, the German Customs Criminal Investigation Office is the competent authority, pursuant to § 3 (6) 1(b) ZFdG.[72]

Cooperation in the framework of the Mutual Assistance Regulation encompasses mutual assistance between the competent national authorities on request of one of those authorities, Articles 4 et seq Regulation (EC) No 515/97, as well as spontaneous assistance between them, Articles 13 et seq Regulation (EC) 515/97. Mutual assistance on request can take the form of a simple transmission of any relevant information, transmission of relevant documents, notification of relevant administrative decisions, or maintaining or arranging for a special watch on persons, places, movement of goods, or means of transport within the operational area of the applicable authority in order to prevent breaches of EU customs law. It also encompasses the execution of administrative enquiries by the applicable authority within its operational area. Spontaneous assistance between competent national authorities covers activities wherein there are serious grounds involving the commitment of breaches of EU customs law as well as the exchange of broadly relevant information and findings.

The Mutual Assistance Regulation also regulates cooperation between the competent national authorities and the European Commission, Articles 17 et seq Regulation (EC) 515/97. The horizontal cooperation between competent national authorities is thereby complemented with a strong element of vertical cooperation and coordination.[73] The competent national authorities are obliged to transmit to the European Commission any general information of relevance without request, see Article 17 Regulation (EC) 515/97. Furthermore, pursuant to Article 18 Regulation (EC) 515/97 they have to transmit information of particular relevance to the EU level regarding concrete breaches or serious grounds for the

[70] von Bogdandy, in: Hoffmann-Riem/Schmidt-Aßmann (eds), 2000, pp 133 et seq (185).

[71] Herrmann, in: Grabitz/Hilf/Nettesheim (eds), 2013, Vol I, Art 33 TFEU, para 7.

[72] Dietrich, 2005, p 71. The German Customs Investigation Service Act: Gesetz zur Neuregelung des Zollfahndungsdienstes (Zollfahndungsneuregelungsgesetz–ZFnrG) vom 16 August 2002, Artikel 1 Gesetz über das Zollkriminalamt und die Zollfahndungsämter (Zollfahndungsdienstgesetz—ZFdG), BGBl I p 3202; last amended 20.06.2013, BGBl I p 1602.

[73] von Bogdandy, in: Hoffmann-Riem/Schmidt-Aßmann (eds), 2000, pp 133–94 (185).

commitment of breaches of EU customs law either at the request of the European Commission or on their own initiative. The European Commission has to convey the information received to the competent authorities of the other EU Member States, see Article 18 paragraph 1 sentence 2 Regulation (EC) 515/97. Indeed, as national authorities transmitting information to the European Commission are no longer obliged to inform other competent national authorities as well, see Article 18 paragraph 2 Regulation (EC) 515/97, the European Commission has become the mainly responsible actor for the distribution of relevant information under the Mutual Assistance Regulation.[74] This means that in practice, direct communication between competent national authorities regarding customs law infringements only takes place in urgent cases.[75] Moreover, based on the information received, the European Commission has the right to coordinate the measures of the competent national authorities in the fight against breaches of EU customs and EU agricultural law, see Article 18 paragraph 1 sentence 1, paragraph 3 Regulation (EC) 515/97. In this context, the European Commission can even demand that competent national authorities carry out administrative enquiries based on the European Commission's own assessment of the situation,[76] pursuant to Article 18 paragraph 4 Regulation (EC) 515/97. The European Commission also has the right to send its own officials to conduct an investigation, see Article 18 paragraphs 4, 5 Regulation (EC) 515/97.

Therefore, in the framework of the Mutual Assistance Regulation, the European Commission has the function of a centre for the receipt and distribution of information as well as for initiation and coordination of cooperation,[77] which strengthens the position of the European Commission also in the horizontal cooperation of the EU Member States.[78] The European Commission is supported by a committee, Article 43 Regulation (EC) 515/97. This committee was established as a scrutiny committee in the sense of Article 5a Decision 1999/468/EC[79] in conjunction with Article 12 Regulation (EU) 182/2011,[80] see Article 43 paragraph 2 Regulation (EC) 515/97, and further has the right to examine all matters relating to the application of the Mutual Assistance Regulation and the Customs Information System, see Article 43 paragraphs 4, 5 Regulation (EC) 515/97.

[74] Dietrich, 2005, p 81; von Bogdandy, in: Hoffmann-Riem/Schmidt-Aßmann (eds), 2000, pp 133–94 (185, 186).

[75] Dietrich, 2005, p 81; von Bogdandy, in: Hoffmann-Riem/Schmidt-Aßmann (eds), 2000, pp 133–94 (185, 186).

[76] Dietrich, 2005, p 82.

[77] Dietrich, 2005, pp 72, 81, 82; von Bogdandy, in: Hoffmann-Riem/Schmidt-Aßmann (eds), 2000, pp 133–94 (185).

[78] von Bogdandy, in: Hoffmann-Riem/Schmidt-Aßmann (eds), 2000, pp 133–94 (185).

[79] Council Decision of 28 June 1999 laying down the procedures for the exercise of implementing powers conferred on the Commission (1999/468/EC), [1999] OJ L184/23–26, amended by Council Decision 2006/512/EC of 17 July 2006 amending Decision 1999/468/EC laying down the procedures for the exercise of implementing powers conferred on the Commission, [2006] OJ L200/11–13.

[80] Regulation (EU) 182/2011 of the European Parliament and of the Council of 16 February 2011 laying down the rules and general principles concerning mechanisms for control by Member States of the Commission's exercise of implementing powers, [2011] OJ L55/13–18.

Although the Mutual Assistance Regulation contains basic rules for administrative assistance in EU customs, its provisions primarily concern the prevention and detection of customs law infringements.[81] Indeed, the main focus of the Mutual Assistance Regulation is on breaches of EU customs law by economic operators and not on cross-national information exchange in the day-to-day work of customs authorities for the improvement of the application of EU customs law by customs officials. It thus does not aim to put into practice the goal of the European Commission to 'act as one administration'.[82]

The centrepiece of the Mutual Assistance Regulation is the Customs Information System (CIS II),[83] which is laid down in Articles 23 et seq Regulation (EC) 515/97 and adds an informational-technical component to the administrative procedure of mutual assistance in matters of customs law infringements.[84] It consists of a common computer network in the form of a central database, which is set up and maintained by the national customs administrations of the EU Member States and the European Commission, each which has access to it via their own terminals—though direct access is restricted to the competent national authorities and the competent departments of the European Commission, see Article 29 paragraph 1 Regulation (EC) 515/97. Because of their EU-transnational character, the data of the CIS II cannot be restricted for national use in certain areas.[85] Therefore, its technical architecture as well as the administrative role of the European Commission serves to strengthening the vertical element in the horizontal cooperation of the EU Member States.[86] On the other hand, Article 32 Regulation (EC) 515/97 established an important horizontal element in the CIS II by giving only the CIS II-partner that created and owns the data the right to change or delete it.[87]

As part of the Mutual Assistance Regulation, the CIS II has the same scope of application and therefore contains data about goods, means of transportation, companies et cetera in order to help to prevent and detect breaches of EU customs law.[88] The CIS II is not an additional institution but an instrument for the quick and systematic exchange of information between the EU Member States as well as with the European Commission.[89] The purpose of the CIS II is to support

[81] von Bogdandy, in: Hoffmann-Riem/Schmidt-Aßmann (eds), 2000, pp 133–94 (184); Dietrich, 2005, p 59.

[82] See for example: European Commission, EU Customs strategy, URL: http://ec.europa.eu/taxation_customs/customs/policy_issues/customs_strategy/index_en.htm; COM (2001) 51 final, p 5; Customs 2013 Programme, Art 5 (f), Recital (2) of Decision 624/2007/EC.

[83] As the Common Information System (CIS) is shared by the Mutual Assistance Regulation and the Naples II Convention based on different legal bases and using different databases within the CIS, for the purpose of differentiation the short form CIS in the context of the Mutual Assistance Regulation is complemented by the Roman numeral 'II' (CIS II), while the short form CIS in the context of the Naples II Convention is complemented by the Roman numeral 'I' (CIS I); see Dietrich, 2005, p 121.

[84] von Bogdandy, in: Hoffmann-Riem/Schmidt-Aßmann (eds), 2000, pp 133–94 (184).

[85] ibid, pp 133–94 (186).

[86] ibid, pp 133–94 (186).

[87] ibid, pp 133–94 (186).

[88] Dietrich, 2005, p 122.

[89] ibid, p 120.

measures under the Mutual Assistance Regulation, which means that its nature is preventive, see Article 23 paragraph 2 Regulation (EC) 515/97. Therefore, while the CIS II increases the effectiveness of customs cooperation and even customs controls by disseminating data and information quickly, it has the same limitations as the Mutual Assistance Regulation; its practicability in day-to-day customs matters for the improvement of uniform customs administration is limited. The EU thus still requires further rules for cooperation between national customs authorities in the EU beyond the scope of the Mutual Assistance Regulation and the CIS II if it is to guarantee coherence of application in the area of EU customs.[90]

Nevertheless, although the main objective of the Mutual Assistance Regulation is to regulate administrative cooperation with regard to breaches of EU customs law, it also contributes to the prevention of distortions in competition resulting from the non-uniform application of EU customs law. It does so through the provision of a permanent exchange of information between the competent customs authorities in the EU by obliging them to transfer information about irregularities to the European Commission or the competent customs authorities of other EU Member States with use of modern information technology.[91] Furthermore, the strong position of the European Commission in this system of mutual assistance also promotes the more uniform administration of EU customs law. The support of the European Commission can facilitate the work of customs authorities and enable them to investigate cross-national cases with the same quality as national ones.[92]

B. Naples II Convention

The other important legal basis for cooperation in EU customs matters is the Naples II Convention on mutual assistance and cooperation between customs administrations of 1997.[93] This convention concerns customs cooperation in criminal matters as part of the former third pillar, what is now the area of freedom, security, and justice in the sense of Article 4 paragraph 2 section (j) and Articles 67–89 TFEU. The Naples II Convention replaced the former Naples I Convention of 1967,[94] which was an international treaty between the EU Member States. It continues the first convention's intergovernmental cooperation but is integrated

[90] Herrmann, in: Grabitz/Hilf/Nettesheim (eds), 2013, Vol I, Art 33 TFEU, para 9.

[91] Kunas, in: Bongartz (ed), 2000, pp 1–24 (15).

[92] ibid, pp 1–24 (15).

[93] Convention drawn up on the basis of Art K3 of the Treaty on European Union, on mutual assistance and cooperation between customs administrations ('Naples II') of 18 December 1997, [1998] OJ C24/1; last amended by Council Decision of 6 December 2007 concerning the accession of Bulgaria and Romania to the Convention of 18 December 1997, drawn up on the basis of Art K3 of the Treaty on European Union, on mutual assistance and cooperation between customs administrations, [2008] OJ L9/21–22.

[94] Convention on mutual assistance between customs administrations, concluded in Naples on 7 September 1967.

into the institutional framework of the EU.[95] Mutual assistance under the Naples II Convention concerns the prevention and detection, prosecution, and punishment of infringements of national customs legislation as well as EU customs law and comprises preventive as well as repressive action.[96] It also takes part in the Common Information System CIS, but has its own database (CIS I)[97] separate from the Mutual Assistance Regulation's database (CIS II),[98] and thus benefits from the possibilities of quick information exchange.

As already alluded to,[99] any kind of intergovernmental customs cooperation in combating crime is not of the same nature and purpose as customs cooperation in the meaning of Article 33 TFEU. The contents of the Naples II Convention cannot significantly support the uniform application of EU customs law in customs administration, because such former third pillar customs cooperation 'intrinsically represents police cooperation of customs authorities'.[100] Therefore, the Naples II Convention is not a part of the administrative cooperation mechanisms existing between customs authorities to ensure their own correct and uniform application of specific EU customs law.[101]

C. Conclusion

The legal acts providing for mutual assistance in the area of EU customs deal mainly with activities directed at the fight against administrative customs offences or even criminal matters outside the scope of Article 33 TFEU. They do not seek as their main purpose to enhance and facilitate the correct and uniform application of EU customs law by national customs authorities. However, the strong cooperation between competent authorities under the Mutual Assistance Regulation regularly has to deal with case specifics of day-to-day customs work, and thus can still enhance customs authorities' awareness of the European character of customs work today. Moreover, it may even facilitate cooperation in other customs areas aside from breaches of EU customs law, as contact between customs authorities of different EU Member States occurs more frequently and thus becomes a normal part of customs work. Although there is no general obligation for customs authorities to consult each other before issuing a customs decision with EU-wide effect and validity, the EU Member States have the right to ask other EU Member

[95] Dietrich, 2005, p 40.

[96] ibid, pp 98, 99.

[97] As the Common Information System (CIS) is shared by the Mutual Assistance Regulation and the Naples II Convention based on different legal bases and using different databases within the CIS, for the purpose of differentiation the short form CIS in the context of the Naples II Convention is complemented by the Roman numeral 'I' (CIS I), while the short form CIS in the context of the Mutual Assistance Regulation is complemented by the Roman numeral 'II' (CIS II); see Dietrich, 2005, p 121.

[98] Dietrich, 2005, p 122.

[99] See Chapter 7.I.

[100] Hobbing, CEPS Papers No 39, June 2011, p 8; Grave, (5) 2010 GTCJ (3), pp 95–111 (104).

[101] Grave, (5) 2010 GTCJ (3), pp 95–111 (105).

States' customs administrations for relevant information in the field of EU customs.[102] Today, customs officials in the EU form an important human network and act in the name of the EU. Therefore, they have to be open to cooperation among themselves and with the European Commission, as the spirit of Article 33 TFEU demands.[103]

III. AD HOC COOPERATION IN EU CUSTOMS ADMINISTRATION PRACTICE

The efficiency of the EU Customs Union depends as much on uniform rules as on the quality of its operational structures.[104] Administrative cooperation is primarily a network of real administrative activity, and involves the use of practical instruments. Therefore, the area of cooperation consists not only of legal provisions but also of real acts.[105] For administrative cooperation, exchange of information is of extreme importance and constitutes the basis of cooperative acts.[106] Information can be provided about actual situations or decisions, legal situations, or concrete activities.[107] Furthermore, informative relations can be either of a direct or indirect nature or a combination of the two, as seen when EU Member States give information to EU institutions, which then distribute it to other EU Member States in the original, as well as in the changed or supplemented, form.[108] In case of direct horizontal exchange of information between national administrations of EU Member States, the number of points of contact between the specific administrative departments is increasing;[109] because administrative cooperation, as a continuous task, requires the reliable exchange of information and thus solid structures of communication.[110] This has led in part to the emergence of contact points for specific administrative areas in the EU Member States which function as components of distinct administrative networks.[111]

Actually, in the area of EU customs—meaning customs administration as the charging of customs duties and not the investigation of customs law infringements—several such contact points for specific customs matters exist in each EU Member State, such as, for example, for binding tariff information (BTI)[112]

[102] Rogmann, in: Kluth/Müller/Peilert (eds), 2008, pp 797–819 (800); Rogmann, 2008 ZfZ 3, pp 57–69 (62).

[103] Moussis, 2011, p 77.

[104] ibid, p 77.

[105] Schmidt-Aßmann, 1996 EuR 3, pp 270–301 (272).

[106] ibid, pp 270–301 (290).

[107] ibid, pp 270–301 (290).

[108] ibid, pp 270–301 (290).

[109] ibid, pp 270–301 (291).

[110] ibid, pp 270–301 (291).

[111] ibid, pp 270–301 (291).

[112] List of customs authorities designated by Member States for the purposes of receiving applications for, or issuing binding tariff information, [2011] OJ C144/8–12, published in accordance with Art 6 para 5 CCCIP. Binding Tariff Information is analysed in detail in Chapter 10.I.E.

and binding origin information (BOI),[113] single authorisation,[114] or authorised economic operators (AEO).[115] Indeed, customs officials have confirmed that direct contact between individual customs officers as well as between central contact points are an important aspect of cooperation between the national customs administrations of the EU Member States. The quantity of direct contact, though, can to some extent depend on the level of authority and the area of EU customs law to which a customs official is appointed. For example, customs officials in the United Kingdom confirmed:

> But yes, no – we have no problems going directly to the individual officers … Yes. With emails it is easier … We have always had very good communications with the rest of Europe on that. And sometimes again because a lot of the stuff is in English, they will sometimes come to us just for definition of things. But we had never had any problems with communicating to Member States … So, from the higher officer's point of view, we have an awful lot of cooperation between them.[116]

Also in interviews with German customs officials it has been confirmed that direct contact via email is customary,[117] though the central contact points are at least equally important, due to the language barriers between national customs administrations.[118]

Decision-making processes in the implementation of EU law are regularly characterised by cooperation between the national authorities of different EU Member States and also with the European Commission.[119] Customs procedures in the EU regularly involve customs administrations of several EU Member States and require information from the European Commission and/or central databases. In EU customs, various possibilities to exchange information on an ad hoc basis, on request, as well as on a permanent basis, have established a kind of network structure for administrative interaction in the implementation phase. Such network structures regulate vertical as well as horizontal relations between national

[113] List of authorities designated by Member States to receive applications for, or to issue, binding origin information, [2011] OJ C106/6–10, published in accordance with Art 6 para 5 CCCIP. Binding Origin Information is discussed in Chapter 10.III.

[114] URL: http://ec.europa.eu/taxation_customs/customs/procedural_aspects/general/centralised_clearance/index_en.htm. Single authorisation is a first step towards centralised clearance, whose advantages are discussed in Chapter 4.I.

[115] URL: http://ec.europa.eu/taxation_customs/resources/documents/customs/policy_issues/customs_security/aeo_contacts_for_traders_en.pdf. The AEO status is discussed in Chapter 4.

[116] Interview of 9 January 2012 on file with author.

[117] 'Eigentlich immer … Also ich muss ziemlich viel … Ob das jetzt per E-Mail ist, weniger per Telefon.' Interview of 1 April 2011 on file with author; 'Also es ist jetzt nicht der Anruf aber Gott sei Dank ja der Email-Verkehr. Und der wird gelebt … Insofern ist genau dieser direkte Weg der richtige Weg um auch das was man bezwecken möchte, nämlich einen lebhaften Informationsaustausch, auch zu gewährleisten. Und da sprechen ja die Praktiker miteinander.' Interview of 20 May 2011 on file with author.

[118] 'Das funktioniert. Ja. Wie gesagt, im direkten Verkehr kommt es gelegentlich vor, aber meistens ziehen die Mitgliedstaaten einfach diesen Verkehr über die Zentralstellen vor, weil sie dann gleichzeitig auch eine Übersetzung bekommen. Ich kann kein Ungarisch.' Interview of 10 May 2011 on file with author.

[119] Weiß, 2010, p 15; Hofmann/Türk, 2007 ELJ (13), pp 253–71 (254).

administrations and the European Commission in order to ensure the uniform implementation and effective enforcement of EU law.[120]

IV. CUSTOMS ACTION PROGRAMME

More cooperation activities can be found in the Customs Action Programme[121] of the EU Customs Union. Beyond its policy objectives, the Customs Action Programme is intimately linked with the wider EU Customs Union. Herein, it primarily has a supporting and enabling role for the implementation and application of EU customs legislation designed to ensure the effective functioning of the Internal Market in the area of EU customs.[122] It has a heavy emphasis on former first-pillar activities,[123] and thus in the future will be legally based on Article 33 TFEU.[124]

In contrast to the Mutual Assistance Regulation, the Customs Action Programme contains no rules for administrative assistance in customs procedures. Rather it constitutes the framework for various forms of cooperation activities oriented on the practical aspects of operations in the administration of EU customs. Specific objectives of such action are: standardisation and simplification of customs systems and controls, development of best working practices, maintaining a system for measuring the performance of customs administrations, ensuring uniform tariff classification, support of the creation of a pan-European electronic customs environment, maintenance and development of communication and information systems, and the development and reinforcement of common training. The main focus of the Customs Action Programme is thus the improvement of the application of EU customs law by customs officials throughout the EU. Indeed, the current[125] Customs Action Programme explicitly declares its purpose is to support the EU's customs strategy, thereby enabling national customs administrations within the EU Customs Union to operate as efficiently and effectively as would a single united EU customs administration, see Recital (2) and Article 4 paragraph 1 section (b) Decision 624/2007/EC.[126] Thus, the Customs Action Programme is part of the EU's strategy to enhance uniform customs administration in the EU Customs Union.

While the EU Customs Union is an exclusive competence of the EU, the EU legal framework in itself cannot sufficiently ensure the proper functioning of the

[120] Hofmann/Türk, 2007 ELJ (13), pp 253–71 (259).

[121] The term 'Customs Action Programme' refers to the Customs Action Programme as such regardless whether it is the Customs 2000, 2002, 2007, 2013 or Customs 2020 programme.

[122] The Evaluation Partnership, Mid-Term Evaluation–Final Report, June 2011, pp 7, 8.

[123] COM (2005) 111 final, p 10.

[124] Future programme (situation as of 31.12.2013): Regulation (EU) 1294/2013 of the European Parliament and of the Council of 11 December 2013 establishing an action programme for customs in the European Union for the period 2014–20 (Customs 2020) and repealing Decision 624/2007/EC, [2013] OJ L347/209–20.

[125] Situation as of 31.12.2013.

[126] Decision 624/2007/EC of the European Parliament and of the Council of 23 May 2007 establishing an action programme for customs in the Community (Customs 2013), [2007] OJ L154/25–31.

EU Customs Union and thus has to be supported by measures promoting the convergent and harmonised application of EU customs legislation throughout the EU.[127] Activities in the customs field are often of a cross-border nature and involve and affect several if not all EU Member States.[128] A continuous process of alignment is needed in order to avoid the development of diverging working practices in the national customs administrations that could lead to distortions in the Internal Market.[129] Without an instrument on the EU level to support EU Member States in acting as if they were a single administration, such distortions would be more likely.[130] The Customs Action Programme is a key tool of the EU for enabling the EU Customs Union to function as a single customs administration rather than a patchwork of 28 separate national customs administrations. It does so by providing them with possibilities for quick and regular exchange of information, data, and expertise.[131]

Therefore, while the EU Member States are responsible for the smooth functioning of their national customs administration systems, the Customs Action Programme emphasises the European dimension of day-to-day customs work in the EU Customs Union.[132] The Customs Action Programme is a driving force for cooperation,[133] as it has established structures for the organised sharing of knowledge and experience between customs officials in the EU, has created a network that facilitates contact-making and problem-solving at an operational working level, and has enhanced confidence between national customs administrations of different EU Member States.[134]

The Customs Action Programme has established a number of contact networks on the level of the customs officials and their national customs administrations by allowing them to get to know their counterparts in all EU Member States on a personal basis. These networks have facilitated decision-making processes as well as solution-building, and have enhanced the effectiveness of the communication between EU Member States and with the European Commission.[135] One of those networks is, for example, the integrated Network of European Customs Laboratories, which consists of the European Customs Inventory of Chemical Substances (ECICS) database and the Group of European Customs Laboratories (GCL)[136]

[127] COM (2011) 706 final, pp 5, 6; COM (2012) 464 final, p 4; SEC (2011) 1318 final, p 3.

[128] SEC (2011) 1317 final, p 16.

[129] Commission Staff Working Document of 15 July 2006, /*SEC/2006/0570*/, 4.6 Answer any future challenges, URL: http://eur-lex.europa.eu/LexUriServ/LexUriServ.do?uri=SEC:2006:0570:FIN:EN:HTML.

[130] ibid, 4.6 Answer any future challenges.

[131] SEC (2011) 1317 final, p 6.

[132] Commission Staff Working Document of 15 July 2006, /*SEC/2006/0570*/, 2. Procedural issues and consultations of third parties.

[133] ibid, 4.6 Answer any future challenges.

[134] ibid, 6.1.3. Loss of impetus for knowledge sharing between Customs administrations.

[135] The Evaluation Partnership, Mid-Term Evaluation–Final Report, June 2011, pp 39, 40.

[136] URL: http://ec.europa.eu/taxation_customs/customs/customs_controls/custom_laboratories/group_ecl/index_en.htm.

that has already been alluded to.[137] The ECICS database provides information of a scientific and statistical nature and product identification based on the Combined Nomenclature (CN). The GCL provides for the structured coordination of the Customs Laboratories of the EU Member States including the Intra Laboratory Inventory of Analytical Determination (ILIAD) database, which is a shared directory of analytical methods and procedures for the correct and coherent application of EU customs law.[138] A network such as the integrated Network of European Customs Laboratories, with uniform and centrally run databases, is essential for uniform results from national analyses, as diversity in this area would have a direct negative impact on results in tariff classifications and customs controls in the EU. Furthermore, it is important for a common understanding and interpretation of health and security standards in order to protect EU citizens.[139] By supporting the Network of European Customs Laboratories, the Customs Action Programme maintains a permanent basis for uniform classification of goods in the EU Customs Union.[140]

Another example of organised cooperation and coordination under the Customs Action Programme is the Common Risk Management System that has to be incorporated in all aspects of customs work to ensure that customs controls are implemented with equal effectiveness throughout the EU Customs Union.[141] Under the umbrella of the Customs Action Programme, common risk criteria and the organisation of high-risk information between all EU Member States and the European Commission has been developed, resulting in a standardised framework for risk management in the customs administrations of the EU,[142] which is actively used by all EU Member States' administrations.[143] Further developments of an electronic Union risk management system are continuing under the Customs Action Programme.[144]

A. History of the Customs Action Programme

The current[145] Customs 2013 Programme[146] (Customs 2013) is the fifth action programme for customs in the EU. Its predecessors were the Customs 2007

[137] See Chapter 4.

[138] Commission Staff Working Document of 15 July 2006, /*SEC/2006/0570*/, 6.2.1. Weaken security and safety within the Community area and the external border, 2. Safety.

[139] ibid, 6.2.1. Weaken security and safety within the Community area and the external border, 2. Safety.

[140] ibid, 6.2.1. Weaken security and safety within the Community area and the external border, 2. Safety.

[141] ibid, 4.3 Reinforce the functioning of the internal market.

[142] http://ec.europa.eu/taxation_customs/resources/documents/framework_doc.pdf.

[143] Commission Staff Working Document of 15 July 2006, /*SEC/2006/0570*/, 6.3.1.3 Risk Management and audit.

[144] ibid, 6.3.1.3 Risk Management and audit.

[145] Situation as of 31.12.2013.

[146] Decision 624/2007/EC of the European Parliament and of the Council of 23 May 2007 establishing an action programme for customs in the Community (Customs 2013), [2007] OJ L154/25–31.

Programme[147] (Customs 2007), which covered the period from 2003 to 2007, the Customs 2002 Programme[148] (Customs 2002), which covered the years 2001 and 2002, the Customs 2000 Programme[149] (Customs 2000), which covered the period from 1996 to 2000, and the Matthaeus Programme[150] (Matthaeus), which ran from 1991 to 1999. Over the course of these programmes, enhancing uniform customs administration progressively became one of the most important objectives of the Customs Action Programme.

While Matthaeus was primarily an action programme for basic and advanced professional training of customs officers, Customs 2000 sought to strengthen cooperation between the national customs administrations of the EU Member States, as well as between them and the European Commission, and thereby to ensure the uniform application of EU customs law.[151] The programme led to a widened definition of customs officers' duties and the further development of their training to increase their flexibility and mobility and foreign language competence.[152] Its successor, Customs 2002, combined the objectives of Customs 2000 with Matthaeus and united all the measures of both programmes in one single concept. A similar agenda to Customs 2002 was continued in Customs 2007. In the Customs 2007 Decision, which was adopted around the same time as the WTO dispute settlement *EC—Selected Customs Matters*,[153] the European Commission for the first time specified the achievement of equivalent results at every point of the EU customs territory as one of the most important goals of EU Customs, see Article 3 paragraph 1 section (b) Decision 253/2003/EC. The explicit naming of this goal in such a prominent position in the decision and its repetition and confirmation in further acts of the EU institutions[154] illustrates that it has become the clear ambition of the EU Customs Union to also constitute an EU Customs Administration Union as part of the strategy for EU customs. Successive action programmes for customs are and will continue to be an important instrument in the realisation of this strategic ambition.

[147] Decision 253/2003/EC of the European Parliament and of the Council of 11 February 2003 adopting an action programme for customs in the Community (Customs 2007), [2003] OJ L36/1–6.

[148] Decision 105/2000/EC of the European Parliament and of the Council of 17 December 1999 amending Decision 210/97/EC adopting an action programme for customs in the Community (Customs 2000) and repealing Council Decision 91/341/EEC, [2000] OJ L13/1–4.

[149] Decision 210/97/EC of the European Parliament and of the Council of 19 December 1996 adopting an action programme for customs in the Community (Customs 2000), [1997] OJ L33/24–31.

[150] Council Decision 91/341/EEC of 20 June 1991 on the adoption of a programme of Community action on the subject of the vocational training of customs officials (Matthaeus Programme), [1991] OJ L187/41–46.

[151] Kunas, in: Bongartz (ed), 2000, pp 1–24 (22).

[152] ibid, pp 1–24 (22).

[153] WT/DS315.

[154] See for example: European Commission, EU Customs strategy, URL: http://ec.europa.eu/taxation_customs/customs/policy_issues/customs_strategy/index_en.htm; Customs 2013 Programme, Recital (2) and Art 4 para 1 character (b) Decision 624/2007/EC; COM (2001) 51 final, p 5; European Court of Auditors, Special Report No 1/2010, [2010] OJ C149/8 and URL: http://eur-lex.europa.eu/LexUriServ/LexUriServ.do?uri=SRCA:2010:01:FIN:EN:PDF, para 34; European Parliament, Resolution of 1 December 2011 (2001/2083(INI)), text adopted P7_TA(2011)0546, para 53.

B. The Customs 2013 Programme

Customs 2013[155] also continues to pursue similar objectives as its predecessor, in particular the ambition to 'act as one customs administration'. Customs 2013 aims to directly address the needs and problems of national customs administrations in the EU.[156] It takes into account the European Commission's strategy for the evolution of the Customs Union as agreed to in 2008:[157] to make EU customs ready to meet the various challenges it has to face by modernising EU customs legislation as part of the 'Better Regulation' Initiative,[158] to build a robust communication chain between all customs offices in the EU through the creation of an EU-wide electronic customs system as part of the Electronic Customs Initiative,[159] and, in doing so, to develop a coherent system of performance management in EU customs administrations as part of the Future Customs Initiative.[160] The mid-term evaluation of Customs 2013 came to the conclusion that the objective to support the ability of the national customs administrations of the EU Member States to act as one is generally perceived as important by the main participants of the programme, namely the national customs administrations themselves.[161]

The European Commission and the participating countries, especially the EU Member States as the main beneficiaries, are implementing Customs 2013 in partnership. The European Commission performs an organising and facilitating role[162] and is supported by the Customs 2013 Committee, which has been established as a management committee in the sense of Decision 1999/468/EC[163] and now falls under the examination procedure pursuant to Article 13 paragraph 1 section (b) in conjunction with Article 5 Regulation (EU) 182/2011.[164] The Customs 2013 Committee has to ensure the overall functioning of the programme and to link programme activities with the overall objectives.[165]

To achieve its objectives, Customs 2013 relies primarily on IT actions; on joint actions including benchmarking, seminars and workshops; on project groups and steering groups; and on working visits, training activities, and monitoring actions.

[155] Decision 624/2007/EC of the European Parliament and of the Council of 23 May 2007 establishing an action programme for customs in the Community (Customs 2013), [2007] OJ L154/25–31.

[156] The Evaluation Partnership, Mid-Term Evaluation–Final Report, June 2011, p 7.

[157] COM (2008) 169 final.

[158] COM (2001) 726 final.

[159] COM (2002) 263 final.

[160] The Evaluation Partnership, Mid-Term Evaluation–Final Report, June 2011, p 33.

[161] ibid, p 7.

[162] ibid, p 39.

[163] Council Decision of 28 June 1999 laying down the procedures for the exercise of implementing powers conferred on the Commission (1999/468/EC), [1999] OJ L184/23–26, amended by Council Decision 2006/512/EC of 17 July 2006 amending Decision 1999/468/EC laying down the procedures for the exercise of implementing powers conferred on the Commission, [2006] OJ L200/11–13.

[164] Regulation (EU) 182/2011 of the European Parliament and of the Council of 16 February 2011 laying down the rules and general principles concerning mechanisms for control by Member States of the Commission's exercise of implementing powers, [2011] OJ L55/13–18.

[165] The Evaluation Partnership, Mid-Term Evaluation–Final Report, June 2011, p 39.

Therefore, Customs 2013 is a tool designed precisely to support cooperation in EU customs by connecting customs services across the EU, fostering their exchange of information, and ensuring their uniform implementation and application of EU customs legislation.[166]

1. IT Action

Regarding IT action, Customs 2013 supports the development and the maintenance cost of central and trans-European IT systems and e-learning modules.[167] IT-related actions consume the largest part of the budget of Customs 2013[168] as was the case with Customs 2007.[169]

Electronic customs systems contribute significantly to the national customs administrations acting as though as they were one single European customs administrations, as the implementation of IT systems enforces uniform procedures among all EU Member States.[170] IT action in Customs 2013, such as meetings of the Electronic Customs Group (ECG) and its technical working groups, evaluation workshops for conformance testing of IT systems and applications and activities related to IT training, have had a positive impact on and clearly contribute to the interoperability, maintenance, and upgrading of existing IT systems as well as to the development and implementation of new IT projects.[171] The main benefit of Customs 2013 in this regard is its funding mechanism for meetings, coordination, exchanges and joint problem solving, to support the EU Member States in the implementation and application of electronic customs systems.[172]

2. Joint Action and Training

Joint actions represent the human element of Customs 2013 and bring together customs officials from national customs administrations of EU Member States and from the European Commission in a variety of formats and bodies.[173] Project groups meet several times over a fixed period of time to achieve specific predefined objectives.[174] Steering groups perform activities of a coordinating nature over a long period of time regarding specific areas of Customs 2013.[175] Those specific areas are: electronic customs, working methods, customs laboratories, training, programme coordination and communication, and implementing provisions for

[166] European Commission, Brochure on the Customs Cooperation Programme 2013, 2009, p 4.
[167] ibid, p 9.
[168] The Evaluation Partnership, Mid-Term Evaluation–Final Report, June 2011, pp 36, 39.
[169] COM (2005) 111 final, p 12.
[170] The Evaluation Partnership, Mid-Term Evaluation–Final Report, June 2011, pp 65, 66.
[171] ibid, p 66.
[172] ibid, p 67.
[173] ibid, p 36.
[174] ibid, p 36.
[175] ibid, p 36.

the new Customs Code.[176] Seminars examine specific topics mainly at a strategic level, but are formal one-off events, for example conferences.[177] Workshops are also one-off events which examine specific topics, but are rather smaller-scale than seminars and deal with more operational matters.[178] Working visits involve the exchanges of customs officials between participating EU Member States' customs administrations to enable the sharing of knowledge and best practices in order to realise a predefined objective.[179] Benchmarking activities involve two or more national customs administrations of EU Member States which work together to undertake systematic research, analysis, and comparison in order to identify and learn from best practices.[180] Monitoring activities are carried out by a joint team that analyses national customs practices for the identification of difficulties in the correct implementation of EU customs legislation in order to make suggestions for improvement.[181] Finally, the European Commission also organises IT training sessions for the customs officials of the EU Member States.[182] Many, if not most, joint actions pursue the harmonisation of working methods and processes as one of their objectives, even if it is not the primary one, while over 25 per cent of the total joint actions explicitly strive towards the 'act as one' ambition as their main objective.[183]

Common training and training infrastructure, such as courses and modules enabling customs officials to acquire common professional skills and knowledge, contribute significantly to a common core of high-quality training. This training has the potential to harmonise working methods, spread best practices, increase coordination, and instil mutual confidence regarding customs controls and methods practiced in the EU Member States throughout the EU.[184]

3. *Effectiveness of the Customs 2013 Programme*

Customs 2013 assists the national customs administrations of the EU Member States in performing their duties more homogeneously by providing a platform for the exchange of information and the development of common guidelines, IT systems and training.[185] Indeed, Customs 2013 supports a large number of activities that are necessary for guaranteeing the proper functioning of the EU Customs Union and that largely depend on the EU's coordination and financial support.[186]

Customs 2013 focuses especially on promoting and facilitating cooperation and coordination between national customs administrations. Thus, it contributes to

[176] ibid, p 39.
[177] ibid, p 36.
[178] ibid, p 36.
[179] ibid, p 36.
[180] ibid, p 36.
[181] ibid, p 36.
[182] ibid, p 36.
[183] ibid, p 63.
[184] ibid, pp 71, 72.
[185] ibid, p 64.
[186] ibid, pp 9, 12.

the EU-wide spread of relevant information and good practices, thereby ensuring coherence of customs operations by improving working methods for customs controls, which in turn leads to a more level playing field between the national customs administrations of the EU Member States.[187] In truth, one of the greatest assets of Customs 2013 is how it brings together and leverages the knowledge and expertise of experts from all EU Member States.[188] Customs 2013 facilitates a large number of personal and direct contacts between national customs authorities and their officials[189] and thus generates harmonisation effects. The outputs of networking, discussions, coordination of approaches, and joint problem solving have a direct, significant, and positive effect on the correct implementation and application of EU customs legislation.[190] Customs 2013 is leading to the gradual closing of the gaps that exist in the interpretation and application of EU customs law.[191] This has been confirmed in interviews with customs officials in Germany, who found that joint actions of Customs 2013 helped them to optimise their day-to-day customs work.[192] Overall, Customs 2013 was assessed to be important in how it promotes the awareness of 'togetherness' between customs officials of different EU Member States.[193] Also stressed was the importance of Customs 2013 in providing an overview of the processes, parallelisms, and differences amongst EU Member States.[194]

Nevertheless, the effectiveness and efficiency of Customs 2013 could be improved. In particular, the dissemination of outputs of Customs 2013 activities within national customs administrations should be enhanced and maximised, and a common framework for monitoring of outputs should be defined. This includes the broader use of the online Programmes Information and Collaboration Space (PICS) as a common platform for disseminating such results.[195] This is especially important with regard to joint actions with a limited number of participants, as the knowledge shared and generated during such programme activities is often only accessible to the participants in an event.[196] However, the simple distribution

[187] ibid, pp 8, 12.
[188] ibid, p 12.
[189] ibid, p 12.
[190] ibid, pp 8, 10.
[191] ibid, pp 8, 10.
[192] 'Aber wir können für unsere tägliche Arbeit da Optimierungspotential herausschöpfen.' Interview of 4 April 2011 on file with author.
[193] 'Also bevor man sich über größere Zeiträume mit Emails immer hin und her kontaktiert, ist es doch, glaube ich, schon sehr [viel] effektiver, wenn man sich dann einmal trifft, ja, für zwei Tage und sich dann halt entsprechend austauscht … 2013 ist wirklich eigentlich recht wichtig.' Interview of 1 April 2011 on file with author; 'Also das ist zu wertvoll, diese, ja diese Erkenntnis,Wir gehören zusammen', Interview of 10 May 2011 on file with author.
[194] 'Also das ist eine wichtige Sache, sich auch in den Mitgliedstaaten zu treffen um einfach auch einmal … auch einfach ein besseres Bild machen zu können über Abläufe, Parallelitäten, aber auch Abweichungen insgesamt. Also zum Gesamtverständnis trägt es schon bei, dass es so etwas gibt.' Interview of 20 May 2011 on file with author.
[195] The Evaluation Partnership, Mid-Term Evaluation–Final Report, June 2011, p 12.
[196] Commission Staff Working Document of 15 July 2006, /*SEC/2006/0570*/, 6.3.2.2 Establishment of information sharing structure.

of information would not be sufficient. A systematic dissemination is required to actually be of use for customs officials. Indeed, in an interview with customs officials in the United Kingdom, the criticism was raised that, at least in part, 'there is an information overload. There is a lot of information which is available. It is finding it, as you say, [that] is one of the problems.'[197] The lack of sufficient systematic dissemination of programme results was also a criticism raised regarding Customs 2007.[198] Additionally, the circle of participants in joint actions should be enlarged. In another interview with customs officials in the United Kingdom, it was pointed out that the same people tend to be involved in joint actions.[199] Furthermore, German officials criticised Customs 2013 for running selective actions and for not providing a permanent exchange, at least not on an operational level.[200]

C. The Customs 2020 Programme

Customs 2020[201] will maintain the support for cooperation between the customs administrations of the EU Member States by concentrating on human networking and competency building through joint actions, enabling the exchange of good practices and operational knowledge, as well as by IT capacity building, see in particular Recitals (2), (5), (6) Regulation (EU) 1294/2013. This kind of EU action is needed because the European dimension of customs work has to be reiterated and reinforced to avoid distortions of the Internal Market and ensure effective protection of the EU external borders, see in particular Recital (2) Regulation (EU) 1294/2013. New joint actions tools will also be introduced, including expert teams as a structured form of cooperation to pool expertise and address specific operational activities, and actions for public administration capacity building in order to support customs authorities that face particular difficulties, see in particular Recital (5) Regulation (EU) 1294/2013. However, a new approach with regard to the systematic dissemination of outputs cannot be found in Customs 2020.

D. Summary

The EU Customs Union cannot function without close cooperation that enhances uniform and effective application of EU customs law, and the Customs Action

[197] Interview of 10 January 2012 on file with author.

[198] Commission staff working document, SEC/2006/0570*/ of 15.07.2006, 6.3.2 Improve structure knowledge sharing.

[199] Interview of 9 January 2012 on file with author.

[200] 'Aber ich meine, dadurch, dass es eben sehr punktuell nur läuft–und es ist ja so, wenn da von den vielen Zöllnern einmal ein paar einzelne das machen–kann die Wirkung auch nicht so übermäßig sein. Was nicht heißt, dass man es zukünftig unterlassen soll. Im Gegenteil, vielleicht sollte man es noch forcieren.' Interview of 20 April 2011 on file with author.

[201] Regulation (EU) 1294/2013 of the European Parliament and of the Council of 11 December 2013 establishing an action programme for customs in the European Union for the period 2014–2020 (Customs 2020) and repealing Decision 624/2007/EC, [2013] OJ L347/209–20.

Programme is crucial for ensuring the efficiency of this cooperation.[202] The Customs Action Programme constitutes an important framework for cooperation between customs officials of different EU Member States. Its possibilities for direct contact, exchange of information and development of common best working methods enhance mutual understanding. Indeed, the Customs Action Programme is an important instrument for the strengthening of uniform customs administration in the EU. Nevertheless, the systematic distribution of outputs has to be significantly improved in order to enhance its effectiveness. However, in this context, Customs 2020 contains no indication of new developments or significant improvement. Both the European Commission and the customs administrations of the EU Member States are thus being called upon to provide a common platform to enable customs authorities and their officials to obtain access to the relevant results of programme actions.

V. CONCLUSION

In conclusion, manifold forms of cooperation exist in the area of EU customs. However, the correct legal basis for rules on cooperation can be difficult discern, as Article 33 TFEU conflicts with other provisions, especially with regard to cooperation in the area of freedom, security, and justice. Explicit rules for administrative cooperation regarding daily compliance issues to enhance uniform customs administration are seldom found. Rules for administrative cooperation in the Community Customs Code, as well as in the Union Customs Code, are selective and contain no detailed provisions for cooperation. Although the Mutual Assistance Regulation provides for various procedural rules on administrative cooperation, these rules focus on the investigation of breaches of EU customs law by economic operators and not on the correct charging of customs duties, the day-to-day customs work of customs officials. Therefore, the contribution of the Mutual Assistance Regulation to improving uniform customs administration is limited, though it still can have positive effects through enhancing awareness of the European character of EU customs work today. Aside from explicit rules for cooperation, there are also central contact points supporting cooperation between customs administrations of different EU Member States, and even direct contact between customs officials is increasing. Nevertheless, the most important instrument regarding customs cooperation is the Customs Action Programme. Its manifold programme actions provide for direct contact, exchange of information and expertise, as well as mutual understanding and the development of common working methods and standards. Though the dissemination of its outputs has to be improved, the programme is still effective and an important strategy of the EU for enhancing uniform customs administration.

[202] SEC (2011) 1317 final, p 8.

8

Role, Competences and Strategies of the European Commission

ABOVE ALL, THE European Commission has to be considered as the leading political organ of the European Union, but it simultaneously also possesses some executive functions regarding EU customs matters. Indeed, in the EU's system of customs administration, the European Commission holds a crucial position in the making of customs legislation as well as in the administration of the customs duty regime.[1]

I. LEGISLATIVE FUNCTIONS AND 'QUASI-LEGISLATIVE' FUNCTIONS

Given its lack of natural legitimacy the EU as well as its EU Customs Union depend on other sources for reflected or derived legitimacy.[2] For this purpose, the enactment of effective law and thereby successful governance play a central role.[3] The effectiveness and efficiency of EU law act as foundations for the legitimacy of the EU.[4]

A. Right of Initiative

With its right of initiative, the European Commission has the responsibility to advance the 'Better Regulation' Initiative by proposing and designing new or amended legal acts.[5] The European Commission's right of initiative is regarded as a basic element in the institutional balance of the EU, laid down as part of the ordinary legislative procedure in Article 294 paragraph 2 TFEU. The effective synthesis of relevant information for developing suitable legislative initiatives in the

[1] Lyons, 2008, p 118.
[2] von Bogdandy, in: Hoffmann-Riem/Schmidt-Aßmann (eds), 2000, pp 133–94 (139); Weiß, 2010, p 34.
[3] von Bogdandy, in: Hoffmann-Riem/Schmidt-Aßmann (eds), 2000, pp 133–94 (139); Weiß, 2010, p 34.
[4] von Bogdandy, in: Hoffmann-Riem/Schmidt-Aßmann (eds), 2000, pp 133–94 (139).
[5] COM (2007) 502 final, p 3.

EU requires a specialised and autonomous institution provided with corresponding competences.[6]

This is also the case in the area of EU customs legislation, where the European Commission's right of initiative is mainly guaranteed by cross reference to the ordinary legislative procedure, namely in Article 207 TFEU regarding the common commercial policy, Article 33 TFEU regarding cooperation in customs administration and, more commonly, in Article 114 TFEU regarding the approximation of laws in achieving the objectives of the Internal Market set out in Article 26 TFEU. These three Articles together thus constitute the legal basis of the Union Customs Code, the Customs Code itself being the greatest example of the crucial role that the European Commission holds in the making of EU customs legislation through its exclusive right of initiative. In addition to such cross references to the ordinary legislative procedure, the European Commission is also explicitly conferred the right of initiative in the area of Common Customs Tariff duties, in Article 31 TFEU.

Furthermore, the European Commission issues implementing provisions of a quasi-legislative and executive character, as well as other measures, in order to improve the working of the EU Customs Union and the administration of EU customs. Since the entry into force of the Customs Code, the European Commission has enacted the accompanying regulation that lays down the provisions for its implementation. To further improve the implementation of EU customs law, the Commission also enacts regulations on classification, issues comments on the combined nomenclature, and provides best practice guidelines to ensure the correct application and uniform implementation of EU customs law in the national customs administrations of the EU Member States.

In the agenda-setting policy phase, which is formally dominated by the European Commission due to its right of initiative, national administrations play a crucial role, as groups of national experts are used for deliberation, brainstorming, intergovernmental conflict solving and developing concepts.[7] In the case of EU customs law, various project groups for different areas of EU customs policy exist; for example, the modernised customs code policy group discusses the modernisation of EU customs and the European Commission's plans for implementing provisions. Private parties are also often involved in various bodies, for example in the Trade Contact Group.

The European Commission's competence regarding tertiary law-making in customs matters has to be considered in more detail, especially with regard to Article 290 TFEU. Implementing acts pursuant to Article 291 TFEU – and also soft law acts – are part of the European Commission's administrative function in the implementation of EU customs.

[6] von Bogdandy, in: Hoffmann-Riem/Schmidt-Aßmann (eds), 2000, pp 133–94 (145).
[7] Hofmann/Türk, 2007 ELJ (13), pp 253–71 (254, 255).

B. Competences Regarding Tertiary Law-Making Pursuant to Article 290 TFEU

In terms of powers, the European Commission's authority to issue delegated acts is part of its competence to enact legal acts according to EU primary law, which includes not only the enactment of EU secondary law but also the enactment of tertiary EU law that can be delegated to the European Commission as executive law-making.[8] Therefore, concretising acts of tertiary law making in areas where the EU has legislative competence are legitimate with regard to the distribution of competences between the EU and the EU Member States.[9] However, according to Article 290 paragraph 1 subparagraph 2 TFEU, essential elements of an area must be regulated by the EU's legislative branch, namely the European Parliament and the Council. This article codifies the requirements of the principle of democracy as long anchored in the case law of the ECJ and since reinforced with the entry into force of the Treaty of Lisbon.[10]

In the institutional balance of the EU, the European Commission is not constituted as a legislative organ but as an executive one, which means that its law-making competences are limited. The functioning of the EU is based on representative democracy pursuant to Article 10 paragraph 1 TEU, whereby representation is not through the European Commission but through the European Parliament and the Council.[11] Thus the latter two should have the decisive influence over EU legislation, giving the necessary democratic legitimacy to the legislative acts.[12] Therefore, in the area of EU customs the legislative organs are the Council or the Council together with the European Parliament pursuant to Articles 31, 33, 114 and 207 TFEU. The European Commission can only adopt delegated acts or implementing acts pursuant to Articles 290 and 291 TFEU, which are formally not of a legislative character pursuant to Article 289 paragraph 3 TFEU. Moreover, Article 290 TFEU allows only for the delegation of amending or supplementing powers regarding the adaption of non-legislative acts of general application, while the essential elements of an area such as EU customs cannot be delegated.[13]

The scope of application of Article 290 TFEU, in comparison to Article 291 TFEU, is an issue that is quite hotly debated,[14] as the differentiation between 'supplementing' and 'implementing' can be troublesome,[15] given that delegated acts

[8] Weiß, 2010, p 40.

[9] ibid, p 40.

[10] Weiß, (2) 2011 JECLAP (5), pp 441–51 (447); European Parliament Resolution of 5 May 2010, (2010/2021(INI)), [2011] OJ C81E/6–10, Recital A.

[11] Weiß, (2) 2011 JECLAP (5), pp 441–51 (448).

[12] ibid, pp 441–51 (448).

[13] ibid, pp 441–51 (448, 449).

[14] See the detailed differentiation in Chapter 5.I.A.1.

[15] Weiß, 2010, p 59; Stelkens, 2012 EuR 5, pp 511–45 (513); Hofmann/Türk, 2012 ZG, pp 105–37 (115); Craig, 2011 ELRev (36), pp 671–87 (672, 673); Nettesheim, in: Grabitz/Hilf/Nettesheim (eds), 2013, Vol III, Art 290 TFEU, para 20.

can also serve to implement their basic legislative acts.[16] However, the correct differentiation between them has practical implications for the involvement of the European Parliament, the Council and the EU Member States in the enactment of such acts and in the control of the European Commission's work.[17] Delegated acts of the European Commission fall under the political control of the European Parliament and the Council pursuant to Article 290 paragraph 2 TFEU, while implementing acts are object under the EU Member States' control pursuant to Article 291 paragraph 3 TFEU.[18] Therefore, the differentiation between Articles 290 and 291 TFEU also reinforces the EU's concept of Executive Federalism. The delegation of quasi-legislative competence to an executive body requires the supervision of the EU legislator, while the exceptional conferral of implementing powers affirms the basic competence of the EU Member States to adopt implementing measures.[19]

The control mechanisms laid down in Article 290 paragraph 2 TFEU protect the horizontal balance of powers, granting the European Parliament and the Council control competences.[20] Yet while these mechanisms constitute a large advance for the European Parliament,[21] and thus also for the democratic legitimacy of the EU, they have simultaneously freed the European Commission from the oversight of EU Member State officials and the veto power of any comitology committee in the most crucial sector of its law-making powers.[22] Although the European Commission intends to consult experts from national authorities, using existing or even creating new expert groups in the context of its preparatory work for the adoption of delegated acts, the European Commission also intends not to grant these consultations any institutional role in the procedure itself.[23] Therefore, it seems that the European Commission has benefited from a substantial inter-institutional power shift in its favour.[24]

However, the Council has been unwilling to abandon any procedural rules regarding the preparatory work of delegated acts and the involvement of necessary expertise.[25] The controls of the European Parliament and the Council and their rights to revoke or object to a delegated act pursuant to Article 290 paragraph 2 TFEU largely depend on the fact that their members first have to understand the delegated act.[26] However, gaining the necessary information could be difficult without the relevant expertise that was formerly provided by comitology

[16] Nettesheim, in: Grabitz/Hilf/Nettesheim (eds), 2013, Vol III, Art 290 TFEU, para 20.
[17] ibid, Vol III, Art 290 TFEU, para 20.
[18] Weiß, 2010, p 58.
[19] Hofmann, 2009 ELJ (15), pp 482–505 (497).
[20] Craig, 2011 ELRev (36), pp 671–87 (674).
[21] Hofmann/Türk, 2012 ZG, pp 105–37 (118).
[22] Bast, 2012 CMLRev (49), pp 885–927 (918).
[23] COM (2009) 673 final, pp 6, 7; see also Hofmann/Türk, 2012 ZG, pp 105–37 (119), who criticise the attitude of the European Commission in this context.
[24] Bast, 2012 CMLRev (49), pp 885–927 (919).
[25] Hofmann/Türk, 2012 ZG, pp 105–37 (119).
[26] Craig, 2010, p 262.

committees.[27] Therefore, it seems that the Council, and perhaps also the European Parliament, will now create advisory committees, although there is no formal mechanism for such committees and they will be distinct from the committees created under Article 291 TFEU and the Comitology Regulation,[28] differing also with regard to their membership.[29] Meanwhile, as a compromise, most legal acts now contain a general reference to the need for the involvement of experts in the preparatory work of delegated acts.[30]

This is also the case in EU customs law. The Union Customs Code explicitly requires that the European Commission carry out appropriate consultations during its preparatory work with regard to delegated acts. In particular it should consult national experts as well as the EU business community in a transparent manner and well in advance, see Recitals (3) and (5) UCC. It must also transmit all relevant documents to the European Parliament and the Council in a timely manner, see Recital (3) UCC. Furthermore, the European Parliament and the Council can revoke any delegation of power in the Union Customs Code at any time, pursuant to Article 284 paragraph 3 UCC, and can also prevent the entry into force of a delegated act by objecting to it within two months of notification, pursuant to Article 284 paragraph 5 UCC.

In contrast to delegated acts pursuant to Article 290 TFEU, the basic act which confers implementation power to the European Commission pursuant to Article 291 TFEU does not have to be a legislative act but simply a legally binding EU act; thus, an implementing act may also be made pursuant to a delegated act.[31] As a consequence, the European Commission is now in the position to enact a delegated act in form of a regulation and to decide simultaneously that uniform implementing conditions are required for some of its provisions and thus confer to itself the power to issue implementing acts in the delegated regulation.[32] Formal constraints on the European Commission could only take place as an ex-post control. The Council or the European Parliament could veto the delegated act pursuant to Article 290 paragraph 2 TFEU, while the EU Member States could exercise some influence on the implementing act through the mechanisms provided in Article 291 paragraph 3 TFEU and Regulation (EU) 182/2011.

However, the committees controlling the adoption of implementing acts in the sense of Article 291 TFEU are chaired by the European Commission, which gives the European Commission some influence. With regard to Article 290 TFEU, the Council and the European Parliament have the power to prevent the entry into force of a delegated act, pursuant to Article 290 paragraph 2 section (b) TFEU, but

[27] ibid, p 262.

[28] Regulation (EU) 182/2011 of the European Parliament and of the Council of 16 February 2011 laying down the rules and general principles concerning mechanisms for control by Member States of the Commission's exercise of implementing powers, [2011] OJ L55/13–18.

[29] Craig, 2011 ELRev (36), pp 671–87 (675).

[30] Hofmann/Türk, 2012 ZG, pp 105–37 (119).

[31] Craig, 2010, p 274; Hofmann/Türk, 2012 ZG, pp 105–37 (109); Nettesheim, in: Nettesheim/Grabitz/Hilf (eds), 2013, Vol III, Art 291 TFEU, para 26.

[32] Craig, 2010, p 274.

have no formal right to propose amendments. Therefore, the Treaty of Lisbon has increased the European Commission's 'quasi-legislative' function and its position in the legislative process as a whole.[33]

1. Requirements for Delegated Acts Pursuant to Article 290 TFEU

Delegated acts can be adopted in the form of regulations, directives or decisions, pursuant to Articles 288 and 297 TFEU. However, other types of acts are also possible because atypical acts are only excluded for legislative acts pursuant *e contrario* to Article 296 paragraph 3 TFEU.[34] Regarding the requirements for delegation to the legislature pursuant to Article 290 TFEU, it is of decisive importance to define the essential elements of an area in EU legislation, as only non-essential elements of the basic legal act—which itself must be a legislative act—can be supplemented or amended, while essential elements cannot be questioned or reversed.[35] Following from the principle of democracy, the essential elements of any area in EU legislation have to be determined and enacted by the EU's legislative organs. Thus, the definition of 'certain non-essential elements' in the sense of Article 290 paragraph 1 sentence 1 TFEU is of specific importance.

According to established case law,[36] even before the entry into force of the Lisbon Treaty the adoption of rules essential to the subject matter was reserved to the EU legislator. However, the ECJ has not yet offered much further guidance on the distinction between essential and non-essential elements of legislation.[37] In *Parliament v Council*,[38] which dealt with an enabling provision based on the former Article 202 TEC, the ECJ missed the opportunity to shed greater light on the issue[39] and merely confirmed that the essential character of an element depends on the policy field concerned.[40]

The newly introduced notion of 'political choices requiring conflicting interests to be weighed up against each other and thus falling within the responsibility of the EU legislator',[41] though intended to help in differentiation, does not provide useful guidance. Also, the amendment or supplementing of non-essential elements of legislation often requires such 'weighing up' on the basis of numerous considerations, which would render the possibility of adopting delegated acts useless if such political choices would indeed fall under the reserved domain of the EU legislator.[42]

[33] ibid, p 274.

[34] Hofmann, 2009 ELJ (15), pp 482–505 (491); Hofmann/Türk, 2012 ZG, pp 105–37 (106).

[35] Weiß, (2) 2011 JECLAP (5), pp 441–51 (449); Weiß, 2010 EWS 7, pp 257 et seq (260); Craig, in: Griller/Ziller (eds), 2008, pp 109–34 (112).

[36] See, inter alia, ECJ of 5 September 2012, Case C-355/10, *Parliament v Council* [2012] ECR I-0, para 64, and the case law cited.

[37] Chamon, 2013 CMLRev (50), pp 849–60 (856).

[38] ECJ of 5 September 2012, Case C-355/10, *Parliament v Council* [2012] ECR I-0.

[39] Chamon, 2013 CMLRev (50), pp 849–860 (859).

[40] ECJ of 5 September 2012, Case C-355/10, *Parliament v Council* [2012] ECR I-0, para 68.

[41] ibid, para 76.

[42] Chamon, 2013 CMLRev (50), pp 849–860 (858).

The ECJ also decided that subject matters concerning fundamental rights have to be dealt with by the EU legislator[43] and thus implied that delegated acts are allowed to only marginally touch upon fundamental rights of persons.[44] With Article 290 TFEU, the notion of essential elements is now codified in EU primary law and thus now has an upgraded role.[45] Therefore, a more systemic approach to the distinction between essential and non-essential elements is required in order to provide for more predictability and legal certainty.[46] For example, technicalities may be delegated to the European Commission, whereas basic issues standing behind these technicalities have to be provided for by the EU's legislators.[47]

However, the determination of the essential elements of the basic act is only the first step in a two-staged test to assess whether the requirements of Article 290 paragraph 1 subparagraph 2 TFEU are fulfilled.[48] The EU legislator not only has to determine any non-essential element in the basic legislative act that can be supplemented or amended by the European Commission, it has to expressly define the objectives, content, scope and duration of the delegation pursuant to Article 290 paragraph 1 subparagraph 2 TFEU.[49] The further conditions to which the delegation is subject, pursuant to Article 290 paragraph 2 TFEU, may allow the European Parliament or the Council to revoke the delegation or enable them to veto the delegated act within a specified period of time.[50] This must be specified in the legislative act itself,[51] which in the case of EU customs would in general be the Customs Code. If the provisions to be supplemented or amended were not clearly established and precisely defined in the basic legislative act, then the European Commission could determine the elements and limits of a delegation, instead of the EU legislator, which would violate the principle of democracy.[52]

Therefore the Customs Code, which is the basic legislative act for any delegation of powers to the European Commission that necessarily has to be exercised in order to make the new Code applicable and its implementation feasible, has to define the specific objectives, content, scope and duration of each delegation pursuant to Article 290 paragraph 1 subparagraph 2 TFEU, as well as its conditions pursuant to Article 290 paragraph 2 TFEU.

2. *Delegated Powers of the European Commission in EU Customs Law*

In EU customs law, the 'Better Regulation' Initiative has led to a simplification of the Customs Code, reducing it to the essential rules of customs legislation,

[43] ECJ of 5 September 2012, Case C-355/10, *Parliament v Council* [2012] ECR I-0, para 77.
[44] Chamon, 2013 CMLRev (50), pp 849–60 (859).
[45] ibid, pp 849–60 (856).
[46] ibid, pp 849–60 (860).
[47] Weiß, (2) 2011 JECLAP (5), pp 441–51 (449).
[48] Chamon, 2013 CMLRev (50), pp 849–60 (857, 859).
[49] European Parliament Resolution of 5 May 2010, (2010/2021(INI)), [2011] OJ C81E/6–10, para 1; Craig, in: Griller/Ziller (eds), 2008, pp 109–34 (112).
[50] Craig, in: Griller/Ziller (eds), 2008, pp 109–34 (112).
[51] ibid, pp 109–134 (112).
[52] Weiß, (2) 2011 JECLAP (5), pp 441–51 (450).

with less important and non-essential elements to be regulated by the European Commission in separated provisions. Thus, there is a special need in EU customs law to delegate corresponding powers pursuant to Article 290 TFEU to the European Commission in order to make the Code applicable and enable its implementation in practice. Furthermore, the adoption of detailed provisions in the form of delegated acts is part of the European Commission's strategy to reduce margins of discretion in the implementation of EU customs law.[53] Thus, the Union Customs Code provides for extensive delegation of power in the sense of Article 290 TFEU.

According to the recitals of the UCC, the customs areas where a delegation of power to the European Commission is possible include: rules taking into account the special fiscal regime of certain parts of the customs territory of the EU;[54] some of the technicalities regarding the Electronic Customs Initiative;[55] rules in the context of customs formalities, customs controls, and customs decisions including those relating to binding information, authorised economic operator and simplifications;[56] determination of origin and customs value of goods;[57] rules relating to customs debt[58] and to the customs status of goods;[59] rules relating to customs declaration and release of goods;[60] rules on special procedures;[61] and many more. In fact, the Union Customs Code contains 39 Articles concerning delegation of power to the European Commission. Most of these delegations of power concern the determination of exceptions, time-limits, conditions and cases that are referred to in the Union Customs Code as non-essential elements to be added to the Code in order to supplement it. For example, Article 24 UCC regarding the delegation of power in the context of customs decisions is precisely defined regarding the scope and content of the non-essential elements that shall be added, referring explicitly to the exceptions, conditions, time-limits and cases that the European Commission can regulate by means of delegated acts.

As a 'quasi-legislative' function of the European Commission, the adoption of delegated acts pursuant to Article 290 TFEU is controlled by the EU legislator, but beyond this the European Commission can act independently from any control of EU Member States. The extensive delegation of power in the Union Customs Code thus has been criticised, as the European Commission will indeed be able to regulate large parts of EU customs law without EU Member States having a voice.[62]

A customs official of the section for the modernised customs code in the United Kingdom declared that there are indeed concerns that the European Commission is trying to push so much into delegated acts as to effectively be proposing

[53] Lux, 2012 AW-Prax 8, pp 257–62 (258).
[54] Recital (14).
[55] Recital (18).
[56] Recital (29).
[57] Recital (31).
[58] Recital (39).
[59] Recital (41).
[60] Recital (46).
[61] Recital (51).
[62] Boysen, in: von Arnauld (ed), 2014, § 9 pp 447–514, para 75.

legislation, without taking notice of EU Member States, even if the content in theory might require the consultation of EU Member States:

> And there are concerns that they will try to, if you like, flex their muscles a bit in terms of what they think is the authority they have to take decisions without necessarily effectively consulting Member States.[63]

Therefore, the EU Parliament and the Council are required to thoroughly control the delegated acts adopted by the European Commission to ensure they fulfil the requirements of Article 290 TFEU.

In the ordinary legislative procedure, the European Parliament emphasised the importance of uniform implementation and application of the Union Customs Code with regard to the fundamental spirit of pan-European e-customs and the unconditional principle of electronic exchange as the keystone principle of the modernisation of EU customs law.[64] Therefore, in the context of e-customs, only technicalities can be delegated to the European Commission, whereas the fundamental issues behind those technicalities have to be provided for in the Union Customs Code itself. For example, with regard to the exchange and storage of data, Article 7 UCC delegates the determination of the necessary common data requirements to the European Commission, while the Union Customs Code lays down the basic rules in Article 6 UCC.

However, in other cases the European Commission had to be reminded by the EU legislator to comply with the restriction to amend or supplement only non-essential elements by way of delegation. For instance, the European Parliament argued that the main conditions for authorised economic operator (AEO) status are essential aspects and therefore must be explicitly laid down in the basic act itself.[65] Therefore, Articles 22 and 23 of the UCC proposal were reviewed and the delegation of power to the European Commission to specify the rules for granting AEO status was removed. In the Union Customs Code, the basic rules relating to conditions and procedure for granting the status of AEO are laid down in Articles 38 and 39 UCC, while the European Commission is only authorised, pursuant to Article 40 UCC, to specify the corresponding simplifications, facilitations and favourable treatment by way of delegated acts.

The Union Customs Code also determines the duration of any delegation of power, as Article 290 paragraph 1 subparagraph 2 TFEU requires. Although the European Commission has been authorised a large scope to adopt delegated acts based on the Union Customs Code, any delegation of power after 30 October 2013 is valid only for a period of five years, pursuant to Article 284 paragraph 2 UCC. However, the Union Customs Code provides for the tacit extension by an identical duration unless the European Parliament or the Council oppose such an extension, see Article 284 paragraph 2 UCC. On the other hand, the European Parliament

[63] Interview of 9 January 2012.

[64] European Parliament, First Reading Report of 26 February 2013, A7-0006/2013, Amendments 10 and 11, pp 11, 12.

[65] ibid, Amendment 24, p 20.

and the Council can revoke any delegation of power in the Union Customs Code at any time, pursuant to Article 284 paragraph 3 UCC, and can also prevent the entry into force of a delegated act by objecting to it within two months of notification, pursuant to Article 284 paragraph 5 UCC. In this regard, the Union Customs Code also meets the conditions of Article 290 paragraph 2 TFEU.

3. *Conclusion*

In conclusion, the extensive delegation of power to the European Commission in various fields of EU customs law illustrates the European Commission's strong position in the management of the EU Customs Union. Its 'quasi-legislative' competences in EU customs legislation—now by way of delegated powers—have been confirmed in the Union Customs Code in order to improve the functioning of the EU Customs Union. In this context, the Union Customs Code follows a more centralised approach than the Community Customs Code. As a consequence, the European Commission could become more independent from the cooperation with EU Member States.

II. ADMINISTRATIVE FUNCTIONS

In addition to its 'quasi-legislative' function, the European Commission is constituted as the central executive organ in the system of the EU and thus has to carry out executive and administrative functions pursuant to Article 17 paragraph 1 sentence 5 TEU. It also has to ensure the application of the EU Treaties pursuant to Article 17 paragraph 1 sentence 2 TEU. Therefore, the European Commission has to work in close partnership with the EU Member States through contacts, networks and regular meetings of national experts to ensure efficient and effective application of EU law and to consider technical updates and ideas for the further development of EU law.[66]

In EU customs, the European Commission has to ensure that scientific expertise, which normally can only be gained by the relevant groups of national experts, is integrated together.[67] It also has to manage formal and informal networks of EU Member State representatives, experts and private parties.[68] As part of its administrative function, the European Commission adopts implementing acts pursuant to Article 291 TFEU to ensure the uniform application of EU customs law. Moreover, the issuing of soft law acts to provide useful guidance for the practical implementation of EU customs law is an important instrument in the EUs' strategy to ensure the uniform administration of EU customs.[69]

[66] COM (2007) 502 final, p 3.
[67] Hofmann/Türk, 2007 ELJ (13), pp 253–71 (257).
[68] ibid, pp 253–71 (257).
[69] Lux, 2012 AW-Prax 8, pp 257–62 (258).

Furthermore, as the EU's representative, the European Commission also has to participate in the work of the WTO and WCO committees related to customs policies. An important part of this work is to ensure a common approach to the various customs fields by the EU and its EU Member States in their dealings with the EU's major trading partners.[70] The European Commission is also chief negotiator in the numerous free trade agreements with third countries, which also concern customs related issues, pursuant to Article 207 paragraph 3, Article 218 TFEU.

In carrying out its administrative functions, the European Commission is subject to the duty of good administration, pursuant to Article 41 of the Charter of Fundamental Rights, and has the duty to analyse and coordinate the various information it receives from EU Member States.[71] Although the duty of good administration is a general duty, the European Commission's obligations in the area of EU customs administration also derive from specific legislation and international agreements, for example in the area of tariff quotas or preferential rates of duty.[72] Such administrative duties of the European Commission often contain the requirement not only to ask EU Member States to keep the European Commission informed about trade flows in relation to customs matters, but also to monitor the correct implementation of EU customs law and international agreements in the EU Member States.[73] Although the European Commission normally has no authority to give instructions to national customs authorities,[74] the integration of centralised and decentralised elements of implementation provides the European Commission with some instruments by which to exercise influence in the implementation of EU customs law.

A. Coordination, Management, Monitoring and Assistance as the Main Administrative Functions

Regarding the administration of the EU customs duties regime, to a large extent the European Commission has a coordinating function and manages and enhances the exchange of information throughout the EU through its operation of several databases such as the TARIC[75] and EBTI,[76] as well as other electronic customs systems such as CIS.[77] The European Commission itself has described its main function regarding customs administration activity to be the management

[70] See also European Court of Auditors, Special Report 23/2000, [2001] OJ C84/1–18, para 17.

[71] Lyons, 2008, p 119.

[72] ibid, p 119, fn 97.

[73] For example: General Court, Case T-23/03, *CAS SpA* [2007] ECR II-289, para 234 (regarding international agreements); General Court of 27 February 2003, Case T-329/00 *Bonn Fleisch Ex- und Import GmbH* [2003] ECR II-287, paras 89, 90 (regarding GATT quotas).

[74] Weiß, 2010, p 25; Kadelbach, in: Joerges/Dehousse (eds), 2003, pp 167–206 (170).

[75] The online integrated Community Tariff, see Chapter 2.III.A.3.

[76] European Binding Tariff Information database, see Chapter 10.I.E.1.

[77] Customs Information System, see Chapter 7.II.A and B.

of customs instruments needed for the application of the EU's common policies.[78] These policies form the basis for measures such as the establishment of a customs nomenclature, the management of tariff databases and the setting up of a system for information exchange regarding controls and checks for fraud and irregular practices.[79]

The coordination of information is of special importance in the EU, as its vertical and horizontal information flows have a unique quality and frequency compared to transnational communication relationships outside of the EU.[80] The functioning of Executive Federalism in the EU Customs Union depends to a large degree on the development of efficient information and communication networks as well as the effective use of information in decision-making processes.[81]

The regulation of information exchange between EU Member States in order to improve the effectiveness of national administrations is one of the central tasks of the EU and results in a strengthened position for the European Commission.[82] The European Commission also has an important function in horizontal cooperation in the area of EU customs through its role in the development and expansion of information technology. As has already been alluded to, the Mutual Assistance Regulation[83] contains important elements of vertical regulation. Especially the introduction of the customs information system (CIS) has strengthened the role of the European Commission, which possesses extensive technical and administrative responsibilities for the management of this centralised IT system.[84]

Indeed, the European Commission manages many central customs databases or common platforms for those databases, such as TARIC, AEO (Authorised Economic Operators), EBTI (Binding Tariff Information), ECICS (European Customs Inventory of Chemical Substances), EORI (Economic Operators Identification and Registration number), EXPORT (tracking goods in export), QUOTA (tariff quotas), SURVEILLANCE (statistical monitoring of imports and exports), SUSPENSIONS (Autonomous Tariff Suspensions), Customs offices (offices where transit declarations can be made), and TRANSIT (Movement Reference Number (MRN) Follow-up Information).[85] The collection and administration

[78] European Commission, Seventeenth Annual Report on monitoring the application of Community law, 1999, COM (2000) 92 final, [2001] OJ C30/1–206, p 17.

[79] ibid, p 17.

[80] von Bogdandy, in: Hoffmann-Riem/Schmidt-Aßmann (eds), 2000, pp 133–94 (139).

[81] Similar: ibid, pp 133–94 (139).

[82] See Chapter 7.II.A.

[83] Council Regulation (EC) 515/97 of 13 March 1997 on mutual assistance between the administrative authorities of the Member States and cooperation between the latter and the Commission to ensure the correct application of the law on customs and agricultural matters, [1997] OJ L82/1–16; last amended by Regulation (EC) 766/2088 of the European Parliament and of the Council of 9 July 2008 amending Council Regulation (EC) 515/97 on mutual assistance between the administrative authorities of the Member States and cooperation between the latter and the Commission to ensure the correct application of the law on customs and agricultural matters, [2008] OJ L218/48–59.

[84] von Bogdandy, in: Hoffmann-Riem/Schmidt-Aßmann (eds), 2000, pp 133–94 (184, 185, 186).

[85] URL: http://ec.europa.eu/taxation_customs/common/databases/. A detailed analysis of the central databases in EU customs administration can be found in Chapter 4.IV.D.

of such information by the European Commission is regularly connected with corresponding obligations for the EU Member States to send information or supply the common databases with the relevant updated information.

The e-customs Decision[86] gives a general overview of the extensive obligations and administrative functions of the European Commission for the operation and management of electronic customs systems to regulate relevant customs information in order to improve and simplify customs work. The European Commission's administrative function regarding the central coordination and analysis of customs-related information can bring it into a position in which it alone is able to detect abuse of the EU Customs system.[87]

B. Exceptional Competence for Administrative Decisions and New Implementing Powers Pursuant to Article 291 TFEU

In the EU's system of customs administration, the European Commission is not designed as a regular decision-making authority as is the case, for example, in the administration of EU competition law. Thus, in EU customs, the European Commission only has the competence to function as a kind of decision maker with its own discretion in exceptional cases. Indeed, the Community Customs Code provides for only two such possibilities, both relating to exceptions from the obligation to pay a customs duty for reasons of equity.

The first exception is the remission or repayment of a customs duty under Article 239 paragraph 1 second indent CCC (Article 120 UCC/former Article 83 MCC) or in case the notion of a special situation is in question, pursuant to Article 905 CCCIP.[88] However, the European Commission is only competent to assess whether special reasons of equity exist when the special circumstances of the case result either from a breach of duty or an error on the part of the European Commission, pursuant to Article 905 paragraph 1 first indent CCCIP; when the case relates to a Union investigation carried out under the Mutual Assistance Regulation,[89] pursuant to Article 905 paragraph 1 second indent CCCIP; or when the amount of customs duty is EUR 500,000 or more, Article 905 paragraph 1 third indent CCCIP. Furthermore, even in these cases the national customs authority is only obliged to

[86] Decision 70/2008/EC of the European Parliament and of the Council of 15 January 2008 on a paperless environment for customs and trade, [2008] OJ L23/21–26.

[87] Lyons, 2008, p 119.

[88] ibid, pp 119, 502; see also Classen, in: Grabitz/Hilf/Nettesheim (eds), 2013, Vol II, Art 197 TFEU, para 63.

[89] Council Regulation (EC) 515/97 of 13 March 1997 on mutual assistance between the administrative authorities of the Member States and cooperation between the latter and the Commission to ensure the correct application of the law on customs and agricultural matters, [1997] OJ L82/1–16; last amended by Regulation (EC) 766/2088 of the European Parliament and of the Council of 9 July 2008 amending Council Regulation (EC) 515/97 on mutual assistance between the administrative authorities of the Member States and cooperation between the latter and the Commission to ensure the correct application of the law on customs and agricultural matters, [2008] OJ L218/48–59.

submit the case to the European Commission if the Commission has not already adopted a decision on a case and is not currently considering cases that regard comparable issues of fact and of law, pursuant to Article 905 paragraph 2 CCCIP.

The second exception is Article 220 paragraph 2 section (b) CCC (Article 119 paragraph 1 UCC/former Article 82 paragraph 1 MCC), according to which the national customs authorities can submit a concrete case to the European Commission in order to assess whether or not an error on the part of the national customs authority could not reasonably have been detected by the person liable for payment who acted in good faith. The European Commission's decision legally binds the national customs authority regarding the subsequent entry into the accounts of the person liable for payment.

Both exceptions, Article 239 paragraph 1 second indent CCC (Article 120 UCC/ former Article 83 MCC) and Article 220 paragraph 2 section (b) CCC (Article 119 paragraph 1 UCC/former Article 82 paragraph 1 MCC), concern the assessment of reasons of equity relating to decisions with direct effect on the EU's financial interests. In this context, the EU has a special interest that the margin of discretion with regard to reasons of equity are uniformly applied, which explains the special competence of the European Commission to actually take a decision in this one customs procedure. The exceptional commitment of the European Commission in such customs procedures is clearly designed to ensure that EU customs law is uniformly applied throughout the EU.[90] Nevertheless, under existing EU customs legislation it is normally the function of the national customs administrations to take customs decisions.[91]

Nevertheless, the new implementing powers pursuant to Article 291 TFEU that the European Commission will have under the Union Customs Code have to be analysed further with regard to generally applicable acts as well as individual acts. Such implementing powers, especially in form of individual acts, could grant the European Commission greater influence on the implementation of EU customs law. Furthermore, the European Commission intends to further reduce margins of discretion in EU customs law and the possibilities for national idiosyncrasies in customs procedures by adopting a wide range of generally applicable implementing acts as part of the EU's strategy to enhance uniform customs administration.[92]

Article 291 TFEU provides for a conferral of implementing powers to the European Commission to give effect to legally binding EU acts.[93] The implementation of EU law through the European Commission is part of its administrative functions in the sense of Article 17 paragraph 1 sentence 5 TEU.[94] By adopting implementing acts, the European Commission supersedes the EU Member States in the implementation of EU law. Under the conditions of Article 291 paragraph 2

[90] See Lyons, 2008, p 503 regarding the customs procedure under Arts 906 to 909 CCCIP.
[91] Similar ibid, p 119.
[92] Lux, 2012 AW-Prax 8, pp 257–62 (258); see also Chapter 4.III.B.
[93] Weiß, (2) 2011 JECLAP (5), pp 441–51 (449).
[94] Ruffert, in: Calliess/Ruffert (eds), 2011, Art 291 TFEU, para 7.

TFEU, a shifting of administrative competences from the EU Member States to the European Commission takes place, and implementing measures in the sense of Article 291 paragraph 1 TFEU replace national measures.[95] Therefore, the control mechanisms under Article 291 paragraph 3 TFEU protect the interests of the EU Member States instead of the EU legislator that has conferred the power, and again, the European Commission seems to have benefitted the most from the conceptual rearrangement in the Lisbon Treaty.[96] Nevertheless, to a certain degree, the European Commission has to cooperate with the EU Member States in the relatively formalised procedures laid down in the Comitology Regulation.[97]

1. *Control Under the Comitology Regulation*

Although the European Commission is controlled by committees of experts composed of national representatives, in the advisory procedure, being the default procedure of the Comitology Regulation, the European Commission is not bound by the committee's opinion.[98] Rather, it has only to take the committee's opinion into account, see Article 4 paragraph 2 Regulation (EU) 182/2011. On the other hand, the conditions under which the examination procedure has to be applied are broad, see Article 2 paragraph 2 Regulation (EU) 182/2011, and thus it is to be expected that this procedure will take place with regard to a considerable range of implementing acts.[99] In the more complex examination procedure, the European Commission's adoption of an implementing act depends to a large degree on the committee's opinion.[100]

Nevertheless, in case of disagreement between the European Commission and the relevant committee the file is referred to the appeal committee, pursuant to Article 3 paragraph 7 in conjunction with Article 5 Regulation (EU) 182/2011. This then means that only a qualified majority of weighted votes is able to block the adoption, pursuant to Article 6 paragraph 1 Regulation (EU) 182/2011, aside from certain exceptions in the field of certain trade policy measures, pursuant to Article 6 paragraph 5 Regulation (EU) 182/2011.[101] Moreover, this appeal committee is chaired by the European Commission, pursuant to Article 3 paragraph 2 Regulation (EU) 182/2011, which provides the possibility for the increased exercise of influence by the European Commission in the appeal procedure.[102] Under

[95] Stelkens, 2012 EuR 5, pp 511–45 (512).

[96] Similar: Hofmann/Türk, 2012 ZG, pp 105–37 (118).

[97] Regulation (EU) 182/2011 of the European Parliament and of the Council of 16 February 2011 laying down the rules and general principles concerning mechanisms for control by Member States of the Commission's exercise of implementing powers, [2011] OJ L55/13–18.

[98] Craig, 2011 ELRev (36), pp 671–87 (678, 680).

[99] ibid, pp 671–87 (678).

[100] For a detailed analysis of the complex modalities of the examination procedure see Craig, 2011 ELRev (36), pp 671–87 (680, 681).

[101] Bast, 2012 CMLRev (49), pp 885–927 (912, 914); Craig, 2011 ELRev (36), pp 671–87 (682).

[102] Hofmann/Türk, 2012 ZG, pp 105–37 (110, 119); Craig, 2011 ELRev (36), pp 671–87 (686).

the former Comitology Decision,[103] in case of disagreement it was for the Council to decide on the adoption of the measure in question, see Article 5 paragraph 4 and Article 5a paragraph 4 Council Decision 1999/468/EC; the new Comitology Regulation provides no such recourse to the Council.[104]

Furthermore, Article 2 paragraph 3 Regulation (EU) 182/2011 as a general provision provides for the possibility to use the advisory procedure instead of a mandated examination procedure in duly justified cases. Although the Comitology Regulation does not specify who makes the determination of whether a duly justified case exists and what criteria should be used for such an assessment, the logic of the Comitology Regulation as control instrument in the sense of Article 291 paragraph 3 TFEU should prevent the European Commission from autonomously shifting from the examination to the advisory procedure against the will of a committee.[105]

Moreover, in urgent cases the European Commission may adopt immediately applicable implementing acts, pursuant to Article 8 Regulation (EU) 182/2011, which constitute a third type of procedure.[106] In this procedure, the European Commission can adopt implementing acts without prior submission to a committee, except for provisional anti-dumping or countervailing measures,[107] see Article 8 paragraph 5 Regulation (EU) 182/2011. Finally, although the European Commission has to review a draft implementing act that is considered to exceed the implementing powers provided for in the basic act, pursuant to Article 11 Regulation (EU) 182/2011, it is not bound to withdraw the draft implementing act but can—after reviewing it—decide to maintain it.[108]

In EU customs, the Customs Code Committee assists the European Commission pursuant to Articles 247a, 248a CCC (Article 285 UCC/former Article 184 MCC) and constitutes a permanent committee in the sense of Article 3 paragraph 2 Regulation (EU) 182/2011. Furthermore, the Committee is not only to assist but also to control the European Commission when issuing implementing acts pursuant to Article 291 paragraph 3 TFEU. For this purpose, the Customs Code Committee has given itself rules of procedure,[109] which are an adaption of the standard rules published by the European Commission.[110]

Because of the various fields of customs rules and the necessary expertise in each of these customs fields, the Customs Code Committee operates in several

[103] Council Decision 1999/468/EC of 28 June 1999 laying down the procedures for the exercise of implementing powers conferred on the Commission, [1999] OJ L184/23–26, and Council Decision 2006/512/EC of 17 July 2006 amending Council Decision 1999/468/EC laying down the procedures for the exercise of implementing powers conferred on the Commission, [2006] OJ L200/11–13.

[104] Craig, 2011 ELRev (36), pp 671–87 (675).

[105] ibid, pp 671–87 (678).

[106] ibid, pp 671–87 (681).

[107] ibid, pp 671–87 (681).

[108] ibid, pp 671–87 (683).

[109] Customs Code Committee, Rules of Procedure, 2012, TAXUD/A2/2011/011 Final–EN.

[110] Standard rules of procedure for committees, [2011] OJ C206/11–13.

departments or sections.[111] Important fields in the work of the Customs Code Committee's departments are customs classification, customs valuation and customs procedures, but also the modernisation of customs. The current rules of procedure provide for 13 different sections pursuant to Article 1 rules of procedure. These are: General Customs Legislation; Tariff and Statistical Nomenclature; Tariff Measures; Duty Relief; Origin; Customs Value; Customs Debt and Guarantees; Import and Export Formalities; Data Integration and Harmonisation; Customs Status and Transit; Special Procedures; Customs Controls and Risk Management; and Enforcement of Intellectual Property Rights. Furthermore, the Customs Code Committee may create working groups to examine particular issues and report back to the Committee, pursuant to Article 7 rules of procedure. The Committee may also decide to invite experts to talk on particular matters, pursuant to Article 6 paragraph 1 and Article 8 paragraph 3 rules of procedure.

The Customs Code Committee consists only of representatives of the EU Member States, while a representative of the European Commission acts as chairman without being a member of the Committee.[112] This composition and voting configuration of the Customs Code Committee is in accordance with Article 3 paragraph 2 sentences 2 and 3 Regulation (EU) 182/2011, which regards committees one of the mechanisms by which EU Member States control the European Commission's exercise of implementing powers.

Pursuant to Article 3 paragraph 2 section (a) and (b) together with Article 5 rules of procedure, the main part of the Customs Code Committee's agenda is to give an opinion on draft implementing acts to be adopted by the European Commission in accordance with the relevant procedures—examination procedure or advisory procedure—laid down in the relevant basic legal acts and together with Regulation (EU) 182/2011. In this context, and as already alluded to, the Customs Code Committee even has the power to prevent the European Commission from issuing implementing acts under certain conditions.

In the past, the Customs Code Committee issued opinions regarding the European Commission's proposals amending the Customs Code and its implementing provisions through the regulatory procedure or – more frequently – the management procedure pursuant to Articles 247a, 248a CCC together with the Comitology Decision. In the Modernised Customs Code, the procedures for participation of the Customs Code Committee had been changed, and the application of the management procedure and thus the authority of the European Commission regarding the enactment of implementing provisions had been reduced.[113] The Modernised Customs Code responded thereby to Council Decision 2006/512/EC,[114] which amended the Comitology Decision and introduced the regulatory

[111] Henke, in: Witte (ed), 2013, Art 247a CCC, para 3.

[112] ibid, Art 247a CCC, para 5.

[113] Witte, in: Witte/Henke/Kammerzell (eds), 2009, p 198.

[114] Council Decision 2006/512/EC of 17 July 2006 amending Council Decision of 28 June 1999 laying down the procedures for the exercise of implementing powers conferred on the Commission, [2006] OJ L200/11–13.

procedure with scrutiny. Accordingly, the Customs Code Committee should act as a Scrutiny Committee pursuant to Article 184 paragraph 4 MCC.

However, the Treaty of Lisbon has fundamentally changed the possibility and procedure for a conferral of implementing powers to the European Commission by introducing Article 291 TFEU and the Comitology Regulation. The Union Customs Code has responded to these changes in Article 285 UCC by establishing the Customs Code Committee as a committee in the meaning of the Comitology Regulation pursuant to Article 285 paragraph 1 UCC. Therefore, more than ever the Customs Code Committee will be a control instrument of the EU Member States with regard to the exercise of implementing powers conferred on the European Commission. However, this control mechanism also ensures that customs experts at the national and European level discuss the provisions to be adopted, and thus holds the potential to enhance common understanding and best practice as well as to facilitate the application and interpretation of those provisions in the national customs administrations.

2. *Legal Nature of Implementing Acts*

The legal nature of possible implementing acts and the term 'measure' in the sense of Article 291 paragraph 2 TFEU is controversial[115] but the predominant view is that such implementing acts can be adopted as generally applicable acts as well as individual acts.[116] Systematic considerations support this opinion, as the term 'measure' in Article 291 paragraph 1 TFEU includes any concretising act while Article 291 paragraph 2 TFEU mentions no restrictions in this regard.[117] Furthermore, implementing acts can have the form of legal acts in the sense of Article 288 TFEU but also of atypical acts such as plans and measures.[118]

It has sometimes been suggested that, at least at present, only the adoption of legal acts by the European Commission is authorised, as advanced rules for the application of Article 291 paragraph 2 TFEU that are necessary pursuant to Article 291 paragraph 3 TFEU can only be found in the Comitology Regulation. However, Recital (11) and Article 2 paragraph 2 Regulation (EU) 182/2011 differentiate only between implementing acts of general scope and specific implementing acts. This kind of differentiation does not automatically have to be equated with the differentiation between legal norms and individual acts: although the German term 'Durchführungsrechtsakt' seems to suggest such an interpretation, other official EU languages, for example the French or the English versions of the Comitology Regulation, leave the term 'implementation' undetermined.[119]

[115] A detailed overview offers Stelkens, 2012, EuR 5, pp 511–45.

[116] COM (2009) 673 final, p 4; Weiß, 2010, pp 59, 60; Bast, 2012 CMLRev (49), pp 885–927 (910, 919 et seq); Ponzano, in: Griller/Ziller (eds), 2008, pp 135–41 (140); Driessen, 2010 ELRev (35), pp 837–48 (845).

[117] Nettesheim, in: Grabitz/Hilf/Nettesheim (eds), 2013, Vol III, Art 291 TFEU, para 13.

[118] Hofmann, 2009 ELJ (15), pp 482–505 (493); Hofmann/Türk, 2012 ZG, pp 105–37 (109).

[119] Stelkens, in: Höfling (ed), 2012, pp 369–417 (385 fn 59).

Article 291 paragraph 2 TFEU does not limit the European Commission's choice of the appropriate legal instrument. Possible implementing acts can, therefore, be any act in the sense of Article 288 TFEU, though a directive would seem to be inconsequential because of its limited binding force, while recommendations and opinions have no binding force at all and thus would also be inappropriate.[120] Substitute performances, on the other hand, cannot be authorised by Article 291 paragraph 2 TFEU, which deals with the control of national implementation in EU Member States.[121]

The possibility of adopting generally applicable implementing acts, for example an implementing regulation concerning the classification of certain goods in the combined nomenclature, raises problems of differentiation regarding the scope of delegated acts. Yet any overlap between the scope of delegated acts and implementing acts is comparably small because of the different requirements in Article 290 TFEU and Article 291 TFEU. The basic legal act in Article 290 TFEU must be a legislative act, whereas the scope of Article 291 TFEU requires that the need for uniform implementing conditions exist already at the time of the adoption of the basic act, which is unlikely to be the case in many legislative procedures.

On the one hand, it would be odd to enact directives and authorise the European Commission to impose uniform implementing conditions given that the nature of directives leaves their concrete implementation to the discretion of the EU Member States.[122] Legislative acts of direct application, on the other hand, are unlikely to require uniform implementing conditions, unless past experience has revealed different implementation conditions within different EU Member States.[123] Therefore, such considerations often do not take place until the implementation has started and difficulties have arisen. Nonetheless, the possibility of adopting individual acts has been criticised because of an alleged conflict with Article 263 paragraphs 3 and 5 TFEU. This provision grants remedy against individual decisions of EU agencies that are precluded by Article 291 TFEU because of the lack of control of EU agencies by EU Member States as required in Article 291 paragraph 3 TFEU.[124]

However, it remains unclear why individual decisions by EU agencies, which indeed are stipulated in Article 263 paragraphs 1 and 5 TFEU, should be prohibited simply because of the European Commission's possibility to adopt individual measures under the conditions of Article 291 paragraph 2 TFEU. Article 291 TFEU does not suspend the possibility to give EU agencies the competence to adopt individual implementing measures, but it does limit the European Commission's ability to interfere in the EU Member States' indirect implementation of

[120] Nettesheim, in: Grabitz/Hilf/Nettesheim (eds), 2013, Vol III, Art 291 TFEU, para 27.

[121] ibid, Vol III, Art 291 TFEU, para 31.

[122] Craig, in: Griller/Ziller (eds), 2008, pp 109–34 (121); Craig, 2010, p 273.

[123] ibid, pp 109–34 (120, 121); Craig, 2010, p 273; similar: Stelkens, 2012 EuR 5, pp 511–45 (542, 543).

[124] Stelkens, 2012 EuR 5, pp 511–45 (517).

legally binding EU acts. This has been confirmed by the ECJ.[125] Article 291 TFEU emphasises the principle of the national implementation of EU law, similar to Article 197 paragraph 1 TFEU.

However, Article 291 TFEU only confirms this principle and does not constitute it. Thus, it does not regulate the conditions for exceptions to this principle but only the requirements for a conferral of implementing powers to the European Commission.[126] As there is no explicit prohibition, it is possible to authorise EU agencies to implement EU law in certain areas,[127] though the conditions for any transfer of administrative competences to EU agencies are of a comparably high standard.[128] At least in EU customs law, the Union Customs Code authorises the European Commission to adopt implementing acts of general application as well as in form of individual acts, or even as atypical acts.

3. *Conferral of Implementing Powers in the Union Customs Code*

In EU customs law, the European Commission has adopted implementing provisions since the coming into force of the Customs Code.[129] The Modernised Customs Code was also intended to be accompanied by modernised implementing provisions in form of a new implementing regulation of the European Commission (MCCIP).[130] However, after the coming into force of the Treaty of Lisbon and the new differentiation between delegated acts pursuant to Article 290 TFEU und implementing acts pursuant to Article 291 TFEU, a single instrument for both types of acts, as was originally planned for in MCCIP, has now been excluded.[131] Therefore, the Union Customs Code provides for the delegation of powers as well as conferral of implementing powers to the European Commission. Furthermore, it is the European Commission's intention to split a completed draft of the MCCIP into two separate acts, with each covering one kind of power exercised by the European Commission.[132]

[125] ECJ of 22 January 2014, Case C-270/12, *United Kingdom v Parliament and Council* [2014] ECR I-0, paras 79, 80, 83.

[126] Similar: Nettesheim, in: Grabitz/Hilf/Nettesheim (eds), 2013, Vol III, Art 291 TFEU, para 38.

[127] ibid, Vol III, Art 291 TFEU, paras 38, 39.

[128] Weiß, 2010, pp 39, 41, 42; see also Chapter 6.II.A.1.

[129] Commission Regulation (EEC) 2454/93 of 2 July 1993 laying down provisions for the implementation of Council Regulation (EEC) 2913/92 establishing the Community Customs Code, [1993] OJ L253/1.

[130] Last version (situation as of 31.12.2013): Consolidated preliminary draft of the MCCIP of 25 November 2011, Document TAXUD/MCCIP/2010/100-3.

[131] Grave, (5) 2010 GTCJ (3), pp 95–111 (111); a detailed analysis of this differentiation can be found in Chapter 5.I.A.1.

[132] See the announcement of the 'splitting-exercise' in the current preliminary draft, last version (situation as of 31.12.2013): Consolidated preliminary draft of the MCCIP of 25 November 2011, Document TAXUD/MCCIP/2010/100-3, p 3 'legal follow-up'.

(a) Atypical Acts

The work programme pursuant to Article 280 TFEU that the European Commission is to draw up relating to the development and deployment of the necessary electronic customs systems is an atypical act that is not contained in Article 288 TFEU. The Union Customs Code explicitly refers to the priorities of the work programme as being the harmonised exchange of information; enhancement of efficient, effective and uniform application through re-engineering of customs and customs-related processes; and enabling economic operators to interact in the same way with the customs authorities of any EU Member State. All these priorities thus correspond with the need for uniform implementing conditions. In the ordinary legislative procedure, the European Parliament had even expressed the opinion that the work programme relating to the development and deployment of electronic systems should be dealt with at the level of delegated acts.[133]

Nonetheless, the programme is being designed as atypical implementing act without reference to the Comitology Regulation, meaning there is no procedure through which the EU Member States can control the European Commission. Nevertheless, the European Commission will have to discuss any work programme drawn up with the EU Member States if it is to have any chance of actually being put into practice.

(b) Generally Applicable Acts and the Examination Procedure

Most of the provisions conferring implementing power to the European Commission are designed for the adoption of generally applicable acts. The European Commission is regularly authorised to specify procedural rules for certain aspects in a specific customs procedure. For example, Article 200 UCC empowers the European Commission to specify the procedural rules for the destruction, the sale, and the abandonment of goods in the customs procedures regarding the disposal of goods in Title V Chapter 4 UCC.

While the Union Customs Code provides for extensive conferral of implementing power with regard to the adoption of generally applicable acts, all these measures must be adopted in accordance with the examination procedure referred to in Article 285 paragraph 4 UCC and as laid down in Article 5 Regulation (EU) 182/2011. Therefore, the European Commission's competence is limited. In this examination procedure, the opinion of the committee composed of national representatives is of significant importance, giving the EU Member States a strong position. The European Commission is not allowed to adopt a draft implementing act in the event of a negative opinion by the committee, though it can submit it to the appeal committee for further deliberation, see Article 5 paragraph 3 Regulation (EU) 182/2011. In case the appeal committee, which is also composed of

[133] European Parliament, First Reading Report of 26 February 2013, A7-0006/2013, Amendment 13, pp 13, 14.

national representatives, also delivers a negative opinion, the draft implementing act is not enacted, pursuant to Article 6 paragraph 3 Regulation (EU) 182/2011.

As the implementation of EU law is mainly the responsibility of the EU Member States, the extensive use of the examination procedure in the Union Customs Code ensures that the European Commission has to respect the EU Member States when adopting implementing acts of general application. This is in line with Article 2 paragraph 2 Regulation (EU) 182/2011. Thus, the EU legislator, namely the European Parliament and the Council, seems to have installed the examination procedure as to offset the empowerment of the European Commission to adopt a wide range of implementing acts, as this procedure allows the EU Member States possibilities for control.

Nevertheless, the European Commission does not have a weak position in the examination procedure. Although the European Commission has no vote, it chairs the committees, which require a qualified majority to agree on an opinion, pursuant to Article 5 paragraph 1 Regulation (EU) 182/2011 together with Article 16 paragraphs 4 and 5 TEU. Furthermore, if the appeal committee cannot agree on an opinion with the necessary qualified majority pursuant to Articles 6 paragraph 1, 5 paragraph 1 Regulation (EU) 182/2011, the European Commission may adopt the draft implementing act. Therefore, the Union Customs Code provides a strong position for the European Commission with regard to competences for the adoption of implementing acts in order to ensure uniform conditions for the Code's implementation.

(c) Individual Acts and the Advisory Procedure

Only three provisions in the Union Customs Code provide for the adoption of individual implementing acts by the European Commission. Furthermore, the impact of these acts on the administration of EU customs law is confined to small areas, as their scope of application is clearly defined and limited in the Union Customs Code.

Article 8 paragraph 2 UCC authorises the European Commission to adopt decisions through implementing acts on derogations allowing one or several EU Member States the exceptional use of techniques other than electronic data-processing. The competences of the European Commission are clearly defined by reference to Article 6 paragraph 4 UCC, allowing the European Commission to grant derogations only for a specific period of time and under certain conditions. The decision must be justified by the specific situation of the EU Member State requesting the derogation even while the EU-wide exchange and storage of information has to be maintained.

The UCC proposal was less clear with regard to the specific extent of competence the European Commission could gain by granting such derogations, see Article 6 paragraph 3 of the UCC proposal. This was criticised by the European Parliament, which in this context emphasised the fundamental spirit of pan-European e-customs as originally outlined in the Modernised Customs Code.

It therefore insisted that clearer specifications were needed and that implementing decisions of the European Commission should be valid only for a limited period of time.[134]

Another example for the authorisation of the European Commission to adopt individual implementing acts is Article 37 paragraph 2 UCC. The European Commission can adopt decisions requesting that EU Member States revoke customs decisions relating to binding information.[135] Therefore, the European Commission is able to ensure that customs decisions relating to binding information are revoked if they are concerned by a change in the interpretation of EU customs law in the sense of Article 33 paragraphs 7 or 8 UCC.

The last example for the authorisation of the European Commission to adopt individual implementing acts based on the Union Customs Code is Article 123 paragraph 3 UCC. The European Commission can adopt decisions granting repayment or remission of duties in cases where the European Commission failed in its obligations or committed an error pursuant to Article 116 paragraph 3 UCC.

Although the European Commission's competence to adopt individual acts based on the Union Customs Code is limited, every adaption of such acts is controlled only in the advisory procedure referred to in Article 285 paragraph 2 UCC and as is laid down in Article 4 Regulation (EU) 182/2011. In this advisory procedure, the European Commission has only to take the utmost account of the conclusions drawn from the discussion within the committee, but can in the end decide on its own about the adoption of the draft implementing act, pursuant to Article 4 paragraph 2 Regulation (EU) 182/2011. Therefore, the Union Customs Code provides for a strong position for the European Commission when adapting individual implementing acts, though these kinds of acts are only single exceptions in the Code.

4. *Conclusion*

In conclusion, a new era of the European Commission's implementing powers does not yet seem to have begun. On the one hand, the European Commission seems to have benefited to a large extent from the conceptual arrangement of Article 291 TFEU, and the Union Customs Code provides for extensive conferral of implementing powers to the European Commission in the administration of the EU Customs Union. However, cooperation with the EU Member States is still necessary. Indeed, the extensive use of the examination procedure of Article 5 Regulation (EU) 182/2011 clearly shows that the EU Member States have the possibility to control the European Commission in this regard. References to the advisory procedure, which grants the European Commission more independence from comitology committees, are the exception.

[134] European Parliament, First Reading Report of 26 February 2013, A7-0006/2013, Amendment 10, p 11.

[135] Binding Tariff Information (BTI) and Binding Origin Information (BOI). Further details can be found in Chapter 10.I.E. and III.

Although the advisory procedure exists for cases in which the European Commission is allowed to adopt individual implementing acts, their limited scope of application confines their impact to small areas in the administration of EU customs. Furthermore, the involvement of the national level in the comitology mechanism offers the potential for cooperation between EU Member States and the European Commission and can provide for a common understanding of the interpretation and application of the provisions finally adopted, as those provisions will have been discussed among experts in the Customs Code Committee.

C. Instruments for Supervision of National Implementation

Generally, the European Commission, as guardian of the Treaty pursuant to Article 17 paragraph 1 sentence 2 TEU, has been given the authority and responsibility to review the implementation of EU law by the EU Member States and makes use of contacts, correspondence and meetings in order to ensure respect for EU law.[136] Complaints with regard to the application of EU law can be reported to the European Commission, which considers and responds to such inputs in accordance with the European Commission's Code of Good Administrative Behaviour.[137]

Furthermore, the European Commission can initiate an infringement proceeding pursuant to Article 258 TFEU in order to stop incorrect application of EU law and thus prevent non-uniform standards of implementation in EU Member States by bringing the matter before the ECJ.[138] However, this possibility does not seem to be used very often in the area of customs administration[139] and there exists no such thing as an enforceable right to an infringement proceeding, because such action lies at the discretion of the European Commission.[140]

1. Inspections and Reporting Obligations

As a kind of supervising instrument, the European Commission has its own rights for inspection in the EU Member States, while the customs administrations of the EU Member States have obligatory duties of notification and must contribute to special reports.[141] In the EU Customs Union, the European Commission is responsible for the protection of the EU's financial interests. Thus, through oversight of the national customs authorities' implementation of EU customs law it seeks to assure that the correct amount of customs duties are collected.[142]

[136] COM (2007) 502 final, p 3.

[137] [2000] OJ L267/63, URL: http://ec.europa.eu/transparency/civil_society/code/_docs/code_en.pdf; Panel Report, *EC–Selected Customs Matters*, WT/DS315/R, para 7.174.

[138] COM (2007) 502 final, p 3, Rogmann, 2008 ZfZ 3, pp 57–69 (61).

[139] Panel Report, *EC–Selected Customs Matters*, WT/DS315/R, para 7.170.

[140] Streinz, 2012, para 396.

[141] Kunas, in: Bongartz (ed), 2000, pp 1–24 (11).

[142] European Court of Auditors, Special Report 23/2000, [2001] OJ C84/1–18, para 19.

The European Commission's right to collect information and to carry out inspections is generally provided for in Article 337 TFEU but needs further definition in EU secondary law. In particular, the national customs administrations have to tolerate inspections by the European Commission pursuant to Article 18 Council Regulation (EC, Euratom) 1150/2000[143] with regard to the collection of the EU's own resources, as customs duties are traditionally own resources of the EU, pursuant to Article 2 paragraph 1 section (a) and paragraph 3 Decision 2007/437/EC, Euratom.[144] Thereby, the European Commission has the right to be included upon request in the inspection measures the national customs administrations carry out, see Article 18 paragraph 2 section (b) Council Regulation (EC, Euratom) 1150/2000. Alternatively it may carry out inspection measures itself, see Article 18 paragraph 3 Council Regulation (EC, Euratom) 1150/2000. In doing so, the European Commission must give notice of the inspection to the EU Member State concerned in a timely and duly substantiated communication, while customs officers of the EU Member State concerned should participate in the inspection measure, see Article 18 paragraph 3 Council Regulation (EC, Euratom) 1150/2000.

Furthermore, Council Regulation (EC, Euratom) 1150/2000 contains various obligations for EU Member States to keep the European Commission informed about the effective collection of the EU's own resources, such as customs duties. In particular Article 6 Council Regulation (EC, Euratom) 1150/2000 contains the obligation to send the European Commission a monthly statement of accounts relating to the collection of the EU's own resources. Article 17 paragraph 5 Council Regulation (EC, Euratom) 1150/2000 obliges the EU Member States to inform the European Commission of the details and results of their inspections by means of annual reports, while Article 3 Council Regulation (EC, Euratom) 1150/2000 contains a general obligation to keep the supporting documents concerning own resources for at least three calendar years.

Reporting obligations of the EU Member States and the authority of the European Commission can also be found in the context of the Electronic Customs Initiative in Articles 11 and 12 of Decision 70/2008/EC.[145] Other notification obligations of national customs authorities vis-à-vis the European Commission can also be found in Articles 17 and 18 Regulation (EC) 515/97,[146] especially regarding

[143] Council Regulation (EC, Euratom) 1150/2000 of 22 May 2000 implementing Decision 2007/436/EC, Euratom on the system of the Communities' own resources, [2000] OJ L130/1–12, amended by Council Regulation (EC, Euratom) 2028/2004 of 16 November 2004 amending Regulation (EC, Euratom) 1150/2000 of 22 May 2000 implementing Decision 94/728/EC, Euratom on the system of the Communities' own resources, [2004] OJ L352/1–7, and also amended by Council Regulation (EC, Euratom) 105/2009 of 26 January 2009 amending Regulation (EC, Euratom) 1150/2000 implementing Decision 2000/597/EC, Euratom on the system of the Communities' own resources, [2009] OJ L36/1–5.

[144] Council Decision of 7 June 2007 on the system of the European Communities' own resources, 2007/436/EC, Euratom, [2007] OJ L163/17–21.

[145] Decision 70/2008/EC of the European Parliament and of the Council of 15 January 2008 on a paperless environment for customs and trade, [2008] OJ L23/21–26.

[146] Council Regulation (EC) 515/97 of 13 March 1997 on mutual assistance between the administrative authorities of the Member States and cooperation between the latter and the Commission to ensure the correct application of the law on customs and agricultural matters, [1997] OJ L82/1–16.

information on any shortcomings or regulatory gaps in EU customs law. The European Commission also regularly seeks information from EU Member States on the basis of this regulation.[147]

A monitoring function for the uniform application of EU customs law was established by the European Commission in 2006.[148] Monitoring activities analyse the implementation of EU customs law in several if not all EU Member States in a specific sector in order to identify problems and weak points and thereby make suggestions for improvement. For example, monitoring programmes for 2009 and 2010 included elements of simplified procedures.[149] The European Commissions has the authority to conduct monitoring actions under the Customs 2013 Programme which is laid down in Article 13 of Decision 624/2007/EC.[150] These monitoring actions are managed by the European Commission in cooperation with EU Member States. They aim to promote the uniform implementation of EU customs law by targeting sensitive fields where incorrect application exists or could possibly exist and to provide guidance that ensures correct understanding and implementation of EU customs law and its administrative procedures.[151]

However, while there are a great many and variety of possible topics that could benefit from direct supervisory activities such as inspections and monitoring, the European Commission has limited resources.[152] It thus relies on risk-analysis techniques to allocate its resources to those areas presenting the highest risk in terms of own resources.[153]

2. *Practice of Revenue Allocation*

Another 'supervisory' instrument, and one of special importance in EU customs, is the European Commission's practice of revenue allocation. The uniform implementation of EU customs law also concerns the protection of financial interests for the EU, as customs duties are traditionally own resources of the EU,[154] pursuant to Article 2 paragraph 1 section (a) and paragraph 3 Decision 2007/437/EC, Euratom.[155]

In the EU Customs Union, customs duties are charged by national customs administrations and then transferred to the EU after deduction of fixed collection

[147] Lyons, 2008, p 127.

[148] European Court of Auditors, Special Report 1/2010, [2010] OJ C149/8 and URL: http://eur-lex.europa.eu/LexUriServ/LexUriServ.do?uri=SRCA:2010:01:FIN:EN:PDF, para 37.

[149] ibid, para 37.

[150] Decision 624/2007/EC of the European Parliament and of the Council of 23 May 2007 establishing an action programme for customs in the Community (Customs 2013), [2007] OJ L154/23–31.

[151] European Commission, Customs 2013 Programme—Monitoring Guide, 2010, p 4.

[152] European Court of Auditors, Special Report 23/2000, reply of the European Commission, summary p 13.

[153] ibid, summary p 13.

[154] Rogmann, 2008 ZfZ 3, pp 57–69 (62); Rogmann, 2008 AW-Prax 5, pp 195–99 (196).

[155] Council Decision of 7 June 2007 on the system of the European Communities' own resources, 2007/436/EC, Euratom, [2007] OJ L163/17–21.

costs in the amount of 25%, pursuant to Article 2 paragraph 3 and Article 8 paragraph 1 Decision 2007/437/EC, Euratom. However, customs duties have to be transferred to the European Commission even if they have not actually been collected by national customs authorities.

In *Commission v Denmark*, the ECJ demonstrated that customs duties do not really have to be charged by national customs administrations, but rather have to correspond to established entitlements pursuant to Article 17 paragraph 1 Regulation (EC, Euratom) 1150/2000.[156] Furthermore, for the establishment of those entitlements, it is sufficient that the conditions provided for by the customs regulations concerning the entry of the entitlement in the accounts have been met in the sense of Article 2 Regulation (EC, Euratom) 1150/2000—whereas a real entry into the accounts is not necessary.[157] EU Member States violate EU law, namely Articles 2 and 8 Decision 2007/437/EC, Euratom, if they fail to establish entitlements of the EU's own resources and to transfer them to the European Commission, unless the conditions laid down in Article 17 paragraph 2 Regulation (EC, Euratom) 1150/2000 have been met.[158]

Therefore, the EU Member States can be charged for amounts of the EU's own resources that have been disbursed elsewhere or have not been imposed by competent national authorities in contravention of EU customs law.[159] Even though national customs authorities are not allowed to carry out a subsequent invoice to correct their error for legal reasons such as, for example, Article 220 paragraph 2 section (b) CCC (Article 119 paragraph 1 UCC/former Article 82 paragraph 1 MCC), this legal impossibility to correct an error does not release the EU Member States from their obligation to establish the EU's entitlements to own resources.[160]

The hard line of the ECJ with regard to the EU Member States' financial responsibility has been criticised for its potential to lead to the nearly unlimited liability of EU Member States.[161] Rather than reducing financial liability to cases of serious and evident violations the current approach holds EU Member States liable for simple failures and errors in their national customs administration, which are bound to occur anywhere people are involved.[162] However, the European Commission's capacities only allow for random controls and the objects of such control are typically not single cases of violation but cases of a higher dimension, where customs authorities have wrongly interpreted EU customs law in a uniform manner, which suggests a failure of guidance of the relevant EU Member State.[163]

[156] ECJ of 15 November 2005, Case C-392/02, *Commission v Denmark* [2005] ECR I-9811, paras 66, 67, 68.

[157] ibid, para 58.

[158] ECJ of 18 October 2007, Case C-19/05, *Commission v Denmark* [2007] ECR I-8597, para 32.

[159] Schoenmakers, in: Gellert (ed), 2008, pp 117–22 (118).

[160] ECJ of 15 November 2005, Case C-392/02, *Commission v Denmark* [2005] ECR I-9811, para 62; ECJ of 18 October 2007, Case C-19/05, *Commission v Denmark* [2007] ECR I-8597, para 32.

[161] Gellert, 2008 AW-Prax 1, pp 31–32 (31).

[162] ibid, pp 31–32 (31).

[163] Stelkens, in: Härtel (ed), 2012, § 42 pp 425–61 (447).

Nevertheless, the national customs authorities are urged to apply and implement EU customs law with as much accuracy as possible,[164] since even in single cases a lack of correctness can lead to financial strains on the national budgets of the EU Member States.[165] Therefore, the practice of revenue allocation raises concrete pressure for harmonisation[166] and thus presents a very effective instrument of the European Commission to ensure the correct and uniform administration of EU customs law by national customs authorities in the decentralised system of EU customs law implementation.

3. *Soft Law Acts as Guidance for Administrative Practice*

In many areas of EU law, the European Commission is shaping the reality of law through soft law acts established in various forms. Thus, the European Commission contributes considerably to the concretisation of the law in order to achieve better applicability, which otherwise would only be achieved through key decisions in EU case law.[167] Indeed, such administrative rule-making is a central tool to guide administrative procedures and the exercise of discretion; it assists the administration in transforming abstract-general legislative provisions into single-case decisions.[168] In general, the main function of soft law acts is to promote the unity of administrative practice, as well as legal certainty and predictability of EU secondary law implementation.[169]

This is also the case for EU customs,[170] where the European Commission relies to a great extent on soft law acts an important strategy to enhance uniform customs administration.[171] Indeed, it has been declared that even the most detailed provisions in the Customs Code and its implementing provisions need further guidance in form of soft law acts.[172]

A customs officer of the section for the modernised customs code in the United Kingdom confirmed that the whole package of soft law acts – such as explanatory notes, opinions, best practice guidelines etc – constitute an important part of customs administration in the EU: 'Those sorts of things, those sorts of notes etc, I think they are a fundamental part of the whole package.'[173] In fact, it was said

[164] Schoenmakers, in: Gellert (ed), 2008, pp 117–22 (119).

[165] Streinz, 2012, § 7 para 586; Rogmann, 2008 ZfZ 3, pp 57–69 (62).

[166] Rogmann, 2008 ZfZ 3, pp 57–69 (62); Streinz, 2012, § 7 para 586.

[167] Weiß, (2) 2011 JECLAP (5), pp 441–51 (441); Weiß, 2010 EWS 7, pp 257–61 (257); Hofmann/Rowe/Türk, 2011, pp 536, 537.

[168] Hofmann/Rowe/Türk, 2011, p 536.

[169] ibid, p 541.

[170] European Commission, 'Nature and legal value of guidelines', TAXUD/1406/2006–EN, para 4.

[171] Lux, 2012 AW-Prax 8, pp 257–62 (258); Kuplewatzky/Rovetta, (7) 2012 GTCJ (11 & 12), pp 454–60 (458, 460).

[172] Lux, 2007 AW-Prax 7, pp 277–80 (280).

[173] Interview of 9 January 2009 on file with author.

that in many cases it would be difficult if not impossible to come to the correct conclusion without them:

> Without them, if we did not have that type of stuff, I think a lot of us would be lost … without that document, or without that opinion or view, you would not have been able to have come to the correct conclusion on this … without it, the system does not work, if you like.[174]

Many guiding concepts for the application of EU customs law are not to be found in EU primary or secondary law but in notices, guidelines and other soft law texts issued by the European Commission. The European Commission itself has declared that soft law acts are to help ensure that in practice the same course of action for a given set of facts is taken by customs authorities throughout the whole EU.[175] Thus they ought to replace national instructions.[176]

The European Commission's soft law acts also have the function of creating a predictable and transparent legal and operational framework for economic operators.[177] Furthermore, the soft law texts in EU customs law are intended to replace numerous detailed rules and instructions found to be inappropriate for inclusion in EU regulations.[178] The kind of details to be found in soft law texts would overload legal acts and prevent their quick modification.[179] Such quickly adaptable details are often necessary to provide instruments for interpretation that are appropriate for the latest developments in technology, safety and security.[180]

Therefore, soft law texts in EU customs contribute to uniform implementation, more transparency and greater currency of EU customs law and thus are part of the 'Better Regulation' Initiative,[181] which has the concept of combining the adoption of legislation with the increased use of instruments such as guidelines and other soft law texts.[182] Since this initiative, it has been the declared intention of the European Commission for such documents to regularly accompany the introduction of new provisions in EU customs law, as well as any modification of already existing ones.[183] Therefore, soft law acts can be found in many fields of EU customs, for example customs procedures with economic impact;[184] procedures for

[174] ibid.

[175] European Commission, 'Nature and legal value of guidelines', TAXUD/1406/2006–EN, para 4.

[176] ibid, para 4.

[177] Gellert, in: Gellert (ed), 2009, pp 51–57 (52).

[178] European Commission, 'Nature and legal value of guidelines', TAXUD/1406/2006–EN, para 4.

[179] Natzel, 2007, pp 42, 43; COM (2001) 428 final, pp 18 et seq; Lux, 2012 AW-Prax 8, pp 257–62 (258).

[180] Natzel, 2007, pp 42, 43; COM (2001) 428 final, pp 18 et seq; Lux, 2012 AW-Prax 8, pp 257–62 (258).

[181] COM (2001) 726 final.

[182] COM (2001) 428 final, pp 27, 30; Gellert, in: Gellert (ed), 2009, pp 51–57 (53).

[183] See COM (2001) 51, p 17.

[184] European Commission, 'Guidelines concerning Title III 'Customs procedures with economic impact' of Commission Regulation (EEC) 2454/93 of 2 July 1993 laying down provisions for the implementation of Council Regulation (EEC) 2913/92 establishing the Community Customs Code', [2001] OJ C269/1-50, amended by: European Commission, 'Amendment to the guidelines concerning Part II, Title III "Customs procedures with economic impact" of Commission Regulation (EEC) No 2454/93 of

the waiving, remission and repayment of customs debts;[185] export procedures;[186] customs value;[187] Community transit;[188] drafting of binding tariff information;[189] and audit procedures.[190]

One of the best examples of this kind of soft law practice in EU customs is the concept of the Authorised Economic Operator (AEO), which was introduced in the EU Customs Union with the Security Amendment of the Community Customs Code[191] in 2005.[192] AEO status can allow participation in simplified customs procedures and/or streamline security compliance requirements. Simplified procedures are highly attractive for economic operators as they imply that few controls are made before the release of goods, while subsequent controls are based on standardised risk analysis methods. AEO status can be given by customs administrations of EU Member States to any economic operator meeting the common criteria laid down in the Customs Code, notably Article 39 UCC (former Article 14 MCC), and has to be recognised by the other EU Member States pursuant to Article 38 paragraph 4 UCC (former Article 13 paragraph 3 MCC).

Although detailed provisions are laid down in amendments of the implementing provisions in the form of Commission regulations,[193] the reality of the application

2 July 1993 laying down provisions for the implementation of Council Regulation (EEC) No 2913/92 establishing the Community Customs Code published in the Official Journal of the European Communities C 269, 24.9.2001, p. 1', [2005] OJ C219/7–18.

185 European Commission, 'Information paper on the application of Articles 220(2)(b) and 239 of the Community Customs Code', URL: http://ec.europa.eu/taxation_customs/resources/documents/customs/procedural_aspects/general/debt/guidelines_en.pdf.

186 European Commission–Customs Code Committee, 'Guidelines on export and exit in the context of Regulation (EC) No 648/2005 (applicable from 1-1-2011)', TAXUD/A3/0034/2010, 25 October 2010, URL: http://ec.europa.eu/ecip/documents/procedures/export_exit_guidelines_en.pdf.

187 European Commission—Customs Code Committee, 'Compendium of Customs Valuation Texts', TAXUD/800/2002/EN, September 2008, URL: http://ec.europa.eu/taxation_customs/resources/documents/customs/customs_duties/declared_goods/european/compendium_2008_en.pdf.

188 European Commission, 'Transit Manual', TAXUD/A3/0007/2010, URL: http://ec.europa.eu/taxation_customs/resources/documents/customs/procedural_aspects/transit/common_community/transit_manual_consolidation_en.pdf.

189 European Commission, 'Application for Binding Tariff Information (BTI)—General Information', URL: http://ec.europa.eu/taxation_customs/resources/documents/common/databases/ebti/ebti_general_information_en.pdf and also European Commission, 'BTI Application Form', URL: http://ec.europa.eu/taxation_customs/resources/documents/bti_application_form_en.pdf.

190 European Commission, 'Standardised Framework for Risk Management in the Customs Administrations of the EU', 30 September 2004, URL: http://ec.europa.eu/taxation_customs/resources/documents/framework_doc.pdf. This chapter will focus on the general characterisation and effects of the European Commission's soft law acts in EU customs administration as part of the European Commission's strategy to enhance uniform customs administration. In Chapter 10, specific soft law measures in certain important areas of EU customs will be discussed, whose varying importance and interaction with legal tools of the EU, as well as with WCO soft law acts in those customs areas, have to be analysed further.

191 Regulation (EC) 648/2005 of the European Parliament and of the Council of 13 April 2005, [2005] OJ L117/13–19.

192 See also Chapter 4.I.

193 Commission Regulation (EC) 1875/2006 of 18 December 2006, [2006] OJ L360/64–125 and Commission Regulation (EC) 1192/2008 of 17 November 2008, [2008] OJ L329/1–51 and Commission Regulation (EU) 197/2010 of 9 March 2010, [2010] OJ L60/9–10.

in practice is significantly shaped by the AEO guidelines[194] issued by the European Commission. These guidelines explain the AEO rules and best practice by reflecting on the experiences gained so far.[195] In doing so, the AEO guidelines not only give general information about the AEO concept (Part 1) and its criteria and categories based on the adopted legislation (Part 2), but also deal extensively with the overall decision-making process concerning both customs authorities and economic operators. It does so by explaining the application and authorisation process as laid down in the Customs Code and its implementing provisions in a detailed manner (Parts 3, 4, 5). Topics include support for determination of the competent EU Member State, guidance for conducting effective and efficient risk analysis and audits, information for speeding up the authorisation process, advice for cooperation between EU Member States regarding information exchange, and the management of granted AEO status through monitoring, reassessment, suspension and revocation.

This detailed explanation of the practical application of EU customs law has not been included in the implementing provisions of the Customs Code in order to avoid any overload of this regulation that would make it somewhat confusing and its application difficult, for this would be incompatible with the 'Better Regulation' Initiative.[196] However, although the European Commission explicitly states the explanatory nature of these practical guidelines, which do not constitute a legally binding act,[197] they nevertheless may have significant influence on the implementation of customs procedures at the operational level. Thus, their legal character and effects have to be analysed further.

(a) Legal Character of Soft Law Acts

The European Commission's practice of issuing soft law through guidelines, notices, and so forth has been criticised, notably in the area of EU competition law, and in particular EU antitrust law as well as EU state aid law.[198] The reason for this criticism lies in the principle of democracy, which demands essential elements of an area be reserved for the EU legislator. This principle cannot be undermined by the European Commission through adopting administrative standards that have considerable legal significance, especially since Article 290 paragraph 1 subparagraph 2 TFEU significantly increased the legal requirements for authorising

[194] European Commission, 'Authorised Economic Operators Guidelines', TAXUD/B2/047/2011—Rev 3, 17 April 2012, URL: http://ec.europa.eu/taxation_customs/resources/documents/customs/policy_issues/customs_security/aeo_guidelines2012_en.pdf.

[195] European Commission, AEO Guidelines, TAXUD/B2/047/2011—Rev 3, p 6.

[196] European Commission, 'Nature and legal value of guidelines', TAXUD/1406/2006–EN, para 4; Natzel, 2007, p 42.

[197] European Commission, AEO Guidelines, TAXUD/B2/047/2011—Rev 3, p 6.

[198] See for example: Weiß, 2010 EWS 7, pp 257–61; Weiß, (2) 2011 JECLAP (5), pp 441–51; Nehl, in: Immenga/Körber (eds), 2012, pp 113–52.

the European Commission to adopt delegated legislation.[199] Any attempt of the European Commission to issue acts with formally binding legal force yet without a corresponding legislative mandate is unlawful.[200]

To adopt measures of directly legally binding effect in the EU Member States, the European Commission requires a specific enabling power.[201] In this context, the general principle of sincere cooperation pursuant to Article 4 paragraph 3 TEU is not a sufficient enabling provision.[202] Although Article 4 paragraph 3 TEU imposes on EU Member States the legal obligation to make EU law effective on a normative, administrative and judicial level, such recourse to general EU primary law cannot result in a concrete obligation for EU Member States when legal obligations are already concretised in relevant provisions of EU secondary law.[203] Article 4 paragraph 3 TEU is subsidiary to specific provisions and thus only of a declaratory or confirmatory character; it does not constitute the required expression of a specific duty of cooperation.[204] Additionally, Article 17 paragraph 1 sentences 2 and 3 TEU (former Article 211 First Indent TEC), which lay down the European Commission's function to ensure the application of EU law, are too indefinite for establishing a specific enabling power.[205]

In EU customs law, the obligation of Union loyalty is already concretised, with the Customs Code as well as its implementing provisions extensively addressing the tasks and obligations of national customs authorities related to making EU customs law effective. However, even the recourse to Article 4 paragraph 3 TEU could only result in the general principle that national courts and authorities have to make EU customs law effective, and thus have to sufficiently consider the interests of the EU when applying EU law—especially if a European institution has officially expressed its opinion.[206] The general principles of effectiveness and equality addressed to the EU Member States when implementing EU law also do not provide a sufficient legal basis for a competence of the European Commission to adopt formal legally binding measures with external effect in EU Member States. These principles of EU law are too general, and thus should be approached carefully with regard to their ability to force national authorities to apply soft law acts.[207]

199 Weiß, (2) 2011 JECLAP (5), pp 441–51 (447); Weiß, 2010 EWS 7, pp 257–61 (259). See also the analysis in Chapter 8.I.B.2.

200 Hofmann/Rowe/Türk, 2011, p 552.

201 ibid, p 568; Schweda, 2004 WuW 11, pp 1133–44 (1139).

202 Hofmann/Rowe/Türk, 2011, p 575; Senden, 2004, p 443; Schweda, 2004 WuW 11, pp 1133–44 (1140, 1141); Gellert, in: Gellert (ed), 2009, pp 51–57 (54); Gellert, 2007 AW-Prax 12, pp 511–13 (512).

203 Thieme, 2011, p 122; Pohlmann, 2005 WuW 10, pp 1005–1109 (1006).

204 Hofmann/Rowe/Türk, 2011, p 575; Senden, 2004, p 443; Schweda, 2004 WuW 11, pp 1133–44 (1140, 1141); Gellert, in: Gellert (ed), 2009, pp 51–57 (54); Gellert, 2007 AW-Prax 12, pp 511–13 (512); Pohlmann, 2005 WuW 10, pp 1005–09 (1006).

205 Natzel, 2007, p 61.

206 ibid, p 68.

207 Senden, 2004, p 442.

This observation follows from the fact that the procedural issues of the European Commission's administrative rule-making generally lie within the European Commission's institutional discretionary power, which thus lacks any kind of scrutiny or control by the EU legislator or the EU Member States.[208] In EU customs law, the procedure for the adoption of soft law sometimes takes the form of a consensus between the European Commission and the EU Member States, but can also be defined case by case.[209] Regularly, soft law acts are issued following intensive discussions between customs experts of the relevant customs area in the Customs Code Committee,[210] which is composed of national experts and chaired by the European Commission.[211] Only exceptionally does a specific legal provision lay down a particular procedure as, for example, in the area of the Combined Nomenclature and TARIC, see Article 9 paragraph 1 section (a) second indent Regulation (EEC) 2658/87.[212]

In this context, it is interesting that the European Commission's proposal for the Modernised Customs Code[213] even contained a regular procedure for the adoption of soft law in the customs area, see Articles 195, 196 paragraph 3 of the MCC proposal. However, these provisions were not transferred to the final Modernised Customs Code or the Union Customs Code – presumably in order to avoid the integration of a procedure regarding the issuing of soft law into the procedures for the adoption of legal implementing provisions, which could have led to too much similarity between soft law with a fixed formal procedure and formal legal texts. Indeed, in general it has been argued that the extension of the comitology mechanism to encompass soft law acts bears the risk of upgrading their legal status.[214]

Because of its lack of legal competence, the European Commission is not allowed to adopt soft law acts amending legal acts, in particular by imposing new obligations on the EU Member States and their national authorities, and must not depart from provisions of EU law.[215] Moreover, the ECJ has often emphasised that soft law acts do not constitute legal obligations and cannot alter the scope of EU legislation.[216] Any effects of soft law can go only so far as they remain in

[208] Hofmann/Rowe/Türk, 2011, p 570.

[209] European Commission, 'Nature and legal value of guidelines', TAXUD/1406/2006–EN, para 9.

[210] Rovetta, (5) 2010 GTCJ (3), pp 129–31 (129).

[211] The function of the Customs Code Committee assisting the European Commission is discussed in Chapter 8.III.

[212] Council Regulation (EEC) 2658/87 of 23 July 1987 on the tariff and statistical nomenclature and on the Common Customs Tariff, [1987] OJ L256/1–675, last amended by Council Regulation (EC) 254/2000 of 31 January 2000 amending Regulation (EEC) 2658/87 on the tariff and statistical nomenclature and the Common Customs Tariff, [2000] OJ L28/16–18. This exception with regard to the European Commission's explanatory notes, whose 'true legal character' causes problems in practice – see Kuplewatzky/Rovetta, (7) 2012 GTCJ (11&12), pp 454–60 (458) – is analysed further in Chapter 10.I.D. See also European Commission, 'Nature and legal value of guidelines', TAXUD/1406/2006–EN, para 9.

[213] COM (2005) 608 final.

[214] Lefevre, 2004 ELRev (29), pp 808–22 (821).

[215] Hofmann/Rowe/Türk, 2011, pp 570, 578.

[216] ECJ of 18 July 2013, Case C-501/11 P, *Schindler Holding Ltd and Others* [2013] ECR I-0, para 66; ECJ of 11 February 2010, Case C-373/08, *Hoesch Metals and Alloys GmbH* [2010] ECR I-951, para 39;

accordance with EU law, for the European Commission cannot change existing EU primary and secondary law.[217]

For example, in *HEKO Industrieerzeugnisse*,[218] the ECJ asserted that the European Commission's list rules, as acts of soft law, were not legally binding and therefore could not alter the law in question and had to be in accordance with it, namely Article 24 CCC.[219] As a further consequence, soft law measures of the European Commission can bind neither national courts[220] nor the European courts in their decision-making.[221] Therefore, the guidelines and notices represent only indicative rules that entail no new obligations and are intended simply to enable national customs administrations to standardise and harmonise their administrative practices.[222]

Within these limits, the adoption of soft law acts by the European Commission is not unlawful,[223] and the European Commission's right of initiative might even allow for the presumption of a certain authority in suggesting how the implementation of the law should be carried out.[224] Nevertheless, because of the European Commission's lack of competence, a directly legally binding effect has not been attributed to soft law.[225] However, the legal principle that unfavourable measures should not have retroactive effects applies also for soft law acts when the retroactive application of a new interpretation concerns a legal provision establishing an unfavourable measure.[226] Indeed, the principle of non-retroactivity is closely linked to the general principles of legal certainty and legitimate expectations.[227] It can also become important with regard to a review of guidelines that change the European Commission's interpretation of EU law and that may have subsequent influence on the national authorities too.[228]

ECJ of 10 December 2009, Case C-260/08, *HEKO Industrieerzeugnisse* [2009] ECR I-11571, paras 20, 21; ECJ of 23 March 2004, Case C-233/02, *France v Commission* [2004] ECR I-2759, para 50; ECJ of 14 November 2002, Case C-112/01, *ATS* [2002] ECR I-10655, para 39; ECJ of 21 January 1993, Case C-188/91, *Deutsche Shell AG* [1993] ECR I-363, paras 16, 17; ECJ of 13 November 1991, Case C-303/90, *France v Commission* [1991] ECR I-5315, paras 23 et seq, 33.

[217] ECJ of 29 April 2004, Case C-91/01, *Italy v Commission* [2004] ECR I-4355, para 45.

[218] ECJ of 10 December 2009, Case C-260/08, *HEKO Industrieerzeugnisse* [2009] ECR I-11571.

[219] ibid, paras 20, 21.

[220] See, inter alia, ECJ of 7 March 2002, Case C-310/99, *Italy v Commission* [2002] ECR I-2289, para 52, and the case law cited.

[221] See, inter alia, ECJ of 30 May 2013, Case C-270/11, *Commission v Sweden* [2013] ECR I-0, para 41, and the case law cited.

[222] European Commission, 'Nature and legal value of guidelines', TAXUD/1406/2006–EN, para 10.

[223] ECJ of 18 July 2013, Case C-501/11 P, *Schindler Holding Ltd and Others* [2013] ECR I-0, para 68.

[224] Hofmann/Rowe/Türk, 2011, pp 539, 569.

[225] ECJ of 10 January 2008, C-70/06, *Commission v Portugal* [2008] ECR I-1, para 34; ECJ of 25 November 2003, Case C-278/01, *Commission v Spain* [2003] ECR I-14141, para 41; ECJ of 4 July 2000, Case C-387/97, *Commission v Greece* [2000] ECR I-5047, para 80.

[226] ECJ of 28 June 2005, Joined Cases C-189/02 P, C-202/02 P, C-205/02 P to C-208/02 P and C-213/02 P, *Dansk Rørindustri* [2005] ECR I-5425, paras 214 et seq.

[227] Hofmann/Rowe/Türk, 2011, p 576; Kuplewatzky/Rovetta, (7) 2012 GTCJ (11 and 12), pp 454–60 (456, 457).

[228] Hofmann/Rowe/Türk, 2011, p 576; Kuplewatzky/Rovetta, (7) 2012 GTCJ (11 and 12), pp 454–60 (456, 457).

Regarding EU customs, the European Commission itself has pointed out that soft law does not constitute a legally binding act but is only of an explanatory nature, a tool designed as interpretation assistance for the purpose of facilitating the correct, as well as the uniform, application of EU customs law by national customs authorities.[229] Although the European Commission's soft law acts can contribute to the uniform implementation and application of EU customs law,[230] they cannot change legal parameters and standards of EU customs law and its interpretation through the ECJ.[231] Soft law texts are normally published either in the form of communications in the Official Journal Series C—as opposed to Series L—or on the DG TAXUD internet site of the European Commission.[232]

With regard to the effects of soft law acts, an important distinction has to be made between the legal versus practical effects of such measures. Further, in respect to legal effects, a further distinction has to be made between direct legal effects which require a specific enabling provision in EU law that soft law measures of the European Commission are missing, and indirect legal effects.[233] Nevertheless, the lack of legal character and the problematic external effect of the European Commission's soft law acts means that administrative authorities on the European or national levels are not allowed to base decisions on soft law.[234]

(b) Indirect Legal Effects of Soft Law Especially in Terms of Self-Binding Commitment

Soft law acts have no direct legal effect, but are also different from recommendations and opinions because of their intention to affect legal reality by defining specific contents of interpretation.[235] They thus constitute their own category of EU acts.[236] Most soft law acts of the European Commission have the purpose to concretise legal norms or the exercise of discretion.[237] They can be a mere compendium of the relevant case law of the ECJ in a specific area, but may also describe the future policy of the European Commission or, increasingly, contain interpretative assistance for the implementation of EU secondary law.[238] Such guidelines, notices and other soft law texts are thus not covered by Article 288 TFEU and given

[229] European Commission, 'Nature and legal value of guidelines', TAXUD/1406/2006–EN, para 7.

[230] Gellert, 2007 AW-Prax 12, pp 511–13 (511).

[231] Lieber, 2007 AW-Prax 10, pp 424–26 (425).

[232] European Commission, 'Nature and legal value of guidelines', TAXUD/1406/2006–EN, para 6; see also Hofmann/Rowe/Türk, 2011, p 537.

[233] Hofmann/Rowe/Türk, p 571.

[234] Similar: Weiß, 2010 EWS 7, pp 257–61 (258).

[235] Thomas, 2009 EuR 3, pp 432–43 (424); Natzel, 2007, p 50.

[236] Thomas, 2009 EuR 3, pp 432–43 (424); Natzel, 2007, p 50; similar Nehl, in: Imenga/Körber (eds), 2012, pp 113–52 (124); different: Hofmann/Rowe/Türk, 2011, pp 544 et seq, who, however, refuse to use the misleading term 'soft law' at all and rather refers to administrative rules, p 536.

[237] Thomas, 2009 EuR 3, pp 432–43 (426).

[238] Natzel, 2007, p 47; Adam, 1999, pp 10 et seq, 58, 59, 61 et seq.

then lack of explicit authorisation in EU primary or secondary law are considered not to be legal acts but mere subsidiary administrative rules of conduct.[239]

However, this purely formal perspective does not mean that guidelines and notices cannot have an indirect legal effect, as their external effects derive from the fact that they are instructions on administrative practice.[240] Despite the lack of a legal character of soft law, the administrative authorities as well as the national courts are requested to take soft law acts of the European institutions into consideration[241] as useful guidance for interpretation.[242] Nevertheless, though taking into consideration a soft law act as guidance for the interpretation of EU law requires a substantive examination of the measure in question, it establishes no obligation for courts and national authorities to follow the suggestions and opinions contained in it.[243]

However, such kinds of instructions can bind the European Commission itself in its role as decision maker due to the fundamental principles of equal treatment and the protection of legitimate expectations,[244] which are manifestations of the European principle of the rule of law pursuant to Article 2 TEU.[245] For example, in EU antitrust law, rules of conduct can – despite their soft law character – impose limitations on the European Commission's exercise of discretion, as they cannot be ignored without constituting a breach of the aforementioned general principles of law.[246]

However, no indirectly binding force of soft law acts can ever be of an absolute character, as soft law acts normally cover only typical cases of application, given their concretising function, and therefore do not regulate an issue area in an encompassing way.[247] In individual cases, the European Commission can deviate from its self-imposed guidelines provided there is an objective substantiation for such an exception that remains compatible with the principle of equal treatment.[248] Furthermore, the European Commission can change and modify its soft law texts at any time because there is no legitimate expectation regarding the continuance of an administrative practice.[249]

[239] Nehl, in: Imenga/Körber (eds), 2012, pp 113–52 (124).

[240] Hofmann/Rowe/Türk, 2011, p 539; similar: Weiß, (2) 2011 JECLAP (5), pp 441–51 (443).

[241] Deimel, 2009 ZfZ 6, pp 157–60 (159); Sonnefeld, 2008 ZfZ 11, pp 476–77 (477); Thomas, 2009 EuR 3, pp 423–43 (437, 438); Gellert, in: Gellert (ed), 2009, pp 51–57 (55); Natzel, 2007, pp 69, 70; European Commission, 'Nature and legal value of guidelines', TAXUD/1406/2006–EN, para 10.

[242] See, inter alia, ECJ of 7 March 2002, Case C-310/99, *Italy v Commission* [2002] ECR I-2289, para 52, and the case law cited.

[243] Natzel, 2007, p 70.

[244] Hofmann/Rowe/Türk, 2011, p 575; Weiß, (2) 2011 JECLAP (5), pp 441–51 (443).

[245] Nehl, in: Imenga/Körber (eds), 2012, pp 113–52 (125).

[246] Weiß, (2) 2011 JECLAP (5), pp 441–51 (443).

[247] Thomas, 2009 EuR 3, pp 423–43 (427).

[248] ECJ of 11 July 2013, Case C-439/11 P, *Ziegler SA* [2013] ECR I-0, para 60.

[249] See, inter alia, ECJ of 23 November 2000, Case C-1/98 P, *British Steel* [2000] ECR I-10349, para 52, and the case law cited.

The possibility of a self-imposed limitation of the European Commission's exercise of discretion due to the adoption of soft law has been confirmed by the ECJ, provided such guidelines or notices concretise the approach of the institution and are in accordance with the rules of the treaty.[250] This leads to an indirect external effect, because legal persons and bodies may be allowed to rely on those soft law acts in any dealing with the European Commission.[251]

In EU competition law, the case law of the European Courts evidences the importance of soft law and its indirect external effects for the judicial control of the European Commission's decisions,[252] although altogether the statements about the relevance of soft law in judicial control are of a differing and sometimes even latently inconsistent nature.[253] Soft law acts should not constitute the legal basis of legal decisions but rather only clarify and concretise the elements of the EU law in question[254]—in the manner of a gap-closing function with the European Commission as a kind of legislator-in-reserve.[255] Nevertheless, soft law acts should fall within the scope of the term 'law' under Article 7 paragraph 1 ECHR, as they can produce indirect legal effects via general principles of law.[256] As already stated, the obligation of the European Commission to apply its own soft law acts is based on the principles of equal treatment and the protection of legitimate expectations.[257]

Despite their asserted legal insignificance, the substantial requirements of soft law acts have been analysed in a very detailed manner in EU competition law.[258] Indeed, the judicial control sometimes has not reviewed merely whether or not the European Commission's exercise of discretion has been based on materially accurate facts and that no manifest error of assessment or misuse of its powers has occurred, but frequently includes considerations as to whether or not the European Commission has observed its own guidelines.[259] For example, in one case regarding EU state aid law, the Court analysed the applicability of a Commission Communication in a detailed manner.[260] In EU competition law, soft law acts have even been counted amongst the legal background for the Court's judicial

[250] See, inter alia, ECJ of 11 July 2013, Case C-439/11 P, *Ziegler SA* [2013] ECR I-0, para 59; ECJ of 29 April 2004, Case C-278/00, *Greece v Commission* [2004] ECR I-3997, para 98; ECJ of 7 March 2002, Case C-310/99, *Italy v Commission* [2002] ECR I-2289, para 52; ECJ of 5 October 2000, Case C-288/96, *Germany v Commission* [2000] ECR I-8237, para 62.

[251] Nehl, in: Imenga/Körber (eds), 2012, pp 113–52 (125, 126).

[252] See, inter alia, ECJ of 11 July 2013, Case C-439/11 P, *Ziegler SA* [2013] ECR I-0, para 59, and the case law cited; and also, inter alia, ECJ of 7 March 2002, Case C-310/99, *Italy v Commission* [2002] ECR I-2289, para 52, and the case law cited.

[253] Weiß, (2) 2011 JECLAP (5), pp 441–51 (443); similar: Thieme, 2011, p 130.

[254] ECJ of 8 February 2007, Case C-3/06 P, *Danone* [2007] ECR I-1331, paras 23–28.

[255] Nehl, in: Imenga/Körber (eds), 2012, pp 113–52 (124).

[256] ECJ of 28 June 2005, Joined Cases C-189/02 P, C-202/02 P, C-205/02 P to C-208/02 P and C-213/02 P, *Dansk Rørindustri* [2005] ECR I-5425, paras 211, 223.

[257] ECJ of 11 July 2013, Case C-439/11 P, *Ziegler SA* [2013] ECR I-0, para 60.

[258] Nehl, in: Imenga/Körber (eds), 2012, pp 113–52 (126); similarly Thieme, 2011, p 129.

[259] Hofmann, Rowe/Türk, 2011, p 570; Nehl, in: Imenga/Körber (eds), 2012, pp 113–52 (126).

[260] General Court of 26 June 2008, Case T-442/03, *SIC-Sociedade* [2008] ECR II-1161, paras 149 et seq.

control[261] and are considered to be useful points of reference.[262] Some statements of the ECJ even approximate the acceptance of a de facto legal quality of soft law acts.[263]

Therefore, the relevance of soft law extends beyond rules of conduct and mere administrative regulations. Moreover, because of its indirect external effects it can even hold the same significance as implementing provisions or legally binding amendments to EU primary and secondary law, as has been criticised in the area of EU antitrust law.[264] Nevertheless, the ECJ recently seems to have shifted toward a stronger orientation on other criteria than soft law for the judicial control of the European Commission's exercise of discretion in the future.[265]

Indeed, with regard to penalties for infringement of EU antitrust law, the ECJ has emphasised the manifold criteria laid down in EU secondary law and developed in established case law that the European Commission has to consider when exercising its discretion, such as, for example, the gravity and the duration of an infringement or the profit derived from the infringement.[266] In the end, the scope and limitation of the juridification of soft law acts still remains problematic and under development, especially in cases where the European Courts tend to upgrade guidelines as criterion for judicial control, as is the case in EU antitrust law.[267]

(c) Indirect Legal Effects of Soft Law in EU Customs Law

Because of the decentralised implementation of EU customs law and the organisational and institutional autonomy of EU Member States, things are different in EU customs law compared to EU competition law. Any indirect legal effect of soft law acts that is based on the self-limitation of the European Commission itself is only relevant with regard to administrative decisions the European Commission has to take, as is frequently the case in EU antitrust law. Even if the European

[261] ECJ of 18 May 2006, Case C-397/03 P, *ADM I* [2006] ECR I-4429, para 19; ECJ of 28 June 2005, Joined Cases C-189/02 P, C-202/02 P, C-205/02 P to C-208/02 P and C-213/02 P, *Dansk Rørindustri* [2005] ECR I-5425, paras 207, 208; General Court of 18 June 2008, Case T-410/03, *Hoechst* [2008] ECR II-881, para 372; General Court of 12 February 2008, Case T-289/03, *BUPA* [2008] ECR II-81, paras 10–13; General Court of 30 September 2003, Case T-203/01, *Michelin* [2003] ECR II-4071, para 292; General Court of 30 April 1998, Case T-16/96, *Cityflyer Express Ltd* [1998] ECR II-757, paras 3, 4.

[262] ECJ of 7 March 2002, Case C-310/99, *Italy v Commission* [2002] ECR I-2289, para 52.

[263] ECJ of 24 September 2009, Joined Cases C-125/07 P, C-133/07 P, C-135/07 P and C-137/07 P, *Erste Group Bank AG* [2009] ECR I-8681, paras 143, 174, 193; ECJ of 19 March 2009, Case C-510/06 P, *ADM II* [2009] ECR I-1843, para 77; ECJ of 18 May 2006, Case C-397/03 P, *ADM I* [2006] ECR I-4429, para 93.

[264] Weiß, (2) 2011 JECLAP (5), pp 441–51 (444).

[265] Nehl, in: Imenga/Körber (eds), 2012, pp 113–52 (138, 139)

[266] ECJ of 8 December 2011, Case C-386/10 P, *Chalkor* [2011] ECR I-0, paras 55–58.

[267] Nehl, in: Imenga/Körber (eds), 2012, pp 113–52 (126, 127). For a detailed critical analysis of the importance of soft law in EU competition law and especially in EU antitrust law, see: Weiß, (2) 2011 JECLAP (5), pp 441–51; Weiß, 2010 EWS 7, pp 257–61; Nehl, in: Imenga/Körber (eds), 2012, pp 113–52.

Commission binds itself in terms of general principles of law by issuing soft law acts,[268] this self-limitation cannot have indirect binding legal effect upon the EU Member States implementing EU law.[269] Such indirect binding legal effect upon EU Member State authorities could only emerge if there was a strictly hierarchical relationship between the European Commission and the national authorities.[270]

However, such a chain of command does not exist between the European Commission and the national authorities of the EU Member States, as the European Commission lacks any general authority to issue instructions to national authorities.[271] The granting of a corresponding authority for the European Commission would change the basic structure and conditions of the relationship between the European Commission and the EU Member States in the indirect implementation of EU law, and would thus require a specific legal basis in EU primary law.[272] Thus, any self-limitation of the European Commission by adopting soft law acts has no externally binding effect on national authorities when such an indirect binding effect cannot be based on a hierarchical relationship.[273]

The self-limitation of the European Commission arises from the general principles of equal treatment and legitimate expectations, as the issuing of soft law acts gives rise to expectations with regard to a certain interpretation of the EU law in question.[274] The EU Member States and their national authorities have not given cause for an expectation of a certain interpretation when the institutionally separated European Commission has issued a soft law act.[275] The European Commission has no competence for taking a customs decision or giving instructions to the national customs authorities. Therefore, if a national customs authority does not follow the interpretation given by guidelines, economic operators cannot rely on these guidelines to assert that the national authority has breached general principles of law based on a self-imposed limitation of the margin of discretion.[276]

In EU customs law, it is for the national customs authorities to take customs decisions in the day-to-day EU customs work. For these national customs authorities, guidelines and other soft law acts that have been issued by the European Commission cannot impose a limit on their exercise of discretion in a formal way, as the European Commission has no authority to give national customs administrations binding instructions.[277] There is no relation in terms of superior and

[268] Hofmann/Rowe/Türk, 2011, p 576.

[269] See, inter alia, ECJ of 4 December 2013, Case C-121/10, *Commission v Council* [2013] ECR I-0, para 75, and the case law cited; ECJ of 4 December 2013, Case C-117/10, *Commission v Council* [2013] ECR I-0, para (90), and the case law cited.

[270] Hofmann/Rowe/Türk, 2011, p 572.

[271] Hofmann/Rowe/Türk, 2011, pp 572, 573; Thomas, 2009 EuR 3, pp 423–43 (436).

[272] Natzel, 2007, p 61; Adam, 1999, pp 90, 92.

[273] Hofmann/Rowe/Türk, 2011, p 572.

[274] ibid, pp 572, 576; Senden, 2004, p 441.

[275] Hofmann/Rowe/Türk, 2011, pp 572, 576; Senden, 2004, p 441; Thieme, 2011, p 117; Thomas, 2009 EuR 3, pp 423–43 (436).

[276] Deimel, 2009 ZfZ 6, pp 157–60 (159).

[277] Natzel, 2007, p 61.

subordinated authority between the European Commission and national customs authorities.

Nevertheless, as has already been alluded to,[278] a kind of indirect binding effect of soft law acts also occurs in the sense that national authorities are requested to take such measures into consideration as useful points of reference, which is also the case in EU customs. Some soft law acts are even regarded to be an important aid for the interpretation of the Common Customs Tariff, especially in the area of tariff classification.[279] Therefore, to disregard useful soft law acts completely when implementing EU customs law raises the potential risk of assessment errors.[280] In this context, an economic operator may indeed rely on soft law acts, claiming a manifest error of assessment resulted from the national customs authority completely ignoring soft law guidance.

(d) Practical Effects of Soft Law Acts

In addition to indirect legal effects, soft law measures of the European Commission addressed to EU Member States and their national administrative authorities when implementing EU law can have practical external effects.[281] By addressing the national authorities of the EU Member States, the European Commission seeks to push EU Member States to harmonise their respective administrative approaches.[282] Soft law measures regularly assist national authorities in their day-to-day application and interpretation of EU law.[283] These national administrations are often in need of guidance in the interpretation of EU law, as EU law and even the case law of the ECJ are often not self-explanatory, especially with regard to the operational level of national administrations.[284]

Because of its administrative function, the European Commission is aware of the difficulties related to the practical implementation of EU law.[285] Indeed, soft law acts such as guidelines are regularly the most helpful source for the interpretation of EU law, next to the case law of the ECJ.[286] Therefore, by providing useful guidance for the operational level, soft law acts are usually quite persuasive, meaning that it can be assumed that such measures will be applied by national authorities.[287] This psychologically binding force[288] of soft law is the result of a

[278] See Chapter 8.II.C.3.b.

[279] ECJ of 12 December 2013, Case C-450/12, *HARK GmbH & Co KG* [2013] ECR I-0, para 32.

[280] Natzel, 2007, p 70.

[281] Hofmann/Rowe/Türk, 2011, pp 576, 569; Gellert, in: Gellert (ed), 2009, pp 51–57 (56); Adam, 1999, p 66.

[282] Hofmann/Rowe/Türk, 2011, p 568.

[283] ibid, p 536; Lefevre, 2004 ELRev (29), pp 808–22 (810).

[284] Lefevre, 2004 ELRev (29), pp 808–22 (810).

[285] ibid, pp 808–22 (812).

[286] Thomas, 2009 EuR 3, pp 423–43 (437).

[287] Hofmann/Rowe/Türk, 2011, p 557; Lefevre, 2004 ELRev (29), pp 808–22 (810); Thomas, 2009 EuR 3, pp 423–43 (437).

[288] Natzel, 2007, p 71.

kind of natural authority based on the presumption of the practical usefulness of soft law acts.[289]

Furthermore, although soft law acts can only impose a self-limitation on the European Commission itself, this fact can have a political effect[290] in that the European Commission cannot blame national customs administrations when the application of soft law has led to mistakes in the national implementation of EU law.[291] Therefore, guidelines and notices can bind the competent national authorities to extensive and close orientation of their administrative practice on soft law measures in order to avoid inconveniences or even a proceeding for breach of contract pursuant to Article 258 TFEU[292]—an option the European Commission explicitly retains, based on the obligation to Union loyalty pursuant to Article 4 paragraph 3 TEU.[293]

Deviation from guidelines and other soft law texts can even give reason for a request pursuant to Article 267 TFEU, former Article 234 TEC, when there is an issue of interpretation of EU law because of a soft law text.[294] However, the subject matter of such a preliminary ruling would not be the soft law act itself, but the correct interpretation of the EU law in question.[295] Nevertheless, this kind of effectively binding character of soft law can further lead national authorities to base their interpretation of EU customs law on the contents of guidelines in order to avoid the annulment of their customs decision by national courts and reduce the risk of being the subject of punitive measures by the European Commission.[296] In the end, the EU Member States will 'take the path of least resistance.'[297] Therefore, soft law acts of the European Commission are likely to influence the practical implementation of EU law by national authorities at the operational level.[298]

(e) Practical Effects of Soft Law in EU Customs

In EU customs administration, soft law acts of the European Commission undoubtedly have external practical effects. They regularly address EU Member States and their national administrative authorities for the purpose of harmonising the implementation of EU customs law at the operational level. This can be seen by the AEO guidelines. The political effect of soft law measures may even be of special importance in EU customs because of the already discussed European Commission's practice of revenue allocation.[299] Therefore, real pressure exists for

289 Thomas, 2009 EuR 3, pp 423–43 (442); Natzel, 2007, p 71.

290 Hofmann/Rowe/Türk, 2011, p 569.

291 Gellert, in: Gellert (ed), 2009, pp 51–57 (56); Gellert, 2007 AW-Prax 12, pp 511–13 (513).

292 Hofmann/Rowe/Türk, 2011, pp 576, 569; Natzel, 2008, p 2.

293 European Commission, 'Nature and legal value of guidelines', TAXUD/1406/2006–EN, p 5 para 13; see also: Gellert, in: Gellert (ed), 2009, pp 51–57 (55).

294 Thomas, 2009 EuR 3, pp 423–43 (438).

295 ibid, pp 423–443 (439).

296 Hofmann/Rowe/Türk, 2011, pp 576, 569; Gellert, in: Gellert (ed), 2009, pp 51–57 (56).

297 Hofmann/Rowe/Türk, 2011, p 569.

298 ibid, p 573; Lefevre, 2004 ELRev (29), pp 808–22 (820).

299 See Chapter 8.II.C.2.

national customs authorities to apply soft law measures of the EU in order to avoid negative consequences and even financial strains. Several EU customs law experts, at least in Germany, consider soft law acts of the European Commission to be of 'quasi-binding' force.[300]

A customs officer of the Section for the Modernised Customs Code in the United Kingdom confirmed the importance of soft law acts with regard to implementation at the operational level:

> Although it does not stand on its own legally, it forms part of the overall package of information ... helping people that need to use it [EU customs law] understand what [EU customs law] actually means in practice. So that type of underpinning work is really important actually in getting people [to] understand what all this [EU customs law] means in practice ... I do not believe that one would be wise to ignore that, because without it, I do not see how you could necessarily draw the right conclusion.[301]

(f) No Authoritative Interpretation of EU Law by the European Commission

National authorities using soft law acts as interpretation instruments have to keep in mind that the European Commission is not automatically authorised to interpret EU law, this being instead the original function of the ECJ.[302] Therefore, soft law acts of the European Commission bear the potential risk of being inconsistent with the ECJ's interpretation of EU law.

The use of soft law acts of the European Commission as part of the regular interpretation method applied to EU law can even be inconsistent with the system of EU law, as when the European Commission was only part of the legislative process and does not possess final decision-making power.[303] Usually, in the ordinary legislative process, the European Commission has the right of initiative but is not among the main legislative organs of the EU, which are the Council and the European Parliament. Therefore, its interpretation of the law is initially just the expression of an opinion—with follow-on power to shape the administrative practice mainly by a kind of guarantee function.[304]

Although the EU Member States are not qualified to interpret EU law in an authoritative manner, and the European Commission is the guardian of the treaties pursuant to Article 17 paragraph 1 sentences 2 and 3 TEU, it is not able to issue an authentic interpretation of EU law in the form of soft law[305]—confirmed early on as obiter dictum[306] by the ECJ.[307] Only if the European Commission

300 See Wolffgang, 2002 AW-Prax 3, p 81; Weerth, 2003 AW-Prax 4, pp 146–48 (147); Natzel, 2007, p 72; Gellert, in: Gellert (ed), 2009, pp 51–57 (56, 57) with further references.

301 Interview of 9 January 2012 on file with author.

302 Hofmann/Rowe/Türk, 2011, p 569; Lefevre, 2004 ELRev (29), pp 808–22 (810); Thieme, 2011, p 126; Thomas, 2009 EuR 3, pp 423–43 (435).

303 Thieme, 2011, p 126.

304 Thomas, 2009 EuR 3, pp 423–43 (426).

305 Hofmann/Rowe/Türk, 2011, pp 569, 571.

306 ibid, p 571.

307 ECJ of 18 June 1970, Case 74-69, *Krohn* [1970] ECR 451, para 9.

has enacted legal acts by itself, such as, for example, delegated acts pursuant to Article 290 TFEU, is its assistance in the form of soft law relevant for the interpretation of these acts.[308]

Furthermore, the case law of the ECJ confirms that the interpretation of EU customs law through soft law acts of the European Commission is to be used with care, as it can be inconsistent with the law and therefore lead to incorrect customs decisions. In *HEKO Industrieerzeugnisse,*[309] the European Commission issued a list of rules as guidelines for the interpretation of the terms 'last, substantial, economically justified processing or working' in Article 24 CCC. These guidelines determined a product's country of origin by relying only on the criterion of a change in the tariff position. The ECJ declared the exclusive recourse to a single criterion to be illegal, because it imposed a limit on the range of Article 24 CCC.[310] The European Commission had argued that the rules were necessary to ensure the uniform implementation of Article 24 CCC and furthermore were in accordance with the obligations contracted by the EU in the context of the WTO regarding rules of origin.

However, the ECJ had stressed that – although EU secondary law regularly must be interpreted in consideration of the relevant WTO agreements[311] – the agreement in question was only a harmonisation working programme, which left a margin of discretion for WTO Members regarding the adoption of rules of origin and determining certain criteria.[312] The WTO agreement in question, therefore, did not constitute a kind of legal application command regarding the European Commission's list rules.[313] Therefore, the interpretation of Article 24 CCC by the European Commission as laid down in its list rules was wrong and could lead to illegal customs decisions when applied by national customs authorities.

(g) Summary

In summary, the European Commission's soft law acts have no directly legally binding force because of their lack of legal character. Soft law cannot derive legally binding force from Article 4 paragraph 3 TEU without violating EU primary law. Indeed, the European Commission has no competence to adopt legally binding soft law acts, as Article 17 paragraph 1 sentences 2 and 3 TEU are too indefinite and general for such an authorisation, which would change the basic structure of indirect implementation of EU law.

308 Thieme, 2011, p 126.

309 ECJ of 10 December 2009, Case C-260/08, *HEKO Industrieerzeugnisse* [2009] ECR I-11571.

310 ibid, para 36.

311 ECJ of 16 November 2004, Case C-245/02 *Anheuser-Busch* [2004] ECR I-10989, para 55; ECJ of 14 December 2000, Joined Cases C-300/98 and C-392/98, *Dior and Others* [2000] ECR I-11307, paras 42–47.

312 ECJ of 10 December 2009, Case C-260/08, *HEKO Industrieerzeugnisse* [2009] ECR I-11571, para 22.

313 Lieber, 2010 AW-Prax 2, pp 55–57 (57).

However, soft law can have indirect legal effects in that by issuing such acts, the European Commission imposes limits on itself with regard to its own margin of discretion. This is of significant importance in EU competition law. However, in EU customs it is for the EU Member States to implement the law, and in this context, the self-limitation of the European Commission cannot have external effect on the national customs authorities' margin of discretion. Nevertheless, national customs authorities have to take soft law measures into consideration as useful guidance for the interpretation of EU customs law. This can create an indirect legal effect in that national authorities should examine the substantive content of soft law acts in order to avoid assessment errors when exercising discretion.

Furthermore, in EU customs, soft law can also have significant practical effects as a psychologically and politically binding force. Soft law acts are frequently a very helpful source for interpretative assistance and best practice standards drawing from the expertise of the European Commission. Even the ECJ regards them to be appropriate instruments for the interpretation of EU customs law, which is why neither national administrations nor national courts should dismiss them without reason. Especially national customs authorities customarily rely on the European Commission's soft law in order to avoid criticism or negative decisions in the European Commission's practice of revenue allocation—or even a procedure for breach of contract pursuant to Article 258 TFEU. Because of these effects, soft law acts of the European Commission can have a kind of de facto binding force in practice.

However, national courts and national customs authorities have to keep in mind that the European Commission's soft law is not an authoritative source of interpretation, because as *HEKO Industrieerzeugnisse*,[314] in the area of EU customs, has clearly shown, only the ECJ has such competence. Nevertheless, the European Commission's soft law acts play an important role in EU customs administration and their effects on the operational level should not be underestimated. Thus, they are one of the main instruments of the European Commission for exercising influence on EU customs law implementation and an important strategy to ensure uniform customs administration.

III. ASSISTANCE BY THE CUSTOMS CODE COMMITTEE

As we have seen, the role of the European Commission is primarily to facilitate the correct application of EU customs law. An important aspect for obtaining uniform application of customs rules in the different EU Member States is the identical interpretation of margins of discretion in those rules with regard to similar cases. In this context, the Customs Code Committee can offer a platform for EU Member States, together with the European Commission, to establish common approaches on certain customs-related questions by agreeing on common rules

[314] ECJ of 10 December 2009, Case C-260/08, *HEKO Industrieerzeugnisse* [2009] ECR I-11571.

or guidelines in order to give opinions on the implementation of EU customs law. Thereby the Customs Code Committee can contribute to ensuring the uniform administration of EU customs law through every national customs administration of the EU Member States.[315]

Furthermore, WTO and WCO topics constitute significant elements of the Customs Code Committee's agenda. Thus, by discussing aspects for meetings in the WTO and the WCO committees, it also contributes to ensuring a common position of the EU towards major trading partners in these organisations.[316] For this reason, the main tasks of the Customs Code Committee are the examination of customs issues, in particular divergent interpretations of EU customs provisions by national customs administrations of the EU Member States, amendments of and guidelines for EU customs rules, and the preparation of common EU positions in the corresponding WTO committees and the corresponding WCO technical committees on customs matters.[317] As already discussed, the Customs Code Committee is organised into numerous sections reflecting the wide range of expertise necessary in different areas of EU customs, and has given itself rules of procedure.[318]

Besides its status as a comitology committee in the sense of the Comitology Regulation,[319] another important part of the Customs Code Committee's agenda is the discussion of other customs related issues put to the Committee to gain information or facilitate a simple exchange of views in accordance with either Article 249 CCC (interim Article 185 MCC) or Article 8 Regulation (EEC) 2658/87,[320] pursuant to Article 3 paragraph 2 section (c) rules of procedure. The Customs Code Committee can examine any question concerning customs legislation raised by its chairman, either on his/her own initiative or at the request of an EU Member State's representative pursuant to Article 249 CCC (interim Article 185 MCC). The Committee can issue opinions but not its own measures, in which it is only involved through the European Commission pursuant to Articles

[315] Rogmann, 2008 ZfZ 3, pp 57–69 (60).

[316] European Court of Auditors, Special Report 23/2000, para 24.

[317] For example: In the area of classification the Harmonised System Committee of the WCO, URL: www.wcoomd.org/en/about-us/wco-working-bodies/tarif_and_trade/harmonized_system_committee.aspx; in the area of valuation the WCO Technical Committee on Customs Valuation, URL: www.wcoomd.org/en/about-us/wco-working-bodies/tarif_and_trade/technical_committee_on_customs_valuation.aspx, and the WTO Committee on Customs Valuation, URL: www.wto.org/english/tratop_e/cusval_e/cusval_info_e.htm; in the area of origin the WCO technical Committee, URL: www.wcoomd.org/en/about-us/wco-working-bodies/tarif_and_trade/technical_committee_on_rules_of_origin.aspx, and the WTO Committee on Rules of Origin, URL: www.wto.org/english/tratop_e/roi_e/roi_info_e.htm.

[318] See Chapter 8.II.B.1.

[319] Regulation (EU) 182/2011 of the European Parliament and of the Council of 16 February 2011 laying down the rules and general principles concerning mechanisms for control by Member States of the Commission's exercise of implementing powers, [2011] OJ L55/13–18.

[320] Council Regulation (EEC) 2658/87 of 23 July 1987 on the tariff and statistical nomenclature and on the Common Customs Tariff, [1987] OJ L256/1–675, last amended by Council Regulation (EC) 254/2000 of 31 January 2000 amending Regulation (EEC) 2658/87 on the tariff and statistical nomenclature and the Common Customs Tariff, [2000] OJ L28/16–18.

247a, 248a CCC (Article 285 UCC/former Article 184 MCC).[321] The Committee has been intensively involved especially in the fields of customs classification and customs valuation.[322] The Customs Code Committee issues opinions in the form of non-binding common rules, guidelines and other common conclusions, but usually without examining individual cases, as the Committee has no power to ask national customs administrations to account for the treatment applied to a certain economic operator.[323]

The opinions of the Customs Code Committee are not legally binding on the national customs authorities in the EU Member States.[324] Furthermore, the Committee has not even been involved in many cases of non-uniform application of EU customs law.[325] Additionally, the European Commission cannot be forced to follow the recommendations of the Committee.[326] Nevertheless, within the limits of its functioning, the Customs Code Committee makes a valuable contribution to the consistent application of EU customs law by giving opinions to assist the European Commission as well as the national customs administrations of the EU Member States.[327] Customs officials in the United Kingdom confirmed:

> If the Customs Code Committee has issued an opinion, then again, it is more the fact that they [the EU level] expect Member States to follow that opinion because again regardless of whether Germany agrees or the UK agrees, if uniformly the majority has agreed to that statement, we are overridden. But again, opinions do form part of our checklist to see why we do them [customs decisions] and how we do them [customs decisions]. So whilst if they are not legal, they are authoritative.[328]

In part, the preference to maintain these competences of the Customs Code Committee has been driven by the desire to ensure an opportunity exists to examine cases where encouraging innovation is appropriate or cases in which the Union Customs Code or its delegated acts or implementing acts may have disproportionate negative consequences.[329] Nevertheless, in the Union Customs Code, Article 249 CCC, respectively Article 185 MCC, can no longer be found. Therefore, in the future such assistance can only be based on Article 8 Regulation (EEC) 2658/87.

The main function of the Customs Code Committee seems to now be to act as an instrument of control with regard to the conferred implementing powers of the European Commission, while the examination of questions concerning customs legislation has become less important. However, the numerous sections of the

[321] Henke, in: Witte (ed), 2013, Art 249 CCC, para 7.

[322] Rogmann, 2008 ZfZ 3, pp 57–69 (61).

[323] European Court of Auditors, Special Report 23/2000, reply of the European Commission, para 29; Lyons, 2008, p 146.

[324] Lyons, 2008, p 174.

[325] Rogmann, 2008 ZfZ 3, pp 57–69 (67).

[326] ibid, pp 57–69 (67).

[327] European Court of Auditors, Special Report 23/2000, reply of the European Commission, summary p 13; Lyons, 2008, p 174.

[328] Interview of 9 January 2012 on file with author.

[329] European Parliament, Committee Amendments of 29 October 2012, PE498.017, 29.10.2012, Amendment 213, pp 116, 117.

Customs Code Committee illustrate the great expertise and intense examination of customs matters that the Committee provides for both EU customs legislation and EU customs implementation. After all, in view of the limited resources of the European Commission—especially its limited staff—the Customs Code Committee provides important assistance in the development and deployment of EU customs. Therefore, the contribution of the Customs Code Committee to enhancing uniform customs administration throughout the EU by providing assistance to the European Commission, as well as to national customs administrations, should not be underestimated. Furthermore, the Customs Code Committee also plays an important role in constituting a platform for EU Member States' customs administrations.

Nevertheless, the agendas for the meetings of the various sections of the Customs Code Committee can be overly ambitious and the structure of the Committee, depending on an agreement of the 28 EU Member States, can slow things down. This was confirmed by customs officials in the United Kingdom:

> No, I think sometimes the agendas can be overambitious … So I think sometimes they are just not as realistic as they could be. And you do simply go over the same things over and over again, and Member States tend to make the same point each time without actually seemingly getting anywhere.[330]

Better preparation of meetings—including the timely translation of documents—and shorter intervals between meetings when important issues have to be discussed could improve the important work of the Customs Code Committee. Customs officials in the United Kingdom partly criticised the management of such meetings, as minor issues could outgrow their importance while more important issues would be delayed:

> So, whether that be down to the number of issues, the fact [remains] that it is not particularly well-managed in terms of the subject may outgrow its importance and throw things off the agenda which should have had [been] longer discussed. Or really a clearer set down plan [is needed], if you like, that each meeting will agree at least [to] these issues, and that never seems to happen, does it?[331]

Furthermore, the number of meetings and their length seems to have been reduced, even though the number of important issues is increasing with the delay of the reform process:

> If you go back in time, there always used to be a meeting every three months for about three days if not four, when there was a coordination for the WCO, but now I mean they have just cut down and you get meetings [once] a year if you are lucky and its only one day … Going back in time, I do not think we had any more problems to resolve back in time than what we have got today, but there were a lot more meetings, and I think it moved things forward a lot quicker by having those meetings quicker.[332]

330 Interview of 10 January 2012 on file with author.
331 ibid.
332 ibid.

The issuing of documents for these meetings was also criticised, as not all members could get their documents translated in time, or had the opportunity to discuss their content within the national customs administration in order to come to the meetings well prepared, in turn slowing things down in the meeting itself:

> They often do not get their documents translated in time and they cannot contribute at all. And there are some Member States who will [not], if there is a chance to debate something, they cannot contribute because they have not had the time to see the document and there is a feeling sometimes that [this] is almost being done on purpose.[333]

Therefore, the important work in the Customs Code Committee could and should be improved in terms of management, which is the main responsibility of the European Commission, as chair of the Committee.

IV. CONCLUSION

In the indirect implementation of EU customs law, the European Commission holds a strong position. Its 'quasi-legislative' function with regard to the exercise of delegated powers pursuant to Article 290 TFEU, which has been introduced into the Union Customs Code, indicates that the EU wishes to enhance the influence of the European Commission.

Concerning its administrative functions, the European Commission is crucial for the coordination and management of exchange of information and cooperative activities. The numerous provisions for conferral of implementing powers in the Union Customs Code demand cooperation between the European Commission and the EU Member States, which have control functions in the Customs Code Committee.

Nevertheless, the European Commission seems to have gained more influence in the new comitology mechanism. Furthermore, as customs duties are traditionally own resources of the EU, the European Commission has a right of inspection in national customs administrations, which also have to fulfil reporting obligations. The practice of revenue allocation, which threatens to place financial strains on the national budgets of the EU Member States, is also an important instrument for supervision. Finally, the European Commission's soft law acts are an important part of its strategy to reduce margins of discretion in the implementation of EU customs law by complementing adopted delegated acts and implementing acts with practical guidance addressed to the operational level. The national experts of the Customs Code Committee and its various sub-committees provide important assistance to the European Commission in the management of the EU Customs Union.

[333] ibid.

9

Summarising the Implementation System of EU Customs Law

AS WE HAVE seen, the EU's agenda to improve uniform customs administration consists of several strategies that are often connected with the initiatives of the great reform of EU customs. Concerning the 'Better Regulation' Initiative, one of the most important strategies is the adoption of detailed legal provisions in order to narrow down the margins of discretion for national customs authorities as much as possible while simultaneously simplifying EU customs legislation to facilitate its application. Therefore, the new Union Customs Code is more coherently structured in comparison to the Community Customs Code, and the allocation of provisions between the Code and its implementing provisions is more balanced.

Actually, the customs procedures and the legal terminology have been simplified, reducing the possibilities for national idiosyncrasies in customs procedures. The EU-wide validity of national customs decisions has been explicitly laid down and first steps towards a harmonisation of administrative penalties in EU customs as well as further harmonisation of appeal procedures have been undertaken. Compared to the current Community Customs Code, under the 'Better Regulation' Initiative the Union Customs Code contributes to the development of an improved customs procedure union. The establishment of a strategy for an electronic customs environment in the Electronic Customs Initiative is also strongly anchored in the Union Customs Code. However, while a modern customs environment does have the potential to significantly contribute to uniform customs administration, the success of the Electronic Customs Initiative is still to be seen.

In the EU Customs Union, there have also been developments towards a stronger administration union. As we have seen, in the decentralised implementation of EU customs law the EU Member States do not possess absolute autonomy and forms of cooperation and interdependencies exist. The Union Customs Code establishes a stronger position for the European Commission by providing for manifold conferral of implementing powers, while the requirements of Article 291 paragraph 2 TFEU are not substantiated. This lack of any substantiation of the essential conditions set out in Article 291 paragraph 2 TFEU negatively affects the EU's credibility regarding its democratic legitimacy. Thus, the European Commission should at least provide for remedy when adopting its implementing provisions. Nevertheless, a centralised EU customs administration has not yet been established and the Community Customs Code and the Union Customs Code only provide for sporadic provisions on the organisation of administration.

As the implementation of EU customs law is still mainly the responsibility of the EU Member States, the promotion of customs cooperation as part of the Future Customs Initiative constitutes an important strategy of the European Commission to improve the uniform functioning of the EU Customs Union. However, the Customs Code and its implementing provisions do not provide for the concrete regulation of cooperation among national customs authorities in customs procedures, but simply stipulates cooperation in transnational customs procedures. Further, the Mutual Assistance Regulation contains no rules with regard to day-to-day customs work and is only relevant with regard to EU customs law infringements. Yet with the Customs Action Programme the EU has gained an effective instrument to improve cooperation amongst national customs authorities. Its various programme actions enable the development of contact networks and the exchange of information in many areas of EU customs and on different levels of customs officials while also contributing to common working standards and understanding in the EU Customs Union. Still, the output of the Customs Action Programme in terms of systematic dissemination of information about programme actions and their results has to be improved. In this context, a common online platform managed by the European Commission could be an effective solution.

The European Commission has expressed its intention to administer the application of EU law in close partnership with the EU Member States through contacts, sector-specific networks and regular meetings with national experts.[1] The function of the European Commission in the administration of the EU Customs Union is not to be underestimated. Its primary role is to coordinate information exchange and cooperation amongst EU Member States' national customs administrations and to facilitate correct and uniform application of EU customs law. As part of the 'Better Regulation' Initiative, the Union Customs Code provides for a great number of delegation of powers and conferral of implementing powers to the European Commission, which enhances the strong position of the European Commission in the management of the EU Customs Union. This enables the European Commission to adopt detailed legal provisions and, in doing so, to follow its strategy to further reduce the national authorities' margin of discretion in the implementation of EU customs.

The wide range of delegated power provided for in the Union Customs Code as a 'quasi-legislative' function of the European Commission, without control of EU Member States, indicates that the EU is following a more centralised approach than it took in the Community Customs Code. In contrast, the adoption of

[1] COM (2007) 502 final, p 4.

implementing acts as administrative function is controlled by the EU Member States through the comitology mechanism. Moreover, this kind of control also ensures cooperation amongst the EU Member States and with the European Commission in the Customs Code Committee, enhancing a common understanding with regard to the interpretation and application of the implementing acts adopted in these procedures and establishing interdependencies in the administration of EU customs. Furthermore, the European Commission's position under the new Comitology Regulation is slightly stronger than it used to be in the former comitology mechanism.

Finally, though there is no hierarchical structure between them, the European Commission has some supervisory instruments vis-à-vis the EU Member States and their national customs administrations. Alongside its rights of inspection and the reporting obligations of the EU Member States, as well as the European Commission's practice of revenue allocation, the European Commission's system to ensure uniform customs administration relies to a great extent on the use of soft law texts that provide important practical guidance for the implementation of EU customs law at the operational level. The kind of information to be found in soft law acts is not appropriate to be put in legal acts, as it regularly concerns the practical aspects of administrative processes. These soft law measures accompanying legal acts are part of the 'Better Regulation' Initiative and thus are an important strategy of the European Commission for influencing the national implementation of EU customs law. While such acts have no legal character, they nonetheless have significant indirect legal effects and important practical ones on national customs administrations. Soft law measures have to be taken into consideration to guide interpretation in order to avoid assessment errors as well as to prevent negative consequences arising from the European Commission. Furthermore, the guidance of the European Commission in the administration of EU customs is approved of by the national customs authorities, as this assistance can greatly facilitate day-to-day customs work.

The interdependencies and various forms of cooperation, together with the guidance of the European Commission, which is also assisted by the Customs Code Committee and its various sub-committees, contribute to a kind of administration in EU customs that can no longer be defined as a strictly decentralised form of administration. In summary, the European Commission together with the EU Member States continue to work on building an EU Customs Administration Union that is not centrally organised on the EU level but consists of integrated levels of administration working together to ensure uniform administration of EU customs and thus the functioning of the Internal Market. In this context, the administration of EU customs in the EU has been recognised as existing 'not merely on paper but in practice, due to a rigid system of compliance control.'[2]

[2] Hobbing, CEPS Papers No 39, June 2011, p 12.

Part V

Specific Areas of EU Customs

10

Special Tools and Mechanisms for 'Uniformisation' of EU Customs Law Implementation in Specific Areas of EU Customs

AS WE HAVE seen, the strategies of the EU, and in particular of the European Commission, to enhance uniform customs administration generally have resulted in an EU customs administration consisting of multiple levels integrated through various forms of cooperation and coordination, as well as guidance from the European Commission. Yet in different areas of EU customs, special instruments exist whose functions and interaction in their specific customs area have to be analysed further. These special tools and mechanisms in the various sectors of EU customs are specifically designed to meet the particular needs for uniform customs administration in these specific areas.

Therefore, though they can partly be included under the strategies already discussed in the general context of EU customs law implementation, these special instruments should be analysed in the context of their specific customs area to identify peculiarities, unique working methods, and novel interactions of instruments. In the *EC—Selected Customs Matters* dispute settlement,[1] the European Commission described in detail many of these special instruments and mechanisms used to guarantee the uniform administration of EU customs law in specific areas.

I. CLASSIFICATION

Throughout the EU, all tariff classification decisions made by the national customs authorities must follow the Combined Nomenclature of the Common Customs Tariff.[2] The classification of goods under the Common Customs Tariff[3] is one of the most important, and most difficult, fields of EU customs. The Customs

[1] WT/DS315.

[2] Grayston, (6) 2011 GTCJ (3), pp 149–55 (150).

[3] Composition and structure of the Common Customs Tariff are explained in Chapter 2.III.A.

Code Committee[4] has a regularly meeting section that addresses tariff classification matters: the Customs Code Committee—Tariff and Statistical Nomenclature Section. The main task of the Committee's Classification Section is the examination of classification issues. Such issues are, in particular, divergent interpretations of tariff headings by national customs administrations of the EU Member States, amendments of and guidelines to EU customs classification rules, and the preparation of common EU positions for the corresponding WCO committee on the Harmonised System—the HS Committee. Although the opinions of the Customs Code Committee are not legally binding, they still may constitute useful guidance for the interpretation and application of EU customs law, as the expertise of the Committee is highly regarded.[5]

Interviews with customs officials of the Section for Classification in the United Kingdom revealed that such opinions of experts are seen as valuable, because referring to EU-wide opinions on the meaning of a code position can help to persuade traders of the correctness of a customs decision: 'So in that respect, it adds weight.'[6] In interviews with customs officials in Germany, a more heterogeneous assessment was given: customs officials of a more specialised customs authority gave more weight to the opinions of the relevant section of the Customs Code Committee than those working in general customs offices of Germany.[7]

Although the Common Customs Tariff's design is that of a systematically edited catalogue of goods and various tariff rates of its single lines of goods, which is why its tariff codes differ from the structure of common legal norms, it still constitutes a legal act, and thus its codes have to be interpreted and applied according to juristic legal interpretative methods.[8] The facts of the case are the goods to be classified; the wording of the tariff positions and sub-positions, together with the legal notes to the sections, chapters and sub-positions, constitute the legal situation in conjunction with applicable general provisions of classification; the legal consequence is the correct tariff rate.[9] In the interests of legal certainty and for ease of verification, the interpretation and application of the Common Customs Tariff has to be based on objective, EU-wide uniform criteria. Thereby, according

[4] A general analysis of the tasks and function of the Customs Code Committee can be found in Chapter 8.II.B.1 and III.

[5] Panel Report, *EC–Selected Customs Matters*, WT/DS315/R, para 4.119.

[6] Interview of 9 January 2012 on file with author.

[7] 'Ja, das ist immer ganz wichtig', Interview of 1 April 2011, German section for single authorisation on file with author; 'Das, also wir sind letztendlich schon gehalten oder sagen wir einmal so, wir berücksichtigen diese Stellungnahmen des Zollkodex[ausschusses] schon.' Interview of 7 April 2011, German educational and scientific centre for customs, office location for expert reports, on file with author; 'aber es ist natürlich von Wichtigkeit'. Interview of 13 April 2011, German section for binding tariff information, on file with author; 'Aber für die Arbeit an sich ist es zweitrangig.' Interview of 10 May 2011, German Main Customs Office, on file with author.

[8] Bleihauer, in: Witte/Wolffgang (eds), 2012, p 403, para 1496; Blechschmidt, 2006 BDZ-Fachteil 12, F89–F90 (F89).

[9] Bleihauer, in: Witte/Wolffgang (eds), 2012, p 403, para 1496; Blechschmidt, 2006 BDZ-Fachteil 12, F89–F90 (F90).

to the ECJ,[10] the decisive criterion for the tariff classification of goods for customs purposes generally is to be sought in the objective characteristics and properties of the goods in question, as defined in the wording of the relevant heading of the Combined Nomenclature.

Various instruments, of legally binding as well as non-legally binding force, exist and constitute valuable aids for customs authorities in the EU Member States when it comes to the correct classification of goods under the Combined Nomenclature, while also enhancing the uniform interpretation and application of the Common Customs Tariff. The chronological order of the application of these instruments follows from the composition of the Tariff positions. All these instruments can be found in the electronic database of the Common Customs Tariff used for day-to-day work, in particular in the TARIC as well as the national working tariffs, as the Common Customs Tariff today is predominantly used by means of IT.[11]

A. General Rules and Legal Notes of the Harmonised System by the WCO

The Combined Nomenclature (CN) of the Common Customs Tariff is based on the international Harmonised System (HS), which includes legal notes as well as six general rules that provide for the correct and uniform interpretation of the Harmonised System. As a result, the first six digits of the Combined Nomenclature correspond exactly to the Harmonised System. The Harmonised System of the WCO and the Combined Nomenclature of the EU also contain the same six general rules for their interpretation, which are binding in EU customs law.[12] The Harmonised System has legal character, as it became legally binding when the EU and the EU Member States joined this agreement.[13] Thus, the general rules for classification under the Harmonised System have to be applied as a first step when using the Common Customs Tariff.[14]

The general rules lay down the basic methods for correct tariff classification and explain in a detailed manner the basic interpretation and application of the six-digit HS-positions to be applied at the beginning of each tariff classification. Unless otherwise provided for, the basic rule is that the wording of each division, subdivision and legal note is leading for every classification, as well as for the

[10] ECJ of 27 April 2006, Case C-15/05, *Kawasaki Motors Europe*, [2006] ECR I-3657, para 38; ECJ of 15 September 2005, Case C-495/03, *Intermodal Transports*, [2005] ECR I-8151, para 47; ECJ of 16 September 2004, Case C-396/02, *DFDS*, [2004] ECR I-8439, para 27; ECJ of 9 February 1999, Case C-280/97, *ROSE Elektrotechnik*, [1999] ECR I-689, para 16.

[11] Bleihauer, in: Witte/Wolffgang (eds), 2012, p 382, para 1462.

[12] Grayston, (6) 2011 GTCJ (3), pp 149–155 (150); Lyons, 2008, p 167.

[13] Council Decision of 7 April 1987 concerning the conclusion of the International Convention on the Harmonized Commodity Description and Coding System and of the Protocol of Amendment thereto, OJ L 198, 20.07.1987, p 3–10.

[14] Bleihauer, in: Witte/Wolffgang (eds), 2012, p 385, para 1468; Lyons, 2008, pp 133, 134.

section and chapter notes. The legal section and chapter notes of the Harmonised System are designed to prevent conflicts of positions and to provide for international definitions to prevent different interpretation of terms.[15] The system also provides classification instructions for specific goods and establishes special rules for exceptions to the general rules.[16] Finally, general rule number 4 constitutes a kind of *ultima ratio* in the event that there is no legal note or other general rule providing a solution for the correct classification, commanding classification under the position containing goods most similar to the good in question.[17]

All together, the general rules and legal notes of the Harmonised System provide clear instruction on how the Harmonised System is to be interpreted and applied in principle. The importance of the general rules and legal notes for classification issues should not be underestimated, for they constitute binding common instruments for every customs authority in the EU and are positioned at an early stage of the hierarchical tariff classification process.

B. HS Explanatory Notes and HS Classification Opinions of the WCO

The Harmonised System is managed by the World Customs Organization (WCO) with the assistance of the specifically arranged Harmonised System Committee operating under the oversight of the Harmonised System Council. One of the main functions of the HS Committee is to ensure the uniform application of the Harmonised System worldwide. For this purpose it issues classification opinions, explanatory notes and recommendations pursuant to Article 7 paragraph 1 HS Convention subject to approval by the HS Council pursuant to Article 8 paragraph 2 HS Convention. HS explanatory notes and HS classification opinions constitute an important aid in the interpretation of the six-digit level of the Combined Nomenclature that corresponds exactly with the Harmonised System.[18] Because the notes and opinions of the HS Committee are not part of the HS Convention itself,[19] they have no legal character, but they can be characterised as soft law as issued by the WCO.

The HS Committee decides on classification issues for certain new goods that are difficult to classify under the Harmonised System, issuing classification opinions. As measures of soft law, they are not directly applicable in the EU. To have effect on customs administrations and economic operators in the EU, the HS classification opinions have to be transformed into EU classification regulations or published in the EU's Official Journal Series C.[20]

[15] Bleihauer, in: Witte/Wolffgang (eds), 2012, pp 386, 387, para 1470.
[16] ibid, pp 386, 387, para 1470.
[17] Lyons, 2008, p 170.
[18] Grayston, (6) 2011 GTCJ (3), pp 149–55 (150).
[19] Lux, in: Rüsken (ed), 2013, Vol III, Introduction CN Regulation, para 167; similar Lyons, 2008, p 172.
[20] Weerth, Witten 2007, pp 166, 169.

The European Commission has been criticised for not publicising every opinion of the WCO regarding the Harmonised System in time, and because to an extent it tends to transform into EU classification regulations only those results that it considers to be of special politico-economic interest.[21] Nevertheless, this attitude of the European Commission towards classification opinions of the HS Committee cannot endanger the uniform application of the Common Customs Tariff in the EU, as the EU Member States are bound to HS classification opinions only if these have been made effective in the EU Customs Union through transformation by the European Commission into an EU classification regulation. Therefore, this approach could only lead to non-uniform application of the Harmonised System with regard to other contracting parties of the HS Convention, which is irrelevant with regard to the EU's obligation for uniform customs administration pursuant to Article X:3(a) GATT 1994 and the EU's principle of uniformity.

Furthermore, it seems questionable whether the European Commission, by refraining from transforming an HS classification opinion into a classification regulation, has the competence to prevent the application of that opinion – at least for interpretative guidance – especially since the Official Journal of the EU only refers to them, without any description of their subject matter. The ECJ has taken HS classification opinions into consideration independently from any publication by the European Commission[22] and regards them to be an important aid in the interpretation of the Combined Nomenclature (CN).[23] In this regard, the ECJ emphasised early on that HS classification opinions are:

> all the more decisive because they emanate from an authority entrusted by the contracting parties with ensuring uniformity in the interpretation and application of the nomenclature.[24]

Therefore, HS classification opinions reflecting the general practice of the contracting parties can only knowingly be set aside by national customs authorities if the suggested classification appears incompatible with the wording of the CN position concerned, or goes manifestly beyond the competence conferred on the HS Committee and the HS Council.[25]

HS explanatory notes issued by the HS Committee constitute the 'official interpretation' of the Harmonised System and are provided in the form of a five volume

[21] ibid, pp 167, 169.

[22] In particular ECJ of 8 February 1990, Case C-233/88, *Gijs van de Kolk* [1990] ECR I-265, paras 9, 10; see also ECJ, Opinion of Advocate General Fennelly delivered on 8 June 2000, Case C-42/99, *Fábrica de Queijo Eru Portuguesa Ldª* [2000] ECR I-7691, para 22.

[23] ECJ of 6 December 2007, Case C-486/06, *BVBA Van Landeghem* [2007] ECR I-10661, para 25; ECJ of 27 April 2006, Case C-15/05, *Kawasaki Motors Europe* [2006] ECR I-3657, para 36; ECJ order of 19 January 2005, Case C-206/03, *SmithKline Beecham* [2005] ECR I-415, paras 24, 26.

[24] ECJ of 19 November 1975, Case 38-75, *Nederlandse Spoorwegen* [1975] ECR 1439, para 24.

[25] ECJ order of 19 January 2005, Case C-206/03, *SmithKline Beecham* [2005] ECR I-415, para 24; ECJ of 8 February 1990, Case C-233/88, *Gijs van de Kolk* [1990] ECR I-265, para 9; ECJ of 19 November 1975, Case 38-75, *Nederlandse Spoorwegen* [1975] ECR 1439, para 25.

compendium issued by the WCO.[26] The WTO considers the HS explanatory notes to be important utilities for the interpretation of the HS nomenclature.[27] Additionally, the ECJ also considers them to be valuable instruments for assistance in interpretation matters,[28] in particular in cases where there is no EU provision or CN explanatory note to the EU's Combined Nomenclature.[29]

Furthermore, the European Commission has made clear that its own CN explanatory notes to the Combined Nomenclature do not replace, but merely supplement, the HS explanatory notes.[30] Furthermore, the ECJ decided early on that the CN explanatory notes to the Combined Nomenclature have to be interpreted in the light of HS explanatory notes,[31] which thus constitute an important aid for the interpretation of the Common Customs Tariff.[32] Therefore, the guidance of HS explanatory notes—and also the HS classification opinions—provide for the correct interpretation of the Common Customs Tariff and cannot be ignored by the customs authorities of the EU Member States.[33] This has been confirmed by customs officials in Germany.[34] Nevertheless, because of their lack of legally binding force, it is necessary to consider whether the content of HS explanatory notes—and also of HS classification opinions—is in accordance with the actual provisions of the Common Customs Tariff, and whether or not they alter the meaning of any given provisions.[35]

[26] Lyons, 2008, p 134.

[27] Appellate Body Report, *EC—Computer Equipment*, WT/DS62/AB/R, WT/DS67/AB/R, WT/DS68/AB/R, para 89.

[28] ECJ of 16 December 2010, Case C-339/09, *Skoma-Lux* [2010] ECR I-13251, para 36; ECJ of 27 April 2006, Case C-15/05, *Kawasaki Motors Europe* [2006] ECR I-3657, para 37; ECJ order of 19 January 2005, Case C-206/03, *SmithKline Beecham* [2005] ECR I-415, paras 25, 26; ECJ of 16 September 2004, Case C-396/02, *DFDS* [2004] ECR I-8439, para 28; ECJ of 28 April 1999, Case C-405/97, *Mövenpick Deutschland* [1999] ECR I-2397, para 18; ECJ of 9 February 1999, Case C-280/97, *ROSE Elektrotechnik* [1999] ECR I-689, para 16; ECJ of 10 December 1998, Case C-328/97, *Glob-Sped* [1998] ECR I-8357, para 26.

[29] In particular ECJ of 4 October 1979, Case 11/79, *Cleton* [1979] ECR 3069, paras 9, 10; ECJ of 8 December 1970, Case 14-70, *Deutsche Bakels* [1970] ECR 1001, paras 9, 10; similar ECJ of 20 November 2008, Case C-375/07, *Heuschen & Schrouff Oriëntal Foods Trading BV II* [2008] ECR I-8691, paras 32, 44; see also ECJ, Opinion of Advocate General Fennelly delivered on 8 June 2000, Case C-42/99, *Fábrica de Queijo Eru Portuguesa Ld*ª [2000] ECR I-7691, para 22.

[30] Lux, in: Rüsken (ed), 2013, Vol III, Introduction CN Regulation, para 176.

[31] ECJ of 4 October 1979, Case 11/79, *Cleton* [1979] ECR 3069, para 13.

[32] ECJ of 20 June 2013, Case C-568/11, *Agroferm A/S* [2013] ECR I-0, para 28; ECJ of 6 September 2012, Case C-524/11, *Lowlands Design Holding BV* [2012] ECR I-0, para 33; ECJ of 14 April 2011, Joined Cases C-288/09 and C-289/09, *British Sky Broadcasting Group* [2011] ECR I-2851, para 64; ECJ of 27 April 2006, Case C-15/05, *Kawasaki Motors Europe* [2006] ECR I-3657, para 37; ECJ order of 19 January 2005, Case C-206/03, *SmithKline Beecham* [2005] ECR I-415, paras 25, 26.

[33] Lux, in: Rüsken (ed), 2013, Vol III, Introduction CN Regulation, para 171.

[34] 'Und im Zweifel werden die dann natürlich schon, müssen die auch berücksichtigt werden.' Interview of 7 April 2011 on file with author; 'Man kann also jetzt nicht sagen, Das steht zwar so und so in den Erläuterungen, aber das beachte ich jetzt einmal gar nicht, weil ich anderer Meinung bin. Das geht natürlich auch nicht.' Interview of 13 April 2011 on file with author.

[35] ECJ of 27 April 2006, Case C-15/05, *Kawasaki Motors Europe* [2006] ECR I-3657, para 37; ECJ of 15 September 2005, Case C-495/03, *Intermodal Transports* [2005] ECR I-8151, para 48; ECJ of 9 February 1999, Case C-280/97, *ROSE Elektrotechnik* [1999] ECR I-689, para 23; ECJ of 16 June 1994, Case C-35/93, *Develop Dr Eisbein* [1994] ECR I-2655, para 21; ECJ of 11 July 1980, Case 798/79,

In conclusion, the case law of the ECJ makes no distinction between the interpretative value of HS classification opinions and HS explanatory notes of the WCO, considering them both to be an important aid in the interpretation of the scope of the various tariff headings of the Combined Nomenclature.[36] Especially in cases where no EU provision or CN explanatory note can be found, the HS classification opinions and HS explanatory notes constitute useful guidance.

Interviews with customs officials in Germany confirmed that HS classification opinions and HS explanatory notes form part of the tariff classification, although not that many of them exist.[37] Customs officials of the Section for Classification in the United Kingdom declared HS explanatory notes, as well as CN explanatory notes, to shape virtually every customs classification decision, for they provide some commonality as to what everybody in the EU thinks about specific code positions in the Common Customs Tariff, and thus are widely recognised.[38]

C. Classification Regulations and CN Legal Notes of the European Commission

The European Commission can enact legally binding EU regulations, in the sense of Article 288 paragraph 2 TFEU, for the interpretation of the Combined Nomenclature pursuant to Article 9 paragraph 1 section (a) First Indent Regulation (EEC) 2658/87[39] (CN) and Article 10 Regulation (EEC) 2658/87.[40] Thus, such regulations are directly applicable, precede national law, and can be referred to in customs decisions of national customs authorities. Such binding EU regulations can take the form of a classification regulation or of a legal note to the Combined Nomenclature, depending on their substantive content.

Classification regulations contain specific tariff classification decisions, while legal notes to the Combined Nomenclature regulate certain facts for the CN positions and sub-positions in a general context.[41] CN legal notes can supplement

Chem-Tec [1980] ECR 2639, paras 11, 12; ECJ of 15 February 1977, Joined Cases 69 and 70–76, *Dittmeyer* [1977] ECR 231, para 4.

[36] Lyons, p 173.

[37] '... gehe ich ja an die Einreihung und dann arbeite ich es natürlich ab nach den Rechtsvorschriften ... Und die Erläuterungen auf HS-Ebene gehen natürlich vor den Erläuterungen auf KN-Ebene ... Also letztendlich sind Erläuterungen ja so eine Art ... Zolltariflexikon.' Interview of 7 April 2011 on file with author; 'Ja, das ist ähnlich wie bei den Erläuterungen der Kommission. Erläuterungen sind halt wichtig für die Einreihung.' Interview of 13 April 2011 on file with author.

[38] Interview of 9 January 2012 on file with author.

[39] Council Regulation (EEC) 2658/87 of 23 July 1987 on the tariff and statistical nomenclature and on the Common Customs Tariff, [1987] OJ L256/1–675, last amended by Council Regulation (EC) 254/2000 of 31 January 2000 amending Regulation (EEC) 2658/87 on the tariff and statistical nomenclature and the Common Customs Tariff, [2000] OJ L28/16–18.

[40] Lux, in: Rüsken (ed), 2013, Vol III, Introduction CN Regulation, paras 152, 153 and Art 9 CN (A4), para 3.

[41] Weerth, Witten 2007, pp 170, 175; Lux, in: Rüsken (ed), 2013, Vol III, Introduction CN Regulation, para 153.

existing CN legal notes or be integrated as new legal notes, and are generally applicable implementing acts. They are added, for example, to determine certain analysis methods or to interpret certain undefined legal terms in more detail.[42] Classification regulations are also generally applicable implementing acts, but are construed as single classification decisions determining the tariff classification of certain goods.[43] The European Commission often transforms HS classification opinions of the WCO into classification regulations.[44] However, the European Commission also issues classification regulations without the existence of an HS classification opinion or a judgment of the ECJ.[45]

Both forms of Commission regulations are implementing acts, which interpret the Combined Nomenclature as the superior EU regulation.[46] When enacting EU regulations in the context of the Common Customs Tariff, the European Commission is bound to the EU's obligation pursuant to Article 3 HS Convention, and thus is not allowed to alter the structure of the HS nomenclature.[47] Furthermore, the European Commission is also bound to the requirements of Article 9 Regulation (EEC) 2658/87, meaning it also has no competence to alter the structure of the EU's Combined Nomenclature.[48] Therefore, CN legal notes, as well as classification regulations of the European Commission, cannot alter the scope of a CN position or sub-position.[49]

The Council can exceptionally enact implementing regulations in the form of classification regulations or CN legal notes for the interpretation of the Combined Nomenclature pursuant to Articles 9, 10 Regulation (EEC) 2658/87.[50] However, in order to actually change and modify the Combined Nomenclature of the Common Customs Tariff, the Council has to rely on its competences pursuant to Articles 31, 207 TFEU, and cannot revert to its competences pursuant to Articles 9, 10 Regulation (EEC) 2658/87.[51]

Classification regulations are especially important tools for the settlement of classification disputes between EU Member States.[52] In particular, they constitute a valuable aid for interpretation in cases where goods have to be classified that are similar to the goods subject to a certain EU regulation. The classification

[42] Weerth, Witten 2007, p 171.

[43] Lux, in: Rüsken (ed), 2013, Vol III, Introduction CN Regulation, para 158.

[44] Weerth, Witten 2007, p 171.

[45] ibid, p 171.

[46] ibid, p 170; Lux, in: Rüsken (ed), 2013, Vol III, Introduction CN Regulation, para 154.

[47] Weerth, Witten 2007, pp 171, 175.

[48] ibid, pp 171, 175.

[49] ECJ of 18 July 2007, Case C-310/06, *FTS International* [2007] ECR I-6749, para 21; ECJ of 4 March 2004, Case C-130/02, *Krings* [2004] ECR I-2121, para 26; ECJ of 28 March 2000, Case C-309/98, *Holz Geenen* [2000] ECR I-1975, para 13; ECJ of 14 December 1995, Case C-267/94, *France v Commission* [1995] ECR I-4845, paras 19, 20.

[50] Weerth, Witten 2007, p 170; Lux, in: Rüsken (ed), 2013, Vol III, Introduction CN Regulation, paras 154, 158.

[51] Weerth, Witten 2007, p 170; Lux, in: Rüsken (ed), 2013, Vol III, Introduction CN Regulation, paras 154, 158.

[52] Weerth, Witten 2007, p 171.

determined by a classification regulation has no binding force on similar goods, but its classification criteria can constitute an important indication of the correct classification for such goods.[53] Thus, classification regulations can become relevant by analogy to products similar to those described in the relevant regulation, as the legal principles leading to correct tariff classification remain the same with regard to similar goods.[54]

The analogous application of classification regulations with regard to similar goods, especially when it comes to electromechanical products, was confirmed in an interview with customs officials of the Section for Classification in the United Kingdom:

> The [classification] regulation is applied by analogy. So, not only can you have [the classification regulation applied to] the exact product, as long as you have got enough similarities, then again, you can invoke the [classification] regulation.[55]

This has also been confirmed by customs officials in Germany, who declared that such analogous application can even lead to a general change of interpretation by the customs authorities.[56]

However, the analogous application of classification regulations has been criticised by at least one customs official in Germany because of their nature as individual decisions and the fact that they lack generally explanatory power, on which he opined that they should have only a limited capacity for analogy.[57] In interviews with customs officials in Germany, it was declared that classification regulations are of high value, especially for appeal procedures and difficult tariff classifications,[58] though they are the exception and only regulate single cases. For this reason, classification regulations are not often applied relative to the total number of classification decisions in day-to-day customs work.[59]

However, while customs officials in Germany did not complain about the number of classification regulations issued by the European Commission, one interviewee opined that the European Commission should refrain from establishing a kind of case law.[60] Conversely, customs officials of the Section for Classification in

[53] ECJ of 4 March 2004, Case C-130/02, *Krings* [2004] ECR I-2121, paras 34, 35.

[54] Panel Report, *EC–Selected Customs Matters*, WT/DS315/R, para 4.111.

[55] Interview of 9 January 2012 on file with author.

[56] 'Diese ähnlichen [Waren] auf die das Recht anwendbar ist, da kommt es jetzt zu einer Änderung der Einreihungsauffassung.' Interview of 13 April 2011 on file with author.

[57] 'Und das sind natürlich wirklich Einzelfälle und da ist auch nichts Verallgemeinerungswürdiges darin.' Interview of 20 April 2011 on file with author.

[58] 'Und ja, die sind sehr hilfreich insofern das sie halt etwas regeln … Also da kann ich dann mein Rechtsbehelfsverfahren dementsprechend abschließen.' Interview of 7 April 2011 on file with author.

[59] 'Es gibt natürlich nicht für jede Art von Waren eine Einreihungsverordnung … und deswegen ist der Fall, dass ich eine Einreihungsverordnung berücksichtigen muss, eher die Ausnahme.' Interview of 7 April 2011 on file with author.

[60] 'Wobei auch wieder problematisch ist, umso mehr solche Einreihungsverordnungen kommen, umso schwerer wird diese ganze Sache überschaubar dann. Also wir tendieren dann zu einer Art Präzedenzrecht, was wir ja eigentlich in unserem Kulturkreis hier nicht haben.' Interview of 20 April 2011 on file with author.

the United Kingdom, who are more familiar with case law, pleaded for more classification regulations. In their view, if a classification opinion was already set, any problem would be pre-empted:

> There is never going to be too many simply because a regulation only covers one product ... So from the legal perspective, having a regulation is great because it means that ultimately, regardless of what the trader wants, we cannot go anywhere. He may favour a different code, but if there is a regulation, we have to adhere to it.[61]

1. *The Relation of Classification Regulations and CN Legal Notes to WTO Law, WCO Law and the Harmonised System*

The European Commission has a wide margin of discretion regarding classification decisions, determined through classification regulations as well as in the content of CN legal notes.[62] The control of the ECJ is limited to the examination of evident errors or abuse of discretion, such as the alteration of the wording of the Common Customs Tariff through a classification regulation.[63] In this context, the European Commission has to comply with higher-ranking EU law when issuing CN legal notes and classification regulations, as well as to consider HS classification opinions and HS explanatory notes.[64]

However, in case of conflict between EU law and HS classification opinions or HS explanatory notes, national customs authorities and national courts have to follow binding EU law if relevant, this according to the interpretation of the ECJ. In the event of doubt, it is for the ECJ to decide whether or not an HS classification opinion is applied.[65] Moreover, the Court can even declare a classification regulation to be invalid.[66]

When examining EU classification regulations, the ECJ even considers the decisions from WTO dispute settlements, although WTO law typically does not constitute an examination criteria and decisions of a dispute settlement cannot bind the Court.[67] A WTO measure can only exceptionally become directly effective, if the EU gives effect to these rules in an EU measure.[68] These exceptions are known

[61] Interview of 9 January 2012 on file with author.

[62] See, inter alia, ECJ of 18 July 2007, Case C-310/06, *FTS International* [2007] ECR I-6749, para 21, and the case law cited.

[63] See, inter alia, ECJ of 22 December 2010, Case C-273/09, *Premis Medical BV* [2010] ECR I-13783, paras 31, 40, and the case law cited.

[64] ibid, paras 31, 41, 46; ECJ of 8 February 1990, Case C-233/88, *Gijs van de Kolk* [1990] ECR I-265, para 9; ECJ of 19 November 1975, Case 38-75, *Nederlandse Spoorwegen*, [1975] ECR 1439, paras 23, 24, 25, 26.

[65] ECJ of 18 July 2007, Case C-142/06, *Olicom A/S* [2007] ECR I-6675, para 31; ECJ of 9 February 1999, Case C-280/97, *ROSE Elektrotechnik* [1999] ECR I-689, paras 23, 24.

[66] ECJ of 27 April 2006, Case C-15/05, *Kawasaki Motors Europe* [2006] ECR I-3657, paras 37, 51.

[67] See, inter alia, ECJ of 27 September 2007, Case C-351/04, *Ikea Wholesale* [2007] ECR I-7723, paras 29, 30, and the case law cited.

[68] Weiß, in: Herrmann/Weiß/Ohler (eds), 2007, para 133; Grayston, (6) 2011 GTCJ (3), pp 149–55 (151).

as the Fediol Doctrine and the Nakajima Doctrine. In the *Fediol* case,[69] the ECJ decided that WTO law can exceptionally constitute criteria for the review of EU secondary law if the EU law in question implements a specific WTO obligation of the EU.[70] In the *Nakajima* case,[71] the ECJ decided that if the EU legal act in question explicitly states that it was adopted for the purpose of implementing a specific WTO legal act and to further interpret and make applicable those WTO provisions, then the EU has to ensure compliance with WTO law in this regard.[72]

However, such direct effect of WTO law is problematic in cases where the EU measure in question does not explicitly recite the reason for its adoption as being the need to implement WTO law as required by the ECJ,[73] yet contains identical provisions to the obligations arising under WTO law and, therefore, must have been adopted in order to achieve such implementation.[74] Meanwhile, any direct effect of WTO law in the EU has been regarded by the ECJ as being highly restricted.[75] Thus, the extension of direct effects of WTO law to EU legal acts that implement WTO law without explicitly referring to it seems unlikely.[76]

However, the ECJ tends to come to decisions independently from any WTO law considerations. Yet its conclusions tend to 'incidentally' match the conclusions in relevant dispute settlements,[77] a tendency which has been called a 'muted dialogue'.[78] In truth, the ECJ regularly avoids inconsistencies between its judgements and WTO Appellate Body decisions.[79] Therefore, to avoid a classification regulation being declared invalid by the ECJ, the European Commission often adjusts CN legal notes and classification regulations to the interpretation preferred by the WCO and the WTO.[80]

[69] ECJ of 22 June 1989, Case 70/87, *Fediol* [1989] ECR 1781.

[70] ibid, paras 19, 22.

[71] ECJ of 7 May 1991, Case C-69/89, *Nakajima* [1991] ECR I-2069.

[72] ibid, paras 28, 29, 30, 31.

[73] ECJ of 1 March 2005, Case C-377/02, *Léon van Parys* [2005] ECR I-1465, paras 39, 40; ECJ of 30 September 2003, Case C-93/02 P, *Biret International v Council* [2003] ECR I-10497, para 53; ECJ of 12 March 2002, Joined Cases C-27/00 and C-122/00, *Omega Air and others* [2002] ECR I-2569, para 94; ECJ of 23 November 1999, Case C-149/96, *Portugal v Council* [1999] ECR I-8395, para 49; ECJ of 5 October 1994, Case C-280/93, *Germany v Council* [1994] ECR I-4973, para 111; ECJ of 7 May 1991, Case C-69/89, *Nakajima* [1991] ECR I-2069, para 31; ECJ of 22 June 1989, Case 70/87 *Fediol* [1989] ECR 1781, paras 19–22.

[74] Grayston, (6) 2011 GTCJ (3), pp 149–55 (151, 152).

[75] ECJ of 27 September 2007, Case C-351/04, *Ikea Wholesale* [2007] ECR I-7723, para 35; ECJ of 1 March 2005, Case C-377/02, *Léon van Parys* [2005] ECR I-1465, paras 50, 51, 52, 53, 54; ECJ of 30 September 2003, Case C-93/02 P, *Biret International v Council* [2003] ECR I-10497, para 52; ECJ of 9 January 2003, Case C-76/00 P, *Petrotub and Republica v Council* [2003] ECR I-79, para 53; ECJ of 12 March 2002, Joined Cases C-27/00 and C-122/00, *Omega Air and others* [2002] ECR I-2569, paras 85–93; ECJ of 23 November 1999, Case C-149/96, *Portugal v Council*, [1999] ECR I-8395, paras 36–49, especially para 47.

[76] Grayston, (6) 2011 GTCJ (3), pp 149–55 (151).

[77] Herrmann, 2008 CMLRev (45), pp 1507–18 (1508); Herrmann/Streinz, in: von Arnauld (ed), 2014, § 11 pp 587–679, para 132.

[78] Bronckers, (11) 2008 JIEL (4), pp 885–98 (886, 889, 890).

[79] ibid, pp 885–98 (889, 890).

[80] Lux, in: Rüsken (ed), 2013, Vol III, Introduction CN Regulation, para 156.4; Grayston, (6) 2011 GTCJ (3), pp 149–55 (151).

2. *Timely Applicability of Classification Regulations*

Regarding the temporal effect of EU classification regulations, there seem to be slightly different opinions.[81] Classification regulations based on the Combined Nomenclature are of legal character and thus cannot affect the past.[82] Nevertheless, the European Commission and most national customs authorities hold the view that EU classification regulations can still be of use for customs decisions regarding classification issues that occurred before the adaption of the EU classification regulation in question.[83] In such a case, classification regulations constitute a valuable aid for interpretation.[84] Furthermore, the ECJ has acknowledged classification regulations as able to reflect and confirm the correct classification of a tariff position also when the interpretation was carried out before the entry into force of the relevant classification regulation.[85] However, in recent case law the ECJ has been more hesitant concerning such effects of classification regulations.[86]

Nevertheless, the retroactive consideration of classification regulations by national customs authorities, which has been tolerated by EU Member States and the European Commission, has been criticised as violating the principles of legal certainty and legal predictability.[87] In this context, one has to differentiate two scenarios. If a classification regulation confirms an interpretation of a tariff position that has already been carried out before the adoption of the classification regulation, the principles of legal certainty and legal predictability have not been violated. However, classification regulations that merely confirm an existing interpretation cannot provide the basis for correct classification with regard to issues that occurred before the adoption of the relevant classification regulation; they can only serve as an argument for the correct interpretation. In such a case, the classification regulation only supports the interpretation that would have been carried out anyway, and thus its consideration has not been objected to by the ECJ. However, if a classification regulation leads to a change in the interpretation of the Common Customs Tariff, any retroactive consideration would indeed be unlawful.

[81] Weerth, Witten 2007, p 170; Lux, in: Rüsken (ed), 2013, Vol III, Introduction CN Regulation, para 155.

[82] Lux, in: Rüsken (ed), 2013, Vol III, Introduction CN Regulation, para 158; Grayston, (6) 2011 GTCJ (3), pp 149–55 (150); Lyons, 2008, p 150.

[83] Lux, in: Rüsken (ed), 2013, Vol III, Introduction CN Regulation, para 155.

[84] Lux, in: Rüsken (ed), 2013, Vol III, Introduction CN Regulation, para 155.

[85] In particular ECJ of 28 March 1979, Case 158/78, *Biegi* [1979] ECR 1103, para 16; similar ECJ of 27 November 2008, Case C-403/07, *Metherma GmbH & Co KG* [2008] ECR I-8921, para 41; ECJ of 7 June 2001, Case C-479/99, *CBA Computer Handels- und Beteiligungs GmbH* [2001] ECR I-4391, para 31.

[86] ECJ of 27 November 2008, Case C-403/07, *Metherma GmbH & Co KG* [2008] ECR I-8921, para 41; ECJ of 7 June 2001, Case C-479/99, *CBA Computer Handels- und Beteiligungs GmbH* [2001] ECR I-4391, para 31.

[87] Kuplewatzky/Rovetta, (7) 2012 GTCJ (11 and 12), pp 454–60 (457, 459).

3. *Summary*

In summary, CN legal notes and classification regulations are of great importance for the interpretation of the Common Customs Tariff. As legally binding means of interpretation, they are valid and have direct effect throughout the EU. They have to be applied and considered by national customs authorities, which can even refer to them when issuing a customs decision. Furthermore, EU classification regulations are also indications for the correct classification of goods imported before the coming into force of the regulation in question as well as for the correct classification of goods similar to those referred to in a given regulation. In these cases, EU classification regulations have no binding force but constitute a valuable aid for the interpretation of the Common Customs Tariff.

D. CN Explanatory Notes of the European Commission

In order to assist national customs administrations in applying the Combined Nomenclature, the European Commission is authorised pursuant to Article 9 paragraph 1 section (a) second indent Regulation (EEC) 2658/87[88] (CN) to adopt explanatory notes to the Combined Nomenclature similar to the HS explanatory notes of the WCO. CN explanatory notes of the European Commission are a compendium of texts for the interpretation of the EU's Combined Nomenclature and constitute an important aid for the application of the Common Customs Tariff.[89]

The CN explanatory notes of the European Commission serve a commentary function, thereby preventing different classification opinions in the EU and facilitating the uniform application of the Combined Nomenclature in day-to-day customs work.[90] For this purpose, the European Commission takes the HS explanatory notes regarding the six-digit HS positions and supplements them with CN explanatory notes regarding the EU's part of the Combined Nomenclature.[91] The subject matter of the European Commission's CN explanatory notes is often a more detailed interpretation of undefined legal terms in the Combined Nomenclature.

CN explanatory notes are issued according to the procedure laid down in Article 9 paragraph 1 section (a) second indent and Article 10 Regulation (EEC) 2658/87, which refers to the management procedure of the Comitology Decision[92]

[88] Council Regulation (EEC) 2658/87 of 23 July 1987 on the tariff and statistical nomenclature and on the Common Customs Tariff, [1987] OJ L256/1–675.

[89] See, inter alia, ECJ of 12 December 2013, Case C-450/12, *HARK GmbH & Co KG* [2013] ECR I-0, para 32; ECJ of 7 May 2009, Case C-150/08, *Siebrand BV* [2009] ECR I-3941, para 25, and the case law cited.

[90] Weerth, Witten 2007, p 183; Lux, in: Rüsken (ed), 2013, Vol III, Introduction CN Regulation, para 179.

[91] Weerth, Witten 2007, p 183; similarly: Grayston, (6) 2011 GTCJ (3), pp 149–55 (151).

[92] Council Decision 1999/468/EC of 28 June 1999 laying down the procedures for the exercise of implementing powers conferred on the Commission, [1999] OJ L184/23–26, and Council Decision 2006/512/EC of 17 July 2006 amending Council Decision 1999/468/EC laying down the procedures for the exercise of implementing powers conferred on the Commission, [2006] OJ L200/11–13.

that has been replaced by the examination procedure of the Comitology Regulation pursuant to Article 13 paragraph 1 section (b) in conjunction with Article 5 Regulation (EU) 182/2011.[93] Nevertheless, CN explanatory notes are publicised in Series C of the Official Journal—as opposed to Series L of the Official Journal, which is for acts with legal character. They are not to be mistaken for the preliminary provisions and legal notes of the Combined Nomenclature, which are an integral part of the Combined Nomenclature pursuant to Article 1 paragraph 2 section (c) Regulation (EEC) 2658/87, and thus have legally binding force.[94]

1. *Soft Law Character of CN Explanatory Notes*

CN explanatory notes are valuable instruments for assistance in interpretation matters, as they explain and describe the existing legal situation and often reflect a common classification practice in the EU.[95] Customs officials of the Section for Classification in the United Kingdom claimed that HS explanatory notes, as well as CN explanatory notes, shaped virtually every decision on customs classification, as they provided some basis for knowing what everybody in the EU thinks about specific code positions in the Common Customs Tariff: 'The HSNs [HS explanatory notes] and the CNNs [CN explanatory notes] are what we actually use.'[96] Although they have no legal character,[97] they have been called 'persuasive', also for economic operators, who often accept a customs decision more easily when the customs authority can refer to an EU-wide explanatory note.[98] Customs officials interviewed in Germany concurred with the sentiment that CN explanatory notes can provide useful guidance.[99]

The European Commission chooses to issue explanatory notes when the comment in question is of a practical character describing the function of certain goods, or their affiliation to a certain position, or refers to non-legally binding

[93] Regulation (EU) 182/2011 of the European Parliament and of the Council of 16 February 2011 laying down the rules and general principles concerning mechanisms for control by Member States of the Commission's exercise of implementing powers, [2011] OJ L55/13–18.

[94] Lux, in: Rüsken (ed), 2013, Vol III, Introduction CN Regulation, para 179.

[95] ECJ of 14 April 2011, Joined Cases C-288/09 and C-289/09, *British Sky Broadcasting Group* [2011] ECR I-2851, para 92; ECJ of 27 April 2006, Case C-15/05, *Kawasaki Motors Europe* [2006] ECR I-3657, para 37; ECJ of 16 September 2004, Case C-396/02, *DFDS* [2004] ECR I-8439, para 28; ECJ of 28 March 2000, Case C-309/98, *Holz Geenen* [2000] ECR I-1975, para 14; ECJ of 28 April 1999, Case C-405/97, *Mövenpick Deutschland* [1999] ECR I-2397, para 18; ECJ of 20 June 1996, Case C-121/95, *VOBIS Microcomputer* [1996] ECR I-3047, para 13.

[96] Interview of 9 January 2012 on file with author.

[97] ECJ of 5 June 2008, Case C-312/07, *JVC France SAS* [2008] ECR I-4165, para 34; ECJ of 27 April 2006, Case C-15/05, *Kawasaki Motors Europe* [2006] ECR I-3657, para 37; ECJ of 15 September 2005, Case C-495/03, *Intermodal Transports* [2005] ECR I-8151, para 48; ECJ of 15 February 1977, Joined Cases 69 and 70-76, *Dittmeyer* [1977] ECR 231, para 4.

[98] Interview of 9 January 2012 on file with author.

[99] 'Das geht gut.' Interview of 7 April 2011 on file with author; 'Das funktioniert … Auch die sind in sich verständlich.' Interview of 13 April 2011 on file with author; similar assessments have been made in Interviews of 10 May 2011 and 23 May 2011.

HS explanatory notes.[100] Because of their relevance to practice, there seems to be a tendency to upgrade CN explanatory notes at the operational level. Customs officials in Germany stressed a problematic tendency that CN explanatory notes are often subject to interpretative legal provisions; this would set the wrong priorities and create too much of a distance to legal provisions when making customs decisions.[101] Indeed, CN explanatory notes are an interpretative aid and thus not subject to interpretation themselves—unlike the CN positions, preliminary provisions and legal notes in the sense of Article 1 paragraph 2 section (c) Regulation (EEC) 2658/87 as integral parts of the Combined Nomenclature. Because of their lack of legal character, national customs authorities cannot base their customs classification decisions on a CN explanatory note. Furthermore, in the event of conflict between a CN explanatory note and the rules of classification applicable to the Combined Nomenclature, the latter must prevail and the CN explanatory note has to be ignored.[102]

However, while some EU Member States use the CN explanatory notes directly for interpretative purposes, other EU Member States transform them into national administrative provisions that do indeed have internal legal force within the relevant national customs administration.[103] In Germany, for example, the CN explanatory notes are part of the German Electronic Customs Tariff,[104] which contains not only the HS explanatory notes, HS classification opinions and CN explanatory notes, as well as binding EU classification regulations, but also relevant case law of the ECJ, national decisions, and national notes of the German Federal Ministry of Finance.

In principle, the EU Member States are not allowed to enact legally binding rules for interpretation of the Common Customs Tariff insofar as there exist directly applicable EU regulations. The mandated uniform application of the Common Customs Tariff would be endangered if the EU Member States were allowed to individually regulate the interpretation of the Combined Nomenclature and the scope of the single tariff position.[105] Nevertheless, the issuing of national explanatory notes for interpretation, having no formal legal character but only internal legal effects, is still permitted, for such self-binding interpretative aids can neither alter scope nor meaning of positions of the Combined Nomenclature.[106]

[100] Lux, in: Rüsken (ed), 2013, Vol III, Introduction CN Regulation, para 172.

[101] 'Also in der Praxis macht man es sicherlich häufig anders. Da kuckt man zuerst in die Erläuterungen. Das ist aber ein Weg, der nicht akzeptable ist … denn ich meine die Rangfolge ist eindeutig: Erst kommt das Recht und dann die Erläuterungen zur Auslegung. Und wenn man über die Auslegung der Auslegung diskutiert, dann wird es schon fatal.' Interview of 20 April 2011 on file with author.

[102] Grayston, (6) 2011 GTCJ (3), pp 149–55 (151).

[103] Weerth, Witten 2007, p 185; Lux, in: Rüsken (ed), 2013, Vol III, Introduction CN Regulation, para 134.

[104] Elektronischer Zolltarif (EZT).

[105] Lyons, 2008, p 178.

[106] Weerth, Witten 2007, p 185; Lux, in: Rüsken (ed), 2013, Vol III, Introduction CN Regulation, para 134.

It has been claimed that such national explanatory notes supplementing CN explanatory notes could lead to non-uniform application of the Common Customs Tariff.[107] Yet in reality, national administrative provisions are only applicable in the EU Member State issuing them, which renders them irrelevant for the uniform interpretation of the Common Customs Tariff throughout the EU. Nonetheless, national explanatory notes have to be in accordance with the actual provisions of the Common Customs Tariff. They are of a descriptive character and comment on the legal situation, which is only meant to additionally facilitate the practical day-to-day work of tariff classification, while the main interpretative aids are the HS classification opinions, HS explanatory notes, CN explanatory notes and EU classification regulations.

In this context, it is important to know that, in practice, every classification process follows the hierarchical structure of the Common Customs Tariff. Therefore, the use of instruments for interpretative assistance proceeds along the hierarchical structure of the Combined Nomenclature. This was confirmed by customs officials in Germany.[108] Therefore, national notes could never replace HS explanatory notes or CN explanatory notes, which precede them and are applied at an earlier stage of the classification process. In many cases, they are not even used because the classification issue has already been clarified by the use of HS explanatory notes and CN explanatory notes.[109]

The priority of EU customs law has been confirmed in interviews with customs officials in Germany.[110] Furthermore, customs officials in Germany declared that in the area of classification, there seems to be no discrepancy between national instructions and EU customs law or soft law acts such as CN explanatory notes.[111] At an earlier time, when the European Commission had not yet issued many instruments for interpretation of the Common Customs Tariff, the ECJ permitted such national explanatory notes.[112] This is why there are no similar judgments in

[107] Weerth, Witten 2007, p 188; Rogmann, 2008 ZfZ 3, pp 57–69 (67).

[108] 'Es beginnt mit dem HS, es geht über die KN, es geht zu den nationalen Vorschriften.' Interview of 10 May 2011 on file with author; similar assessments have been made in Interviews of 7 April, of 13 April 2011, and of 23 May 2011 on file with author.

[109] 'Diese anderen Entscheidungen, also wie was einzureihen ist, das wird ja doch meist früher schon eben vorgegeben auf Ebene der Erläuterungen oder vorher schon auf Ebene der Verordnung beziehungsweise der Rechtsvorschriften.' Interview of 7 April 2011 on file with author; similar assessments have been made in interviews of 1 April 2011, of 13 April 2011, of 20 April 2011, of 10 May 2011, of 20 May 2011, and of 23 May 2011 on file with author.

[110] 'Die Einreihungsverordnung, Änderung HS und so weiter, die bewerte ich als europäisches Recht was höher angesiedelt ist in der Hierarchie.' Interview of 13 April 2014 on file with author; similar assessments have been made in interviews of 1 April 2011, of 7 April 2011, of 20 April 2011, of 10 May 2011, of 20 May 2011, and of 23 May 2011 on file with author.

[111] 'Was in Leitlinien steht reflektieren dann die Dienstanweisungen.' Interview of 20 April 2011 on file with author; similar assessments in interviews of 1 April, of 7 April 2011, of 13 April 2011 and of 20 April 2011 in file with author.

[112] ECJ of 8 December 1970, Case 14-70, *Deutsche Bakels* [1970] ECR 1001, paras 3, 4, 5; ECJ of 18 June 1970, Case 74-69, *Krohn* [1970] ECR 451, para 4; ECJ of 18 February 1970, Case 40-69, *Bollmann* [1970] ECR 69, para 4.

recent case law – national explanatory notes are no longer used as the basis for tariff classification decisions.

2. *The Problematic* De Facto *Binding Force of CN Explanatory Notes*

In addition to the facts outlined above, there has been criticism that—just as with soft law acts of the European Commission in general—CN explanatory notes also have a kind of de facto binding force and in practice are seen as alternatives to legally binding EU classification regulations.[113] This misbelief in the binding force of CN explanatory notes that have been published in the Official Journal of the EU Series C was confirmed in interviews with customs officials in Germany.[114] At a more functional level, the fundamental difference between these two instruments seems to have been largely missed, overlooking the fact that classification regulations are legally binding acts of the European Commission, while CN explanatory notes have no legal character and have even been regarded as having retroactive effect.[115] In truth, although they do not constitute a legislative measure in legal theory, CN explanatory notes have been used with retrospective impact because they show how certain goods should be classified in general, which has been regarded as to also show how these goods should have been correctly classified in the past.[116]

However, CN explanatory notes are granted a kind of binding force on national customs authorities in the context of issuing binding tariff information (BTI). A BTI decision is valid EU-wide for a specific period of time and determines the correct classification of a certain product, meaning the economic operator addressed by this decision can rely on this classification vis-á-vis every customs authority in the EU.[117] In the context of BTI, CN explanatory notes have a certain procedural status in EU customs law pursuant to Article 12 paragraph 5 section (a) CCC (now Article 34 paragraph 7 section (a) UCC and also Article 124-307 paragraph 3 draft-MCCIP together with Article 124-3-08 paragraphs 8 and 9 draft-MCCIP). The adoption of a new CN explanatory note has the effect of cancelling all existing national BTIs given in relation to the heading concerned. In this context, a CN explanatory note has the same impact as a judgment of the ECJ, even though a CN explanatory note is issued by the European Commission as mere guidance, following consultation with the EU Member States through the Customs Code Committee.[118]

[113] Grayston, (6) 2011 GTCJ (3), pp 149–155 (155).

[114] 'Doch. Geänderte KN-Erläuterungen und geänderte HS-Erläuterungen sind als Rechtsakt genauso zu bewerten wie Verordnung. [Zustimmung des Kollegen] … Das sind … wenn wir nationale Änderungen der Erläuterungen haben, dann hat das nicht den Rechtscharakter wie eine Erläuterung, die durch das Amtsblatt auch veröffentlicht wird.' Interview of 13 April 2011 on file with author.

[115] Grayston, (6) 2011 GTCJ (3), pp 149–55 (155).

[116] ibid, pp 149–55 (151).

[117] A detailed analysis of Binding Tariff Information (BTI) can be found in Chapter 10.I.E.

[118] Grayston, (6) 2011 GTCJ (3), pp 149–55 (151).

Furthermore, the ECJ—referring to this content of Article 12 paragraph 5 section (a) CCC—has decided that national customs authorities must comply with CN explanatory notes when issuing BTIs in order to ensure the uniform application of EU customs law in the EU.[119] This is the case even if applying the relevant CN explanatory note appears to lead to a conflict with the Combined Nomenclature. In such a case of conflict, the EU Member State in question is to refer the matter to the Customs Code Committee as provided for in Article 247 CCC in accordance with the procedure referred to in Article 8 Regulation (EEC) 2658/87.[120]

Although the content of Article 12 paragraph 5 CCC cannot be found in the Modernised Customs Code itself, it reappears in the draft-modernised implementing provisions, namely Article 124-307 paragraph 3 draft-MCCIP together with Article 124-3-08 paragraphs 8 and 9 draft-MCCIP. Article 32 paragraph 3 and Article 33 section (a) of the UCC proposal corresponded to these draft-implementing provisions by authorising the European Commission to define cases in which a BTI loses its validity. Moreover, the final Union Customs Code now similarly states that BTI decisions shall be revoked when they are no longer compatible with the interpretation of the Combined Nomenclature because of newly issued CN explanatory notes or because of a judgement of the ECJ, see Article 34 paragraph 7 Section (a) UCC. Therefore, CN explanatory notes, which in legal theory are construed as a guidance instrument of non-legal character, in practice have been elevated to the status of law insofar as they relate to BTI issuance[121] and this character will persist despite the great reform.

Regarding the criticism surrounding the dispute settlement in *EC—Selected Customs Matters,*[122] where the Panel encouraged the EU to focus on improving consistency of application, the concern of the EU to ensure the uniform application of the Combined Nomenclature is understandable.[123] Nevertheless, even if the EU Member States push the European Commission to deliver a high level of mandatory guidance,[124] classification decisions have to be made by national customs authorities, and thus such guidance should only provide information that has to be taken into account when customs officials take their own customs decisions and should not prevent the own considerations of customs officials.[125] Therefore, the European Commission's request that national customs administrations view CN explanatory notes as akin to opinions by a higher authority in order to ensure uniform implementation of EU customs classification law should be treated with caution.[126]

[119] ECJ of 14 April 2011, Joined Cases C-288/09 and C-289/09, *British Sky Broadcasting Group* [2011] ECR I-2851, para 93.

[120] ibid, paras 93, 95, 96.

[121] Kuplewatzky/Rovetta, (7) 2012 GTCJ (11 and 12), pp 454–60 (456).

[122] WT/DS315.

[123] Panel Report, *EC—Selected Customs Matters*, WT/DS315/R, for example paras 7.191; 7.295, 7.304.

[124] Grayston, (6) 2011 GTCJ (3), pp 149–55 (155).

[125] Grayston, (6) 2011 GTCJ (3), pp 149–55 (155).

[126] Kuplewatzky/Rovetta, (7) 2012 GTCJ (11 and 12), pp 454–60 (456).

Regarding CN explanatory notes, the tendency of the European Commission, and even of the ECJ, to grant soft law acts of the European Commission a strong de facto binding force seems to have been an open secret for a long time.[127] However, the de facto binding force of CN explanatory notes risks the EU being held potential liable before the WTO under Article X:1 GATT 1994 and Article X:2 GATT 1994. In fact, the Panel in *EC—IT Products* found that CN explanatory notes—despite their soft law character in EU customs law—are measures that can be challenged in WTO dispute settlements.[128]

Furthermore, the Panel found the lack of legally binding force of CN explanatory notes under EU customs law did not preclude them from being contemplated by 'law, regulations, judicial decisions, and administrative rulings' under Article X:1 GATT 1994[129]—provided they have the potential to affect trade and traders.[130] This potential to affect trade and traders requires a certain degree of authoritativeness, which the Panel found to be assigned to CN explanatory notes because of their de facto binding force.[131] One of the most interesting findings of the Panel was the lack of relevance of the legal character of the measure in question, because the Panel found it to be sufficient that the CN explanatory note lead to a change in the interpretation of an EU regulation[132]—notwithstanding that the alleged violation was the result of interpretation rather than of a regulation.[133]

The European Commission's CN explanatory notes have to be used with care to avoid the violation of obligations pursuant to Article X GATT 1994. According to *EC—IT Products*, the European Commission's CN explanatory notes can be challenged because of their de facto binding force. Therefore, in the future a panel in a WTO dispute settlement could demolish the system of soft law guidance that the European Commission is relying on. This could eventually put in question the uniform administration of EU customs law in the EU and result in a second WTO dispute settlement because of an alleged violation of Article X:3(a) GATT 1994.[134]

Furthermore, a HS classification opinion, which is a measure of soft law issued by the WCO and thus in the end is very similar to CN explanatory notes with regard to their function and legal nature, has been successfully challenged before the ECJ. Surprisingly, in *DHL Danzas*,[135] the ECJ declared HS opinions to not have legally binding force, being merely an important aid in the interpretation of the Common Customs Tariff,[136] but nevertheless compared HS explanatory notes

[127] ibid, pp 454–60 (456).

[128] ibid, paras 7.158–7.160, 7.777, 7.778.

[129] ibid, paras 7.1017–7.1029.

[130] ibid, para 7.1026.

[131] ibid, paras 7.1028, 7.1029.

[132] ibid, paras 7.1110.

[133] Van Den Hende, (6) 2011 GTCJ (4), pp 215–16 (215).

[134] Kuplewatzky/Rovetta, (7) 2012 GTCJ (11 and 12), pp 454–60 (458).

[135] ECJ order of 19 January 2012, Case 227/11, *DHL Danzas* [2012] ECR I-0 (full text only available in French and Dutch).

[136] ibid, para 40.

with classification regulations with regard to their legislative nature.[137] This comparison only makes sense if the ECJ thereby wanted to refer to the de facto binding force of soft law measures such as HS classification opinions or CN explanatory notes in the area of classification. Customs experts therefore argue that in this order, the ECJ implicitly declared soft law measures with de facto binding force to be contestable. Thus this order also carries the potential to demolish the system of non-binding guidance measures used by the European Commission.[138]

Therefore, the lesson to be learned from the Panel in *EC—IT Products* and also from the ECJ in *DHL Danzas* is that soft law measures of the European Commission have to be judged by their own standards. The European Commission and national customs administrations of EU Member States grant soft law measures in the area of customs classification a de facto binding force. As a consequence, the application of those soft law measures has to comply with general principles of law to avoid judicial consequences. The need to be careful in the use of the de facto binding force of CN explanatory notes in the area of tariff classification is of special relevance with regard to the prohibition on retroactive use, which has to be analysed further.

3. *The Problematic Combination of* De Facto *Binding Force and Retroactive Effect of CN Explanatory Notes*

In addition to the functions described above, CN explanatory notes have been used with retroactive effect. However, the retroactive use of CN explanatory notes can run contrary to the principles of legal certainty and predictability,[139] for example when the new interpretation is used for the retroactive collection of customs duty from traders. As already alluded to,[140] soft law acts changing the interpretation of a legal act cannot retroactively lead to an unfavourable decision based on the new interpretation.[141]

Nevertheless, in the past such practice seems to have been accepted by the European Commission, national customs administrations and traders alike.[142] In fact, Article 222 CCC (Article 108 UCC/former Article 72 MCC) allows national customs authorities in the EU Member States to collect an import duty retroactively going back up to three years. The issuing of a CN explanatory note by the European Commission has regularly led national customs authorities to apply the newly harmonised classification to all imports that took place over the last three years and to collect the additional duty if the previous classification resulted in

[137] ibid, para 42: 'caractère constitutive'.

[138] Kuplewatzky/Rovetta, (7) 2012 GTCJ (11 and 12), pp 454–60 (458).

[139] Hofmann/Rowe/Türk, 2007, p 576.

[140] See Chapter 8.II.C.3.a.

[141] ECJ of 28 June 2005, Joined Cases C-189/02 P, C-202/02 P, C-205/02 to C-208/02 and C-213/02 P, *Dansk Rørindustri* [2005] ECR I-5425, paras 214 et seq.

[142] Kuplewatzky/Rovetta, (7) 2012 GTCJ (11 and 12), pp 454–60 (456, 457).

the charge of a lower duty.[143] Such retroactive application of a new interpretation of a legal provision establishing an unfavourable measure in the form of a higher customs duty violates the principles of legal certainty and predictability. Indeed, it has already been stated that the European Commission, as well as national customs administrations and even traders in this context, have stretched the use of CN explanatory notes 'to the breaking point.'[144]

Any retrospective use of CN explanatory notes should be avoided, taking into account that CN explanatory notes are contestable because of their de facto binding force. Indeed, the prohibition of retroactive effect could include all measures, whether they are legally binding or not.[145] In fact, the Panel in *EC—IT Products*, as has already been alluded to,[146] found the conditions for violation with regard to Article X:2 GATT 1994 to be fulfilled by the CN explanatory note in question because its retroactive use affected 'an advance in a rate of duty'.[147]

Moreover, the ECJ in *DHL Danzas* decided that HS classification opinions of the WCO, which in the end are very similar to CN explanatory notes, cannot be applied retroactively before their date of adoption.[148] Indeed, the ECJ denied the retroactive application of the HS classification opinion in question, which had provided the basis for declaring a classification regulation invalid that had been used for the classification of goods imported before the new HS classification opinion had been issued.[149] This places a clear bar on the retroactive usage of interpretative guidance instruments for the uniform implementation of EU customs law in classification matters, insofar as this usage leads to a change of the interpretation used so far.[150]

4. *Summary*

In summary, the CN explanatory notes are considered to be a valid aid in the interpretation of the Combined Nomenclature and constitute an important means of ensuring the uniform application of the Common Customs Tariff by the customs authorities of the EU Member States. Therefore, when proceeding a tariff classification, the customs authorities have to take into consideration not only the wording and scheme of the Common Customs Tariff, but also the content of the CN explanatory notes. In practice, CN explanatory notes seem to be considered to be binding EU measures and thus possess a de facto binding force, which is not unproblematic. The long accepted practice in the European Customs Union of

[143] Van Den Hende, (6) 2011 GTCJ (4), pp 215–16 (216).
[144] Kuplewatzky/Rovetta, (7) 2012 GTCJ (11 and 12), pp 454–60 (458).
[145] ibid, pp 454–60 (457).
[146] See Chapter 10.I.D.2.
[147] Panel Report, *EC–IT Products*, WT/DS375,376,377/R, para 7.1110.
[148] ECJ order of 19 January 2012, Case 227/11, *DHL Danzas* [2012] ECR I-0, paras 41–44 (full text only available in French and Dutch).
[149] ibid, para 43.
[150] Kuplewatzky/Rovetta, (7) 2012 GTCJ (11 and 12), pp 454–60 (458).

granting measures of interpretative guidance such as CN explanatory notes both a de facto binding force similar to legal measures and a retroactive effect bears the potential risk of demolishing the European Commission's system for ensuring the uniform administration of EU customs law, as this system relies to some extent on the use of soft law measures of interpretative customs guidance.

E. Binding Tariff Information (BTI)

The Binding Tariff Information (BTI) pursuant to Article 12 CCC (Article 33 UCC/former Article 20 MCC) is an instrument of legal certainty for both economic operators and customs authorities.[151] It constitutes a special kind of information in the form of a customs decision given in writing by a customs authority of an EU Member State that determine the tariff classification of a certain good for the applicant and which is valid for a period of six years pursuant to Article 12 paragraph 4 CCC, henceforth three years pursuant to Article 33 paragraph 3 UCC (former Article 20 paragraph 3 MCC). During the period of its validity, a BTI can be used as often as necessary, provided the goods are identical to the goods described in the BTI decision.[152]

However, BTI is only given for the purpose of importing from or exporting to non-EU countries, as such classification decisions are not required for trade within the EU, given that the EU forms a single market.[153] Additionally, a BTI can only be invoked by the person or entity to whom or to which it is addressed—the holder of the BTI.[154] Furthermore, while BTI provides certainty with regard to the tariff classification of the goods described therein, all other customs controls may still be carried out by customs authorities.[155]

Because of the importance of the BTI system for the functioning of the EU Customs Union, the European Commission organises training in the form of at least four sessions annually, targeted at customs officials working in the designated customs authorities responsible for the issuance of BTI.[156] Furthermore, if required, participating customs official are expected to train their colleagues back in their national customs administration, and EU Member States also generally provide for some training on BTI.[157]

151 Weerth, Witten 2007, p 189.
152 European Commission, EBTI Monitoring Report (2007–2008), 2012, p 14.
153 ibid, p 14.
154 ibid, p 14.
155 ibid, p 15.
156 ibid, p 68.
157 ibid, pp 68, 69.

1. The EBTI Database

The key element of the BTI system is the EBTI database,[158] which allows the European Commission to query whether the BTI applications, BTI decisions and annulled or invalidated BTI are promptly entered in the central database.[159] There are two versions of the EBTI database: one is a public EBTI database, the so-called Data Dissemination System (DDS database), which is accessible via the internet to the public[160] and contains only valid BTI. The other one is the so-called EBTI-3 database,[161] which is accessible only to national customs authorities designated to issue BTI—with each EU Member State designating one national customs authority with exclusive responsibility for BTI[162]—and a limited number of officials in the European Commission.[163]

The EBTI-3 database contains BTI applications, issued BTI and even invalid BTI, along with the reasons for their invalidity, as well as additional confidential data, for example the name and address of the holder and commercial information.[164] The national customs authorities, specially designated by each EU Member State for the purpose of receiving BTI applications or issuing BTI, are obliged to enter such information without delay, pursuant to Articles 8 and 13 CCCIP. Therefore, the EBTI database provides national customs authorities with important information that can be crucial when deciding whether or not to issue BTI.[165] Some EU Member States have developed their own national BTI systems that run parallel with the EBTI database, offer the same functions, and are connected to EBTI for publishing applications and BTI. Germany, for example, has the ZEUS database, while the United Kingdom has the BERTI database.[166]

The EBTI database not only contains a detailed description of the goods in question, but also pictures of these goods, which facilitates categorising them and increases their recognition factor—after all, BTI are issued in any one of 24 official languages without translation.[167] Furthermore, the BTI issuing customs authorities have the possibility to index the decision, using a special purpose thesaurus to translate key terms into the other official languages. While neither images nor keywords are obligatory, they are useful tools for customs authorities to understand

[158] European Court of Auditors Special Report No 2/2008 concerning Binding Tariff Information (BTI) together with the Commission's replies, [2008] OJ C103/1–17, para 7.

[159] European Court of Auditors Special Report No 2/2008, para 22.

[160] URL: http://ec.europa.eu/taxation_customs/dds2/ebti/ebti_home.jsp?Lang=en.

[161] Hereinafter, the term 'EBTI database' refers only to the EBTI-3 database, which is used by customs authorities designated to issue BTI.

[162] Pursuant to Art 6 para 5 CCCIP, a list of the customs authorities designated by the EU Member States must be published in the Official Journal of the European Union, Series C. The present list of customs authorities designated by the EU Member States for receiving applications for BTI and issue BTI can be found in the EU's Official Journal, [2013] OJ C8/3–7.

[163] European Commission, EBTI Monitoring Report (2007–2008), 2012, p 39.

[164] ibid, p 42.

[165] ibid, pp 27, 42.

[166] ibid, p 21.

[167] ibid, pp 50, 51.

BTI in different languages and thus should be used as often as possible by the customs authorities issuing BTI.[168]

The EBTI database enables the European Commission to monitor the issuing of BTI by the national customs authorities in order to ensure that the same goods get classified into the same sub-positions of the Combined Nomenclature in the different EU Member States.[169] If BTI applications and issued BTI were not entered into the EBTI database, there would be no practical means to prevent the issuance of divergent BTI by different EU Member States for identical goods.[170] Therefore, it is also important for EU Member States to ensure that they accurately and promptly upload data in EBTI, as any delays could have serious repercussions and negative consequences for the functioning of the BTI system and enhance BTI-shopping.[171]

2. The Problematic Potential of BTI-Shopping

BTI are of special importance for the uniform application of the Combined Nomenclature, as they are valid EU-wide, pursuant to Article 11 CCCIP (Article 26 UCC/former Article 17 MCC), and thus oblige customs authorities throughout the EU to accept the tariff classification determined by another customs office. Therefore, the clear benefit of possessing a BTI is that it states from the outset the tariff classification of the goods described therein, and that all customs authorities in the EU Member States have to accept this decision when the goods are declared, no matter where the customs declaration is made in the EU.[172]

However, a BTI is only binding on customs authorities in respect to the goods the BTI has been applied for and for which customs formalities are completed after the date at which the decision takes effect, pursuant to Article 12 paragraph 2 sentence 2 CCC (Article 32 paragraph 2 section (a) UCC/former Article 20 paragraph 2 sentence 2 MCC). The introduction of BTI decisions in EU customs law was the response of the EU to a recommendation by the WCO in 1996 that its members establish a kind of binding pre-entry classification information.[173]

However, since it is not obligatory for traders to have a BTI, economic operators are still free to import or export goods without one.[174] Furthermore, under current customs legislation, holders of a BTI decision are not obliged to use them. Therefore, while a BTI is binding on the customs authorities of the EU Member States, so far it has not been binding on its holder, who was nevertheless allowed to rely on it. This has been criticised because the lack of binding force on the holder of a BTI could induce economic operators to not use an unwanted BTI in

168 ibid, pp 52, 79.
169 Lux, in: Rüsken (ed), 2013, Vol I, Art 12 CCC, para 130.
170 European Court of Auditors Special Report No 2/2008, para 32.
171 European Commission, EBTI Monitoring Report (2007–2008), 2012, pp 39, 75, 78.
172 ibid, p 14.
173 Lux, in: Rüsken (ed), 2013, Vol I, Art 12 CCC, para 3; Weerth, Witten 2007, p 189.
174 European Commission, EBTI Monitoring Report (2007–2008), 2012, p 14.

the hopes of a different tariff classification decision when delivering the customs declaration to a different customs office.[175] An economic operator is not allowed to possess more than one BTI for identical goods, as there is no need for another BTI regarding the goods covered by the BTI that has already been received. Nevertheless, a trader could always try to circumvent EU customs legislation and apply again for a BTI at another customs authority in a different EU Member State.[176]

Requests for BTI are possible in the home EU Member State, in EU Member States in which the trader has established a representative acting as applicant, and also in every EU Member State a trader intends to import or export goods to. The European Court of Auditors' Special Report 2/2008 on Binding Tariff Information[177] confirmed that BTI were seldom presented in the past and that if the existence of a BTI had not been declared, it was difficult for customs officers to verify whether the applicant possessed a BTI for the goods and whether the classification was correct.[178]

This can even lead to 'BTI shopping'—the systematic selection of customs authorities that issue the most favourable BTI decisions. Article 6 paragraph 3A section (j) CCCIP has been found not to be clear enough regarding the possibilities and compelling reasons for rejection of a BTI application by customs authorities.[179] To date, if a trader has submitted more than one application for identical goods, the relevant customs authorities contact each other, and between them decide which one will issue the BTI, while regardless of any rejection, each application has to be uploaded in the EBTI-3 database to inform all customs authorities in the EU.[180] However, henceforth an application for a BTI decision should not be accepted if the application has already been made at the same or another customs office in the EU by or on behalf of the particular holder of a BTI decision in respect to the same goods, pursuant to Article 33 paragraph 1 section (a) UCC (former Article 20 paragraph 1 section (a) MCC). Furthermore, BTI decisions will be binding on the holder, who in case of disagreement with a BTI decision has to lodge an appeal against it, while customs authorities in the EU have to consider existing BTI decisions officially and independently of any presentation on behalf of its holder.[181] This means that the risk of liability for customs debts, and even customs penalties when abstaining from presenting a BTI, lies entirely with the holder.[182] This newly introduced binding force of BTI decisions on the

[175] Weerth, Witten 2007, p 190; Witte/Henke, in: Witte/Henke/Kammerzell (eds), 2009, p 56.

[176] European Commission, EBTI Monitoring Report (2007–2008), 2012, p 14.

[177] European Court of Auditors Special Report No 2/2008 concerning Binding Tariff Information (BTI) together with the Commission's replies, [2008] OJ C103/1–17.

[178] European Court of Auditors Special Report No 2/2008, p 4 summary III (e) and para 26.

[179] Witte/Henke, in: Witte/Henke/Kammerzell (eds), 2009, pp 55, 56.

[180] European Commission, EBTI Monitoring Report (2007–2008), 2012, p 37.

[181] Witte/Henke, in: Witte/Henke/Kammerzell (eds), 2009, p 56.

[182] ibid, p 56.

holder corresponds with a recommendation of the European Court of Auditors[183] and will significantly reduce the risk of BTI shopping.

The European Commission declared the provision of equal treatment of traders and uniform application of the Combined Nomenclature to be one of the aims of the BTI system.[184] By attributing an EU-wide classification to a given good and providing legal certainty about the tariff classification of those goods for both economic operators and customs authorities, BTI contribute to the correct tariff classification of goods and the correct charging of customs duties throughout the EU.[185] In its Special Report No 2/2008 on Binding Tariff Information, the European Court of Auditors found the BTI system to be well-designed overall.[186] The determination of the correct tariff code can present difficulties; in this regard, BTI helps to limit the potential for divergent tariff classifications for the same goods.[187]

A similar assessment was made by customs officials of the Section for Classification in the United Kingdom: 'If you have already got BTIs from a different European country that has previously classified it, then we cannot be knowingly divergent, so we have to go with that as well.'[188] The BTI system therefore helps the EU to fulfil its obligation under Article X:3(a) GATT 1994, as it contributes to ensuring the uniform treatment of the same goods in all EU Member States.[189]

3. *BTI as an Interpretative Aid*

Beyond their legal character as EU-wide valid customs decisions, BTI are also an important aid for the correct interpretation of the Common Customs Tariff. Although a BTI is binding on customs authorities—and henceforth also on its holder—only in respect to the actual goods the BTI has been applied for, it can also constitute an instrument for the correct classification of similar or identical goods from other economic operators than the holder of the BTI. Actually, the EBTI database—with extensive data, detailed description of goods covered by BTI and even pictures of those goods—can make BTI a very helpful and easily accessible instrument for interpretation in practice.

Furthermore, as some information from EBTI is available to the general public through the DDS database, economic operators may refer to a BTI issued to another economic operator in support of their own declaration for tariff classification, provided the goods in question are identical or similar. Nonetheless, in such cases an economic operator cannot rely on the legal certainty of a BTI that

[183] ibid, p 56; European Court of Auditors Special Report No 2/2008, [2008] OJ C103/1–17, p 4 summary IV(c) and para 47(a).

[184] European Commission, 'Frequently asked questions about BTI', p 4 question number 20.

[185] European Court of Auditors Special Report No 2/2008, p 4 summary II and para 39.

[186] ibid, p 4 summary III and paras 13, 39.

[187] ibid, para 3.

[188] Interview of 9 January 2012 on file with author.

[189] European Court of Auditors Special Report No 2/2008, para 5.

has been issued to another trader, for customs authorities are not obliged to accept the classification opinion contained by a BTI in another case.[190]

However, the BTI can still be a helpful tool for finding the correct classification. There is no reason for customs officials to disagree with a reasonable classification opinion determined in a BTI, even if this decision is not legally binding. In fact, while only the designated national customs authorities have access to the EBTI-3 database, all national customs authorities have access to the public EBTI database, the DDS, which also contains much helpful information on the tariff classification of certain goods: registration number, issuing EU Member State, start and end dates of validity, description of the goods and any images attached to the BTI (provided such images are not confidential), the date of issue, the justification of the classification, and keywords.[191] Therefore, the public version of EBTI, the DDS, can also constitute a simple and searchable interpretive guidance instrument for classification matters by offering keywords and images.

This function of BTI as an interpretative aid in similar or identical cases, and especially the assistance EBTI can provide, was confirmed in interviews with customs officials in Germany.[192] Additionally, customs officials of the Section for Classification interviewed in the United Kingdom also agreed that BTI can be a helpful interpretation aid, especially with regard to electromechanical goods, and that looking into the EBTI database to see what other EU Member States are doing is of high importance:

> They [the economic operators] have got no legal certainty unless they actually own it [the BTI decision] … But yes, by the same token, it is very difficult to say no [to the interpretation the BTI provides for a certain good], especially with electromechanical because they all tend to be very similar models with very similar specs. So in that area it is quite difficult to say 'no, it is not the same'.[193]

Yet, in such cases, the customs authorities are not obliged to follow the classification opinion exercised in a BTI in another case regarding similar goods or identical goods of a different trader. When taking a customs classification decision, the common national customs authorities are also not required to consult the EBTI database for assistance. However, administrative guidelines of the European Commission advise the designated national customs authorities to check the EBTI database before issuing a BTI, and in the event of disagreement with the classification in a BTI, the customs administrations concerned should consult each other to resolve the problem and, if such consultations fail, submit the problem to the

[190] European Commission, EBTI Monitoring Report (2007–08), 2012, p 15.

[191] ibid, p 40.

[192] 'Ja, weil man muss ja immer wieder reinschauen, wenn es um das Thema, Einreihung geht.' Interview of 1 April 2011 on file with author; 'Hauptinstrument', Interview of 7 April 2011 on file with author; 'Natürlich ist es bedeutsam für unsere tägliche Arbeit', Interview of 13 April 2011 on file with author; 'Und dann ist es eine Riesenhilfe für den operativen Bereich.', Interview of 20 May 2011 on file with author; 'Es erleichtert uns die Arbeit und deswegen ist eine vZTA [verbindliche Zolltarifauskunft] auch wichtig für uns.' Interview of 23 May 2011 on file with author.

[193] Interview of 9 January 2012 on file with author.

Customs Code Committee.[194] Only in respect of the goods for which the BTI has been applied must every customs authority in the EU accept the tariff classification as laid out in the BTI, even if the competent customs authority has a different classification opinion.

This situation will continue under the Union Customs Code. The fact that BTI decisions will be binding on the holder once the Union Customs Code is applied only reduces the potential for divergent BTI decisions concerning the same applicant—preventing BTI shopping—but not regarding different holders of the same kind of goods. Also, the national customs authorities' newly installed obligation to consider each BTI independently from any presentation on behalf of its holder is only relevant with regard to this specific holder and their declaration of the goods for which the BTI has been issued; it constitutes no obligation to consider an existing BTI decision in another case. Therefore, a customs authority can decide upon a different interpretation of the Common Customs Tariff with regard to identical goods from a different economic operator.

For this reason, not even the EBTI database can prevent the non-uniform application of the Combined Nomenclature and the Common Customs Tariff by customs authorities of different EU Member States when issuing BTI. This means there is still a possibility for divergent BTI in the EU, and this will continue to be so under the Union Customs Code. Unfortunately, this can endanger the uniform administration of EU customs law, a problem that was also considered by the European Court of Auditors in its Special Report No 2/2008. However, at least for the national customs authorities designated to issue BTI, the most efficient way to ensure uniformity when applying EU customs legislation is by systematically consulting the EBTI database.[195]

4. *Inconsistencies in Decisions Relating to BTI*

The European Commission, as well as the EU Member States, are aware of the risk for divergent BTI decisions, although inconsistencies in decisions relating to BTI are the exception, as confirmed by customs officials of the Section for Classification in the United Kingdom: 'It is a small percentage. It is not a huge problem.'[196] Similar statements were made by customs officials in Germany.[197] Nevertheless, each case of divergent BTI decisions for different holders of the same kind of goods is an example of non-uniform tariff classification in the EU that persists as long as those BTI decisions are valid.

[194] European Court of Auditors Special Report No 2/2008, para 31; European Commission, EBTI Monitoring Report (2007–08), 2012, pp 43, 76.

[195] European Commission, EBTI Monitoring Report (2007–08), 2012, p 43.

[196] Interview of 9 January 2012 on file with author.

[197] 'Liegt im Rahmen des üblichen Erwartbaren.' Interview of 1 April 2011 on file with author; 'Im Verhältnis zur Masse der erteilten vZTAen [verbindlichen Zolltarifauskünfte] … sind die Fälle nicht häufig.' Interview of 13 April 2011 on file with author; 'Also das ist kein überschäumendes Problem.' Interview of 20 April 2011 on file with author.

Therefore, EU customs law provides a procedure in order to repeal divergent BTI in order to avoid different classification that would persist during the validity of the relevant BTIs. If divergent BTI have been issued by different national customs authorities for the same goods of several economic operators then, as a first effort, the EU Member States in question are to solve the divergent national classification opinions on a bilateral level.[198] Customs officials of the Section for Classification in the United Kingdom have confirmed that many problems with regard to divergent BTI can be solved on the bilateral level, as different classification opinions can simply be the result of different information being given to different customs authorities:

> Sometimes, it is the fact that they have different information to what we have been given, or the fact that they have found a different set of information. So, it works both ways. Sometimes we do revoke them because we have missed something or the officer who issued it has missed something and we are more than happy that they actually found it.[199]

A similar assessment was made by customs officials of the BTI Section in Germany.[200]

However, if no bilateral solution can be found, the procedure pursuant to Article 9 paragraph 1 CCCIP takes place and the Customs Code Committee places the item on the agenda of the next meeting, while the European Commission's administrative guidelines instruct EU Member States to issue no other BTI regarding the issue of this very classification until the matter is resolved.[201] After an agreement has been found, the European Commission has to adopt a measure in accordance with the committee procedure to ensure the uniform application of the Combined Nomenclature as soon as possible, and no later than six months following the meeting. Normally the European Commission chooses to issue a classification regulation that dictates the correct classification with binding force on the national customs authorities.

Although divergent BTI should be resolved as quickly as possible,[202] the European Court of Auditors has criticised the six-month time limit as being difficult to meet,[203] which has been acknowledged by the European Commission itself.[204] This is because of the difficulties in coming to an agreement within the Committee, and also because of the time needed afterwards for drafting, translating and

[198] European Court of Auditors Special Report No 2/2008, para 17; European Commission, EBTI Monitoring Report (2007–08), 2012, p 43.

[199] Interview of 9 January 2012 on file with author.

[200] 'Also die versuchen das bilateral zu klären indem man sich gegenseitig die Einreihungsauffassungen darlegen lässt. Und häufig kommt es dann schon dazu, dass entweder die anderen sagen "Ok, wir ziehen unseres zurück, wir sehen eure Argumente ein" oder umgekehrt.' Interview of 13 April 2011 on file with author.

[201] European Court of Auditors Special Report No 2/2008, European Commission reply, p 14 summary III.(a); European Commission, EBTI Monitoring Report (2007–2008), 2012, p 43.

[202] European Court of Auditors Special Report No 2/2008, paras 17, 18.

[203] ibid, para 18.

[204] ibid, para 19.

publishing a legal measure, with a lack of human resources within the European Commission making it all the more difficult.[205] Therefore, the numerous delays accompanying the present procedure can lead to non-compliance with the time limit pursuant to Article 9 paragraph 1 CCCIP and extend the period of time during which divergent BTI and thus inconsistent tariff classification might exist.[206]

Although in general, problems with divergent BTI can be resolved within reasonable periods of time, there are some cases of inconsistencies between BTI decisions that have taken several years to be resolved, during which time the uniform tariff classification in the EU was not ensured. In interviews with customs officials in Germany, heterogeneous opinions were expressed with regard to the functioning of the procedure to solve problems with divergent BTI. Some believed that problems with divergent BTI regularly can be and are solved within a reasonable time and that only in exceptional cases was a timely solution not found.[207] Others declared that the time needed by the Customs Code Committee, together with the European Commission, was too long.[208] An interview with customs officials of the Section for Classification in the United Kingdom revealed that such classification issues are regularly not being discussed for six months to a year, as the Customs Code Committee is very busy: 'Though the Customs Code [Committee] is trying to be quicker, we are still finding that smaller issues tend to be lost.'[209]

In order to improve the functioning of the Customs Code Committee and reduce the time needed to find an agreement on the correct tariff classification, the European Commission has introduced a standardised template for the submission of classification queries, requiring from the outset that all the information be provided, in order to eliminate unnecessary delays.[210] Indeed, up to now the Committee has regularly been postponing such classification issues to future meetings, declaring that more information was needed to find a solution, and even once obtained, EU Member States' representatives would continue to disagree on the correct classification.[211]

The reform of EU customs law was taken as an opportunity to strengthen the implementation provisions and the administrative guidelines regarding binding information in general, and the procedure for inconsistencies in decisions relating

[205] ibid, para 18.

[206] ibid, para 43.

[207] 'Liegt im Rahmen des üblichen Erwartbaren.' Interview of 1 April 2011 on file with author; 'Im Grunde funktioniert es.' Interview of 13 April 2011 on file with author; 'Aber ich denke einmal, das funktioniert schon.' Interview of 20 April 2011 on file with author; 'Funktioniert … Also das, was ich gesehen habe, ist alles in einer akzeptablen Zeit … abgearbeitet worden.' Interview of 10 May 2011 on file with author.

[208] 'Also ich habe da meine leichten Zweifel, dass das in einem angemessenen Zeitraum in den meisten Fällen zum Ergebnis führt.' Interview of 7 April 2011 on file with author; 'Also ich kann mir nicht vorstellen, dass man das angemessen löst.' Interview of 20 May 2011 on file with author.

[209] Interview of 9 January 2012 on file with author.

[210] European Court of Auditors Special Report No 2/2008, European Commission reply, p 14 summary IV.(a), observations p 15 para 18(a), p 16 conclusion and recommendations paras 43, 44(a).

[211] European Court of Auditors Special Report No 2/2008, paras 18(a), 18(b).

to binding information in particular.[212] In the context of the Modernised Customs Code, the draft for the modernised implementing provisions[213] planned to introduce a strict deadline for replying to bilateral consultations between EU Member States, and also to introduce a more realistic time limit for the resolution of divergent BTI in the Customs Code Committee, pursuant to Article 124-3-13 draft-MCCIP. According to this draft provision, the European Commission intends to set a time-limit of three months for bilateral consultations before the classification issue has to be submitted to the European Commission without delay, and they then have to put it on the agenda of the Customs Code Committee within three months, which then has to come to an agreement within six months.

Although the European Commission tried to improve the Committee procedure by introducing more defined time-limits, there is still the possibility for delays. The placement on the agenda of a classification issue regarding divergent BTI still depends on the availability of the information needed by the Committee pursuant to Article 124-3-13 paragraph 5 draft-MCCIP. It remains to be seen whether the final implementing provisions in the context of the Union Customs Code will constitute an improvement of the Committee procedure pursuant to Article 9 paragraph 1 CCCIP.

5. *Summary*

Although the primary purpose of BTI is to provide traders with legal certainty regarding the tariff classification of their goods, BTI also contribute to the uniform application of the Combined Nomenclature. Though BTIs are issued by national customs authorities, they are EU-wide valid customs decisions that have to be recognised and applied with regard to their specific holders by every national customs authority throughout the EU. Beyond their binding force concerning the actual goods of the specific BTI holder, BTIs also serve as non-binding interpretative aids with regard to similar or identical goods of different traders.

In this context, the EBTI database is the key instrument for information exchange and practical aspects of BTI decisions throughout the EU. The problem of BTI shopping will be significantly reduced under the Uniform Customs Code, but the possibility for divergent BTIs with regard to similar or identical goods of different holders of a BTI will continue. Although this is not a huge problem in practice, the European Commission has been requested to mend the relevant procedure in order to resolve such problems of uniform classification within a reasonable time.

[212] ibid, European Commission reply, p 14 summary IV.(a), observations p 15 para 16.

[213] Last version (situation as of 31.12.2013): Consolidated preliminary draft of the MCCIP of 25 November 2011, Document TAXUD/MCCIP/2010/100-3.

F. Conclusion

In the area of tariff classification, the EU customs law system provides many instruments for the correct interpretation and application of the Common Customs Tariff. This is of special importance in the field of classification, as the correct application of the Common Customs Tariff is a difficult task, not least because of technological progress and the perpetual introduction of unlimited new products by economic operators. However, it is important for both the European Commission and the national customs administrations to differentiate between instruments for interpretation that are of a binding character, such as classification regulations, and those of a non-binding character, such as CN explanatory notes.

The instruments for interpretation of the Common Customs Tariff should help customs officials throughout the EU to find the correct tariff classification, but also not discourage them from making customs decisions on their own or lead to prefer waiting for further instructions. Customs officials also will not always have the time—or the will—to take a large amount of information into account, as the time to make a decision is regularly limited. EU classification regulations can only be the solution in single cases; they can never constitute a comprehensive catalogue with the correct classification for all goods. In view of the unlimited kinds of potential products, this would be an impossible task. Finally, the practice of granting some soft law measures de facto binding force and simultaneously allowing them to have retroactive effect can under certain circumstances violate fundamental legal principles of both EU law and WTO law. While the de facto binding force of soft law measures contributes to uniform customs administration, the retroactive use of such measures raises the risk of demolishing the possibility to rely on soft law acts when implementing EU customs law in the future.

Finally, binding tariff information is an important instrument in the customs area of classification. Nevertheless, as long as BTI decisions are not binding towards their holders and thus need not be presented, there is a potential for BTI shopping, as there is always the possibility of economic operators asking for another BTI decision in a different EU Member State hoping for a different classification. This can lead to non-uniform tariff classification with regard to the same goods of the same BTI holder, constituting diverging BTI decisions addressed to the same person. This potential risk will be reduced once the Union Customs Code is applied, for BTI decisions will then be binding towards their holders. However, the potential for divergent BTI decisions regarding the same or identical goods of different holders will remain, as BTI decisions will still be only binding in the individual case, and not constitute a general binding tariff classification of the kind of goods they concern.

Regarding the procedure in case of inconsistencies in BTI decisions, there still seems to be need for further improvement, although the European Commission has amended the time-limits in the committee procedure. However, it is also up to the EU Member States to avoid delays by reaching a mutual agreement in case of divergent classification opinions. After all, the prompt removal of divergent BTIs, which demonstrate a non-uniform application of the Combined Nomenclature in the EU, is in the common interest of the European Commission and the EU Member States, as ensuring uniform customs administration in reasonable time is an international obligation of the whole EU pursuant to Article X:3 (a) GATT 1994.

II. VALUATION

In the field of customs valuation, EU customs law intends to be a fair, uniform and neutral system to prevent the application of arbitrary or fictitious customs values.[214] Significant rules for customs valuation can be found in Articles 28 to 37 CCC (Article 69 to 76 UCC/former Articles 40 to 43 MCC) and Title V of its CCCIP (Title II Chapter 2 draft-MCCIP). The principles for determination of customs value are based on WTO law, namely the WTO Customs Valuation Agreement,[215] whose rules have been transposed into the directly applicable EU customs law enumerated above. The great reform of EU customs law leaves the rules for customs valuation largely unaffected due to the close connection to the WTO Customs Valuation Agreement and its widely approved methods.[216]

The primary basis for the customs value of goods is the transaction value, pursuant to Article 29 CCC (Articles 70, 71 and 72 UCC/former Article 41 MCC). This is an individualised valuation method, meaning that the customs value must be calculated on the basis of the conditions on which the individual sale was made.[217] Overall, the WTO Customs Valuation Agreement, and thus also the Customs Code, provide six methods to determine the correct customs value. However, only if the method of customs valuation based on the transaction value fails to succeed can secondary methods of customs valuation be applied in their predetermined order pursuant to Articles 30 and 31 CCC (Article 74 UCC/former Article 42 MCC).

Customs value is not only important for the calculation of customs duties, but also in several other areas, for example for some tariff quotas and some rules of origin. To ensure the uniform interpretation and implementation of EU customs law with regard to customs valuation, the Customs Code Committee[218] has a regularly convened section addressing EU customs valuation matters: the Customs Code Committee—Customs Valuation Section. The tasks of the Committee's Valuation Section include the examination of valuation issues, in particular divergent interpretations of EU customs valuation rules by national customs

[214] Wolffgang, in: Witte/Wolffgang (eds), 2012, p 412, para 1511.

[215] WTO, 'Agreement on Implementation of Article VII of the General Agreement on Tariffs and Trade 1994' of 15 April 1994, [1994] OJ L336/119–37, and also URL: www.wto.org/english/docs_e/legal_e/20-val.pdf.

[216] Witte, in: Witte/Henke/Kammerzell (eds), 2009, p 75.

[217] Hesselink, (7) 2012 GTCJ (3), pp 80–91 (81).

[218] A general analysis of the tasks and function of the Customs Code Committee can be found in Chapter 8.II.B.1. and III.

administrations of the EU Member States, amendments of and guidelines to EU customs valuation rules, and the preparation of common EU positions for the WTO Committee on Customs Valuation[219] and the WCO Technical Committee on Customs Valuation.[220]

According to customs officials of the Section for Valuation in the United Kingdom, the chairman of the Customs Code Committee regularly voices the opinion of the 28 EU Member States in the WCO committee and reflects the vast experience of the collective EU Member States: 'As I said, we only have one vote but he does a grand job in the committee and certainly speaks as much as any of the others to get our voice heard.'[221] These officials further stated that while the EU tends to solve problems with regard to customs valuation within the Customs Code Committee before taking it to the WCO committee, less experienced countries go directly to the WCO committee where they are then able to draw on the experience of the other WCO members:

> Because normally we can resolve it – we do not take anything to the WCO … It is the other countries, or members, that probably have lesser experience that take the problems there … we would resolve it, we would know the answer.[222]

Therefore, it seems that the EU Member States, having several of the most experienced countries with regard to customs and customs valuation amongst them, can have quite an influence on the guiding measures of the WCO committee when they voice a common position.

Although the opinions of the Customs Code Committee are not legally binding, they may still constitute useful guidance for the interpretation and application of the EU's valuation rules.[223] In truth, the expertise of the Customs Code Committee's Valuation Section plays an important role in the area of customs valuation by elaborating on commentaries and drawing conclusions on numerous topical issues relating to the administration of customs valuation rules.[224]

Customs officials of the Section for Valuation in the United Kingdom confirmed that they follow the opinions of the Customs Code Committee because, although they are not legally binding, they are persuasive given the expertise behind them: 'We will use it to support an argument, let us say. Yes, we know it is not legally binding but it does hold a lot of sway because it has been looked at by the experts.'[225] Nevertheless, they also pointed out that abstract Committee opinions are rare in the Valuation Section, as every case is different, and thus it is rather the essence

[219] Established pursuant to Art 18 WTO Customs Valuation Agreement, URL: www.wto.org/english/tratop_e/cusval_e/cusval_info_e.htm.

[220] URL: www.wcoomd.org/en/about-us/wco-working-bodies/tarif_and_trade/technical_committee_on_customs_valuation.aspx and URL: www.wto.org/english/tratop_e/cusval_e/cusval_info_e.htm; Lyons, 2008, p 284.

[221] Interview of 10 January 2012 on file with author.

[222] ibid.

[223] Panel Report, *EC—Selected Cusoms Matters*, WT/DS315/R, paras 4.138, 4.291.

[224] ibid, para 4.291.

[225] Interview of 10 January 2012 on file with author.

of such texts that can help point to the correct solution: 'It is more the spirit of it because you are sort of looking through to find what set of circumstances might suit the particular case that comes along next.'[226] It was also noted that most measures will be introduced in the Customs Valuation Compendium.[227]

This is also the case for measures of the WCO Technical Committee on Customs Valuation, which prepare a range of instruments for additional guidance on implementation at the international level as well as tools for effective administration of valuation matters by national customs administrations.[228] These instruments are not legally binding but nevertheless constitute helpful guidance and thus contribute to uniform customs administration in the EU. Customs officials of the Section for Valuation in the United Kingdom stated that they follow the – rare – notes of the WCO in the area of customs valuation even though they are not legally binding because, again, they reflect collective expert opinion and thus are persuasive:

> And again because the WCO itself [the HS committee opinions] is not legal binding so we give it [the HS committee opinions] a similar sort of weight and we will use it exactly the same we would the Customs Code [Committee] opinions, would be fair to them and … yes, they are persuasive but as I say they are not legally binding … These WCO notes are also introduced into a WCO compendium on valuation.[229]

To ensure the uniform application of the EU's valuation rules, EU customs law provides for a number of mechanisms, though the available tools are not as numerous as those in the area of tariff classification. The EU's valuation rules leave relatively little room for specific additional interpretations or for the discretion of national customs authorities, as these provisions are extremely detailed and constitute an almost exhaustive regulation of customs valuation.[230] In most cases, it is not possible to lay down the value of a particular good in the abstract, as customs valuation typically depends on evaluations carried out on the basis of the single case in question.[231] This was confirmed by customs officials of the Section for Valuation in the United Kingdom: 'I think it is fair to say that no two cases are the same.'[232]

Further instruments to ensure the uniform implementation of EU customs law with regard to customs valuation are amendments to the EU's valuation rules contained in the Implementing Regulation and its annexes. They are issued by the European Commission in accordance with Article 247 CCC (Article 75 in conjunction with Article 284 UCC and Article 76 in conjunction with Article 285 UCC/former Article 43 in conjunction with Article 183 paragraph 1 MCC). These amendments constitute legally binding acts in all EU Member States and can be

[226] ibid.
[227] ibid.
[228] URL: www.wcoomd.org/en/about-us/wco-working-bodies/tarif_and_trade/technical_committee_on_customs_valuation.aspx.
[229] Interview of 10 January 2012 on file with author.
[230] Panel Report, *EC—Selected Cusoms Matters*, WT/DS315/R, paras 4.136, 4.286.
[231] ibid, paras 4.136, 4.289.
[232] Interview of 10 January 2012 on file with author.

regarded as functionally similar to classification regulations in the area of tariff classification.[233] The European Commission can also decide to issue non-binding soft law acts for further guidance. There is also a specific instrument for the assistance of national customs authorities in the area of customs valuation, namely Customs Valuation Compendium.

A. Customs Valuation Compendium

To provide further information on customs valuation, the European Commission issues and publishes a Customs Valuation Compendium[234] which contains the interpretation of certain customs valuation rules brought to the attention of the Customs Code Committee's Valuation Section. These can include the Committee's conclusions and commentaries on specific valuation topics, an overview of the case law of the ECJ in the field of customs valuation, and references to the instruments and tools for additional guidance on implementation and effective administration adopted by the WCO Technical Committee on Customs Valuation. There is also a WCO compendium, containing the notes and opinions of the WCO Technical Committee on Customs Valuation. Customs officials of the Section for Valuation in the United Kingdom believe that both compendiums work together quite well: 'In a sense it is the EU's equivalent of the WCO explanatory notes'.[235]

The Customs Valuation Compendium has been prepared primarily for the national customs administration in the EU Member States, though it is available to all interested parties in all official languages of the EU on the European Commission's TAXUD website.[236] It provides guidance for national customs authorities, as well as for economic operators, with regard to the interpretation of the rules on customs valuation in the EU, namely the relevant provisions in the Customs Code and its implementing provisions, by illustrating particular problems and their solutions with the help of concrete examples.

However, the Customs Valuation Compendium is not of a legally binding character and contains no authentic texts. Rather, the authentic texts of EU regulations are published in the Official Journal of the EU, while the authentic texts of the judgements of the ECJ are given in the reports of cases before the ECJ.[237] Commentaries, conclusions and other measures contained in the Compendium

[233] Panel Report, *EC—Selected Cusoms Matters*, WT/DS315/R, paras 4.137, 4.291.

[234] Updated edition 2008, TAXUD/800/2002-EN, Brussels, September 2008, URL: http://ec.europa.eu/taxation_customs/resources/documents/customs/customs_duties/declared_goods/european/compendium_2008_en.pdf.

[235] Interview of 10 January 2012 on file with author.

[236] URL: http://ec.europa.eu/taxation_customs/customs/customs_duties/declared_goods/european/index_en.htm; European Commission, 'Compendium of Customs Valuation texts', 2008, TAXUD/800/2002-EN, p 2.

[237] European Commission, 'Compendium of Customs Valuation texts', 2008, TAXUD/800/2002-EN, p 2.

are the opinions of the Customs Code Committee's Valuation Section and do not constitute legal instruments.[238] Commentaries give guidance on how to apply a certain provision, while conclusions are the result of examinations of specific problematic cases; both reflect the view of the Committee's Valuation Section in order to support uniform interpretation and application of EU customs law with regard to customs valuation.[239]

Therefore, while the Compendium can be a helpful instrument for guidance in the area of EU customs valuation, customs decisions cannot be based on its texts and have to rely on EU customs legislation. Customs officials in Germany expressed the view that the Compendium is primarily an instrument for valuation experts in the national customs administration and not one for regular day-to-day customs work, given its content focuses on specific cases and peculiarities.[240]

This view was expressed also by customs officials of the Section for Valuation in the United Kingdom, who stated that the Customs Valuation Compendium of the European Commission was an important tool for their work and was used on a regular basis, while customs officials from a different section or a lower level would simply go to the specific experts for customs valuation with their questions: 'But generally the staff on the workface, no, they will not look at it. They will rely on the advice given by their regional specialists or by ourselves.'[241] Nevertheless, guidance by experts – and the members of the Customs Code Committee's Valuation Section can indeed be counted amongst experts in customs valuation – can constitute important assistance in the complicated and rambling field of EU customs.

B. Binding Valuation Information (BVI) as Part of the Reform

The EU's rules on customs valuation are based on and fully integrate all the rules contained in the WTO Valuation Agreement, and there is no obligation under WTO law to institute a system of binding information for customs valuation matters.[242] Furthermore, unlike customs tariff classification, customs valuation is based on sets of data which can change with every transaction as well as from importer to importer, which makes the use of Binding Valuation Information (BVI) as a tool for ensuring uniformity far less clear than it is for BTI, as its content would have to differ significantly.[243]

[238] ibid, p 2.

[239] ibid, p 2.

[240] 'Da gibt es andere, die das auswerten, lesen müssen [...] sich sehr viel stärker damit beschäftigen als jetzt ein Hauptzollamt.' Interview of 10 May 2011 on file with author; similar assessment have been made in interviews of 1 April 2011, 7 April 2011, 13 April 2011, 20 April 2011, 20 May 2011, and 23 May 2011, all on file with author.

[241] Interview of 10 January 2012 on file with author.

[242] Panel Report, *EC—Selected Cusoms Matters*, WT/DS315/R, paras 4.287, 4.288.

[243] ibid, paras 4.289, 4.290.

This was confirmed by customs officials of the Section for Valuation in the United Kingdom, who stated that, with regard to customs valuation, every single case is different: 'I think the problem again with valuation is, each valuation ruling is going to be so specific to one particular scenario that it would become a nightmare.'[244] Therefore, it would be impossible for BVI decisions to lay down the value of a good in the abstract. Rather, they would have to focus on, for instance, the characterisation of specific elements inherent in certain recurrent transactions between the same parties, taking on a much more nuanced and specific character than seen in BTI.[245] In fact, customs officials of the Section for Valuation in the United Kingdom regarded the whole idea of binding valuation information to be a very troublesome challenge, given the manifold complexities connected with customs valuation, such as transfer pricing, early sales, or royalties, together with different terms of agreement for different countries.[246] Therefore, they feared that inconsistencies and simply wrong—but nevertheless binding—decisions would appear on a regular basis, forcing the Customs Code Committee Valuation Section to meet on a permanent basis: 'I do not know whether it would end up where every issue would almost have to go to the Committee, every application.'[247]

Nevertheless, the idea of introducing EU-wide BVI decisions—similar to BTI decisions but addressing customs valuation instead of customs tariff classification—has been discussed for several years now. Neither the Community Customs Code nor its Implementing Regulation contained the option for BVI. However, the Customs Code Committee's Valuation Section discussed the possibility to propose this kind of binding information as EU-wide valid customs decisions into the draft-modernised implementing provisions of the Modernised Customs Code, but without concrete results so far.[248] The last publicly available agenda of the twelfth meeting of the Customs Code Committee's Valuation Section, held on 9 March 2012, did not explicitly contain a discussion point on Binding Valuation Information.[249] Customs officials of the Section for Valuation in the United Kingdom confirmed that discussion on the topic seemed to have been put on hold by the European Commission and that up to that point, there was no solution on the horizon: 'The Valuation Committee does not seem to want to talk about it.'[250]

Further, the European Commission's proposal for the Union Customs Code contained no possibility for BVI. However, the European Parliament's report of the first reading in the ordinary legislative procedure[251] proposes amendments[252]

[244] Interview of 10 January 2012 on file with author.

[245] Panel Report, *EC—Selected Cusoms Matters*, WT/DS315/R, para, 4.290.

[246] Interview of 10 January 2012 on file with author.

[247] ibid.

[248] Customs Code Committee, Conclusions of 30 September 2011, TAXUD/B4/MN/D(2011)1287374, pp 5, 6; Customs Code Committee, Conclusions of 2 December 2011, TAXUD/B4/MN/D(2012)94162, p 7.

[249] Customs Code Committee, Conclusions of 9 March 2012, TAXUD B4/NM/D(2012)226869.

[250] Interview of 10 January 2012 on file with author.

[251] European Parliament, First Reading Report of 26 February 2013, A7-0006/2013.

[252] ibid, Amendments 37, 38, 39, pp 28–32.

with regard to Articles 32 and 33 of the UCC proposal in order to introduce a BVI system in the EU Customs Union. The final Union Customs Code does not contain these detailed amendments but nevertheless the possibility exists to introduce BVI decisions based on Article 35 UCC. Similar to BTI in the area of customs classification, BVI is to lead to uniform customs valuation practices in all EU Member States and provide legal certainty for both national customs authorities and economic operators. However, detailed requirements and the necessary development of a centrally managed database—similar to the EBTI database—would have to be created by the European Commission, which does not appear to be likely in the near term.

C. Conclusion

The EU's customs valuation rules, based on the WTO Customs Valuation Agreement, have proven to be of value. Therefore substantive changes are not foreseen within the great reform. Overall, the exhaustive regulation of customs valuation rules in the EU does not leave much room for further interpretation instruments or room for discretion by national customs administrations of the EU Member States. Yet the Customs Code Committee and the Customs Valuation Compendium can provide helpful guidance and expertise, although their opinions, recommendations and other texts are not legally binding and do not constitute authentic texts. Indeed, soft law measures in this area are regarded to be significantly less important and authoritative when compared to their importance and de facto binding force in the area of classification. Finally, so far the instrument of BVI has not advanced far enough to be able to draw any concrete conclusions on its effectiveness and possible contribution to the enhancement of uniform customs administration in the area of customs valuation.

III. ORIGIN

Due to customs tariff preferences, the EU grants favourable rates of duty for many import goods to the EU Customs Union. These cost-effective customs tariff preferences can also be applied for exporting goods to third countries.[253] Therefore, customs tariff preferences are important with regard to import and export of goods because they can improve the conditions for economic competition.[254]

In the EU, numerous preferential tariff measures exist due to international preferential trade agreements, but also due to autonomous granting.[255] Although

[253] Wolffgang, in: Witte/Wolffgang (eds), 2012, p 444, para 1558.
[254] ibid, p 444, para 1558.
[255] ibid, p 445, para 1560.

customs tariff preferences generally violate the most-favoured-nation treatment clause of Article I GATT 1994, this principle is suspended with regard to customs unions and free trade areas pursuant to Article XXIV GATT. Furthermore, the enabling clause[256] allows one-sided customs tariff preferences for developing countries.

The application of customs tariff preferences requires the determination of the origin of the goods. The rules on determination of the origin of goods can be found in Articles 22 to 27 CCC (Articles 59 to 66 UCC/former Articles 35 to 39 MCC) and in Articles 35 to 140 CCCIP. These rules have been maintained without significant substantive changes in the ongoing reform process, and the basic principle of the rules on determination of the origin of goods remains the guide to differentiating between preferential origin and non-preferential origin of goods.[257]

The general mechanisms for providing uniform interpretation and application of EU law also apply in the area of customs preferences and rules of origin. Furthermore, the Customs Code Committee[258]—Origin Section contributes to uniformity by elaborating on commentaries and conclusions on numerous topical issues relating to the interpretation and administration of rules of origin. Although, as in other areas, the opinions of the Customs Code Committee's Origin Section are not legally binding, the expertise contained therein means they still can constitute useful guidance for the interpretation and application of EU customs law.

Customs officials of the Section for Preferences in the United Kingdom confirmed the importance of the work of the Customs Code Committee—Origin Section for their own work:

> No, it [an opinion of the Customs Code Committee] is not [legally binding]. It [an opinion of the Customs Code Committee] is based on making sure the whole Origin system works properly ... Yes, it is a very important Committee.[259]

They also declared that soft law measures of the European Commission, as well as opinions of the Committee, are highly regarded, for they also are a persuasive argument in relation to traders: 'So although it might not technically be law, it is the preferred way of doing things.'[260] In fact, it was stated that the place to voice objections is the Customs Code Committee meeting before the European Commission has issued a measure, while afterwards one has to accommodate and follow the European Commission, as otherwise the system of customs administration in the EU would not work: 'Then each Member State is obliged to follow that line.'[261] Again, such statements illustrate the strong position of soft law in the EU's system of customs administration.

[256] WTO, Decision of 28 November 1979 (L/4903).

[257] Kammerzell, in: Witte/Henke/Kammerzell (eds), 2009, p 71.

[258] A general analysis of the tasks and function of the Customs Code Committee can be found in Chapter 8.II.B.1 and III.

[259] Interview of 9 January 2012 on file with author.

[260] ibid.

[261] ibid.

Furthermore, in order to ensure the uniform application of EU customs law in the area of rules of origin, the European Commission can amend the EU's rules of origin by issuing legally binding implementing provisions in accordance with Article 247 CCC (Article 62 in conjunction with Article 284 UCC and Article 63 in conjunction with Article 285 UCC/former Article 38 in conjunction with Article 183 paragraph 1 MCC) and provide for further guidance by issuing non-binding soft law acts. Indeed, in the area of Origin, soft law acts of the European Commission are highly regarded, as Customs officials of the Section for Preferences in the United Kingdom expressed: 'Basically, what the Commission say, we will do.'[262] The Customs Code Committee's Origin Section also prepares the common position of the EU Member States for the WTO Committee on Rules of Origin[263] and for the WCO Technical Committee on Rules of Origin.[264]

Finally, in the area of origin, there is also the option for economic operators to obtain an EU-wide Binding Origin Information (BOI) decision for both non-preferential origin as well as preferential origin. The instrument of BOI is very similar to but independent from the instrument of BTI in the area of customs tariff classification, and BOI decisions also have to be transmitted to the European Commission pursuant to Articles 8 and 13 CCCIP.[265] The changes and improvements in the ongoing reform process with regard to BTI also apply to BOI and therefore were covered in the explanations on binding information above.[266] Overall, BOI decisions are much less frequently applied for than BTI decisions, and thus are less controversially discussed. This was confirmed by customs officials of the Section for Preferences in the United Kingdom: 'We do not get that very often but I would say it is not as widespread as binding tariff because it is much newer than binding tariff.'[267]

IV. CONCLUSION

In conclusion, the EU's system of customs administrations contains various mechanisms and instruments of both a legally binding and non-binding character, intended to ensure the uniform interpretation and application of EU customs law. However, the number of instruments specifically designed for the needs of a specific customs area differs to a great extent, as does the importance of soft law measures for each area. The EU provides the most instruments for the guidance

[262] ibid.

[263] URL: www.wto.org/english/tratop_e/roi_e/roi_info_e.htm.

[264] URL: www.wcoomd.org/en/about-us/wco-working-bodies/tarif_and_trade/technical_committee_on_rules_of_origin.aspx.

[265] The list of national customs authorities designated to issue BOI, which has to be published in the Official Journal of the European Union, Series C, pursuant to Art 6 para 5 CCCIP, can be found in the EU's Official Journal, [2011] OJ C106/6–10.

[266] See Chapter 10.I.E.

[267] Interview of 9 January 2012 on file with author.

of national customs administrations in the area of customs tariff classification, as this constitutes the majority of customs decisions in day-to-day customs work and affects many other areas of EU customs. Herein, soft law measures are of great importance, and the European Commission relies to a great extent on soft law acts to ensure the proper application of the Common Customs Tariff. In practice, with regard to the difficult application of the Common Customs Tariff, instruments of a legal character and those of a non-legal character complement one another in the hierarchically structured classification process.

Nevertheless, the fundamental differences between legally binding instruments and soft law acts have to be respected, for only legal acts can be subject to legal scrutiny, while in legal theory soft law acts—being mere guidance without legally binding character—can have retroactive effect. Therefore, non-binding instruments of interpretation, as mere soft law acts, are not to be misused, in view of the danger posed of violating the fundamental principles of legal certainty and predictability.

This is especially the case in the area of classification, where the retroactive use of a new interpretation has led to additional customs duties, even though soft law measures must not result in unfavourable measures. In particular, with regard to CN explanatory notes, the Panel in *EC—IT Products*[268] asserted a violation of Article X:2 GATT 1994 in this context, and has even provided for the possibility to contest soft law measures if they are regarded to be of de facto binding force. The ECJ made a similar assessment in *DHL Danzas*[269] with regard to HS classification opinions. Henceforth, any semblance of retrospective use of soft law measures with potential effect on trade and traders bears the risk of a WTO dispute settlement resulting in the destruction of the European Commission's system of soft law guidance. Again, this could eventually put into question the EU's fulfilment of its obligation under Article X:3(a) GATT 1994, as the correct functioning of the European Customs Union relies to some extent on the use of soft law guidance in order to ensure the uniform administration of EU customs law.

Furthermore, the European Commission as well as the national customs administrations in the Customs Code Committee have to be aware that providing guidance should not lead customs officials to rely too much on further instructions, especially with regard to non-binding instruments, or discourage them from making genuine customs decisions on their own. After all, the numerous instruments and mechanisms in EU customs are intended to assist customs officials in making correct customs decisions in a uniform manner; they do not remove the responsibility of customs officials to correctly apply EU customs law itself.

Also of great importance in the area of classification are BTI decisions, which are EU-wide valid customs decisions that provide economic operators with legal certainty with regard to the tariff classification of their goods. Although BTI, together

[268] Panel Report, *EC—IT Products*, WT/DS375,376,377/R.

[269] ECJ order of 19 January 2012, Case 227/11, *DHL Danzas* [2012] ECR I-0 (full text only available in French and Dutch).

with the important EBTI database, contribute to uniform customs administration and can even be applied in analogy, they also cause problems. One of these negative effects, 'BTI shopping', will be reduced once the Union Customs Code is applied, as BTI decisions will become binding for their holders, making it much more difficult for one trader to try to get a more favourable classification for the same goods in a different EU Member State. However, the possibility of divergent BTI decisions relating to the same kind of goods will persist with regard to BTI decisions held by different economic operators. Although this is not a huge problem in practice, each case constitutes a non-uniform application of the Common Customs Tariff that persists as long as the divergent BTI decisions are valid. In this context, the European Commission is trying to improve the relevant procedure for the removal of divergent BTIs.

Compared to the area of classification, the areas of customs valuation and of origin do not have a corresponding number of instruments for uniform customs administration. Furthermore, while still important instruments for guidance, in the area of customs valuation soft law measures are of a less authoritative character, as general conclusions are unlikely to take into account the variable details of each customs valuation decision. Furthermore, an instrument comparable to binding tariff information is unlikely to be introduced in the area of customs valuation in the near future because the much more nuanced nature of these decisions make creating EU-wide valid decisions difficult. As a final point, compared to the areas of classification and valuation, the customs area of origin does not face many problems.

Part VI

Final Conclusion

11

Potential for Improving Uniform Customs Administration

THE DEMAND FOR uniform customs administration in the EU comes not only from the WTO and the international obligations of the EU incurred under Article X:3(a) GATT 1994, it is also strongly anchored in EU law, as the principle of uniformity is a requirement for the correct and effective implementation of EU law in general and EU customs law in particular. At least since the WTO dispute settlement in *EC—Selected Customs Matters*,[1] the various institutions of the EU, as well as the EU Member States and to some extent their national customs administrations, have been aware of the special importance that uniform implementation has for the functioning of the EU Customs Union. Therefore, the EU emphasises its goal that national customs administrations of the EU Member States should operate as efficiently and effectively as if they were a single customs administration, and should achieve homogeneous results at every place in the customs territory of the EU Customs Union.[2]

The decentralised organisation of customs administration in the EU has its weaknesses, for instance different administrative traditions and training, as well as translation errors because of different official languages. Thus, this system has some potential for non-uniform interpretation and application of EU customs law. However, neither EU law nor WTO law demand absolute uniformity. Rather, the implementation of EU customs law must not lead to necessarily non-uniform results on a regular basis in concrete cases.

For several years, the EU has been undertaking the biggest reform of EU customs since the adoption of the Community Customs Code. One of the aims of this

[1] WT/DS315.

[2] See, inter alia, European Commission, EU Customs strategy, URL: http://ec.europa.eu/taxation_customs/customs/policy_issues/customs_strategy/index_en.htm; COM (2001) 51 final, p 5; Customs 2013 Programme, Recital (2) and Art 4 para 1 section (b) of Decision 624/2007/EC; European Court of Auditors, Special Report 1/2010 'Are simplified customs procedures for imports effectively controlled?', [2010] OJ C149/8 and URL: http://eur-lex.europa.eu/LexUriServ/LexUriServ.do?uri=SRCA:2010:01:FIN:EN:PDF, para 34; European Court of Auditors, Special Report 23/2000 concerning valuation of imported goods for customs purposes (customs valuation), together with the Commission's replies, [2001] OJ C84/1–18, summary p 3 and para 8; Council Resolution of 30 May 2001 on a strategy for the Customs Union, [2001] OJ C171/1–3, p 2; European Parliament, Resolution of 1 December 2011 (2001/2083(INI)), text adopted P7_TA(2011)0546, para 53.

great reform, which was started soon after the WTO dispute settlement in *EC—Selected Customs Matters*, is the improvement of uniform customs administration in the EU Customs Union. To prepare EU customs for the various challenges it will have to face in order to preserve and enhance the competitiveness of the EU and ensure its safety in a modern, globalised and fast-moving environment, the reform has lofty ambitions. It not only encompasses the development of a new Customs Code and new implementing provisions in the context of the 'Better Regulation' Initiative, but also includes the Electronic Customs Initiative establishing an electronic customs environment and the Future Customs Initiative with regard to human resources.

The 'Better Regulation' Initiative's agenda is the improvement of EU customs law through simplification and a better balance between the Customs Code and its implementing provisions. The initiative thereby aims to facilitate the application of EU customs law, while simultaneously also seeking to reduce the margin of discretion available to national customs authorities through the adoption of detailed rules. The Future Customs Initiative aims to enhance cooperation and common training methods in order to promote best practices and common understanding.

The Electronic Customs Initiative aims to establish a modern customs environment using central databases and inter-operable national IT systems, leading to standardised processes with standardised working methods. This system is intended to not only enhance the EU Customs Union's competitiveness but also ensure correct and uniform customs administration. In particular, the standardisation of customs procedures is expected to reduce margins of discretion and the possibilities for systemic divergence. In this context, business process modelling is to ensure a strong coherence between the functioning of the electronic customs systems and the implementing provisions. Therefore, the establishment of an electronic customs environment has the potential to significantly improve the functioning of the EU Customs Union.

However, the European Commission's agenda in this context remains highly ambitious, and its success cannot be guaranteed. The deployment of a paperless environment for EU customs has turned out to be even more difficult than expected. In times of limited financial and human resources, EU Member States have faced problems developing the manifold electronic customs systems in parallel that are to be connected at the EU's level. The lack of progress in the Electronic Customs Initiative was the main reason for the recast of the great reform and the deadline for the full operability of the electronic customs systems has been delayed until approximately 2020, while the Union Customs Code and its new delegated acts and implementing acts will be applied from 1 June 2016.[3] With the great reform still ongoing and—up to now—no final version of either the implementing provisions or all the aspired to electronic customs systems, it is not possible to predict the final success and effectiveness of these efforts.

[3] Boysen, in: von Arnauld (ed), 2014, § 9 pp 447–514, para 75.

Nevertheless, the EU pursues many strategies to enhance uniform customs administration, most of them more or less connected with the three initiatives of the EU customs reform. As part of the 'Better Regulation' Initiative, the Union Customs Code has been simplified in terms of customs procedures and legal terminology, and thus the possibility for national idiosyncrasies has been significantly reduced. The EU-wide validity of customs decisions taken by national customs authorities of the EU Member States will be explicitly stated in the Union Customs Code, and first steps have been taken even with regard to the harmonisation of administrative penalties and appeal procedures. Therefore, compared to the current Community Customs Code, with its complicated structure and various references to the national administrative law of the EU Member States, the Union Customs Code will significantly contribute to a stronger EU Customs Procedure Union. However, the Union Customs Code also introduces the electronic customs environment aspired to in the Electronic Customs Initiative, while the application of the Modernised Customs Code failed precisely because of its dependency on electronic customs. Thus this risk continues under the Union Customs Code.

The EU Customs Union is not a centrally managed customs administration union, but nevertheless constitutes a kind of integrated network of national customs administrations that are coordinated to a great extent by the European Commission. Indeed, while it is not a requirement of a customs administration union to be centrally organised, in the decentralised administration of EU customs law the EU Member States' organisational autonomy is limited by general principles of EU law, and forms of cooperation and interdependencies exist.

While a centralised EU customs administration has not yet been created, the promotion of cooperation amongst national customs administrations, as well as between the national level and the EU level, is an important strategy of the European Commission. The Community Customs Code, as well as the Union Customs Code, contain only single and indefinite rules on cooperation, and the Mutual Assistance Regulation also does not provide rules for cooperation in day-to-day customs work but only for rules in the context of EU customs law infringements. However, there is ad-hoc cooperation in the form of direct contact, and the EU Member States have to provide specific centralised contact points for specific areas of EU customs. In particular, the Customs Action Programme, which is managed jointly by the European Commission and the EU Member States, establishes an effective instrument for cooperation, common standards, common working methods, and also common understanding between national customs administrations. The Customs Action Programme and its various activities address various levels of EU customs administration, ranging from highly specialised expert groups to general working visits of customs officials from different EU Member States, though the output of these activities should in the future be professionally summarised and made more widely accessible within the EU customs administration.

The European Commission plays a crucial role in the administration of EU customs and has important legislative, 'quasi-legislative' and administrative competences. One of its main functions is the coordination of information exchange and cooperation activities. In this context, its functions are the central management of electronic customs systems and databases at the EU level, such as, for example, the TARIC or EBTI, as well as the coordination of projects, training and other activities in the Customs Cooperation Programme. The European Commission also chairs and coordinates the Customs Code Committee. Furthermore, the European Commission possesses instruments for the supervision of national implementation of EU customs law, namely the right to conduct its own inspections, to place reporting obligations on the EU Member States, the practice of revenue allocation, and the passing of soft law acts for guidance on administrative practice.

In this context, soft law acts of the European Commission are an important strategy to ensure uniform customs administration. Soft law acts are not of a legal character, but regularly have indirect effects; when taking a decision, national authorities are requested to examine the substantive contents of such measures as useful guidance for avoiding manifest errors of assessment. Moreover, soft law measures have important practical effects, because they facilitate day-to-day customs administration at the operational level. Indeed, soft law measures are often welcomed by national customs authorities, and the European Commission relies to a great extent on such soft law acts in order to ensure uniform customs administration in the EU.

The extent to which the European Commission's system of enhancing uniform customs administration is based on the use of soft law can be seen in several different areas of EU customs, although the importance of soft law acts varies across these. Especially in the area of classification, which represents the vast majority of day-to-day customs work, the European Commission provides for numerous mechanisms and instruments of both legally binding and non-binding character in order to assist national customs authorities when implementing EU customs law. Indeed, in the implementation of the 'Better Regulation' Initiative, the European Commission's strategy has been to narrow down as much as possible any margin of discretion by adopting detailed delegated acts and implementing acts pursuant to Articles 290, 291 TFEU, and to complement these with soft law measures for administrative practice at the operational level.

The extensive delegation of power, in the sense of Article 290 TFEU, as well as conferral of implementing powers, in the sense of Article 291 TFEU, to the European Commission in various fields of EU customs law illustrates the European Commission's growing position in the management of the EU Customs Union. The manifold delegated powers, as the 'quasi-legislative' function of the European Commission exercised independently from any control of the EU Member States, imply a more centralised approach to EU customs administration under the Union Customs Code, and thus have been criticised. While the exercise of implementing powers in the sense of Article 291 TFEU is controlled by the EU Member States, the involvement of the Customs Code Committee is also a form of cooperation between the EU Member States and the European Commission, as the Committee is chaired by the latter. Therefore, the conferral of implementing powers in the Union Customs Code ensures that the European Commission and the EU Member States have to work together to implement the Code, and under the new Comitology Regulation, the position of the European Commission is slightly stronger compared to the former comitology mechanism.

The European Commission's eagerness to regulate the administration of EU customs in the EU Member States in order to ensure uniformity is understandable when considering the WTO dispute settlement in *EC—Selected Customs Matters* and its allegation of violation of Article X:3(a) GATT 1994. Even EU Member States seem to an extent to expect more coordination and instructions from the European Commission, thus neglecting their own responsibilities regarding the implementation of EU customs law. However, there are tendencies to neglect the constitutional requirements for delegation and conferral of implementing powers pursuant to Articles 290, 291 TFEU. The term 'non-essential elements', set out as an important condition in Article 290 TFEU, is still quite indefinite. Moreover, there has been criticism that the European Commission is over-stepping its authority with regard to its delegated powers, in order to act more independently from any EU Member State control. Furthermore, the extensive conferral of implementing power to the European Commission lacks any substantiation as required in Article 291 paragraph 2 TFEU, which raises questions and even alarm regarding the EU's democratic legitimacy. Such practice risks undermining the European Commission's system of enhancing uniform customs administration, as such actions make this system contestable. The European Commission should at least address these concerns by substantiating the reasons for its implementing action in the sense of Article 291 paragraph 2 TFEU when adopting implementing provisions, though this originally would have been the task of the EU legislator.

The extensive use of soft law measures is also troublesome. In the customs area of classification, soft law acts of the European Commission and also of the WCO have been granted a de facto binding power similar to measures of a legal character such as classification regulations. However, the European Commission and EU Member States have to be aware of the fundamental differences between legal acts and soft law measures in order to ensure the legitimacy of their action and prevent endangering of the EU's system of ensuring uniform customs administration. Granting soft law acts a de facto binding power means simultaneously imposing higher standards on those measures, ones which to some extent have to be comparable to legal acts. In particular, the retroactive use of soft law measures for providing the legal basis of unfavourable customs decisions in the area of classification has already been successfully challenged in a WTO dispute settlement as well as in an order of the ECJ because of the de facto binding power of those measures in the area of classification. Therefore, soft law acts of the European Commission have to be judged by their own standards, meaning that a de facto binding force requires soft law acts comply with the same fundamental legal principles that are binding for legal measures.

Furthermore, the extensive use of soft law acts, and in parts also the use of detailed implementing regulations such as classification regulations, carries the risk of preventing customs officials from finding their own solutions through the interpretation of the law, as it invites them to either wait for further instructions, or results in them getting lost in too much information. After all, not every customs decision can be pre-prepared. Therefore, the European Commission should not shy away from calling on the EU Member States, their national customs administrations and their customs officials to take personal responsibility.

In specific customs areas of high importance, the EU provides for special instruments of a legal and non-legal character. In particular, in the area of classification various instruments such as HS explanatory notes, CN explanatory notes and classification regulations complement each other in the graduated application of tariff positions that is strongly oriented on the hierarchical structure of the Common Customs Tariff. Furthermore, binding tariff information (BTI) is of great importance in the area of tariff classification. These customs decisions with EU-wide validity contribute to uniform customs administration by determining the classification of specific goods of a particular economic operator. They also constitute a valuable aid for correct interpretation of the Common Customs Tariff with regard to similar or identical goods of different economic operators, as BTIs are collected in the EBTI database, which includes detailed information, key words and even pictures to facilitate its application.

However, BTIs also cause problems that have the potential to endanger uniform customs administration. The possibility for 'BTI shopping', where the holder of a BTI applies for an additional BTI in a different EU Member State hoping for a more favourable decision, will be reduced when BTI decisions become binding for their holder once the Union Customs Code is applied. Nevertheless, the problem of divergent BTIs will continue regarding BTIs of different economic operators, as a BTI decision is still only binding concerning the specific goods of the particular holder of the decision. Although such cases of divergent BTIs are not a huge problem in practice, each case establishes a non-uniform implementation of EU customs law for the time the divergent BTIs are valid, and thus should be resolved as soon as possible. In this context, the European Commission has been intending to improve the procedure already provided for in such cases, but the final implementing provisions have not been adopted yet, which means their effectiveness cannot be evaluated.

Compared to the area of tariff classification, the instruments and mechanisms in the customs areas of valuation and origin are less numerous, and soft law acts do not have a comparable strong de facto binding power. Especially in the area of customs valuation, the conditions for the implementation of EU customs law are significantly different, as the circumstances and relevant facts of each case differ. Thus generally applicable solutions are difficult to find.

In summary, EU customs law contains very detailed provisions, especially regarding the Customs Code Implementing Regulation, accompanied by expertise in the form of the opinions and commentary of the Customs Code Committee and to some extent those of the WCO and the WTO. Best practice guidelines and standardised procedures enhance the harmonisation of working processes. Overall, the system is functioning very well and provides much information on the implementation of EU customs.

In comparison to the administration of the Schengen area, the European Customs Union has been called a 'model EU administration, with full regulatory command over its areas of competence'.[4] Indeed, the Schengen regime governing the border control of persons as administered by police officers or similar units is regulated by an agreement that originally was established outside the sphere of EU law, and heterogeneity and patchwork structures still exist, while not every EU Member State is part of the Schengen area, even though some non-EU Member States are.[5] While there will continue to be scope for improvement, the EU Customs Union can be regarded as an EU Customs Administration Union that will become even stronger once the Union Customs Code is applied.

Finally, the impact of WTO obligations on uniform customs administration in the EU has turned out to be less than expected and generally only subtle – an assessment that complies with observations regarding other established EU policies, which to some extent may be based on the policy continuity that is usually the default position of established policies.[6] Although the European Parliament, as well as the European Commission and to some extent also the EU Member States, pays attention to compliance with WTO rules in principle, the political balance within the EU is considered to be more important than potential WTO dispute settlements.

This is certainly true for the operational level of customs administration. Customs officials in the United Kingdom declared that WTO issues regularly do not filter down into the national customs authority unless there is a practice that has to be changed.[7] Furthermore, even in such cases, often only higher levels in the national customs administration realise the WTO to be the reason for such a change, while the operational level is not aware of the international context, a view confirmed by customs officials in Germany.[8] Even the WTO dispute settlement *EC—Selected Customs Matters* seems to have gone unnoticed by national customs officers, unless they were in a specific section that the European Commission asked for information from. Indeed, WTO issues are to a large part dealt with at the level of the European Commission, while national customs administrations send their experts to assist the European Commission. In contrast, the meetings of the Customs Code Committee and bilateral discussions between different EU Member States are much more often noticed by customs officials of different ranks. This was confirmed in several interviews with customs officials in the United Kingdom,

[4] Hobbing, CEPS Papers No 39, June 2011, p 12.

[5] ibid, p 12; Jørgensen/Sørensen, (37) 2012 ELRev (3), pp 249–67 (264).

[6] Young, in: Costa/Jørgensen (eds), 2012, pp 23–41 (36).

[7] Interview of 9 January 2012 on file with author.

[8] 'Wenn die sich auf dem Panel geeinigt haben und die Amerikaner erheben Strafzölle auf Kekse dann ist das nun einmal so. Dann kriegen wir mitgeteilt "Strafzölle auf Kekse" und den einzelnen Zöllner interessiert nur "So, jetzt muss ich eben statt 20 Prozent 100 Prozent nehmen".' Interview of 20 April 2011 on file with author; 'Wir kriegen dann nur mit, dass es auf eine bestimmte Ware aus China ab Tag X 50 Prozent Anti-Dumping-Zoll zu erheben ist. Und warum, weswegen, ist für uns nicht von Bedeutung.' Interview of 23 May 2011 on file with author.

who stated with regard to the general awareness of the influence of the WTO: 'It does not actually come into our part, does it?',[9] or, 'I have little if anything to do with them.'[10] Similar assessments were made by customs officials interviewed in Germany.[11] Only single customs officers in Germany and in the United Kingdom had noticed—in most cases by chance—the WTO dispute settlement *EC—Selected Customs Matters.*

Yet the theory has been proposed that WTO rules and rulings effectively influence EU regulatory politics in a decentralised way by affecting social mobilisation that then leads to a reconfiguration of an established policy of the EU.[12] However, social mobilisation, understood as the mobilisation of exporters that are possible victims of non-compliance with WTO rules and rulings, has been called implausible, as possible disadvantages for exporters are far too uncertain owing to the vagueness of WTO law.[13] Any influence of WTO law more likely derives from the conceptualisation of WTO rules and rulings, which serves as a frame of reference and a rhetorical device for it to promote its own interests in EU regulatory politics.[14] However, in the reform process of the EU Customs Union, neither compliance with Article X:3(a) GATT 1994 nor the dispute settlement *EC—Selected Customs Matters* have been significantly used as an argument to promote certain aspects in EU customs.

While the great reform of EU customs must have started with full awareness of WTO obligations, given that the WTO dispute settlement *EC—Selected Customs Matters* took place immediately prior to its start, the main reasons for the reform—or at least the reasons presented in public—were different ones. In fact, EU customs is facing a rapidly changing environment, with globalisation leading to increasing numbers of imports and exports, while terrorism has led to new functions in the areas of safety and security for customs administration. Moreover, EU customs also face the challenge of achieving an effective balance between trade facilitation and regulatory invention. This demands new initiatives in order to maintain and enhance the EU's competitiveness. Compliance with WTO rules, in particular Article X:3(a) GATT 1994, seems not to have been a major motivation for reform, at least not one the European Commission admits to.

[9] Interview of 9 January 2012 on file with author.

[10] Interview of 10 January 2012 on file with author.

[11] 'Aber uns ist es nicht bewusst.' Interview of 1 April 2011 on file with author; 'Aber die Welthandelsorganisation in dieser Form ist für uns eigentlich in der täglichen Praxis gar nicht im Fokus, gar nicht im Bewusstsein.' Interview of 7 April 2011 on file with author; 'In den zwei Jahren, wo ich das hier mache, ist es mir nicht aufgefallen.' Interview of 13 April 2011 on file with author; 'Spielt keine Rolle, überhaupt keine.' Interview of 20 April 2011 on file with author; 'Ach Gott, durch Presse, Funk und Fernsehen.' Interview of 10 May 2011 on file with author; 'Also als Privatmann, letztendlich, was man in der Zeitung liest. Aber jetzt so auf dem tatsächlich 100 Prozentig dienstlichen Bereich Null.' Interview of 20 May 2011 on file with author.

[12] Goldstein, in: Narlikar/Daunton/Stern (eds), 2012, pp 64–82 (79).

[13] De Ville, (19) 2012 JEPP (5), pp 700–18 (703, 704).

[14] ibid, pp 700–18 (705, 706).

Nevertheless, in EU customs, there is a clear focus on improving implementation and enhancing uniform administration, whether some influence of WTO obligations has been admitted to or not. Indeed, it seems that the influence of the European Commission, namely DG TAXUD, in EU customs policy and its uniform administration has increased. A significant part of the changes in EU customs pertains to increasing standardisation, best practice guidelines and other guidance by the European Commission, and this seems to have been welcomed, if not requested, by the EU Member States' national customs administrations and economic operators—an assessment that concurs with observations in other EU policy areas.[15]

Even if the EU, as well as the EU Member States, do not want to admit publicly that there exists (and that there is a reaction to) some external pressure on the part of the WTO to comply with its international obligations as they relate to EU customs policy, it cannot be denied that Article X GATT 1994 has received some publicity, including also specifically Article X:3(a) GATT 1994. Article X GATT 1994 has been called a launch pad for ongoing negotiations on the broader topic of trade facilitation, because it can have some impact on enhancing transparency and good governance in transition economies, such as China or Russia.[16] In this context, it seems possible that alternative dispute settlements with regard to Articles I, II and III GATT 1994 would often be unable to address the problem, such claims requiring a high degree of certainty regarding administration and treatment of traders, while uncertainty about such treatment often constitutes the main problem.[17]

Therefore, compared to other possibilities, claims under Article X GATT 1994 seem to be preferable. In the end, although a new panel regarding the EU's compliance with Article X:3(a) GATT 1994 is not on the horizon, caution is to be exercised. The WTO dispute settlement in *EC—IT Products*[18] has shown that to some extent, the European Commission's system for enhancing uniform customs administration bears the risk of being contestable.

[15] Young, in: Costa/Jørgensen (eds), 2012, pp 23–41 (35).
[16] Pauwelyn, 2009 (8) WTR (1), pp 45–48 (46).
[17] ibid, pp 45—48 (47).
[18] WT/DS375,376,377.

Bibliography

BOOKS, MONOGRAPHS AND ESSAYS

Heike Adam, *Mitteilungen der Kommission: Verwaltungsvorschriften des Europäischen Gemeinschaftsrechts?* (Baden-Baden, Nomos, 1999).
Citation: Adam, 1999, p (…).

Panayota Anaboli, 'Customs Violations and Penalties in Europe: Harmonization on the Horizon?' (2010) *Global Trade and Customs Journal*, Vol 5, Issue 9, pp 389–93.
Citation: Anaboli, (5) 2010 GTCJ (9), pp 389–93 (…).

Jürgen Bast, 'New Categories of acts after the Lisbon reform: dynamics of parliamentarization in EU law' (2012) *Common Market Law Review*, Vol 49, pp 885–927.
Citation: Bast, 2009 CMLRev (49), pp 885–927 (…).

Raj Bhala, *Modern GATT Law. A Treatise on the General Agreement on Tariffs and Trade* (London, Sweet & Maxwell, 2005).
Citation: Bhala, 2005, p (…).

Cindy Blechschmidt, 'Die Auslegung unbestimmter Rechtsbegriffe im Zolltarif', Teil 1 (2006) *BDZ-Fachteil*, Vol 12, F89–F90.
Citation: Blechschmidt, 2006 BDZ-Fachteil 12, F89–F90 (…).

Cindy Blechschmidt, 'Die Auslegung unbestimmter Rechtsbegriffe im Zolltarif', Teil 2 (2007) *BDZ-Fachteil*, Vol 1–2, F3–F5.
Citation: Blechschmidt, 2007 BDZ-Fachteil 1–2, F3–F5 (…).

Armin von Bogdandy, 'Information und Kommunikation in der Europäischen Union: föderale Strukturen in supranationalem Umfeld', in Wolfgang Hoffmann-Riem and Eberhard Schmidt-Aßmann (eds), *Verwaltungsrecht in der Informationsgesellschaft*' (Baden-Baden, Nomos, 2000), pp 133–94.
Citation: von Bogdandy, in: Hoffmann-Riem/Schmidt-Aßmann (eds), 2000, pp 133–94 (…).

Carolin Eve Bolhöfer, 'Trade facilitation—WTO law and its revision to facilitate global trade in goods' (2008) *World Customs Journal*, Vol 2, No 1, pp 31–40.
Citation: Bolhöfer, (2) 2008 WCJ (1), pp 31–40 (…).

Sigrid Boysen, 'Das System des Europäischen Außenwirtschaftsrechts', in Andreas von Arnauld (ed), *Europäische Außenbeziehungen* (Baden-Baden, Nomos, 2014), § 9 pp 447–514.
Citation: Boysen, in: von Arnauld (ed), 2014, § 9 pp 447–514, para (…).

Marco Bronckers, 'From "Direct Effect" to "Muted Dialogue"—Recent developments in the European Court's Case Law on the WTO and Beyond' (2008) *Journal of International Economic Law*, Vol 11, Issue 4, pp 885–98.
Citation: Bronckers, (11) 2008 JIEL (4), pp 885–98 (…).

Christian Calliess and Matthias Ruffert (eds), *EUV/AEUV—Das Verfassungsrecht der Europäischen Union mit Europäischer Grundrechtecharta*, 4th edn (Munich, CH Beck, 2011).
Citation: (Author), in: Calliess/Ruffert (eds), 2011, Art (…), para (…).

Merijn Chamon, 'How the concept of essential elements of a legislative act continues to elude the Court. *Parliament v. Council*' (2013) *Common Market Law Review*, Vol 50, pp 849–60.
Citation: Chamon, 2013 CMLRev (50), pp 849–60 (...).

Paul Craig, 'The European Parliament under the Lisbon Treaty', in Stefan Griller and Jacques Ziller (eds), *The Lisbon Treaty* (Wien, Springer, 2008), pp 109–134.
Citation: Craig, in: Griller/Ziller (eds), 2008, pp 109–134 (...).

Paul Craig, *The Lisbon Treaty: Law, Politics and Treaty Reform* (New York, Oxford University Press, 2010).
Citation: Craig, 2010, p (...).

Paul Craig, 'Delegated Acts, Implementing Acts and the New Comitology Regulation' (2011) *European Law Review*, Vol 36, pp 671–87.
Citation: Craig, 2011 ELRev (36), pp 671–87 (...).

Paul Craig, EU Administrative Law, 2nd edn (Oxford, Oxford University Press, 2012).
Citation: Craig, 2012, p (...).

Ernst Czakert, *Das Harmonisierte System 1996* (Cologne, Bundesanzeiger, 1995).
Citation: Czakert, 1995, p (...).

Renaud Dehousse, 'Misfits: EU Law and the Transformation of European Governance', in Christian Joerges and Renaud Dehousse (eds), *Good Governance in Europe's Integrated Market* (New York, Oxford University Press, 2002), pp 207–29.
Citation: Dehousse, in: Joerges/Dehousse (eds), 2003, pp 207–29 (...).

Klaus Deimel, 'Rechtsnatur und Bindungswirkung von Leitlinien der Europäischen Kommission—Zum Vorabentscheidungsverfahren C-260/08' (2009) *Zeitschrift für Zölle und Verbrauchsteuern* Vol 6, pp 157–60.
Citation: Deimel, 2009 ZfZ 6, pp 157–60 (...).

Markus Dierksmeier, 'EG-Zollrecht im Konflikt mit dem Recht der WTO' (Dissertation, Westfälische Wilhelms-Universität Münster, 2007).
Citation: Dierksmeier, 2007, p (...).

Markus Dierksmeier, 'Uneinheitliche Anwendung des EG Zollrechts. Zwingt das WTO-Recht die EG zur Schaffung eines "Europäischen Zollamtes"?' (2008) *Außenwirtschaftliche Praxis* Vol 5, pp 200–03.
Citation: Dierksmeier, 2008 AW-Prax 5, pp 200–03 (...).

Heike Dietrich, 'Amtshilfe im Zollwesen' (Dissertation, Westfälische Wilhelms-Universität Münster, 2005).
Citation: Dietrich, 2005, p (...).

Bart Driessen, 'Delegated legislation after the Treaty of Lisbon: An analysis of Article 290 TFEU' (2010) *European Law Review* Vol 35, pp 837–48.
Citation: Driessen, 2010 ELRev (35), pp 837–48 (...).

Daniel H Erskine, 'The US–EC Dispute over custom matters: trade facilitation, customs unions, and the meaning of WTO obligations' (2006) *Florida Journal of International Law*, Vol 18, No 2, pp 423–84.
Citation: Erskine, (18) 2006 Florida Journal of International Law (2), pp 423–84 (...).

Karl Fuchs, 'Modernisierter Zollkodex und Komitologie' (2011) *Zeitschrift für Zölle und Verbrauchssteuern* Vol 11, pp 281–88.
Citation: Fuchs, 2011 ZfZ 11, pp 281–88 (...).

Lothar Gellert, 'Nichtpräferenzieller Ursprung gemäß Artikel 24 ZK' (2007) *Außenwirtschaftliche Praxis*, Vol 12, pp 511–13.
Citation: Gellert, 2007 AW-Prax 12, pp 511–13 (...).

Lothar Gellert, 'Anmerkung zu EuGH, U v 18.10.2007–Rs C-19/05—(Finanzielle Haftung der Mitgliedstaaten. EuGH verfolgt harte Linie)' (2008) *Außenwirtschaftliche Praxis*, Vol 1, pp 31–32.
Citation: Gellert, 2008 AW-Prax 1, pp 31–32 (…).

Lothar Gellert, 'Rechtsverbindlichkeit von Leitlinien der Europäischen Kommission', in Lothar Gellert (ed), *Zollunion und e-Government: Tagungsband des 21. Europäischen Zollrechtstags des EFA am 18. und 19. Juni 2009 in Linz* (Witten, Mendel, 2009), pp 51–57.
Citation: Gellert, in: Gellert (ed), 2009, pp 51–57 (…).

Lothar Gellert, 'Zum Stand der Arbeiten an der MZK-DVO. Ein Zwischenbericht' (2011) *Außenwirtschaftliche Praxis*, Vol 4, pp 124–25.
Citation: Gellert, 2011 AW-Prax 4, pp 124–25 (…).

Judith Goldstein, 'Trade Liberalization and Domestic Politics', in Amrita Narlikar, Martin Daunton and Robert M Stern (eds), *The Oxford Handbook on the World Trade Organization* (Oxford, Oxford University Press, 2012), pp 64–82.
Citation: Goldstein, in: Narlikar/Daunton/Stern (eds), 2012, pp 64–82 (…).

Laurence W Gormley, *EU Law of Free Movement of Goods and Customs Union* (New York, Oxford University Press, 2009).
Citation: Gormley, 2009, p (…), para (…).

Eberhard Grabitz, Meinhard Hilf and Martin Nettesheim (eds), *Das Recht der Europäischen Union*, 51st edn (Munich, CH Beck, 2013), Vols I–V.
Citation: (Author), in: Grabitz/Hilf/Nettesheim (eds), 2013, Vol (…), Art (…), para (…).

Jean-Michel Grave, 'The Modernised Customs Code: Progress Concerning its Implementation', in Lothar Gellert (ed), *Zollunion und e-Government, Tagungsband des 21 Europäischen Zollrechtstags des EFA am 18 und 19 Juni 2009 in Linz* (Witten, Mendel, 2009), pp 13–25.
Citation: Grave, in: Gellert (ed), 2009, pp 13–25 (…).

Jean-Michel Grave, 'The Impact of the Lisbon Treaty on Customs Matters: A Legal Assessment' (2010) *Global Trade and Customs Journal*, Vol 5, Issue 3, pp 95–111.
Citation: Grave, (5) 2010 GTCJ (3), pp 95–111 (…).

John Grayston, 'The Panel Report on Tariff Treatment of Certain Information Technology Products: Classification Is the Key to Effective Implementation' (2011) *Global Trade and Customs Journal*, Vol 6, Issue 3, pp 149–55.
Citation: Grayston (6) 2011 GTCJ (3), pp 149–55 (…).

Armin Hatje, *Die gemeinschaftsrechtliche Steuerung der Wirtschaftsverwaltung* (Baden-Baden, Nomos, 1998).
Citation: Hatje, 1998, p (…).

Lode Van Den Hende, 'Does the Panel Report in EC-IT Products Imply that Article X:2 of the GATT 1994 Prohibits the restroactive Application of Interpretative Customs Guidance?' (2011) *Global Trade and Customs Journal*, Vol 6, Issue 4, pp 215–16.
Citation: Van Den Hende, (6) 2011 GTCJ (4), pp 215–16 (…).

Christoph Herrmann, 'Case C-351/04, *IKEA Wholesale Ltd v Commissioners of Customs & Excise*, Judgment of the Court of Justice of 27 September 2007, Second Chamber [2007] ECR I-7723' (2008) *Common Market Law Review*, Vol 45, pp 1507–18.
Citation: Herrmann, 2008 CMLRev (45), pp 1507–18 (…).

Christoph Herrmann and Thomas Streinz, 'Die EU als Mitglied der WTO', in Andreas von Arnauld (ed), *Europäische Außenbeziehungen* (Baden-Baden, Nomos, 2014), § 11 pp 587–679.
Citation: Herrmann/Streinz, in: von Arnauld (ed), 2014, § 11 pp 587–679, para (…).

Christoph Herrmann, Wolfgang Weiß and Christoph Ohler (eds), *Welthandelsrecht*, 2nd edn (München, CH Beck, 2007).
Citation: (Author), in: Herrmann/Weiß/Ohler (eds), 2007, para (…).

Tim Hesselink, 'EU Customs Valuation: Wake-Up Call for MNE' (2012) *Global Trade and Customs Journal*, Vol 7, Issue 3, pp 80–91.
Citation: Hesselink, (7) 2012 GTCJ (3), pp 80–91 (…).

Meinhard Hilf/Stefan Oeter, *WTO-Recht. Rechtsordnung des Welthandels* (Baden-Baden, Nomos, 2005).
Citation: (Author) in: Hilf/Oeter (eds), 2005, p (…).

Peter Hobbing, 'Customs Cooperation in the Area of Freedom, Security and Justice: The role of customs in the management of the EU's external border', Justice and Home Affairs, CEPS Papers on Liberty and Security in Europe No 39, June 2011, http://aei.pitt.edu/32072/1/No_39_Hobbing_on Customs_Cooperation.pdf.
Citation: Hobbing, CEPS Papers No 39, June 2011, p (…).

Bernhard M Hoekmann and Petros C Mavroidis, 'Nothing dramatic … regarding administration of customs laws' (2009) *World Trade Review*, Vol 8, No 1, pp 31–44.
Citation: Hoekmann/Mavroidis, (8) 2009 WTR (1), pp 31–44 (…).

Herwig CH Hofmann, 'Legislation, delegation and implementation under the Treaty of Lisbon: typology meets reality' (2009) *European Law Journal*, Vol 15, pp 482–505.
Citation: Hofmann, 2009 ELJ (15), pp 482–505 (…).

Herwig CH Hofmann and Alexander Türk, 'The Development of Integrated Administration in the EU and its Consequences' (2007) *European Law Journal*, Vol 13, No 2, pp 253–71.
Citation: Hofmann/Türk, 2007 ELJ (13), pp 253–71 (…).

Herwig CH Hofmann and Alexander Türk, 'Die Ausübung übertragener Normsetzungsbefugnisse durch die Europäische Kommission' (2012) *Zeitschrift für Gesetzgebung*, pp 105–37.
Citation: Hofmann/Türk, 2012 ZG, pp 105–37 (…).

Herwig CH Hofmann, Gerard C Rowe and Alexander H Türk, *Administrative Law and Policy of the European Union* (Oxford/New York, Oxford University Press, 2011).
Citation: Hofmann/Rowe/Türk, 2011, p (…).

Walter Hübschmann, Ernst Hepp and Armin Spitaler (eds), 'Abgabenordnung, Finanzgerichtsordnung. Kommentar', core manual (Köln, Dr. Otto Schmidt, 1951), 221th supplementary sheet 2013, Vol I–XV.
Citation: (Author), in: Hübschmann/Hepp/Spitaler (eds), 2013, Vol (…), Art (…), para (…).

Carsten Willemoes Jørgensen and Karsten Engsig Sørensen, 'Internal Border Controls in the European Union: Recent challenges and Reforms' (2012) *European Law Review*, Vol 37, No 3, pp 249–67.
Citation: Jørgensen/Sørensen, (37) 2012 ELRev (3), pp 249–67 (…).

Stefan Kadelbach, 'European Administrative Law and the Law of a Europeanized Administration', in Christian Joerges and Renaud Dehousse (eds), *Good Governance in Europe's Integrated Market* (New York, Oxford University Press, 2002), pp 167–206.
Citation: Kadelbach, in: Joerges/Dehousse (eds), 2003, pp 167–206 (…).

Anton Klösters, *Kompetenzen der EG-Kommission im innerstaatlichen Vollzug von Gemeinschaftsrecht* (Cologne/Berlin/Bonn/Munich, Carl Heymanns, 1994).
Citation: Klösters, 1994, p (…).

Siegmar Kunas, 'Der Zoll in Europa', in Matthias Bongartz (ed), *Europa im Wandel* (Cologne/Berlin/Munich, Carl Heymanns, 2000), pp 1–24.
Citation: Kunas, in: Bongartz (ed), 2000, pp 1–24 (…).

Nicolaj Kuplewatzky and Davide Rovetta, 'The Divergence in Theoretical and Practical Use of Combined Nomenclature Explanatory Notes and Tariff Classification Regulations in the EU' (2012) *Global Trade and Customs Journal*, Vol 7, Issues 11 and 12, pp 454–60.
Citation: Kuplewatzky/Rovetta, (7) 2012 GTCJ (11 and 12), pp 454–60 (…).

Silvère Lefevre, 'Interpretative communications and the implementation of Community law at national level' (2004) *European Law Review*, Vol 29, pp 808–22.
Citation: Lefevre, 2004 ELRev (29), pp 808–22 (…).

Carl Otto Lenz and Klaus-Dieter Borchardt, *EU-Verträge—Kommentar*, 6th edn (Cologne, Bundesanzeiger, 2013).
Citation: (Author), in: Lenz/Borchardt (eds), 2013, Art (…), para (…).

Tim Lieber, 'Nichtpräferenzieler Ursprung gem. Art 24 ZK' (2007) *Außenwirtschaftliche Praxis*, Vol 10, pp 424–26.
Citation: Lieber, 2007 AW-Prax 10, pp 424–26 (…).

Tim Lieber, 'Wesentliche Be- oder Verarbeitung gem. Art 24 ZK: EuGH v. 10.12.2009 zu den Listenregeln der Europäischen Kommission' (2010) *Außenwirtschaftliche Praxis*, Vol 2, pp 55–57.
Citation: Lieber, 2010 AW-Prax 2, pp 55–57 (…).

Michael Lux, 'Die Modernisierung der Zollverfahren' (2007) *Außenwirtschaftliche Praxis*, Vol 7, pp 277–80.
Citation: Lux, 2007 AW-Prax 7, pp 277–80 (…).

Michael Lux, '40 Jahre Zollunion—wie geht es weiter?' (2008) *Außenwirtschaftliche Praxis*, Vol 7, pp 283–86.
Citation: Lux, 2008 AW-Prax 7, pp 283–86 (…).

Michael Lux, 'Der Modernisierte Zollkodex. Eine Einführung' (2009) *Zeitschrift für Zölle und Verbrauchssteuern*, Special Vol 1, pp 1–36.
Citation: Lux, 2009 ZfZ Special Vol 1, pp 1–36 (…).

Michael Lux, 'Risikoanalyse bei Waren, die in die EU verbracht werden' (2011) *Außenwirtschaftliche Praxis*, Vol 8, pp 257–61.
Citation: Lux, 2011 AW-Prax 8, pp 257–61 (…).

Michael Lux, 'Der Zoll im Jahre 2020: Ein Ausblick auf die ausstehenden Herausforderungen' (2012) *Außenwirtschaftliche Praxis*, Vol 8, pp 257–62.
Citation: Lux, 2012 AW-Prax 8, pp 257–62 (…).

Michael Lux and Pierre-Jacques Larrieu, 'Der Vorschlag für einen modernisierten Zollkodex–Teil I' (2006) *Zeitschrift für Zölle und Verbrauchssteuern*, Vol 10, pp 301–06.
Citation: Lux/Larrieu, 2006 ZfZ 10, pp 301–06 (…).

Michael Lux and Pierre-Jacques Larrieu, 'Der Vorschlag für einen modernisierten Zollkodex–Teil II' (2006) *Zeitschrift für Zölle und Verbrauchssteuern*, Vol 11, pp 329–41.
Citation: Lux/Larrieu, 2006 ZfZ 11, pp 329–41 (…).

Timothy Lyons, *EC Customs Law*, 2nd edn (Oxford/New York, Oxford University Press, 2008).
Citation: Lyons, 2008, p (…).

Thomas Möller, 'Europäisches Strafrecht und das Zollstrafrecht' (2011) *Zeitschrift für Zölle und Verbrauchssteuern* (ZfZ), Vol 2, pp 39–42.
Citation: Möller, 2011 ZfZ 2, pp 39–42 (…).

Thomas Möller, Gesa Schumann and Peter Sibum, *ZollPraxis* (Sternenfels, Wissenschaft & Praxis, 2010).
Citation: Möller/Schumann/Sibum, 2010, p (…).

Nicholas Moussis, *Access to European Union law, economics, policies*, 19th edn (Rixensart, European Study Service, 2011).
Citation: Moussis, 2011, p (…).

Julia Maren Natzel, 'Der zugelassene Wirtschaftsbeteiligte–Entwicklung und Ergebnis des Rechtsetzungsprozesses' (Dissertation, Westfälische Wilhelms-Universität Münster, 2007).
Citation: Natzel, 2007, p (…).

Hanns Peter Nehl, 'Kontrolle kartellrechtlicher Sanktionsentscheidungen der Kommission durch die Unionsgerichte', in Ulrich Immenga and Torsten Körber (eds), *Die Kommission zwischen Gestaltungsmacht und Rechtsbindung* (Baden-Baden, Nomos, 2012), pp 113–52.
Citation: Nehl, in: Imenga/Körber (eds), 2012, pp 113–52 (…).

Marian Niestedt and Roland M Stein, 'Ist das europäische Zollrecht WTO-widrig? Zugleich eine Anmerkung zu den Berichten des Panels und des AB in Sachen EC-Customs' (2006) *Außenwirtschaftliche Praxis*, Vol 12, pp 516–18.
Citation: Niestedt/Stein, 2006 AW-Prax (12), pp 516–18 (…).

Christoph Ohler, 'Rechtmäßige Errichtung der Gemeinschaftsagentur ENISA' (2006) *Europäische Zeitschrift für Wirtschaftsrecht*, Vol 12, pp 369–74.
Citation: Ohler, 2006 EuZW 12, pp 369–74 (…).

Thomas Oppermann, Claus Dieter Classen and Martin Nettesheim (eds), *Europarecht*, 4th edn (Munich, CH Beck, 2009).
Citation: (Author), in: Oppermann/Classen/Nettesheim (eds), 2009, para (…).

Thomas Oppermann, Claus Dieter Classen and Martin Nettesheim (eds), *Europarecht*, 5th edn (Munich, CH Beck, 2011).
Citation: (Author), in: Oppermann/Classen/Nettesheim (eds), 2011, para (…).

Joost Pauwelyn, 'Comment: Nothing dramatic (… regarding administration of customs laws)' (2009) *World Trade Review*, Vol 8, Issue 1, pp 45–48.
Citation: Pauwelyn, 2009 (8) WTR (1), pp 45–48 (…).

Petra Pohlmann, 'Keine Bindungswirkung von Bekanntmachungen und Mitteilungen der Europäischen Kommission' (2005) *Wirtschaft und Wettbewerb*, Vol 10, pp 1005–09.
Citation: Pohlmann, 2005 WuW 10, pp 1005–09 (…).

Paolo Ponzano, '"Executive" and "delegated" acts: The situation after the Lisbon Treaty', in Stefan Griller and Jacques Ziller (eds), *The Lisbon Treaty* (Wien, Springer, 2008), pp 135–41.
Citation: Ponzano, in: Griller/Ziller (eds), 2008, pp 135–41 (…).

Kathrin Przybilla, 'The "WTOisation" of the customs administration: Uniformity of the administration of law according to Article X:3(a) GATT 1994 and its implications for EU customs law' (2010) FÖV Discussion Papers 58.
Citation: Kathrin Przybilla, 'The "WTOisation" of the customs administration: Uniformity of the administration of law according to Article X:3(a) GATT 1994 and its implications for EU customs law', 2010 FÖV Discussion Papers 58.

Alexander Retemeyer and Thomas Möller, 'Strafrechtliche Bekämpfung von gegen die finanziellen Interessen der EU gerichtetem Betrug–Neues für das Zollstrafrecht?' (2013) *Zeitschrift für Zölle und Verbrauchssteuern*, Vol 2, pp 29–32.
Citation: Retemeyer/Möller, 2013 ZfZ 2, pp 29–32 (…).

Andrea Reuter, 'Modernisierung des Modernisierten Zollkodex. Überlegungen zu einer bereits geraume Zeit andauernden Diskussion über den Recast des MZK' (2012) *Zeitschrift für Zölle und Verbrauchssteuern*, Vol 6, pp 147–50.
Citation: Reuter, 2012 ZfZ 6, pp 147–50 (…).

Andrea Reuter and Karl Fuchs, *Das neue EG-Zollrecht* (Wien, Verlag Österreich GmbH, 2008).
Citation: Reuter/Fuchs, 2008, p (…).

Achim Rogmann, 'Rechtsvollzug und Rechtsschutz im europäischen Zollrecht unter WTO-Einfluss', in Winfried Kluth, Martin Müller and Andreas Peilert (eds), *Wirtschaft—Verwaltung—Recht, Festschrift für Rolf Stober* (Köln/München, Carl Heymans, 2008), pp 797–819.
Citation: Rogmann, in: Kluth/Müller/Peilert (eds), 2008, pp 797–819 (…).

Achim Rogmann, 'Die Wirksamkeit der gemeinschaftsrechtlichen Mechanismen zur einheitlichen Auslegung und Anwendung des Gemeinschaftsrechts—Zum System der Verwaltung des Zollrechts der EG' (2008) *Zeitschrift für Zölle und Verbrauchssteuern*, Vol 3, pp 57–69.
Citation: Rogmann, 2008 ZfZ 3, pp 57–69 (…).

Achim Rogmann, '40 Jahre Zollunion—alles im Gleichklang?' (2008) *Außenwirtschaftliche Praxis*, Vol 5, pp 195–99.
Citation: Rogmann, 2008 AW-Prax 5, pp 195–99 (…).

Davide Rovetta, 'Are Tariff Explanatory Notes Subject to Judicial Supremacy?' (2010) *Global Trade and Customs Journal*, Vol 5, Issue 3, pp 129–31.
Citation: Rovetta, (5) 2010 GTCJ (3), pp 129–31 (…).

Davide Rovetta and Michael Lux, 'The US Challenge to the EC Customs Union' (2007) *Global Trade and Customs Journal*, Vol 2, Issue 5, pp 195–208.
Citation: Rovetta/Lux, (2) 2007 GTCJ (5), pp 195–208.

Reinhart Rüsken (ed), *Dorsch. Zollrecht—Recht des grenzüberschreitenden Warenverkehrs. Kommentar*', core manual, 3rd edn (Munich, Stollfuß, 2001), 144th supplementary sheet 2013, Vols I–IV.
Citation: (Author), in: Rüsken (ed), 2013, Vol (…), Art (…), para (…).

Eberhard Schmidt-Aßmann, 'Verwaltungskooperation und Verwaltungskooperationsrecht in der Europäischen Gemeinschaft' (1996) *Zeitschrift für Europarecht*, Vol 3, pp 270–301.
Citation: Schmidt-Aßmann, 1996 EuR 3, pp 270–301 (…).

Alexander Schoenmakers, 'Anlastungen durch die Europäische Kommission: Verwaltungsfehler auf Kosten der Wirtschaft?', in Lothar Gellert (ed), *40 Jahre Zollunion: Tagungsband des 20. Europäischen Zollrechtstags des EFA am 5 und 6 Juni in Luxemburg* (Witten, Mendel, 2008), pp 117–22.
Citation: Schoenmakers, in: Gellert (ed), 2008, pp 117–22 (…).

Ulrich Schrömbges, 'Bruchreis statt Langkornreis–Führt die falsche Warenbezeichnung zum Entzug aus der zollamtlichen Überwachung?' (2009) *Zeitschrift für Zölle und Verbrauchssteuern*, Vol 8, pp 204–10.
Citation: Schrömbges, 2009 ZfZ 8, pp 204–10 (…).

Marc Schweda, 'Die Bindungswirkung von Bekanntmachungen und Leitlinien der europäischen Kommission' (2004) *Wirtschaft und Wettbewerb*, Vol 11, pp 1133–44.
Citation: Schweda, 2004 WuW 11, pp 1133–44 (…).

Linda Senden, *Soft Law in European Community Law* (Oxford, Hart, 2004).
Citation: Senden, 2004, p (…).

Catherine Soanes and Angus Stevenson (eds) *Oxford Dictionary of English*, 2nd edn, revised (Oxford, Oxford University Press, 2005).
Citation: Oxford Dictionary of English, 2005, p (...).

Axel Sonnefeld, 'Verbindlichkeit der Leitlinien der Kommission' (2008) *Zeitschrift für Zölle und Verbrauchsteuern*, Vol 11, pp 476–77.
Citation: Sonnefeld, 2008 ZfZ 11, pp 476–77 (...).

Ulrich Stelkens, 'Art 291 AEUV, das Unionsverwaltungsrecht und die Verwaltungsautonomie der Mitgliedstaaten—zugleich Abgrenzung der Anwendungsbereiche von Art 290 und Art 291 AEUV' (2012) *Europarecht*, Vol 5, pp 511–45.
Citation: Stelkens, 2012 EuR 5, pp 511–45 (...).

Ulrich Stelkens, 'Rechtsetzungen der europäischen und nationalen Verwaltungen', in Wolfram Höfling (ed), *Grundsatzfragen der Rechtsetzung und Rechtsfindung*, Band 71, (Berlin/Boston, Veröffentlichungen der Vereinigung der Deutschen Staatsrechtslehrer, 2012), pp 369–417.
Citation: Stelkens, in: Höfling (ed), 2012, pp 369–417 (...).

Ulrich Stelkens, 'Die Haftung zwischen Bund und Ländern', in Ines Härtel (ed), *Handbuch Förderalismus—Förderalismus als neue demokratische Rechtsordnung und Rechtskultur in Deutschland, Europa und der Welt.* Band II: Probleme, Reformen, Perspektiven des deutschen Förderalismus (Berlin/Heidelberg, Springer, 2012), § 42 pp 425–61.
Citation: Stelkens, in: Härtel (ed), 2012, § 42 pp 425–61 (...).

Rolf Stober, *Globales Wirtschaftsverwaltungsrecht* (Cologne/Berlin/Bonn/Munich, Carl Heymanns, 2001).
Citation: Stober, 2001, p (...).

Rolf Stober, 'Rezension: Peter Witte (Hrsg), Zollkodex. Kommentar. Mit Durchführungsverordnung und Zollbefreiungsverordnung, 3. Auflage München 2002' (2003) *Neue Juristische Wochenschrift*, Vol 8, p 572.
Citation: Stober, 2003 NJW 8, p 572 (...).

Rudolf Streinz, *Europarecht*, 9th edn (Heidelberg, CF Müller, 2012).
Citation: Streinz, 2012, para (...).

Ben JM Terra and Peter J Wattel (eds), *European Tax Law*, 2nd edn (New York, Kluwer Law International/ Aspen Publishers, 2012).
Citation: (Author), in: Terra/Wattel (eds), 2012, p (...).

Anna Thieme, *Mitteilungen der Europäische Kommission—insbesondere im europäischen Vergaberecht* (Zurich, Schulthess, 2011).
Citation: Thieme, 2011, p (...).

Stefan Thomas, 'Die Bindungswirkung von Mitteilungen, Bekanntmachungen und Leitlinien der EG-Kommission' (2009) *Europarecht*, Vol 3, pp 423–43.
Citation: Thomas, 2009 EuR 3, pp 423–43 (...).

Ferdi De Ville, 'European Union regulatory politics in the shadow of the WTO: WTO rules as frame of reference and rethorical device' (2012) *Journal of European Public Policy*, Vol 19, Issue 5, pp 700–18.
Citation: De Ville, (19) 2012 JEPP (5), pp 700–18 (...).

Carsten Weerth, 'Leitlinien für die besondere Verwendung' (2003) *Außenwirtschaftliche Praxis*, Vol 4, pp 146–48.
Citation: Weerth, 2003 AW-Prax 4, pp 146–48 (...).

Carsten Weerth, *Der neue Zollkodex—Was sich in der Praxis ändert* (Cologne, Bundesanzeiger, 2007).
Citation: Weerth, Bundesanzeiger 2007, p (...).

Carsten Weerth, 'Einheitliche Anwendung des Gemeinsamen Zolltarifs beim Zugang zum Europäischen Binnenmarkt?' (Dissertation, Westfälische Wilhelms-Universität Münster, Witten, 2007).
Citation: Weerth, Witten 2007, p (…).

Carsten Weerth, 'Halloween ist endlich europaweit ein Fest!' (2007) *Außenwirtschaftliche Praxis*, Vol 9, pp 357–58.
Citation: Weerth, 2007 AW-Prax 9, pp 357–58 (…).

Carsten Weerth, 'Das Modell der Zollarbitrage: Ausnutzung von Zolldifferenzen durch die Wirtschaft, Teil 1' (2008) *Außenwirtschaftliche Praxis*, Vol 1, pp 23–25.
Citation: Weerth, 2008 AW-Prax 1, pp 23–25 (…).

Carsten Weerth, 'Das Modell der Zollarbitrage: Ausnutzung von Zolldifferenzen durch die Wirtschaft, Teil 2' (2008) *Außenwirtschaftliche Praxis*, Vol 2, pp 68–72.
Citation: Weerth, 2008 AW-Prax 2, pp 68–72 (…).

Carsten Weerth, '50 Jahre EWG, 40 Jahre Zollunion/-Zolltarifunion ein Grund zum Feiern? Eine kritische Bestandsaufnahme und Analyse' (2008) *Zeitschrift für Zölle und Verbrauchssteuern*, Vol 7, pp 178–85.
Citation: Weerth, 2008 ZfZ 7, pp 178–85 (…).

Carsten Weerth, 'Die MZK-DVO—eine Sachstandsanalyse und Darstellung der Probleme: Verschiebung auf 2015/2016?' (2012) *Zeitschrift für Zölle und Verbrauchssteuern*, Vol 1, pp 8–14.
Citation: Weerth, 2012 ZfZ 1, pp 8–14 (…).

Carsten Weerth, 'Verschiebung des MZK? Der MZK sollte ab 24. Juni 2013 gelten—nun droht die Verschiebung auf nach 2015' (2012) *Außenwirtschaftliche Praxis*, Vol 1, pp 14–17.
Citation: Weerth, 2012 Aw-Prax 1, pp 14–17 (…).

Carsten Weerth, 'Customs Sanctions of the EU-27: A Detailed Analysis and a Preview on the Modernized Customs Code of the EU and the European Union Customs Code' (2013) *Global Trade and Customs Journal*, Vol 8, Issue 2, pp 42–52.
Citation: Weerth, (8) 2013 GTCJ (2), pp 42–52 (…).

Wolfgang Weiß, *Der Europäische Verwaltungsverbund—Grundfragen, Kennzeichen, Herausforderungen* (Berlin, Duncker & Humblot, 2010).
Citation: Weiß, 2010, p (…).

Wolfgang Weiß, 'Das Leitlinien(un)wesen der Kommission verletzt den Vertrag von Lissabon' (2010) *Europäisches Wirtschafts- und Steuerrecht*, Vol 7, pp 257–61.
Citation: Weiß, 2010 EWS 7, pp 257–61 (…).

Wolfgang Weiß, 'After Lisbon, can the European Commission continue to rely on 'Soft Legislation' in its Enforcement Practice?' (2011) *Journal of European Competition Law & Practice*, Vol 2, Issue 5, pp 441–51.
Citation: Weiß, (2) 2011 JECLAP (5), pp 441–51 (…).

Wolfgang Weiß, 'Agencies versus Networks: From Divide to Convergence in European Administrative Governance', in Herwig CH Hofmann and Russell L Weaver (eds), *Transatlantic Perspectives on Administrative Law* (Brussels, Bruylant, 2011), pp 221–50.
Citation: Weiß, in: Hofmann/Weaver (eds), 2011, pp 221–50 (…).

Izaak Wind, 'HS 2007: What's it All About?' (2007) *Global Trade and Customs Journal*, Vol 2, pp 79–86.
Citation: Wind, 2007 GTCJ (2), pp 79–86 (…).

Peter Witte, 'Editorial: Vorteile schon heute leben' (2012) *Außenwirtschaftliche Praxis*, Vol 4, p 119.
Citation: Witte, 2012 AW-Prax 4, p 119 (…).

Peter Witte, 'Compliance im Zollrecht—Teil 1, Gedankenanstöße zur Risikoerkennung' (2012) *Außenwirtschaftliche Praxis*, Vol 5, pp 185–89.
Citation: Witte, 2012 AW-Prax 5, pp185–89 (…).

Peter Witte (ed), *Zollkodex. Kommentar*, 6th edn (Munich, CH Beck, 2013).
Citation: (Author), in: Witte (ed) 2013, Art (…), para (…).

Peter Witte and Hans-Michael Wolffgang (eds), *Lehrbuch des Europäischen Zollrechts*, 7th edn (Herne, Neue Wirtschafts-Briefe, 2012).
Citation: (Author), in: Witte/Wolffgang (eds), 2012, p (…), para (…).

Peter Witte, Reginhard Henke and Nadja Kammerzell (eds), *Der Modernisierte Zollodex: Was ändert sich, was bleibt gleich? Praxisleitfaden zu den Änderungen im europäischen Zollrecht* (Cologne, Bundesanzeiger, 2009).
Citation: (Author), in: Witte/Henke/Kammerzell (eds), 2009, p (…).

Hans-Michael Wolffgang, 'Dienstanweisung aus Brüssel?' (2002) *Außenwirtschaftliche Praxis*, Vol 3, p 81.
Citation: Wolffgang, 2002 AW-Prax 3, p 81 (…).

Alasdair R Young, 'Less than you might think: the impact of WTO rules on EU policies', in Oriol Costa and Knud Eric Jørgensen (eds), *The influence of international institutions on the EU* (Houndmills/New York, Palgrave, 2012), pp 23–41.
Citation: Young, in: Costa/Jørgensen (eds) 2012, pp 23–41 (…).

Anton Zeilinger, 'Sachstand beim Zollkodex der Union', in Gerda Koszinowski (ed), *Grenzerfahrung in der Europäischen Union: Tagungsband des 24. Europäischen Zollrechtstags des EFA am 14 und 15 Juni 2012 in Erfurt* (Witten, Mendel, 2013), pp 103–07.
Citation: Zeilinger, in: Koszinowski (ed), 2013, pp 103–07 (…).

DOCUMENTS OF THE EUROPEAN COMMISSION

Communication from the Commission to the Council, the European Parliament and the European Economic and Social Committee of 8 February 2001, 'concerning a strategy for the Customs Union', COM (2001) 51 final, http://eur-lex.europa.eu/LexUriServ/LexUriServ.do?uri=COM:2001:0051:FIN:EN:PDF.
Citation: COM (2001) 51 final, p (…).

European Commission, 'European Governance—A White Paper' COM (2001) 428 final, http://eur-lex.europa.eu/LexUriServ/site/en/com/2001/com2001_0428en01.pdf.
Citation: COM (2001) 428 final, p (…).

Communication from the Commission of 5 December 2001, 'Simplifying and improving the regulatory environment', COM (2001) 726 final, http://eur-lex.europa.eu/LexUriServ/LexUriServ.do?uri=COM:2001:0726:FIN:EN:PDF.
Citation: COM (2001) 726 final, p (…).

Communication from the Commission to the Council, the European Parliament, the European Economic and Social Committee and the Committee of the Regions of 28 May 2002, 'eEurope 2005: An information society for all', COM (2002) 263 final, http://eur-lex.europa.eu/LexUriServ/LexUriServ.do?uri=COM:2002:0263:FIN:EN:PDF.
Citation: COM (2002) 263 final, p (…).

Communication from the Commission to the Council, the European Parliament and the European Economic and Social Committee of 24 April 2003, 'A simple and paperless environment for Customs and Trade', COM (2003) 452 final, http://eur-lex.europa.eu/LexUriServ/LexUriServ.do?uri=COM:2003:0452:FIN:EN:PDF.
Citation: COM (2003) 452 final, p (…).

Communication from the Commission to the Council, the European Parliament, the European Economic and Social Committee and the Committee of the Regions of 26 September 2003, 'The Role of eGovernment for Europes' Future', COM (2003) 567 final, http://eur-lex.europa.eu/LexUriServ/LexUriServ.do?uri=COM:2003:0567:FIN:EN:PDF.
Citation: COM (2003) 567 final, p (…).

Report from the Commission to the European Parliament and the Council, Report on the implementation of the Customs 2002 programme (1998–2002), Brussels, 11 November 2003, COM (2003) 672 final, http://eur-lex.europa.eu/LexUriServ/LexUriServ.do?uri=COM:2003:0672:FIN:EN:PDF.
Citation: COM (2003) 672 final, p (…).

Communication from the Commission to the European Parliament and the Council of 18 May 2004, 'enhancing police and customs cooperation in the European Union', COM (2004) 376 final, http://eur-lex.europa.eu/LexUriServ/LexUriServ.do?uri=COM:2004:0376:FIN:EN:PDF.
Citation: COM (2004) 376 final, p (…).

European Commission, 'Standardised Framework for Risk Management in the customs administrations of the EU', 30 September 2004, http://ec.europa.eu/taxation_customs/resources/documents/framework_doc.pdf.
Citation: European Commission, Standardised Framework for Risk Management, p (…).

Communication from the Commission to the Council and the European Parliament of 6 April 2005, 'Community Programmes Customs 2013 and Fiscalis 2013', COM (2005) 111 final, http://eur-lex.europa.eu/LexUriServ/LexUriServ.do?uri=COM:2005:0111:FIN:EN:PDF.
Citation: COM (2005) 111 final, p (…).

European Commission, Proposal 2005/0246 (COD) of 30 November 2005 for a regulation of the European Parliament and of the Council laying down the Community Customs Code (Modernised Customs Code), COM (2005) 608 final, http://eur-lex.europa.eu/LexUriServ/LexUriServ.do?uri=COM:2005:0608:FIN:EN:PDF.
Citation: COM (2005) 608 final, p (…).

European Commission, Proposal 2005/0247 (COD) of 30 November 2005 for a decision of the European Parliament and of the Council on a paperless environment for trade and customs, COM (2005) 609 final, http://ec.europa.eu/taxation_customs/resources/documents/common/legislation/proposals/customs/COM609_F_en.pdf.
Citation: COM (2005) 609 final, p (…).

Press release of the European Commission on 30 November 2005, 'Customs: European Commission proposes a new customs environment to face globalisation challenges', IP/05/1501, http://europa.eu/rapid/pressReleasesAction.do?reference=IP/05/1501.
Citation: European Commission, IP/05/1501.

European Commission—Customs Code Committee, Section for General Customs Rules, 'Nature and legal value of guidelines', TAXUD/1406/2006—EN, 5 April 2006, http://ec.europa.eu/taxation_customs/resources/documents/customs/procedural_aspects/general/community_code/1406-en-lignes_directrices.pdf.
Citation: European Commission, TAXUD/1406/2006–EN, p (…).

Commission Staff Working Document of 15 July 2006, 'Annex to the Proposal for a Decision of the European Parliament and of the Council establishing an action programme for customs in the Community (Customs 2013) (COM (2006) 201 final)—Impact assessment', /*SEC/2006/0570*/, http://eur-lex.europa.eu/LexUriServ/LexUriServ.do?uri=SEC:2006:0570:FIN:EN:HTML.
Citation: Commission Staff Working Document of 15 July 2006, /*SEC/2006/0570*/.

Press Release of the European Commission on 18 December 2006, 'Commission reinforces the security of the EU supply chain while facilitating international trade', IP/06/1821, http://europa.eu/rapid/pressReleasesAction.do?reference=IP/06/1821&format=HTML&aged=0&language=en&guiLanguage=en.
Citation: European Commission, Press Release on 18 December 2006, IP/06/1821.

Communication from the Commission of 5 September 2007, 'A Europe of Results—Applying Community Law', COM (2007) 502 final, http://ec.europa.eu/eu_law/eulaw/pdf/com_2007_502_en.pdf.
Citation: COM (2007) 502 final, p (…).

Communication from the Commission to the Council, the European Parliament and the European Economic and Social Committee of 1 April 2008, 'Strategy for the evolution of the Customs Union', Brussels, COM (2008) 169 final, http://ec.europa.eu/taxation_customs/resources/documents/customs/com(2008)169_en.pdf.
Citation: COM (2008) 169 final, p (…).

Press Release of the European Commission on 2 April 2008, 'Customs beyond 2013: Commission launches a debate on the future evolution of Customs', IP/08/492, http://europa.eu/rapid/press-release_IP-08-492_en.htm?locale=en.
Citation: European Commission, Press Release on 2 April 2008, IP/08/492.

European Commission—Customs Code Committee, Customs Valuation Section, 'Compendium of Customs Valuation texts', updated edition 2008, TAXUD/800/2002-EN, Brussels, September 2008, http://ec.europa.eu/taxation_customs/resources/documents/customs/customs_duties/declared_goods/european/compendium_2008_en.pdf.
Citation: European Commission, 'Compendium of Customs Valuation texts', 2008, TAXUD/800/2002-EN, p (…).

Report from the Commission to the European Parliament and the Council, Final evaluation of the Customs 2007 programme in accordance with Article 19 of Decision 253/2003/EC of the European Parliament and the Council of 6 February 2003 adopting an action programme for customs in the Community (Customs 2007), Brussels, 7 October 2008, COM (2008) 612 final, http://eur-lex.europa.eu/LexUriServ/LexUriServ.do?uri=COM:2008:0612:FIN:EN:PDF.
Citation: COM (2008) 612 final, p (…).

European Commission, 2008 E-customs progress report, Taxud.c.1 (2009)172599, http://ec.europa.eu/taxation_customs/resources/documents/customs/policy_issues/e-customs_initiative/2008_progress_report_after_ecg_en.pdf.
Citation: 2008 E-customs progress report, Taxud.c.1(2009)172599, p (…).

Electronic Customs Multi-Annual Strategic Plan (MASP) 2008 yearly revision (MASP Rev 9), TAXUD/477/2004—Rev.9—EN, Brussels, 22 September 2008, http://ec.europa.eu/taxation_customs/resources/documents/customs/policy_issues/e-customs_initiative/masp_strategic_plan_en.pdf (no longer available; manuscript in possession of the author).
Citation: MASP 2008, TAXUD/477/2004—Rev.9—EN, p (…).

European Commission, TAXUD Brochure 'Participating in Customs and Fiscalis Cooperation Programmes 2013', Brussels 20 January 2009, http://ec.europa.eu/taxation_customs/resources/documents/taxation/tax_cooperation/fiscalis_programme/brochure.pdf.

Citation: European Commission, Brochure on the Customs Cooperation Programme 2013, 2009, p (...).

Communication from the Commission to the European Parliament and the Council of 9 December 2009, 'Implementation of Article 290 of the Treaty on the Functioning of the European Union', COM (2009) 673 final, http://eur-lex.europa.eu/LexUriServ/LexUriServ.do?uri=COM:2009:0673:FIN:EN:PDF.

Citation: COM (2009) 673 final, p (...).

European Commission, 2009 E-customs progress report, Taxud.a.1(2010) 364729, http://ec.europa.eu/taxation_customs/resources/documents/customs/policy_issues/e-customs_initiative/2009_progress_report_en.pdf.

Citation: 2009 E-customs progress report, Taxud.a.1 (2010) 364729, p (...).

Communication from the Commission of 3 March 2010, 'Europe 2020—A strategy for smart, sustainable and inclusive growth', COM (2010) 2020 final, http://eur-lex.europa.eu/LexUriServ/LexUriServ.do?uri=COM:2010:2020:FIN:EN:PDF.

Citation: COM (2010) 2020 final, p (...).

European Commission—Customs Code Committee, Import/Export Formalities Section, 'Guidelines on export and exit in the context of Regulation (EC) 648/2005 (applicable from 1-1-2011)', TAXUD/A3/0034/2010, 25 October 2010, http://ec.europa.eu/ecip/documents/procedures/export_exit_guidelines_en.pdf.

Citation: European Commission, Export Guidelines, TAXUD/A3/0034/2010, p (...).

European Commission, 2010 E-customs progress report, Taxud.a.1 (2011) 806750, http://ec.europa.eu/taxation_customs/resources/documents/customs/policy_issues/e-customs_initiative/2010_progress_report_en.pdf.

Citation: 2010 E-customs progress report, Taxud.a.1 (2011) 806750, p (...).

European Commission DG TAXUD Brochure, 'European customs laboratories: Experience you can rely on', 2010, http://ec.europa.eu/taxation_customs/resources/documents/customs/customs_controls/custom_laboratories/brochure_gcl.pdf.

Citation: European Commission, Brochure on the European Customs Laboratories, 2010, p (...).

European Commission, 'Transit Manual', TAXUD/A3/0007/2010, http://ec.europa.eu/taxation_customs/resources/documents/customs/procedural_aspects/transit/common_community/transit_manual_consolidation_en.pdf.

Citation: European Commission, 'Transit Manual', TAXUD/A3/0007/2010, p (...).

European Commission, Customs 2013 Programme–Monitoring Guide, 2010, http://ec.europa.eu/taxation_customs/resources/documents/customs/cooperation_programmes/background_papers/monitoring_guide_en.pdf.

Citation: European Commission, Customs 2013 Programme–Monitoring Guide, 2010, p (...).

Communication from the Commission to the European Parliament, the Council, the Economic and Social Committee and the Committee of the Regions of 13 April 2011, 'Single Market Act—Twelve levers to boost growth and strengthen confidence—"Working together to create new growth"', COM (2011) 206 final, http://ec.europa.eu/internal_market/smact/docs/20110413-communication_en.pdf.

Citation: COM (2011) 206 final, p (...).

Communication from the Commission to the European Parliament, the Council, the European Economic and Social Committee, and the Committee of the Regions and the Court of Auditors of 24 June 2011 'on the Commission Anti-Fraud Strategy', COM (2011) 376 final, http://ec.europa.eu/anti_fraud/documents/preventing-fraud-documents/ec_antifraud_strategy_en.pdf.
Citation: COM (2011) 376 final, p (...).

Report from the Commission to the European Parliament, the Council, the European Economic and Social Committee and the Committee of the Regions, 'Midterm evaluation of the Customs 2013 Programme', Brussels, 5 September 2011, COM (2011) 537 final, http://eur-lex.europa.eu/LexUriServ/LexUriServ.do?uri=COM:2011:0537:FIN:EN:PDF.
Citation: COM (2011) 537 final, p (...).

Commission Staff Working Paper of 24 June 2011, 'Action plan to fight against smuggling of cigarettes and alcohol along the EU Eastern Border', SEC (2011) 791 final, http://ec.europa.eu/anti_fraud/documents/preventing-fraud-documents/eastern_border_action_plan_en.pdf.
Citation: SEC (2011) 791 final, p (...).

European Commission, Proposal 2011/0341 (COD) of 9 November 2011 for a Regulation of the European Parliament and of the Council establishing an action programme for customs and taxation in the European Union for the period 2014–2020 (FISCUS) and repealing Decisions 1482/2007/EC and 624/2007/EC, COM (2011) 706 final, http://ec.europa.eu/taxation_customs/resources/documents/com_2011_706_en.pdf.
Citation: COM (2011) 706 final, p (...).

Commission Staff Working Paper of 9 November 2011, 'Impact assessment accompanying the document "Proposal of the European Commission of 9 November for a regulation of the European Parliament and the Council establishing an action programme for customs and taxation in the European Union for the period 2014–2020 (Fiscus) and repealing Decisions 1482/2007/EC and 624/2007/EC" Vol 1/2', SEC (2011) 1317 final, http://ec.europa.eu/taxation_customs/resources/documents/sec_2011_1317_part1_en.pdf.
Citation: SEC (2011) 1317 final, p (...).

Commission Staff Working Paper of 9 November 2011, 'Executive summary of the impact assessment accompanying the document "Proposal for a Regulation of the European Parliament and of the Council establishing an action programme for customs and taxation in the European Union for the period 2014–2020 (FISCUS) and repealing Decisions No 1482/2007/EC and No 624/2007/EC"', SEC (2011) 1318 final, http://ec.europa.eu/taxation_customs/resources/documents/sec_2011_1318_en.pdf.
Citation: SEC (2011) 1318 final, p (...).

European Commission—Customs Code Committee—Customs Valuation Section, 'Summary of conclusions reached during the 10th meeting of the Customs Code Committee—Valuation, held on 30 September 2011', TAXUD/B4/MN/D(2011)1287374, Brussels, 11 November 2011, manuscript in possession of the author.
Citation: Customs Code Committee, Conclusions of 30 September 2011, TAXUD/B4/MN/D(2011)1287374, p (...).

European Commission, Consolidated preliminary draft of the MCCIP of 25 November 2011, Document TAXUD/MCCIP/2010/100-3, manuscript in possession of the author.
Citation: Consolidated preliminary draft of the MCCIP of 25 November 2011, Document TAXUD/MCCIP/2010/100-3, p (...).

Communication from the Commission to the Council and the European Parliament of 2 December 2011, 'Report on Progress on the Strategy for the Evolution of the Customs Union', COM (2011) 922 final, http://eur-lex.europa.eu/LexUriServ/LexUriServ.do?uri=COM:2011:0922:FIN:EN:PDF.
Citation: COM (2011) 922 final, p (…).

European Commission, 2011 E-Customs progress report, Taxud.a.3 (2013) 1630576, http://ec.europa.eu/taxation_customs/resources/documents/customs/policy_issues/e-customs_initiative/2011_progress_report_en.pdf.
Citation: 2011 E-Customs progress report, Taxud.a.3 (2013) 1630576, p (…).

European Commission—Customs Code Committee, Customs Valuation Section, 'Summary of conclusions reached during the 11th meeting of the Customs Code Committee—Valuation, held on 2nd December 2011', TAXUD/B4/MN/D (2012)94162, Brussels, 26 January 2012, manuscript in possession of the author.
Citation: Customs Code Committee, Conclusions of 2 December 2011, TAXUD/B4/MN/D(2012)94162, p (…).

European Commission, Proposal 2012/0027 (COD) of 20 February 2012 for a Regulation of the European Parliament and of the Council laying down the Union Customs Code (Recast), COM (2012) 64 final, http://eur-lex.europa.eu/LexUriServ/LexUriServ.do?uri=COM:2012:0064:FIN:EN:PDF.
Citation: COM (2012) 64 final, p (…).

European Commission–Customs Code Committee, Customs Valuation Section, 'Agenda of the twelfth meeting of the Customs Code Committee,—Section Valuation; which will be held in Brussels on 9th March 2012 at the Albert Borschette Center', Brussels, 22 February 2012, TAXUD B4/NM/D(2012)226869, manuscript in possession of the author.
Citation: Customs Code Committee, Conclusions of 9 March 2012, TAXUD B4/NM/D(2012)226869, p (…).

European Commission, 'Authorised Economic Operators Guidelines', TAXUD/B2/047/2011—Rev.3, 17 April 2012, Brussels, http://ec.europa.eu/taxation_customs/resources/documents/customs/policy_issues/customs_security/aeo_guidelines2012_en.pdf.
Citation: European Commission, AEO Guidelines, TAXUD/B2/047/2011—Rev 3, p (…).

European Commission—Customs Code Committee, 'Rules of procedure for the Customs Code Committee', Brussels, 30 May 2012, TAXUD/A2/2011/011 Final—EN, http://ec.europa.eu/taxation_customs/resources/documents/customs/procedural_aspects/general/community_code/rulesofprocedureofthecommittee_en.pdf.
Citation: Customs Code Committee, Rules of Procedure, TAXUD/A2/2011/011 Final—EN.

European Commission, 'European Binding Tariff Information–Report of the first phase of the exercise to monitor the issuing of BTI and the application of the relevant Community legal provisions in the Member States 2007 and 2008', June 2012, http://ec.europa.eu/taxation_customs/resources/documents/common/publications/info_docs/customs/ebti_report_phase1_en.pdf.
Citation: European Commission, EBTI Monitoring Report (2007–08), 2012, p (…).

European Commission, Proposal 2012/0193 (COD) of 11 July 2012 for a directive of the European Parliament and of the Council on the fight against fraud to the Union's financial interests by means of criminal law, COM (2012) 363 final, http://eur-lex.europa.eu/LexUriServ/LexUriServ.do?uri=COM:2012:0363:FIN:EN:PDF.
Citation: COM (2012) 363 final, p (…).

European Commission, Amended Proposal 2011/0341/a (COD) of 29 August 2012 for a Regulation of the European Parliament and of the Council establishing an action programme for customs in the European Union for the period 2014–2020 (Customs 2020) and repealing Decision 624/2007/EC, Brussels, COM (2012) 464 final, http://ec.europa.eu/taxation_customs/resources/documents/com_2012_464_en.pdf.
Citation: COM (2012) 464 final, p (...).

Communication from the Commission to the European Parliament, the Council and the European Economic and Social Committee of 21 December 2012, 'on the State of the Customs Union', COM (2012) 791 final, http://ec.europa.eu/taxation_customs/resources/documents/common/publications/com_reports/customs/com(2012)791_en.pdf.
Citation: COM (2012) 791 final, p (...).

Communication from the Commission to the European Parliament, the Council and the European Economic and Social Committee of 8 January 2013, 'on Customs Risk Management and Security of the Supply Chain', COM (2012) 793 final, http://ec.europa.eu/taxation_customs/resources/documents/customs/customs_controls/risk_management/customs_eu/com_2012_793_en.pdf.
Citation: COM (2012) 793 final, p (...).

European Commission, 2012 E-Customs annual progress report, taxud.a.3(2013) 3213327, http://ec.europa.eu/taxation_customs/resources/documents/customs/policy_issues/e-customs_initiative/2012_progress_report.pdf.
Citation: 2012 E-Customs annual progress report, taxud.a.3(2013) 3213327, p (...).

European Commission, DG Taxation and Customs Union Management Plan 2012, http://ec.europa.eu/atwork/synthesis/amp/doc/taxud_mp.pdf.
Citation: DG Taxation and Customs Union Management Plan 2012, p (...).

Electronic Customs Multi-Annual Strategic Plan 2012 Revision—MASP Rev 11 Version 3.0, Taxud.a.3 ARES (2012) 1677638, Brussels, 4 December 2012, http://ec.europa.eu/taxation_customs/resources/documents/customs/policy_issues/e-customs_initiative/masp_strategic_plan_en.pdf (no longer available, manuscript in possession of the author).
Citation: MASP 2012 Revision, TAXUD.a.3 ARES (2012) 1677638, p (...).

MASP Annex 1 timetable (2012), http://ec.europa.eu/taxation_customs/resources/documents/customs/policy_issues/e-customs_initiative/masp_timetable.pdf.
Citation: MASP Annex 1 on the detailed timetable (2012), p (...).

MASP Annex 2 Consolidated Project Fiches (2012), 4 December 2012, Ref. Ares(2012)1450710—06/12/2012, http://ec.europa.eu/taxation_customs/resources/documents/customs/policy_issues/e-customs_initiative/annex_2_consolidated_fiches_en.pdf.
Citation: MASP Annex 2 on the consolidated project fiches (2012), p (...).

European Commission, MASP Annex 3 Governance Scheme for the Implementation of the MASP and its related Electronic Customs Projects (2012), 4 December 2012, Taxud.a.3(2012) 1677638, http://ec.europa.eu/taxation_customs/resources/documents/customs/policy_issues/e-customs_initiative/annex_3_governance_scheme_en.pdf.
Citation: MASP Annex 3 on the governance scheme (2012), p (...).

MASP Annex 4 Trade Contact Group Terms of Reference, 18 December 2008, no longer referred to under the MASP 2013, working document TAXUD/1426/2007 Revision 2,

http://ec.europa.eu/taxation_customs/resources/documents/customs/policy_issues/e-customs_initiative/annex_4_terms_reference_en.pdf.
Citation: MASP Annex 4 on the Trade Contact Group terms of reference (2008), no longer referred to under the MASP 2013, working document TAXUD/1426/2007 Revision 2, p (…).

MASP Annex 5 Business Process Modelling Policy (2012), Ref Ares(2012)1450710—06/12/2012, http://ec.europa.eu/taxation_customs/resources/documents/customs/policy_issues/e-customs_initiative/annex_5_bpm_policy_en.pdf.
Citation: MASP Annex 5 on the BPM policy (2012), p (…).

MASP Annex 6 IT strategy (2012), 4 December 2012, Taxud.r.5 (2012), http://ec.europa.eu/taxation_customs/resources/documents/customs/policy_issues/e-customs_initiative/annex_6_it_strategy_en.pdf.
Citation: MASP Annex 6 on the IT strategy (2012), p (…).

European Commission—Taxation and Customs Union (2013), 'Report on EU customs enforcement of intellectual property rights—Results at the EU border 2012', http://ec.europa.eu/taxation_customs/resources/documents/customs/customs_controls/counterfeit_piracy/statistics/2013_ipr_statistics_en.pdf.
Citation: European Commission, 2012 Report on Intellectual Property Rights Enforcement, p (…).

European Commission, DG Taxation and Customs Union Management Plan 2013, http://ec.europa.eu/atwork/synthesis/amp/doc/taxud_mp_en.pdf.
Citation: DG Taxation and Customs Union Management Plan 2013, p (…).

Electronic Customs Multi-Annual Strategic Plan 2013 Revision–MASP Rev 12 Version 1.2, Taxud.a.3 (2013) 3763373, Brussels, 19 November 2013, http://ec.europa.eu/taxation_customs/resources/documents/customs/policy_issues/e-customs_initiative/masp_strategic_plan_en.pdf.
Citation: MASP 2013 Revision, Taxud.a.3 (2013) 3763373, p (…).

MASP Annex 1 timetable (2013), http://ec.europa.eu/taxation_customs/resources/documents/customs/policy_issues/e-customs_initiative/masp_annex1.pdf.
Citation: MASP Annex 1 on the detailed timetable (2013), p (…).

MASP Annex 2 Consolidated Project Fiches (2013), 19 November 2013, Taxud.a.3 (2013) 3763373, http://ec.europa.eu/taxation_customs/resources/documents/customs/policy_issues/e-customs_initiative/masp_annex2_en.pdf.
Citation: MASP Annex 2 on the consolidated project fiches (2013), p (…).

European Commission, Governance Scheme for the Implementation of the MASP and its related Electronic Customs Projects, Taxud.a.3 (2013)3651276 MASP Annex 3 Revision 12 v1.1, Brussels, 4 November 2013, http://ec.europa.eu/taxation_customs/resources/documents/customs/policy_issues/e-customs_initiative/masp_annex3_en.pdf.
Citation: MASP Annex 3 on the governance scheme (2013), p (…).

MASP Annex 4 EU Customs Business Process Modelling Policy (2013), 4 November 2013, Taxud.a3 (2013)3651276, http://ec.europa.eu/taxation_customs/resources/documents/customs/policy_issues/e-customs_initiative/masp_annex4_en.pdf.
Citation: Annex 4 on the BPM policy (2013), p (…).

Annex 5 on the IT strategy (2013), 4 November 2013, Taxud.(2013)3651276, http://ec.europa.eu/taxation_customs/resources/documents/customs/policy_issues/e-customs_initiative/masp_annex5_en.pdf.
Citation: Annex 5 on the IT strategy (2013), p (…).

European Commission, 'Guidelines for import controls in the area of product safety and compliance', http://ec.europa.eu/taxation_customs/resources/documents/common/publications/info_docs/customs/product_safety/guidelines_en.pdf.
Citation: European Commission, Import Control Guidelines, p (…).

European Commission, 'Information paper on the application of Articles 220(2)(b) and 239 of the Community Customs Code', http://ec.europa.eu/taxation_customs/resources/documents/customs/procedural_aspects/general/debt/guidelines_en.pdf.
Citation: European Commission, Information Paper on Articles 220(2)(b) and 239 CCC, p (…).

European Commission, 'Application for Binding Tariff Information (BTI)—General Information', http://ec.europa.eu/taxation_customs/resources/documents/common/databases/ebti/ebti_general_information_en.pdf.
Citation: European Commission, BTI–General Information, p (…).

European Commission, 'BTI Application Form', http://ec.europa.eu/taxation_customs/resources/documents/bti_application_form_en.pdf.
Citation: European Commission, 'BTI Application Form', p (…).

European Commission, 'Frequently asked questions about BTI', http://ec.europa.eu/taxation_customs/dds2/ebti/faq/ebtifaq_en.pdf?Lang=en&Screen=0&PageName=+%26gt%3b+FAQ&DomainNameLink=ebti_home.jsp&DomainName=European+Binding+Tariff+Information+(EBTI)&callbackuri=CBU-4.
Citation: European Commission, 'Frequently asked questions about BTI', p (…).

DOCUMENTS OF THE EUROPEAN PARLIAMENT

European Parliament Resolution of 19 June 2008 on the fortieth anniversary of the Customs Union, text adopted P6_TA(2008) 0305, www.europarl.europa.eu/sides/getDoc.do?pubRef=-//EP//TEXT+TA+P6-TA-2008-0305+0+DOC+XML+V0//en.
Citation: European Parliament Resolution of 19 June 2008, text adopted P6_TA(2008) 0305, p (…).

European Parliament Resolution of 1 December 2011 on modernisation of customs (2001/2083(INI)), text adopted P7_TA(2011)0546, www.europarl.europa.eu/sides/getDoc.do?pubRef=-//EP//NONSGML+TA+P7-TA-2011-0546+0+DOC+PDF+V0//EN.
Citation: European Parliament Resolution of 1 December 2011 (2001/2083(INI)), text adopted P7_TA(2011)0546, para (…).

European Parliament, Study 'Implementation of the Modernised Customs Code', Policy Department, Economic and Scientific Policy, Brussels February 2012, IP/A/IMCO/ST/2011-11, PE 475.094, www.europarl.europa.eu/document/activities/cont/201203/20120302ATT39810/20120302ATT39810EN.pdf.
Citation: European Parliament, Study 2012, IP/A/IMCO/ST/2011-11, PE 475.094, p (…).

European Parliament, Committee on the Internal Market and Consumer Protection, amendments tabled in committee, PE498.017, 29.10.2012, www.europarl.europa.eu/sides/getDoc.do?pubRef=-//EP//NONSGML+COMPARL+PE-498.017+01+DOC+PDF+V0//EN&language=EN.
Citation: European Parliament, Committee Amendments of 29 October 2012, PE498.017, 29.10.2012, p (…).

European Parliament, Report of the first reading in the ordinary legislative procedure (Union Customs Code. Recast), 26 February 2013, A7-0006/2013, www.europarl.europa.eu/sides/getDoc.do?pubRef=-//EP//NONSGML+REPORT+A7-2013-0006+0+DOC+PDF+V0//EN.
Citation: European Parliament, First Reading Report of 26 February 2013, A7-0006/2013, p (…).

DOCUMENTS OF THE COUNCIL OF THE EUROPEAN UNION

Council of the European Union, Press Release, 2866th Council Meeting, Economic and Financial Affairs, ECOFIN Council Conclusions of 14 May 2008, 8850/08 (Presse 113), www.consilium.europa.eu/ueDocs/cms_Data/docs/pressData/en/ecofin/100339.pdf.
Citation: ECOFIN Council Conclusions of 14 May 2008, 8850/08 (Presse 113), p (…).

Council of the European Union, 'Conclusions on the Progress on the Strategy for the Evolution of the Customs Union', 328th Competitiveness (Internal Market, Industry, Research and Space) Council meeting, 10 and 11 December 2012, www.consilium.europa.eu/uedocs/cms_data/docs/pressdata/en/intm/134129.pdf.
Citation: Council, Customs Union Strategy Conclusions of 10 and 11 December 2012, p (…).

Council of the European Union, General Secretariat (2013), List of Council Preparatory Bodies, Doc. 12111/1/13 REV 1, Brussels, 10 July 2013, http://register.consilium.europa.eu/doc/srv?l=EN&t=PDF&gc=true&sc=false&f=ST%2012111%202013%20REV%201&r=http%3A%2F%2Fregister.consilium.europa.eu%2Fpd%2Fen%2F13%2Fst12%2Fst12111-re01.en13.pdf.
Citation: Council of the European Union, General Secretariat (2013), List of Council Preparatory Bodies, Doc. 12111/1/13 REV 1, p (…).

DOCUMENTS OF THE WCO AND THE WTO AND DISPUTE SETTLEMENT BODY COMMENTARY (DSC)

WTO, 'Differential and more favourable treatment reciprocity and fuller participation of developing countries', Decision of 28 November 1979 (L/4903), www.wto.org/English/docs_e/legal_e/enabling_e.pdf.
Citation: WTO, Decision of 28 November 1979 (L/4903), p (…).

WTO, Ministerial Conferences, Fourth Session, Doha, Ministerial Declaration adopted on 14 November 2001, WT/MIN(01)/DEC/1, www.wto.org/english/thewto_e/minist_e/min01_e/mindecl_e.pdf.
Citation: WTO, Doha Ministerial Declaration adopted on 14 November 2001, WT/MIN(01)/DEC/1, para (…).

WTO, Doha Work Programme of 1 August 2004, WT/L/579, www.wto.org/english/tratop_e/dda_e/ddadraft_31jul04_e.pdf.
Citation: WTO, Doha Work Programme of 1 August 2004, WT/L/579, p (…).

2006 WorldTradeLaw.net LLC, Dispute Settlement Commentary (DSC), Appellate Body Report, *European Communities–Selected Customs Matters*, (WT/DS315/AB/R)/DSR 2006:IX, 3791.
Citation: DSC, (WT/DS315/AB/R)/DSR 2006:IX, 3791, p (…).

WCO, 'Safe Framework of Standards to Secure and Facilitate Global Trade', June 2007, Brussels, http://ec.europa.eu/taxation_customs/resources/documents/customs/policy_issues/customs_security/normes_wco_en.pdf.
Citation: WCO, Safe Framework Standards, 2007, p (…).

WTO, Negotiating Group on Trade Facilitation, Draft Consolidated Negotiating Text of 14 December 2009, TN/TF/W/165, https://docs.wto.org/dol2fe/Pages/FE_Search/FE_S_S009-DP.aspx?language=E&CatalogueIdList=105253,100546,104461,92230,91953,101999,92226,99337,105218,101912&CurrentCatalogueIdIndex=1&FullTextSearch=.
Citation: WTO, Draft Consolidated Negotiating Text of 14 December 2009, TN/TF/W/165, p (…).

WCO, 'Glossary of International Customs Terms', 2013, D/2013/0448/20, www.wcoomd.org/en/topics/facilitation/resources/~/media/949B39871CE147BAB2667EC6758F29C8.ashx.
Citation: WCO, 'Glossary of International Customs Terms', 2013, D/2013/0448/20, p (…).

WTO, Negotiating Group on Trade Facilitation, Draft Consolidated Negotiating Text of 23 October 2013, TN/TF/W/165/Rev.18, https://docs.wto.org/dol2fe/Pages/FE_Search/FE_S_S006.aspx?Query=(%20@Symbol=%20tn/tf/w/165*%20)&Language=ENGLISH&Context=FomerScriptedSearch&languageUIChanged=true#, see also https://docs.wto.org/dol2fe/Pages/FE_Search/FE_S_S009-DP.aspx?language=E&CatalogueIdList=120332,118449,117057,115814,113890,84890,65554,96148,96764,99878&CurrentCatalogueIdIndex=0&FullTextSearch=.
Citation: WTO, Draft Consolidated Negotiating Text of 23 October 2013, TN/TF/W/165/Rev.18, p (…).

MISCELLANEOUS DOCUMENTS AND REPORTS

American Chamber of Commerce to the European Union, Information Paper, 'Explaining AmCham EU's position on the Modernised Customs Code', Brussels, 5 August 2011, www.amchameu.eu/DesktopModules/Bring2mind/DMX/Download.aspx?TabId=165&Command=Core_Download&EntryId=6929&PortalId=0&TabId=165.
Citation: AmCham EU, Information Paper, 5 August 2011, p (…).

American Chamber of Commerce to the European Union, Position Statement, 'AmCham EU position on the proposed changes to EU customs valuation', 24 April 2012, www.amchameu.eu/DesktopModules/Bring2mind/DMX/Download.aspx?TabId=165&Command=Core_Download&EntryId=7715&PortalId=0&TabId=165.
Citation: AmCham EU, Position Statement, 24 April 2012, p (…).

American Chamber of Commerce to the European Union, Position Statement, 'AmCham EU's position on the Union Customs Code and the recast of the Modernised Customs Code', Brussels, 25 May 2012, www.amchameu.eu/DesktopModules/Bring2mind/DMX/Download.aspx?TabId=165&Command=Core_Download&EntryId=7785&PortalId=0&TabId=165.
Citation: AmCham EU, Position Statement, 25 May 2012, p (…).

DBB, 'Strategie für die Zollunion', *dbb-Europathemen* No 21, April 2006.
Citation: DBB, dbb-Europathemen Nr. 21, April 2006, p (…).

Delloitte, Final Report on Task 2.3 'Options for improvement of the functioning of the Customs Union', TAXUD/R3/VDL D(2010) 433216, May 2011, manuscript in possession of the author.

Citation: Delloitte, Final Report on Task 2.3, TAXUD/R3/VDL D(2010) 433216, 2011, p (...).

The Evaluation Partnership, 'Mid-Term evaluation of the Customs 2013 programme, final report', London 15 June 2011, TAXUD/2010/AO-06, http://ec.europa.eu/taxation_customs/resources/documents/common/publications/studies/customs2013_mid_term_report_en.pdf.

Citation: The Evaluation Partnership, Mid-Term Evaluation–Final Report, June 2011, p (...).

The Evaluation Partnership, 'Mid-Term evaluation of the Customs 2013 programme, Annex II', London 15 June 2011, TAXUD/2010/AO-06, http://ec.europa.eu/taxation_customs/resources/documents/common/publications/studies/customs2013_mid_term_an2_en.pdf.

Citation: The Evaluation Partnership, Mid-Term Evaluation–Annex II, June 2011, p (...).

Algirdas Šemeta, EU Commissioner for Taxation and Customs Union, Audit and Anti-Fraud, 'Pooling our efforts to build a modern Customs Union', Speech at the 78th meeting of the Directors General for Customs of the EU Member States and Turkey, Vilnius, 19 May 2011, http://europa.eu/rapid/pressReleasesAction.do?reference=SPEECH/11/358&format=HTML&aged=0&language=EN&guiLanguage=en.

Citation: Algirdas Šemeta, EU Commissioner, Speech of 19 May 2011.

Algirdas Šemeta, EU Commissioner for Taxation and Customs Union, Audit and Anti-Fraud, 'Making customs' modernization a high priority', Speech in the Internal Market Committee of the European Parliament, Brussels, 25 May 2011, http://ec.europa.eu/commission_2010–2014/semeta/headlines/speeches/2011/05/speech_0525.pdf.

Citation: Algirdas Šemeta, EU Commissioner, Speech of 25 May 2011, p (...).

Trade Contact Group, European Business Statement on the Recast of the Modernised Customs Code, 30 May 2012, www.amchameu.eu/DesktopModules/Bring2mind/DMX/Download.aspx?TabId=165&Command=Core_Download&EntryId=7790&PortalId=0&TabId=165.

Citation: Trade Contact Group, Statement, 30 May 2012, p (...).

PRESENTATIONS

European Commission, 'The Modernised Customs Code: why, how, what and when?', 1 November 2008, 26 slides, http://ec.europa.eu/taxation_customs/resources/documents/customs/procedural_aspects/general/community_code/pres_mccc_en.pdf.

Citation: European Commission, Presentation 'The Modernised Customs Code: why, how, what and when?', 1 November 2008, slide (...).

European Commission, 'The Modernised Customs Code: Conditions and state of its implementation', 1 November 2008, 10 slides, http://ec.europa.eu/taxation_customs/resources/documents/customs/procedural_aspects/general/community_code/mcc_implement_en.pdf.

Citation: European Commission, Presentation 'The Modernised Customs Code: Conditions and state of its implementation', 1 November 2008, slide (...).

European Commission, 'Implementation of the Modernised Customs Code (MCCIP)', 20 May 2010, 17 slides, http://ec.europa.eu/dgs/secretariat_general/admin_burden/docs/enterprise/administrative-burdens/high-level-group/files/2010_05_20_presentation_customs_en.pdf.

Citation: European Commission, Presentation 'Implementation of the Modernised Customs Code (MCCIP)', 20 May 2010, slide (…).

European Commission, 'Union Customs Code (recast)', 26 April 2012, 11 slides, www.europarl.europa.eu/document/activities/cont/201205/20120521ATT45426/20120521ATT45426EN.pdf.

Citation: European Commission, Presentation 'Union Customs Code (recast)', 26 April 2012, slide (…).

Index

www.ingramcontent.com/pod-product-compliance
Lightning Source LLC
LaVergne TN
LVHW052226200926
848481LV00001B/226